WORKING THE
WELSH COAST

A COASTFUL OF
WALES

[NIGHT-TIME REFUGES]
2003
7 - Dec

DULAS

PRESTATYN

R. DEE

CHESTER

r. conwy

NEWBOROUGH

ABERDARON

BARMOUTH

ABERDYFI

SOMEWHERE HERE

WELSH - ENGLISH BORDER

NEWQUAY

r. teifi

the last invasion

FISHGUARD

MILFORD HAVEN

CARMARTHEN

r. towy

r. wye

APPROX

CHEPSTOW

R. SEVERN

TENBY

RHOSILI

PORTHCAWL

r. taff

r. usk

CARDIFF

BARRY

MAJOR
LIGHTHOUSE

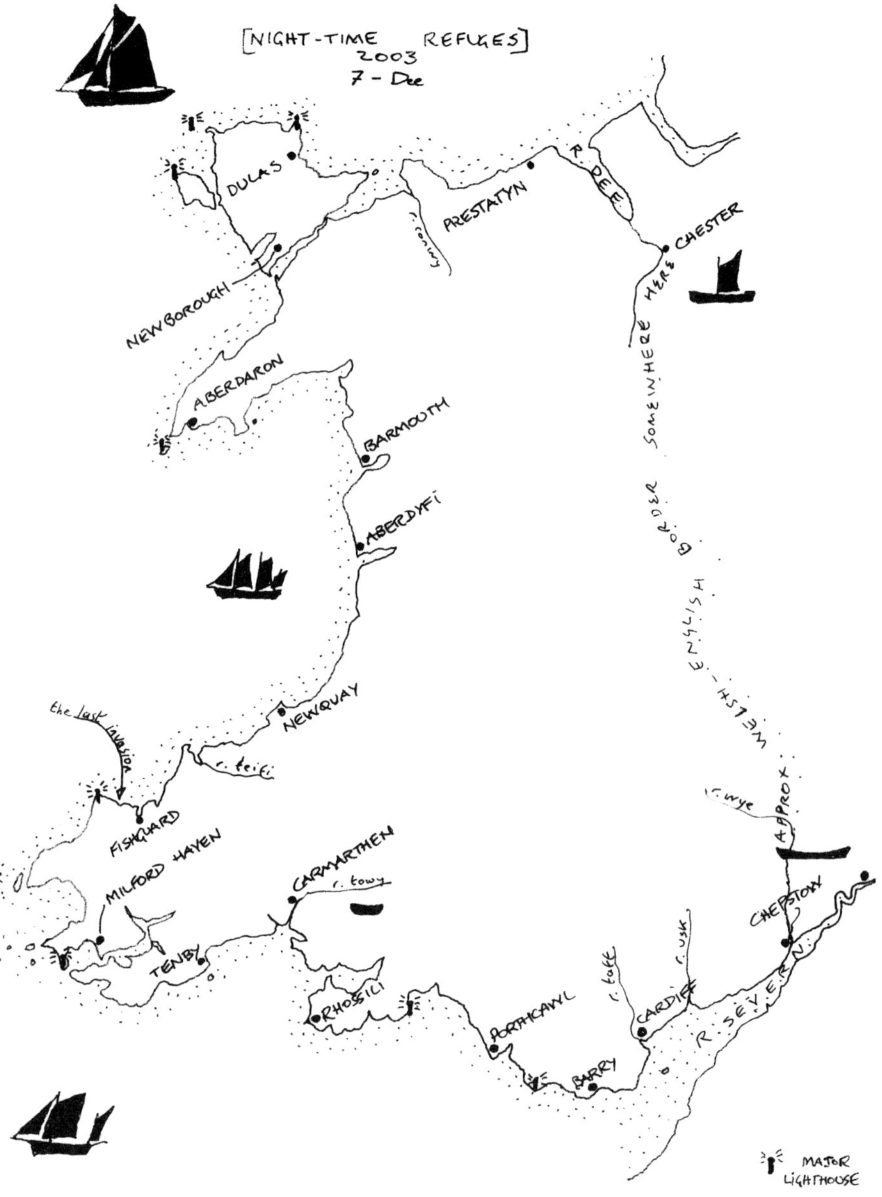

WORKING THE WELSH COAST

Or 'No Dogs Allowed on the Beach!'

Mike Smylie

I fy mab Christoffer, y gwir Cymro
To my son Christoffer, the true Welshman

First published 2005

Tempus Publishing Ltd
The Mill, Brimscombe Port
Stroud, Gloucestershire GL5 2QG
www.tempus-publishing.com

British Library Cataloguing in Publication Data.
A catalogue record for this book is available from the British Library.

ISBN 0 7524 3244 3

Typesetting and origination by Tempus Publishing.
Printed and bound in Great Britain.

CONTENTS

ACKNOWLEDGEMENTS

Thanks to the dog for keeping me entertained and sane during this journey, and to the Ford Motor Company for ensuring my engine didn't grind to a halt! Thanks to all those people I spoke to en route – especially Simon & Ann Cooper, Alan, Gordon and Dexter on the river Severn, Ann Bayliss, Raymond Rees, Roger Hall, Paul Welch, Chris Partington, Scott Metcalfe, Malcolm and Ken Williams and Vic Williams – as well as those spoken to during the subsequent writing of the book. Also to all those authors dead and alive whose books or articles I've found myself endlessly referring to. Again thanks to Maria Stromsholm for proof-reading and to all at Tempus for their continued support.

All photographs and drawings are by the author unless otherwise stated.

THE AUTHOR

Mike Smylie – otherwise known as 'Kipperman' – is a naval architect, maritime historian, fisheries ethnologist, maritime archaeologist and herring smoker. He runs the Centre for Maritime Vernacular Culture and has recently completed two years' research at the Scottish Institute of Maritime Studies at St Andrew's University, where he gained an MPhil. He is the author of five previous books of fishing and fishing boats and has written widely in various magazines and *Fishing News* on maritime matters. In 1995 he co-founded the 40+ Fishing Boat Association, Britain's only organisation dedicated to all types of fishing boats, and edits their magazine *Fishing Boats*. Since 1996, he has been travelling around Britain each summer with the 'Herring Exhibition' to maritime festivals, for which he was presented with the BBC Radio 4 Food Campaigner/Educator Award in November 2004. He alternates between Wales and Greece.

By the same author:
The Herring Fishers and other Vignettes (London, 1995)
The Herring Fishers of Wales (Llanrwst, 1998)
The Traditional Fishing Boats of Britain and Ireland (Shrewsbury, 1999)
Anglesey and its Coastal Tradition (Llanrwst, 2000)
Kipperman and the Red Herring (Llangaffo, 2000)
Herring – A History of the Silver Darlings (Stroud, 2004)

DAY ONE

ON THE RIVER SEVERN

Eels. That seems a good place as any to start. The nocturnal slithery snake-like creatures that come out of their hiding places in the muddy riverbed on dark moonless nights. Or when the river is especially murky and fast flowing after much rain upstream. We'd set the conical eel nets the evening before and the initial job this morning was to check first the eel pot, followed by the eel putchin and then row upstream to empty the nets. This was, of course, following the daily pattern of the fishermen of the river Severn (*Hafren*).

To me, eels are horrible and slimy and beady eyed, but they are truly remarkable creatures. They breed in the Sargasso Sea in the Atlantic at a depth in excess of 500 fathoms. Once hatched they begin a 2,500-mile journey towards Western Europe, pushed on by the Gulf Stream, where three or four years later they arrive as small elvers, otherwise known as glass eels. These enter rivers on Europe's western seaboard in the early spring and thus spread upstream. They then reach maturity between eight and twenty years later, at which time they return to the Atlantic and back to their distant breeding grounds – unless man gets to them first.

Eels have been caught in a number of British rivers for centuries, using one of several methods. In the Severn wicker eel pots are widely used. These are long and narrow with a constricted entrance in the middle that prevents eels escaping and are set with their mouths facing downstream. Two versions exist, the smaller *putcheon* and the larger *weel*. They have a wooden bung in one end, the removal of which allows the eels to be taken out. Similar traps in Norfolk are called *grigs* or, as smaller versions, *hives*, and these appear to be even narrower. On the river Thames they use fyke nets. The putcheon, not to be confusing, is a modern version of the pot, in that it is a wire cage. The gleaving or stanging of eels is the spearing of them using a specially designed head with flat tines that don't damage the eel. But spears are rarely used on the Severn nowadays. It is the eel net, a sort of hoop net some 30ft long, that is most likely to have a good catch of the writhing ugly creatures trapped in it in the morning. Let me explain: I was out on the river Severn with local fisherman Alan Osment, his fishing partner Gordon and friend Simon, alone in his long-net punt.

Pot and putcheon were empty. The nets had but a few eels, although two mullet had also found their way in. Heavy rain two nights before had brought freshwater downriver, as well as a load of rubbish in the form of branches, litter and anything else that floats. Alan and Gordon were doubtful of much and they were dead right. A miserable catch, but being out on the river in the early morning almost made up for this.

We found an elver in the eel pot after it sneaked out into the punt. Elvers, along with whitebait, are the only fish fry that are legally caught as food. When I'd been to this part of the river a few years before, they were realising such a high price in the Far East that it seemed almost everybody was out having a crack at them. Thus the price fell once the market was flooded, as did the stocks, and today elvers are much scarcer.

We returned to Bollow for a cup of tea, me walking along the bank as I'd been put ashore to photograph the net lifting from a different angle. Simon cheated and used his outboard motor to keep up with Alan and Gordon in their fibreglass boat. I took my time, standing at the edge of the river throwing sticks for the dog who wouldn't go into the browny slow-moving water. This was, I knew, the very beginning of a journey that was to take me from river to sea, from rocky coast to sandy beach back to another river seemingly an age away, and I liked it. The irony, though, is that although this journey will take me hundreds of miles from Severn to Dee, this is a far cry from the mere twenty-five miles that separates their sources in the Welsh hills to the north.

Simon and Ann Cooper, in the maritime field, are a rare couple. They have a real passion for the traditional skills of the Severn and surrounding area, skills that are on the cusp of totally disappearing from our modern world. Many people eulogise about the loss of the craftsmanship and dexterity that was, to the fishermen, part of the job such as net mending, eel pot making, and even boatbuilding. Few, though, assemble a collection of traditional vessels such as a Wye stopping boat, a long-net punt, a coble, coracles and items ancillary to the fishery. It was with Simon that I first came to Bollow some five or six years before, when I met Frank, outside whose house we were camping. Unfortunately, Frank himself had recently had a stroke and was laid up in hospital, and so he wasn't able to share with us the wealth of knowledge he has after living next to the river for most of his life. However, Simon and Ann had brought their salmon punt upon which we had been long netting the previous day, and with which we were about to shoot once more. Alan, in whose name the licence to fish this draft is in, Gordon and Simon were to go on the punt, whilst Ann, Moe and I were to watch and film from the far bank and young Dexter was to be the debut-man (he who walks the net up the far sandy, flat, riverbank). The net is shot from the back of the punt as it is rowed across the river from the far bank (they were using the outboard again) until it is set almost across the river, leaving a gap for a fish to pass. With the punt holding one end – the muntle – and the debut-man the other, the net and punt drift downstream as the debut-man walks. The skill, though, is the watching of the net to ensure it stays in a clean arc, and recognising if, and when, a fish gets caught. When the other end of the draft (the part of the river where they can fish) is reached, slowly the punt brings the muntle back across the river and onto the bank below the debut-man and the muntle is brought ashore and the net is closed. A steady but slow haul of the top and bottom of the net can begin.

As the net comes in Dexter holds its bottom edge to the riverbed to stop any fish escaping. The excitement increases since Alan thinks he's felt movement. Perhaps a mullet, he explained, as there was too much freshwater in the river for salmon. Suddenly there's movement in the shallow water and the top edge of a salmon appears. He swims upstream as the net comes in and Alan swears because he's forgotten the ring-net to land him, such was his doubt that we'd get anything. He splashes in and flicks the salmon, which was about to make an escape over the top of the net. He's ashore, flapping about in the mud and nearly makes it back to the water. We've no priest to kill him and an old brush makes do. Five minutes later we have the net in and what later is weighed as a 12lb 9oz fish, a fine specimen who must have been swimming downriver ahead of the freshwater. There was no debate about having another shoot! Second time, though, the net came in empty. The salmon was later taken up to the Severn and Wye Smokery where Alan sells the majority of his catch, including the eels.

Simon's long net punt once worked this draft before he saved it from a certain rotting demise. These flat-bottomed punts were used above Newnham and were developed to suit the conditions of the river. This one is 26ft long and about 3ft in the beam. Built out of oak, the boat weighs almost one ton with the net aboard. We found that rowing it as the net is shot is almost impossible, although it was the only mode of propulsion before an outboard motor was attached. And that was a recent modernisation of Simon's! Scottish cobles were introduced at some time and subsequently built locally and Simon has been able to add one of those to his collection of salmon boats. Long net fishing is only licensed between June and August and only three drafts are in use these days, such is the state of the salmon stocks in the river.

Fish weirs were another mode of catching salmon on a commercial scale and only a few remain in use. The rights to fishing these, like the stop- and long-nets, were 'the lord's preserve', I'd read somewhere. Fixed rents were paid and/or a portion of the catch handed over in the same way that the netsmen paid their rents. I photographed the one at Broadoak where a double height putcher weir has thirty-six putchers in its length, making seventy-two in total. A putcher is a loosely woven conical basket and is some 5 or 6ft in length, into which a salmon will swim and become trapped. Some are five or six baskets high and can amount to hundreds of baskets. Putts, on the other hand, are much bigger and more complicated because they consists of three parts – the *kype, butt* and *forewheel*. The kype might be as much as 6ft in diameter and the whole putt 15ft long. Both of these 'fixed engines' cannot be used out of the season. The putcher is dismantled and stored ashore while the much heavier putt is closed off to salmon by the fitting of two withy rods cross-wise at the rear of the kype, so that eels and other small fish can continue to be caught.

From Broadoak the road goes to Newnham, where I took the dog for a walk along the river. The little road we took I noted was called Severn View, although the river was hidden by the houses. The village is renowned for its export of oak bark and cider, although this was lost at the beginning of the nineteenth century. Bullo Pill and its tiny harbour are next, and were used for the export of coal, and it is said that it superceded Newnham as a harbour because of its proximity to the railway line. Downstream, at Awre, the Cadogan family has been fishing their four ranks of putchers since the 1920s. Much earlier, John of Box is said to have had a fishery in the parish before 1300. In Blakeney, set away from the river, I found the turning to Etloe and Gatcombe.

I have been to Gatcombe three times now and each subsequent visit seems as refreshing as the first. It's probably something to do with its hide-way situation, which gives the tiny hamlet the appearance of being surrounded by a shroud of trees so that it survives in a veil of secrecy. It is easily overlooked by even the most inquisitive of travellers. Nowadays that is, because in times long gone this was a thriving port. Francis Drake is reputed to have stayed at the Sloop Inn when visiting the Forest of Dean to view the quality of the timber here for shipbuilding. Walter Raleigh is also said to have come here for the same reason. The Spanish are reputed to have hatched a (failed) plan to burn the entire forest, such was its reputation in contributing to Britain's mastery of the oceans.

Sitting almost astride the bank of the river Severn, Gatcombe's only protection from the swirling silt-filled waters is the main Gloucester to South Wales railway line. Beneath this grand structure an archway allows access to the water, which is almost ravenous in its flow. Just back from the archway, on the grassy bank, lie the forlorn shells of three boats, moss-covered and fatigued by old age. Three out of a handful of the last remaining of the Severn stop-net boats. In fact it was these boats that had first drawn me to Gatcombe that first time five years earlier. For, measured once by renowned maritime historian Eric McKee, these are the remaining vestiges of an industry that once played supreme in the hamlet. As in many other rivers throughout the world, it was the salmon that brought an income to those that dwelt alongside this proud river.

The first time I came here I met Ann Bayliss. Her great-great-grandfather, Charles Morse, bought the fishing rights in 1878. A century before they belonged to George Smith, then to John Shaw who passed them on to his son William. He, his brother Thomas, and local fisherman Thomas Margrates were bringing their stop-net boat upriver when it hit the nearly completed Severn railway bridge which, when opened the following year, connected Sharpness and Purton. Tragically, William Shaw drowned so the rights passed to his brother who then sold the lease to the Morse family. Shaw's body was brought to the Sloop Inn soon after the accident. Ann today lives in the same Court House in which her ancestors exercised their rights to fish their 'chains' upon the river.

Paradoxically, in this instance a 'chain' is a wire cable and it was stretched out between an anchor in the deep water of the river and a stake on the lower part of the beach. Here a fisherman would come and attach his boat with up to a maximum of six boats working one chain. In all there were ten stop-net boats – sometimes called stopping boats – at Gatcombe, although there were other licensees in the river fishing a total of twenty-four nets, including those of Gatcombe. I'll explain the workings of the fishing in a minute.

Although the practise of fishing with stop-nets is said to predate the Civil War, it was not until the 1860s that the British Government took strides to control what was by then deemed to be over-fishing. William Shaw gave evidence to the 1866 Special Commission for the Salmon Fisheries who reported in 1866. Thus the Shaws established their fishing rights. The Wellhouse Bay fishery belonged to Lord Bledisloe of Lydney while those at Gatcombe itself belonged to the Crown at the Highgrove Estate. The latter fishery was the more dangerous of the two and, after a fisherman called Fenner was drowned while at work in 1937, use of the stop-net ceased there and the seven 'chains' of Wellhouse Bay retained. These were each named as *Haywards Rock*, *Long Ledge* (where there were two), *Round Rock*, *Fish House*, *Old Dunns* and *The Flood*.

The stop-net is a bag-net suspended on two 24ft-long stout pieces of wood called rames, made from Norwegian spruce. These are held in a 'V' by a spreader and weights at the apex of the rames complete the frame. Once the stop-net boat is moored to the 'chain', broadside on to the river, the frame is lowered into the tide so that the bag opens up below the shallow-drafted boat. Five feeling strings are attached to different parts of the net and to a 'tuning fork' – a wooden stick – which is held by the fisherman. A wooden prop supports the weighted apex. Once a fish is determined to be in the net, the prop is kicked out – called 'knocking out' – and, helped by the weight of the fisherman, the mouth of the net brought to the surface. If there is in fact a fish, the 'cunning hole' is opened by undoing a cord and revealing a concealed entrance to the cod end of the net, and the prize killed by a quick thump with the 'knobbling pin'. The hole is closed and the net dropped back into the river and the prop replaced.

The secret was to stay absolutely silent during the three hours or so that fishing was possible in one tide, for the wily salmon would have been put off by idle chatter. I write this in the past tense because that is where it belongs: Ann's husband Raymond was the

last to fish and he ceased in 1986. I'd first visited Gatcombe with Simon who had
arranged the trip and together we met Raymond when he showed us his home-cured
bacon. Sadly Raymond has since died, so that chapter in the life of the river has finally
passed on. I remember him saying that the best time to fish was with a good
southwesterly wind and a 21–22ft tide in the river. Then they might get two or three
fish. When the tide was strong or the water flat calm, they might go for days without a
fish; not fun in the cold conditions of the river.

On that same occasion Ann showed Simon and me her father's records of the fishing.
These are mostly in leather-bound volumes whose pages illustrate the pride and
thoroughness with which the fishing was run. In an exquisite, almost copperplate, style
every aspect of the business is captured. The 'salmon accounts' detail each fish caught, its
weight and selling price, while the 'wages book' state the earnings of the stop-net fishermen
employed by the Morses. One volume names each of the lave-net fishermen (more of these
later) and the number of salmon so caught while another lists his annual expenses. Each
leaves us today with a glimpse of how the fishery was operated and how much an average
fisherman earned. In 1913 this was about 8*s* for every 10lb of fish caught and each fish
weighed on average within the range 10-20lb. The record for a salmon caught in a stop-
net is, I read, 62lb, but this was caught a few years later. In February 1913 a fish fetched 2*s*
3*d*, reducing to 1*s* 6*d* in March and 1*s* 2*d* in July. The fisherman received about half of this
and the Morses the other half, for which they paid all the rents, licences, boat and net costs
and transportation. In total 1,179 salmon were caught during that season that commenced
on 2 February and continued through to its closure on 15 August. Total sales for the year
were just over £1,070, with the expenses at about £646, giving a gross profit of almost
£424. A licence in 1893 cost £3 which had risen to £12 by 1961. In 1932, as an example,
the telephone bill was nearly £16, repairs to the boats £40, three stop-nets £9, insurance
about £16, rent to Highgrove £15 and Wellhouse Bay £30. Sales that year had increased
to £1,411 and expenditure £1,147 with a reduced profit of £254. Some years produced
losses, which were usually counteracted by good years. But Alan had explained the night
before exactly how he and his wife kept their records and apparently not much has changed!

Raymond Bayliss in his stop-
net boat with a good salmon.
(Courtesy Ann Bayliss)

Some Great Welsh Recipes

With this book concerned principally with the coast, most of these recipes contain ingredients from the sea in some form or other. Potatoes have been included because many a Scottish fisherman was said to help himself to a few spuds when cooking his fish at a time when these fishermen camped by the shore. Furthermore, they were not averse to stealing the odd egg, although it should be added that they sometimes traded these for fish. It's not inconceivable that Welsh fishermen were of the same thinking. I did consider including Welsh lamb, but concluded that sheep rustling, once a hanging offence, was not to be encouraged. The mutton in the Gower oyster soup is not to be obtained this way!

Smoked Welsh eel

Skin the eel and cut into thin strips. Serve with lemon and granary bread and Welsh butter.

Fried whitebait

Wash the fish and fry in a little oil for a few minutes before tossing. Serve with lemon and granary bread.

Wyau Sir Fon – *Anglesey eggs*

Peel and boil 1lb potatoes and add six chopped up leeks for the last ten minutes. Darin and mash until fluffy. Hard-boil four eggs, cool and shell. At the same time make a cheese sauce from flour, butter, milk and Cheddar cheese. Place the potato and leek mixture around the edge of a warm plate and the eggs in the middle. Cover with the cheese sauce, sprinkle a bit of grated cheese on top and place under the grill for a few minutes to brown.

Welsh cheese potato cakes

Make pastry in the normal manner and place cut out circles into greased patty tins. Peel and boil 1⁄2lb potatoes, drain and add 1⁄4lb each of currants, sugar and butter. Fill the pastry cases and cook in a hot oven (400F or Gas Mark 6) for twenty– twenty-five minutes.

Welsh Rarebit

Toast four slices of bread. Grate 1⁄2lb Cheddar cheese into a pan and heat gently until it melts. Add 1tsp butter, 2tsp Worcester sauce, 1tsp dry mustard, 2tsp flour, 2tbsp beer and salt and pepper to taste. Spread this mixture over the toast and brown under a grill.

Add some hot laverbread on top and a dash of lemon juice for a variation or add a poached egg on top of each slice to make Buck Rarebit

Gower oyster soup

Wash 2lb scrag end of mutton, cut off the fat and boil in three pints of water. Add 2oz pearl barley, one chopped onion, one diced carrot and one diced turnip. Add salt, pepper and mace to taste and boil the mixture for three hours. Melt some butter in a pan and add a little flour and pour the broth over this to thicken it. Serve with opened oysters.

Bara Lawr – *Laverbread*

Laverbread can be eaten in a number of ways. Portion it and roll in oatmeal and fry in bacon fat. Serve with lemon juice or fried bacon. It tastes just as good on hot buttered toast, with or without bacon. It can also be added to any fish or chowder with advantage.

Cockle pie

Leave one quart of cockles to stand overnight in salted water with oatmeal added to cleanse. Drain and wash thoroughly before boiling until the shells open. Remove the cockles from their shells. Meanwhile make some pastry and line a dish with it. Chop one bunch of spring onions and four rashers of bacon. Fill the dish with alternate layers of cockles, onions and bacon, finishing with a layer of cockles. Add half a cup of milk and salt and pepper. Cover with pastry and cook in a hot oven (425F or Gas Mark 7) for twenty– twenty-five minutes.

Limpets can be used in place of the cockles and layers of hard-boiled eggs included.

Mussel broth

Scrub, wash and boil three quarts of mussels until the shells open. Fry a chopped onion, 2oz mushrooms and some garlic. Add the liquid from the mussels, 3oz breadcrumbs, a glass of sweet sherry and the juice of one lemon. Bring to the boil again, add the mussels and remove from the heat to mix in an egg yolk. Simmer for another five minutes before serving with chopped parsley.

Herring rolls

Clean four herrings and split up the belly, removing the guts and backbone. Spread the insides with a little mustard, roll up the fillets and secure with a cocktail stick. In a greased ovenproof dish place some peeled and sliced potatoes on the bottom. Add the herring fillets, one large sliced cooking apple and one sliced onion. Sprinkle with chopped sage, add more potatoes, some butter and salt and pepper to taste. Cover and bake in a moderate oven (350F or gas Mark 4) for forty-five minutes, removing the lid after that and cook for another thirty minutes to brown the top.

Sgadan Abergwaun – Fishguard herring

Lay out eight medium-sized herring fillets, sprinkle with salt and pepper, and paint over a little bit of mustard on each, then roll up the fillets. Lightly grease an ovenproof dish and line it half of 2lb of peeled and sliced potatoes. Add one large apple, peeled, cored and sliced, then a large peeled and sliced onion, the herring rolls. Sprinkle with chopped sage and season again before covering with the remaining sliced potatoes. Half fill with boiling water, add a good knob of butter, and cover and bake in a moderate oven (350F) for forty-five minutes. Remove the lid and allow the top to brown for a further half an hour.

Mackerel, anchovies, pilchards, tuna or John Dory can be used in this recipe, and half cider and half water used if preferred.

Saws Eog Teifi – Teifi salmon sauce

Wash 2lb of salmon, remove the skin, bones, etc., and cut into chunks. Boil up the trimmings in a cup of water well seasoned for half an hour, then strain it and reserve the liquid. It should have reduced and be strongly favoured. Mash up one anchovy fillet, add the salmon, half a cupful of Port, 8oz butter and one teaspoonful of mushroom ketchup, as well as the stock. Place in an ovenproof dish and bake in hot oven (400F) for about forty minutes.

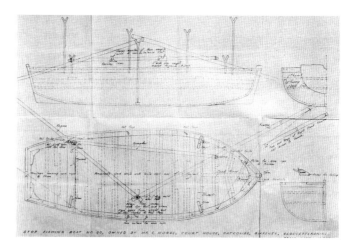

Stop fishing boat No.30,
owned by Mr C. Morse,
Blakeney, Gloucestershire.

Ann Bayliss next showed us her outside workshop. Here, as a child, she would help her father to set up the nets. The nets were made from hemp before 1965 and the raw material came from Bridport in panels 76ft long by 30ft deep. The top three feet of the net had a 7in mesh, decreasing every 2ft to 6, 5 and then 4.5ins, thence to 4in for the bottom 18ft of the net. Together they would knit the various meshes into one net. The mesh pins, wooden needles and the wooden winder are still there, amongst the boatbuilding tools. On the lid of the chest two lists still hang, dated 1899 and 1923, containing the names of the fishermen of that year, the particular boat they used and the size of net required. It's as if nothing has been touched in a century! Once a net was completed it was carried outside and tarred in the copper boiler that still sits outside the blacksmith's shop. Immersed nets would stay in the mixture of tar and tar oil for several days before they were hauled out on the pulley that was suspended above and left to drip. Then they were hung up to thoroughly dry. Nets seldom lasted more than a season so they were only barked at the beginning.

The boats built specifically for stop-netting were 26ft long and 7ft in beam. They had the minimum of keel to reduce sideways drag when moored to the chain and to prevent the net being obstructed underneath. They were heavily constructed with oak frames and larch and elm planking. Gunwales were ash to cope with the stresses of the frame of the net. Other than a grey strip above the rubbing strake, they were pitched inside and out.

Ann remembers her father describing the way his father and fisherman Joe Wathen built the last boat in 1922. This was the *Margaret*, No.30 as she was, and is one of the three lying on the slope by the archway. The timber had come from the sawmills at the edge of the Forest of Dean, chosen by Charles Morse (her grandfather) himself. It took about three months to build and was named after her father Christopher's youngest sister. Repairs were likewise undertaken outside the workshop after the season's close. This was the time of 'bringing' the boats in. On the August high tide, just after the full moon, all ten boats were dragged up under the railway line, one by one, with the help of horses and all the fishermen and their families. This day became a celebration of the salmon fishing, a form of thanksgiving after a successful annual harvest from the river. Once each boat had been blocked up to dry out, everyone went up to Court House for a meal of cold salt beef, beetroot and mashed potato, followed by home-made apple pie, accompanied by ample supplies of cider and fishermen's stories that rolled on and on…

Winter was also the time to earn a living outside of the fishing. The Morse family undertook general carpentry repairs and made ladders to sell. Then there was plum-picking and cider-making. They had cows also that needed milking and calves that had to be tended. Ann remembers milking the fourteen cows and taking the churns to the top of the lane to await collection by Cadbury's. Her grandfather on her mother's side looked after the lights on the Severn Railway Bridge while her father also ran the local Blakeney Gas, Light & Coke Company. Also in winter the galvanised cables in the river needed relaying and I read a note in the carpenter's shed dated 1915 that noted their lengths: Length of slack wire: 40 fathom, Gatcombe: 83 (fathom), Fish House Head: 73, Low Water Wire: 45, Middle: 83, Dunns: 65. The Fish House referred to was situated at Wellhouse Bay and was a small stone building with two rooms, one with bunks, cupboards and a fireplace and the other a storeroom for fishing gear. Here the fishermen would sit around the open fire or sleep, waiting for the right state of the tide. When the house was destroyed in a very high tide in 1950, Christopher Morse built a wooden shed higher up the railway embankment.

And so, looking around this tiny hamlet, the three stopping boats are all that remain visible without digging into the personal memories of Court House. These boats, the tools of those hard-working fishermen, are fast falling apart and are beyond repair. Soon, as has happened often before, there will be none left. The Heritage Centre in the Forest of Dean has its own example standing outside in a fragile state, which I photographed at the time of my second visit to the area, for this boat is also unlikely to stay in one piece for much longer without dire attention. There is also one in Chepstow, which I would be viewing soon.

Which brings me back to the present day and it was my third time standing on the grassy slope staring out over the muddy waters of the freely flowing river, towards Purton where three weeks earlier I had stood by the seventeenth-century pub gazing towards Gatcombe. The Severn Bridge once stood here, before it was demolished. Downstream a bit, Sharpness and the entrance to the Gloucester Canal were clearly visible. Both upstream and downstream the river widens out, and Gatcombe was situated on the neck or constriction of the river.

From there we briefly went to Lydney. Ships were built here in Tudor times but the shifting sands made the navigation of large ships dangerous. Oak and iron were the exports from the Forest of Dean but the railway finished off the last remnants of trade within the harbour. From here the road heads fast towards the Welsh border at Chepstow, although we detoured to Beachley, where the remains of a salmon weir can be seen on the edge of the river. We – dog and I – walked upstream along the river's edge to exercise and view its remains. They didn't amount to much. A bit further on we came to Slimeroad Pill, above which is the southern extremity of Offa's Dyke footpath, and I remembered standing here ten years previously at the beginning of a 190-odd mile walk along the path to Prestatyn in the north. I surmised that by the time I'd almost finished this present journey around the coast I would have circumnavigated Wales! We re-traced our steps back to the fish weir.

Thomas Sanders rented a fishery here in 1786–95. The Special Commissioners who were investigating the fishery in 1865 allowed 754 putchers at this particular fishery and another 400 putchers at Horse Pill and 376 at Lyde Rock, which is almost underneath the old Severn Bridge. These were latterly owned by the Wye River Authority and leased to private tenants. Today, though, almost all the signs of this have gone. Two drift-nets 200ft long by 2 yards deep were once licensed to operate here. These worked four hours at a tide. The Old Passage ferry quay is all that remains. There's a pub there, but I decided to drive the two miles to Chepstow. A pint in the Boat Inn seemed a good idea. And it was time to cross the river Wye and head into Wales.

DAY TWO
CHEPSTOW TO CARDIFF

The museum at Chepstow doesn't open until 11 a.m. so the dog and I spent a couple of hours walking along the river. The Old Wye Bridge – *Hen Bont Afon Gwy* – is dated 1816 and commemorates the junctioning of Monmouth and Gloucester, according to the ironwork at its halfway point. Poking about outside the Chepstow Boat pub around the point where the salmon boats were once kept is fascinating, for here, two hundred years ago, was a dry-dock and shipyard, as well as several more pubs, the Customs House and a collection of warehouses. Downstream, beyond the railway bridge, were timber yards and more shipyards. Today this whole area would be unrecognisable to a nineteenth-century sailor now that the maritime flavour of the town has disappeared, replaced by the present ubiquitous waterfront housing and twenty-first-century fluff. Even more recently, the construction of a flood barrier has made access to the river hazardous. These modernisations, though, are part of the so-called 'advance', the progression towards a richer society, and are apparent throughout Britain. We shall come across much more of them in our travels.

Thus we headed up town, finding a second-hand bookshop en route. Its owner appeared to be highly eurosceptical, judging by the monologue that he was giving to two poor Irish customers who'd only come in to buy a book from the 50 pence tray outside. Some of what he said made sense but there was a lot of dogma, the sort of stuff you've heard before. Politics and book buying don't go hand in hand in my opinion so I didn't dare mention the Brussels affect upon the fisheries. After all, I did want to be at the museum by opening time!

This I achieved and by coincidence saw an advertising poster there declaring that the Chepstow Bridge was to open in a ceremony on Wednesday 24 July 1816 and that the procession was to assemble at one o'clock in the Square. This bridge, though, was not the first bridge by any means across the Wye (*Afon Gwy*). The earliest crossing dated from the thirteenth century and was a wooden affair said to be the highest in Britain at the time. By 1785 the wooden piers on the Welsh side had been replaced by ones of stone and within a few years a new bridge was under construction. It was designed by John Rennie and John Urpeth Rastrick – referred to as engineer and surveyor in the poster – and sufficed until the modern A48 Bridge was completed in 1988.

Chepstow was well described by William Coxe in *A Historical Tour through Monmouthshire* at the end of the eighteenth century when he saw that 'a singular intermixture of buildings, vessels, cliffs, water and wood is presented to view'. He also produced a fine drawing of the old bridge – one of the last. However, the town's association with water goes back to before the Norman Conquest of 1066 and the subsequent plan to quell the Welsh into submission by building castles. Chepstow was one of the first and has innovative structures in its construction which, it has to be said, has been significantly altered over the centuries.

Opening of the landing stage at Chepstow in 1907.

Giraldus Cambrensis – otherwise known as Gerald of Wales – during his journey around Wales in 1188 found plentiful supplies of fish in the river and noted that 'the Wye has more salmon and the Usk more trout'. Defoe, in 1725, doesn't mention the fisheries but notes 'a Place of very good Trade' and 'a Noble Bridge over the *Wye*: To this Town Ships of good Burthen may come up, and the Tide runs here with the same impetuous Current as at *Bristol*'. Corn, he states, is exported, chiefly to Portugal. Thus we perceive a town with strong maritime traditions in both the shipbuilding and trade, and the more localised, vernacular fishery.

Wine, it is said, was the principal import into England in the time after 1066. This attracted a tax called *prisage* by which the king took a tun of wine from before and one from behind the mast from every English vessel importing twenty or more tuns of wine. Not for the last time do we see the establishment robbing the populace of their belongings to pay for the more opulent lifestyles of those in charge! However, Chepstow, as with other towns under the control of the Marcher Lords, was considered to be exempt to this duty although there were complaints that non-payment 'en le port de Chipstouwe a graunt damage du roi'. Wine passed through Chepstow, up the Wye, on a number of occasions in the thirteenth century to satisfy the demands of travelling kings. Wool was next to be taxed in 1275, as were exported hides soon after. Collectors of Customs were set up around the country to levy these taxes and Chepstow became under the control of Bristol. But wine continued to be imported into the port and loaded onto smaller boats, thus escaping the full dues once carried across the Severn estuary into England. Bristol customs officers intervened in an attempt to stamp the practise out by levying customs in Chepstow, leading to subsequent complaints of their activities. However, the privileges of the Lords of the Marches survived longest at Chepstow, until 1536 and in 1573 the Customs House was opened which eventually resulted in a decline in trade in the port. Oak bark to Ireland became the chief export in the eighteenth century, reaching almost 9,000 tons by the end of it. This was brought down the river from Monmouth, Llandogo, Brockweir and Tintern in trows, the river barges that were native to the Bristol Channel. The export of oak, elm, ash and beech for shipbuilding declined as de-forestation took effect after centuries of felling and little replanting. Even as early as 1664 the diarist John Evelyn was advocating to the landowners the sense behind replanting of the land but his pleas fell on deaf ears. A first rate ship took 3,000 loads of timber, one load being an average sized tree. This amounted to 60 acres of century-old oak and it has been estimated that half the timber used by the Navy during the Napoleonic era for building and repairs came from the Forest of Dean. Not surprisingly then, as trade declined, the Customs House closed in 1882.

Trows have been the subject to much research and debate, and the first registered one seems to have been at Chepstow in 1797, although this by no way means they hadn't been around for ages. These early vessels were flat-bottomed, open boats that were suited to the conditions of the Severn and Wye. In Bristol the *Llandogo Trow* is an ancient pub down by the harbour, its name an obvious association between Llandogo, which is on the Wye, and the city. A typical trow was the *Joseph & Elizabeth*, 64 tons and 52½ft, built in 1761 and rebuilt 1797, which ran between the lower Wye and Bristol. Later they were twice that size, up to 120 tons.

Shipbuilding only emerges in documentation in the eighteenth century when there were three yards – Rock, Middle and Upper – along the riverbank. Prior to that the first recorded building in the area is at Lydney in 1657 although it is presumed vessels were built before this, owing to the proximity to the Forest of Dean and its timber. Some boats were also built at Monmouth. At Chepstow, vessels up to some 600 tons were normal and Ivor Waters, in *The Port of Chepstow*, notes the increase in commodities such as hemp, flax, pitch, tar, cables, handspikes, cordage and oars from Russia and Norway about this time. Other imports include Baltic pine for masts and North American timber. However, Graham Farr in *Chepstow Ships* tells the full story of shipbuilding in the port and thus repetition would be pointless. Shipbuilding at this time, as we shall see, was prolific along the Welsh coast so that large ships were being built in what we consider today to be the most inaccessible of places. Nevertheless, in an era when the sea was the principal mode of transport until the advent of the railway, these so-called inaccessible places were no more or less accessible than the rest of the entire coast. Roads were few and far between and unsurfaced and travellers often took days to get anywhere. The sea was their crossroads, as they say! However, it must be added that shipbuilding did survive on the river until 1925, albeit on a much reduced scale to the nineteenth-century level, and even after that seven floating cranes were built immediately after the Second World War, after which all such activity ceased.

It wasn't until 1852 that the Brunel-designed tubular suspension bridge was opened to a single-file railway, bringing the railway connection from England to Chepstow. The following year it was complete and, except for modifications by British Rail in 1962, it remains much the same. The irony is, of course, that although it was designed with shipping in mind – a 300ft span and a height of 50ft above the highest known tide – it was ultimately the railway that was responsible for the decline of the port. But then again, that's an often-repeated saga as one mode of transport succeeds another. Correct me if I'm wrong, but hasn't the motor car unfortunately done the same to the railway?

Just as the Severn fishery has attracted our attention, the Wye fishery must too. Edward I attempted to bring conservation into the salmon fishery in 1307 by protecting the parr. A fisherman, Roger Carey, was outlawed for fishing the river for salmon and an accomplice was punished by having his nets burnt. But not a lot else was done to help the stocks breed. Numerous weirs were built, so many in fact that it was said that they prevented the upstream journey of the fish so that the river was 'swollen with a sea of salmon'. For example, the Abbey of Tidenham is recorded as having sixty weirs in the Severn and twenty in the Wye. The monks at Tintern had others. Even the coming of the railways contributed to the general decline in salmon by making the sending of fish to the London markets much quicker and easier.

It wasn't until the setting up of the Commissioners on Salmon Fisheries in 1860 that any formal regard to the plight of the salmon was taken notice of. In their first report the following year, the Commissioners noted the use of stone piers and stop-nets that they considered caught every fish. Only by the establishment and recognition of fishing rights, proven through usage and set in concrete, so to speak, could the total collapse of the salmon be thwarted, as we've previously discovered at Gatcombe.

In the Wye, between Monmouth and Chepstow, these rights had passed to the Duke of Beaufort after the dissolution of the monasteries, and the Special Commission of 1866 later confirmed these claims to the fishing rights, as the Shaws had done on the Severn. In 1863 these rights were leased to brothers Alexander and David Miller. These two had come down from Scotland, where, as boys, they had learned about salmon on the river Tay. Subsequently, Alexander and another brother John had managed salmon fisheries in Galway, before Alexander came to Chepstow after gaining the lease, along with David. They also had leases to fishing at Newnham on the Severn and at Dunn Sands, which are just off the mouth of the Wye. In 1864 they opened a fish house in the town, selling to the public as well as supplying markets in Bristol and London. They named their newly built house Stuart House, after their best customers in London – a firm called Stuart! Alexander became superintendent water-bailiff of the Wye Preservation Society and this house later became its headquarters.

However, it was Frank Buckland as Inspector of Fisheries who did more than anyone to preserve the salmon in the river. He brought 700 small salmon from the Rhine and introduced them into the river. He worked hard on in building fish ladders, helped by the Millers, although it has been said that they and their sons probably did more harm than anyone else in over-fishing the rivers with their multitude of nets.

At that time the Commissioners declared that the Wye was 'principally fished by stop-nets', the number of which was uncertain because they were unsure of the number fishing between Llandogo and Monmouth. They did estimate the number in the rest of the river up to Hereford – twenty-three between the estuary and Chepstow bridge, fifteen from there to Llandogo and another forty between Monmouth and Hereford. In more recent times there were thirty-six boats operating some two hours at low water at Chepstow, these being drawn up onto the riverbank at the end of the season and repaired.

So what of these stopping boats?, I thought. There were none at all lying by the riverside, which wasn't really surprising. Obviously there was Simon's back in his collection. However, peering through the iron railings behind the museum I found another I'd heard about from him. I asked the museum about its age, but no one knew. I also knew the Evironment Agency had another, although I was unsure of its whereabouts.

Looking at the Ordnance Survey map of the Wye I found a number of weirs with evocative names such as Walter's Weir, Liveoaks Troughs Weir and Riding Stream Weir, and then the less obscure Bigs Weir, Wall Weir, Chit Weir, Hook Weir and, of course, Brooksweir. I had a sudden desire to drive up to Llandogo because of the Bristol pub named the Llandoger Trow, and a second-hand bookshop in Tintern I know of. But I didn't because of another urge to press on, to get to the coast, to reach the sea.

By this time I had decided to follow the footsteps of Mr and Mrs S.C. Hall, who travelled from Gloucester to Milford Haven in the late 1850s by the newly opened railway. Their autobiographical story is told in *The Book of South Wales, the Wye and the Coast*, first published in 1861, but a special impression was produced to mark the inauguration of Alcoa's new rolling mill for aluminium Rigid Container Sheet, Waunarlwydd Works, Swansea, 21 July 1978. That last bit comes directly from the book, so don't ask me what 'aluminium Rigid Container Sheet' means! The imprint on the hard cover informs me that 'Alcoa chose Wales for the first aluminium RCS mill in Europe'. However, the Hall's seemed a way of adding some comparison to today's social and cultural upheavals that would become obvious as I travelled along the coast. Glancing at the map, it is easy to see how they managed to almost hug the coast as today's rail, although dismantled over a few old sections, is largely still in operation. Some lines have been abandoned, such as that along the coast of Glamorgan (I later found it hadn't been built in their time anyway) and a few detours would be needed, but mirroring the majority of their route almost 150 years later would be exciting, I surmised. Dog wagged his tail at such thrilling news and looked at me with his peppercorn eyes – eyes that pleaded, 'When were we going to the beach?'

So we went to Black Rock where information boards told us that a Celtic Iron Age tribe – the Silures – had established a strong fortress at Sudbrook with walls over 16ft high to dominate the cross channel trade. These people introduced the wheel, reaping machines and soap into this part of Wales. Cor, I thought, from the wheel to soap in one easy move. How, I wondered, would they react to today's society when almost equal importance is paid to both the wheel and soap, yet reaping machines are somewhat obsolete.

Black Rock was the site of one of the ferries across the estuary. A landing stage was established in Roman times to carry away goods associated with charcoal burning, iron smelting, ceramics and mining. The ferry was initiated some time later and became known as the 'New Passage'. The story goes that Charles I crossed over this way to escape the pursuing Cromwellians. When the boatmen returned to the Welsh side, they were forced to take the awaiting Parliamentarians across to where they had landed Charles on the English side. However, instead they took them to the large area midstream known as English Rock and told them they could easily walk to the far shore. But before they were halfway across, the tide came in and all the soldiers drowned. So incensed was Cromwell himself that he closed the ferry down (I'm surprised he wasn't a bit more punitive!). It didn't reopen until 1718. Travellers wanting to cross to Wales had to light bundles of straw to attract the attention of the boatmen who lived across at Black Rock and wait fifteen minutes for the boat to cross. In 1787 the mail coach used the route for the first time until Thomas Telford suggested switching it back to the Old Passage in 1823 because he regarded this passage safer than the other. Construction and the subsequent opening of a ferry in 1863 between two rail termini, one at Portskewett pier – 774ft long – and the other at New Passage pier – 1,635ft long – with steamers plying the ferry route between, created a relatively quick link between Bristol and the South Wales Junction. However, this was short-lived because ten years later the Victorian engineers began the Severn Tunnel which was to become one of their great feats of work. At the height of work this employed 3,628 men and some 76 million bricks were cemented in. By the time it was opened in 1882 there were forty electric lights along the route and a telephone line linked both sides. It wasn't until the motor car began its mark upon our lives that a vehicle ferry was opened in 1931, over a hundred years after Telford first muted the idea of a bridge. A scheme had been adopted four years before, but was passed over in preference to the building of the Forth Bridge. It wasn't until 1966 that the present Queen opened what is now considered to be the 'old bridge', for the second road crossing arrived in the 1990s. Thankfully, though, the rail tunnel is still in operation. We walked over to Sudbrook where workmen were digging. Tens of feet below where they were working trains full of people were rushing to and fro, just as I had on many an occasion. Well, perhaps there are not so many trains or people these days, but this link remains today an essential part of the network of infrastructure across this waterway!

Portskewett, according to the Halls, was once 'probably the port to Caerwent', the nearby Roman city. Men from the village, and from Sudbrook, have fished the Black Rock Lave-Net Fishery for generations, and this is the only remaining lave-net fishery in Wales. Fishing can only take place 1½ hours over the low water during spring tides, and the season begins with the first spring tides in June and ends with the last ones in August. Hereabout, the fishermen use local terms such as Monkey's Tump, Nester's Rock and Lighthouse Vear, places certainly not found on the map.

The beach suffers from dumping here for it is littered with broken sections of reinforced concrete and clumps of bricks from some demolished building. Further along, it is nature that is changing its appearance as the red cliff falls away in constant erosion. Indeed, the beach itself has become a smoothened floor of red rock as the wind and sea chew away at the cliff's edge. Perhaps the concrete and brick are from fallen buildings I surmised. No, the only thing that has fallen, I guess, is man's standards.

Caldicot has an appearance of sadness today, with its modern town centre of brick-faced one-storey shops and bland streets. The motorway acts as a barrier between town and sea, strangling it at the neck and chopping away the life-blood of the people. For here, surprisingly, was a strong tradition of looking seaward, and one of shipbuilding. There's a fine castle, built in the Norman times, where some remains of an ancient planked boat were discovered in 1988 during the construction of a lake in the Caldicot Castle Country Park. These fragments of a boat have been dated to 1700 BC and remain the oldest excavated boat parts in existence in Wales to date.

Furthermore, there's an association with Nelson in that parts of HMS *Foudroyant*, an 80-gun ship of the line built in 1789 and later Nelson's flagship for one year, are scattered about the castle. These include the figurehead, a cannon, ashtrays made from salvaged copper from the hull and plans and photographs. The ship, once decommissioned, was purchased by Geoffrey Cobb, who restored her to train young lads. On a voyage around Britain, she was wrecked off Blackpool in 1897. Cobb, whose father owned the castle, went on the buy HMS *Trincomalee* to continue his sail training of boys.

We walked along the coastal footpath, past the Sudbrook pumping station, and the papermill, and under the motorway to Caldicot Pill. This whole area from Black Rock almost to Magor Pill is termed the Caldicot levels and has been subject of much archaeological interest over the last fifty years or so. Here at Caldicot Pill, according to the evidence, is the point on the coast that Roman vessels ascended the stream up to Caerwent. Here, too, a flourishing shipbuilding business developed in the late eighteenth and early nineteenth centuries. Henry Wise lived in the hall, and owned at various times sixteen vessels, sometimes as sole owner. He financed the local shipbuilding usually speculatively, diverting the Nedern stream to construct a shipyard. Vessels were taken over to Bristol or up to Chepstow for fitting out. A typical vessel was the brigantine *Lion*, built in 1785, 132 tons, 74ft 6in in length overall, owned by H. Wise, merchant of Caldicot and Master Thomas Barrow. However, after the *Sisters*, 314 tons, was built by Giles Viner in 1801, the building of large vessels ceased. Henry Wise died in 1805 and his son Samuel just retained a share in two boats. Very small coastal sloops continued to be built and the last recorded activity was the rebuilding of a ship's longboat *Recovery* in 1823, with the work being done by the owner who was probably a local fisherman.

One of the most fascinating aspects of maritime history is the discovery of wrecks lying in the ground which have become covered with clay or peat, thus preventing a breakdown of the organic matter. Four such wrecks (not including the aforementioned fragments at Caldicot) have been unearthed in the area between Magor Pill and the mouth of the Usk. The oldest is inland, at the site of the Tesco warehouse, close to what was Barland's Farm, at Magor. This vessel, termed by many as a Romano-Celtic boat, was in excess of 10m long and was discovered lying alongside a wooden and stone pier. Dendrochronology – tree-ring dating – suggests that the trees used in its construction were felled between AD 283 and AD 326. The bottom is flat with frames fixed to this and planks subsequently fixed to the frames using large iron nails that are clenched over. This boat is presumed typical of that type in use along the European Atlantic seaboard by the Celts over many centuries. Today's contemporary types would include the beach boats of Holland and Belgium, notably the *scute*, a replica of which has recently been built in Belgium.

Debate rages amongst the academic world as to the nature of vessels in use in the period after the Norman Conquest up to the fourteenth century. Many point to a strong Scandinavian influence in boatbuilding techniques and suggest that most of Britain's native craft have evolved from such craft. On the other hand, others point to the existence of Saxon vessels long before the Vikings ever raided these coasts. As a third ingredient to the eventual mix-match of influences, the Roman practise of boatbuilding, which is altogether different from the other two, affected parts of the coast. Although the writer does have opinions of the way boat design was influenced by others from outside the country, these pages are not the place to elucidate on such matters, given that the subject could fill an entire volume much thicker than this meagre book. What I will state though is that it is my opinion that all along the western fringe of England, Wales and Scotland, the East Irish coast and the Isle of Man, when it comes to influences that have contributed to boat design, there has been a 'clash of culture'. The vessels in use up to the end of the sail era, all unique in their own area, developed from this Roman-Celtic boat with a later dressing of distinct Scandinavian flavour.

What is surprising, though, is that we don't seem to have progressed very far in the last thirty years. Recently I was reading a book on boatbuilding, written thirty years ago, and it seems to me our knowledge then has been little improved upon, even though there seems to be a flood of eager and enthusiastic academics – possibly they are enthused about their own skills rather than the sifting of evidence. The earliest known 'ship' in Wales is still the ceremonial Caergwrle Bowl, carved in oak and depicting a sea-going vessel. We know that rafts, hollowed out logs, bark boats and skin boats were the earliest craft, and that curraghs and coracles, constructed from willow or ash and covered in hide, were described by Pliny, and that Caesar found the same. Caesar also noted the flat-bottomed, carvel-built craft with high ends. These craft developed into what is generally regarded as the Romano-Celtic boat described very briefly above. Then came the

Germanic Saxons with their craft followed closely by the Vikings and their vessels with painted sails and dragonheads. Into the Middle Ages and vessels became bigger and beamier, bluff in the bow and fuller in shape. Rigs developed and then the slow realisation that more masts enabled the setting of more sail, thus increasing speed and the carrying capability – and the sailing range.

The wreck at Magor Pill, the second of our four wrecks, does exhibit strong Norse traditions in its construction. This double-ended vessel, the building of which has been dated to AD 1240, was found in the intertidal zone off the mouth of the pill, in an area that is believed to have been the documented landing area *Abergwaitha*, which was destroyed by flooding in the fourteenth century. Unlike the Romano-Celtic boat, which was built of edge-joining planks with caulking in between, this boat is built of overlapping planks – in other words, clinker built. These planks were of oak and had been fastened to the frames and floors using treenails whilst the floors were not fastened to the keel. That links between the Irish Sea and Denmark existed is verified by the fact that the timber used in the building of one wreck found in Denmark – called the Skuldelev 2 wreck – has been found to come from this area. Viking settlements in Dublin and all around the coast of Wales, the Bristol Channel and into the West Country further seem to confirm this. A reconstruction of the part of the boat that was excavated, commissioned by the National Museums and Galleries of Wales, shows flat floors and a considerable sheerline. However, it should perhaps be stressed that this model and the associated drawings were interpreted from only a few surviving floors and appear to take no account of any sagging of the timber. What is sure is this wreck is the most complete of its type found in Welsh waters.

In April 1878 the remains of a boat were found near the mouth of the Usk during the excavations for the Alexander Dock and this has been termed the 'Ancient Danish Vessel' by Octavius Morgan, although it is clinker-constructed from Danzig oak. Although the find was only part of one (possibly port) side of the vessel, Morgan suggested this was 70ft long and between 17 and 20ft in breadth and was therefore capable of sailing long distances. More recent research has shown that, contrary to Morgan's thesis, the vessel was Danish, it had similar features to many other of its contemporary north European boats and thus neither its form nor origin can be confirmed.

The fourth wreck, in terms of its discovery, is much more recent. In the summer of 2002, during excavations of the below-ground orchestral pit for a new arts centre in the middle of Newport, alongside the Usk, the wreck of a large, beamy oak-built vessel was discovered. Some of the oak has been dated to 1465 and testing suggests origins from South Gloucestershire. This, then, was an important Middle Ages ship find, enough to halt work on the site and persuade – after public pressure was brought to bear – the Welsh Assembly to fund a full excavation of the wreck. This was completed by the autumn and the timbers remain at present in conservationary tanks at the nearby Llanwern steelworks. Until a proper investigation is carried out, further details are not available. However, like projected ideas for the Magor Pill wreck, it is envisaged that some future exhibition in Newport will feature the wreck, its finds and a full interpretation of shipbuilding of that era. The intention with the Magor Pill wreck is, I believe, to make it centrepiece in a new National Maritime Museum for Wales, thus replacing the one that was shut down when the ground beneath it was needed for the Cardiff Bay waterside development project. Heritage, as we all know, takes the back seat when developers move into a site and erect their idea of paradise in the form of waterfront housing!

Bridges and Tunnels

Communication routes in and out of Wales, as well as around the country, have created problems for travellers for thousands of years. With rivers flowing down from the mountainous hinterland into estuaries indenting all along the coastline, and major rivers – specifically the Severn, Wye and Dee – blocking the border between England, it has been these that primarily have caused the obstacles. It's less than surprising then that Wales has some spectacular bridges and tunnels. From Thomas Telford's graceful Suspension Bridge and Robert Stephenson's Britannia Railway Bridge, both spanning the Menai Strait, to two modern road bridges and one rail tunnel, all crossing the river Severn, the country has structures of engineering of their time and, at the same time, wonderfully aesthetic.

Telford was responsible for building much of today's A5 route from Shrewsbury to Holyhead after the Post Office had demanded the improvement of the route from London, all the way to Holyhead. This was virtually complete by 1830. River crossings were numerous and the major bridges included the Stanley Embankment to Holy Isle (1822), the Menai Suspension Bridge (1826) and the Waterloo Bridge across the river Conwy at Bettws-y-Coed (1815).

The river Conwy also caused a major obstacle on the North Wales coast. This was crossed by ferry until the first bridging was made by Telford's suspension bridge, six months after he opened the Menai Bridge in 1826. The coastal route was improved because of the importance of the Chester to Holyhead mail coach, which carried the Irish mail, following the decision to make Holyhead the port for Ireland. Robert Stephenson followed Telford with his tubular railway bridge alongside the first, completed for rail traffic in 1849. This bridge, consisting of two tubes, was the forerunner to the larger Britannia Bridge (1850). Another road bridge, alongside the tubular rail bridge, was opened in the 1950s, increasing traffic in the town, a problem that was not solved until the route under the river, built using concrete tubes that were sunk into the seabed, opened in 1991.

Ferries were of course the only way of crossing all the Welsh rivers until bridges were constructed. Some were free such as the ferry at Queensferry on the river Dee between 743 and 1897. That year, the first Victoria Jubilee Bridge was opened which was demolished and replaced by another in 1926. Another bridge to carry the dual carriageway was built in the 1960s, while the newest bridge at Flint was opened in the 1998.

Likewise South Wales has its own peculiar crossings, other than the Severn bridges. Bridges of note are the 1816-built Old Wye Bridge that crossed that river at Chepstow, the Transporter Bridge at Newport – unique to Wales and completed in 1902 – and over the Neath river at Briton Ferry, crossed for the first time as late as 1955. Telford suggested a suspension bridge here in the early nineteenth century but no action was taken. The M4 motorway crossing followed in the 1980s. The Cleddau Bridge collapsed during its construction in 1970 and thus added delays to its eventual completion and opening in 1975.

Of course, each river has its own bridge crossing of some kind or other. Many of the major ports – Newport, Cardiff, Swansea, Carmarthen, Cardigan, Aberystwyth and Conwy for example – rose out of a need to cross a river at that particular spot. Estuaries such as the Mawddach and Dyfi have not, as yet, been crossed by road bridges close to their confluence into the sea, although railway crossings upon wooden bridges to do exist. Porthmadog's cob is a good example of the way the Victorian engineers reclaimed land as well as crossed wide estuaries.

The final type of river crossings that are seldom mentioned are the small so-called humpback bridges that cross so many of Wales's rivers, but are usually sited well up rivers,

Above: The old bridge at Chepstow built in 1816 thus joining Monmouthshire to Gloucestershire.

Right: The Newport Transporter Bridge.

away from the coast. One exception though that immediately comes to mind is the old stone bridge across the little river at Aberffraw, on Anglesey's West Coast. Although not of any particular note, it mirrors hundreds of tiny stone bridges – some bigger and higher arched than others – that appear in out of the way places amongst the mountains and hills. Some carried the narrow gauge tramways from the quarries while others followed old drovers' routes. Some are barely wide enough for a horse to cross while others can take two lanes of today's traffic. What they all do have in common is survival – survival from an era of building excellence – are vernacular in design and serve a purpose that many continue to serve today. That they share with their grander contemporaries. For a thorough record of the country's bridges, viaducts and aqueducts, see Gwyndaff Breese's *The Bridges of Wales* (Llanrwst, 2001).

As Britain's communication routes are improved to cope with increasing traffic, there are of course plans afoot to build more roads that will necessitate more bridges. A southern motorway route around Newport will incorporate another crossing of the river Usk. A third bridge across the Menai Strait has been mooted, such is the bottleneck on the A55 route across the Britannia Bridge where the dual carriageway becomes a single carriageway. Another mistake that will need rectifying is the lack of a double tunnel at Penmaenbach on the A55, which has led to congestion to traffic travelling eastwards. One final project that has been mentioned, although is never likely to happen, is the building of a tunnel all the sixty miles to Ireland. However, with tunnels under the English Channel, amongst the Danish archipelago and in Japan, and others planned such those from China to Taiwan and Spain to Morocco, perhaps just one day this will be a reality. One that might be of more use to Wales, though, would be a tunnel from Southwest Wales to Devon, reinvigorating ancient trading routes and sparing the need to journey over 150 miles to complete a distant of some thirty miles by the way the crow flies. Some hope!

The rights of the fishing at Goldcliff and the lands of the Benedictine Priory were given to Eton College at its founding in the reign of Henry VI, although their ownership has since changed. Stout frameworks across the tidal flow, onto which were fixed putchers, has existed for generations, and only in 1952 was sea-resistant wire adopted instead of the traditional willow baskets. Three ranks each named separately – Flood, Ebb and Putt – amounted to a total of 2,327 putchers. The posts still stick up from the mud, transfixed by a few crosspieces. The sign, in red flaking paint, still remains on the old fish store and reads 'private – persons interfering with these fisheries will be prosecuted, By Order:- Goldcliff Fisheries'. But the fisheries are as redundant as the flaky paint, the same as at Beachley, the salmon gone! All around was quiet. I looked for somebody to ask questions but found not a soul.

Upstream, at Porton, another rank of some 600 putchers was once equally proficient at catching salmon but now remain but a distant memory. A brick smokehouse was built in the twentieth century but its use appears to have been short-lived.

Across the milky brown water distant shapes betrayed the conurbation around the mouth of the river Avon. Upstream of that river, towards Bristol, lies Sea Mills, the third-century harbour of Roman settlement of *Abona*. Presumably the majority of vessels working these waters called in there. In more recent times, Sea Mills became important as a harbour because, when it was built in 1712, it was only one of three tidal harbours in Britain where vessels could remain afloat. However, as the Bristol docks were developed in the nineteenth century, this former port fell into disrepair, so that today all that remains is part of the harbour wall inland of the railway bridge that carries the line between Bristol and Avonmouth.

It was raining and even the dog seemed to sense the madness, the sadness of it all. We'd only gone a tiny proportion of the distance we had to cover, and already the depression of almost everything being either redundant or from the past hovered like a black cloud. We retraced our path back to van and drove quickly to the Transporter Bridge across the Usk (*Afon Wysg*).

The gondola was moving off as we arrived but the sign said the last run across was at 8.30 p.m., so I parked up. The bridge is quite extraordinary, given its age and the fact that it still worked. Here, then, was what appeared to be a relic from the past that still carried cars and light vehicles across for 50 pence and pedestrians, cyclists and motorcyclists for free. However, having only been opened in 1906, amid a fanfare and the appearance of Viscount Tredegar, in actual fact it isn't so old comparatively, though it almost closed until being listed as a structure of special interest in 1982 and refurbished ten years later.

One piece of fact occurred to me as the gondola moved away. In 1907, eighteen-year-old Ada Hathaway jumped overboard just as the gondola was coming into this eastern side but the quick-thinking conductor, Peter Lynbert, rescued her. Obviously Ada had wished to end her life here because she declared to Lynbert as he was saving her that, 'I do not want to be picked up. I do not want to go home'. She was lucky indeed, having jumped when the tide was three-quarters in flood. Perhaps, though, wanting to die, she wouldn't have agreed.

The gondola was originally the brainchild of French engineer Ferdinand Arnodin who was given the brief after congestion on the Town Bridge and a swift growth in Newport's fortunes necessitated a second crossing of the river. It is said that Arnodin designed his bridge so as to appear as being a ferry that glided over the water rather than lifting up into the air. People, he suggested, were wary of new ideas (aren't we still?) and so a bridge of this nature would appear to act as a ferry in that it travelled from one side to the other in a straight line, but could operate regardless of tide. Innovative it certainly was – only fifteen were ever built in the world, between 1893 and 1916. Of only six remaining, three are in Britain.

To today's visitor it simply appears functional – masses of criss-crossing steel a bit like something made out of meccano. One elongated 'A' frame stands either side of the river, connected by a boom with rails, along which, and below, the gondola runs, pulled by cables operated from electric motors in the winding house situated on the eastern side. The span is 645ft and I timed the returning gondola to two minutes to make the crossing. The maximum speed is said to be 12mph, the speed of a trotting horse! Even though there was a fair wind blowing, the transverse moment of the gondola was negligible. The gondola, though, seems to come direct from a Victorian storybook, such is its decorative appearance. It has been likened to 'the gaiety of a seaside pavilion' with its kingfisher blue paintwork, ornate ironwork, pagoda roofs and pilot house complete with weather vane, although I could not understand how the driver could actually see from what direction the wind was blowing, given the vane was hidden by the roof above his head! Still, in no time the six vehicles it can carry were aboard and we were off with hardly a bump or sound, and in two minutes we, too, were across the Usk, the blue gates opened, and away.

Newport museum and library was closed by the time I arrived. Still, I had been inside earlier, viewing the exhibits on the Roman era, the port and associated industries that accounted for the city's sudden growth in the mid-nineteenth century. For Newport, whose name comes from the New Fort (Casnewydd to give it its proper Welsh name) built by the Normans in the twelfth century, and not the port, has only recently transferred from town status to a new millennium city.

John Leland found 'a bigge town' and described it as a 'town yn ruine' whereas an earlier writer, according to the Halls, wrote that 'many saile to Bristowe from that port'. Defoe found a place of good trade with similar imports as Chepstow. Giraldus, as already noted, found a surplus of trout, although he did add that salmon abounded in the Usk in the summer. Indeed, a photograph of Caerleon dated 1910 shows three salmon boats anchored in the river with their nets hanging above to dry. Some sixteen stop-nets were in use on the river, and in 1910 there were 603 salmon thus netted. Numbers fell rapidly after that, decreasing to sixteen in 1919, and by 1934 this had further fallen to just three. The practise ceased altogether the following year.

But it was not the fish that Newport expanded upon, but the iron ore and coal. Pococke noted one occupation of the locals: 'They have a way of collecting coals on the slub on each side of the river, when the tide is out, and have boats for that purpose: amongst it there is a great deal of charcoal.' Presumably they were law-abiding folk because he continues, 'When a tax was imposed on coal they left off collecting it, and took it up again when it was taken off.' He found a poor town with 'two or three good inns'. Archdeacon Coxe, in 1800, deemed the streets to be 'dirty and ill paved; the houses in general wear a gloomy appearance', while Macpherson's *Annals of British Commerce* (1801) declares it 'a good town, near the mouth of the Usk, which makes a harbour for small vessels. Shipbuilding is the principal business of the place'. This mention of shipbuilding is interesting, because so far I was led to believe it was solely the coal and iron that sparked off the surge of prosperity in the town.

The bookplate of Newport Library.

A canal was built between Newport and Pontnewydd (Newbridge) and opened in 1796 with, three years later, an arm to Crumlin, and thus the first foundations that led to the building of one of the principal coal ports of Britain had begun. In 1800, a canal between Brecon and Gilwern was opened but it wasn't for another twelve years that the link south to Pontnewydd was achieved, thence completing what is now known as the Monmouthshire & Brecon Canal, stretching forty-two miles from Newport to Brecon and another eleven miles in the arm to Crumlin. Tramways connected the canal to the various works and mines so that ironwork, coal and limestone was brought down in huge quantities.

Another interesting archaeological find occurred in 1984 at Tredunnoc, further upstream of the river Usk. Here a flat-bottomed, double-ended, barge-like boat, dating from about 1800 and of about 60ft in length, was excavated. Whether or not this vessel was typical of all the towing barges working on the river at the time is unclear, but it does seem quite probable.

But Newport was also a ferry harbour and embarkation port. The first steamer into the Usk was the *Cambria* that began a service from the town to Bristol in 1822. Between 1825 and 1850 passenger ships brought in Irish immigrants from Southern Ireland, these often being landed at the mouth of the river to avoid licensing problems. In 1849 the master of the schooner *Mary* was found guilty of having over 200 aboard his little vessel and putting them ashore in a boat so that they had to clamber up the mud by the lighthouse to get ashore.

By the time the Halls arrived the Town Dock had been opened (1842), thus they noted 'the banks of the river on the Newport side being a mass of docks, quays, and creeks…the tall forest of shipping stands out sharply against the afternoon sky…' The first boat in was the Newport-owned barque *Great Britain* that was lost the following year in the Atlantic. In 1872 the first iron-screw steamer was built by the Uskside Iron Company and launched from their yard on the west side of the river above the bridge.

This was the 126ft *Blanche*, described as being 'stiff as a church' when she had floated. In 1878, when the Alexander Dock was opened, its sea lock was the largest in the world, and the mouth of the river the deepest in Britain. The growth of Newport from a town in ruin to a major prosperous deep port was indeed rapid, but also rapid was its decline once the railway altered the nature of transport, and shipping died off. Newport possibly benefited briefly from the major rail junction between the northern line and the main South Wales line, but that was short-lived. Incidentally, Brunel first came here in 1844 and is upon the list of famous visitors, as is Voltaire who arrived in 1729 after a period of exile in England. Brunel then returned in 1850, driving the first train on the new Chepstow to Swansea railway.

Then came the closure of the coal, followed on by today's pain as the steel industry collapses. This is, of course, the result of the so-called 'globalisation' that nobody seems to have asked for or wants. Even with city status, the future for Newport is bleak, words echoed by Alan Roderick in 1994 when he wrote that 'no-one, but no-one, not even John Frost himself, could possibly accuse Newport of being a beautiful place'.

We drove out, crossing the river Ebbw (*Afon Ebwy*), otherwise known as 'Newport's Other River', that leads up to Ebbw Vale and followed the Lighthouse Road. A light twinkled low and ahead. At St Brides we turned left off this road and found the Lighthouse Inn. There was a sign saying 'No Dogs'. That seemed a suitable place to stop for the night. Another sign stated that, owing to vandalism, the gates would be locked at the close of business and reopened at 7.45 a.m. That was even better. Now that the rain had stopped the sky was orange from the distant lights of the metropolis that is Cardiff. Dog sniffed the 'No Dogs' sign with an air of contempt! I went for a quick pint in an almost empty pub, followed by a peer over the seawall over to distant England, a lungful of sea air in the freshening wind, then back to the van and out like a light!

DAY THREE
CARDIFF TO BARRY

The Halls refer to Marshfield as being the only station in the twelve miles between Newport and Cardiff and that the 'name indicates the nature of the locality'. Today the area remains a drained part of the coast marked as 'Wentlooge Level' on the map. The railway station at Marshfield has gone. The road winds past Peterstone Gout and New Quay Gout, although nobody in the locality knew why it was called 'New Quay'. *The Welsh Port Books* identify havens along this part of the coast between Newport and 'Rompney' (Rhymney) as being at 'Ebothey creeke or pylle', 'Westhowcke creeke' and 'Peterstone creek called the great Goulte', each having deputies appointed there. Presumably these first two relate to the Ebbw River and Wentlooge, although correct me if I am wrong.

Soon, we are driving past the beginnings of industrial Cardiff, past the Lamby refuse tip and along the Lamby Way, over the river Rhymney (*Afon Rhymni*). A few boats lie moored in the lower reaches of the river, below the bridge, but nothing of significance, although I'm afraid that the owners may disagree! If any of you do, by the slimmest of chance, read this, please, no disgruntled letters.

I don't like cities, never have, but Cardiff isn't as bad as many. Probably because of its relatively small size, it doesn't seem quite as sprawling as other capitals. It lies, nominally, sandwiched between the Rhymney and the eastern bank of the river Taff (*Afon Taf*) which flows down from the vale of the same name. The Taff flows out to sea over the Penarth Flats where it joins the Ely River (*Afon Elai*). However, those incessant developers have changed the whole nature of the Flats by the building of the Cardiff Bay Barrage which opened in 1998, flooding the Flats so that they are no longer tidal. Of course, this meant 'developing' the whole area, which generally translates to the building of a mass of trendy waterside housing, evicting existing tenants from the older docklands in the process – including the National Maritime Museum of Wales, which is no longer – and creating both an air of tackiness and a lack of individualism. I heard a story that they were also trying to charge boat owners for the use of the Taff which upset many that have moored their boats there for decades.

But Cardiff is the capital of Wales and therefore we must linger. It is home to the new Assembly, the new talking shop of Welsh government, the building of which hasn't yet begun, although its start is only days away. Or so I was told. Only time will tell if their formation actually filters any benefit down to those that pay their wages, whereas at present it does seem that a majority of the inhabitants are suspicious and doubt the presence of the Assembly will alter their lives. Add to this that only a tiny majority voted for devolution, and something like only half the population voted in the first place, it's hardly surprising that the people are not bubbling with enthusiasm for what does seem, on the face of it, to be yet another tier of government with its associated costs to the tax payer.

Ships belonging to 'Kerdif' were mentioned in a 1233 Tewkesbury Abbey document, which points to some kind of harbour or shelter upon the river. In the fourteenth century tolls were levied on, amongst other goods, timber, at what was described as a 'sea-landing place'. Cardiff was at the time the principal place of maritime trade with links with Bristol, Somerset, the West Country, the South Coast of England and Brittany at least. Documentary evidence of its quay only surfaces in the early 1550s but presumably one existed previously. By the time of the late sixteenth century it had become 'a faire Key and a safe harborowe for Shippinge' and 'to which both Ships and Botes resort'.

However, the initial growth of the Port of Cardiff can only be attributed to the development of the iron industry. Ironworks had been in existence in Glamorgan since before the Roman times but it wasn't until the late sixteenth century that a significant amount of iron was exported into Bristol and Somerset, and later to London and the Netherlands. In the next century improvements in furnaces saw a rapid growth in the industry, which continued in the eighteenth century. Alongside this, coal mining developed to satisfy the furnace demand, and a further need for domestic heating and other industrial requirements. The export of coal reached a maximum in 1913 when in excess of 36 million tons where exported from the South Wales ports. This, ironically, coincided with the peak year of herring exports from Britain as a whole when over a million tons were landed. When Defoe arrived in Cardiff in 1725 he found 'a very good Harbour opening onto the Severn'.

In the mid-eighteenth century, coal and iron was being transported across mountain ridges and through the green valleys by horseback until a roadway was built to enable wheeled carts to be pulled by horses. However, in an expanding era, this was obviously not sufficient to satisfy the demand. Canal building around Britain was in its infancy but was fast evolving and so the idea of a Glamorgan Canal was first mooted in the early 1780s. With Parliamentary approval, building commenced in 1790 and the whole twenty-five-mile canal from Cardiff to Merthyr Tydfil completed in 1798 when it was opened and the sloop *Cardiff Castle* was the first vessel to enter. The canal dropped 568ft from its head to the sea and consisted of fifty locks, such was the splendour of the project. A further section from Abercynon to Aberdare was completed in 1812. Thus both the collieries and the ironworks were able to increase output once vessels of 200 tons could enter the sealock and load up with their cargo.

To get the coal down to these vessels, flat-bottomed barges were used. None are known to exist any longer – except the Tredunnoc boat mentioned the previous day – but fortunately Philip Oke prepared a rough sketch of one in the 1930s as part of his work compiling details of working craft around Britain for the Coastal Craft Committee of the Society for Nautical Research. Photographs are in existence as well. These all show barges of about 60ft in length and between 9 and 10ft in beam and the rudder added another 5ft to its length. They are said to have been influenced in shape by the barges designed by James Brindley for the Duke of Bridgewater's colliery canal at Worsley. The draught was some 13ins when empty and each could hold some 21 tons of coal. Some were entirely open boats while others had a very short forepeak and a cabin aft. Many were owned by the Glamorganshire Canal Co. and used for either hauling or maintenance duties on the canal. The company also operated an icebreaker on the canal, which was built in oak and iron clad. It had a transom stern and, as would be expected, it was sharp in the bow. Whilst being towed along by horse, the crew, who could number ten men, gripped the two handrails, one on either side, and rocked the boat from side to side thus breaking up the ice.

The coal barges were weighed by being lifted in the Weighing Machine at North Road, Cardiff. The machine there, built by Brown Lennox of Pontypridd in 1836 and capable of weighing up to 40 tons, was dismantled and taken to the Waterways Museum at Stoke Bruerne, Northamptonshire, in 1963.

Chappell says the canal served the port well until the 1840s and was the prime reason that Cardiff developed on the scale it did. In the previous year, some 211,214 tons of coal were exported down the canal and through the port. However, with the development of railways and the subsequent building of a line up to the port meant shipping competed with trains, although the former continued to increase traffic until the 1870s after which an increase of the movement of goods by railway saw a decline in the fortunes of the canal. Today, the canal has been built over much of its route, thus preventing a re-opening as has been the case in many other waterways.

Shipbuilding was not significant in the growth of Cardiff as a port because most of the vessels coming there were owned from other ports. One of the earliest builders was James Davies who built a half-tide dock at the old Town Quay in 1813. In the 1830s, with the massive increase in trade that Cardiff experienced, a proper dock was deemed vital to the interests of shipping. Thus the West Bute Dock was planned and subsequently opened in 1839 with the entry of the vessel *Manulus* through the sea-lock into what was at first called the Ship Canal. Richard Tredwen had a shipyard at the head of the dock. However, the dock itself soon became insufficient for the port's needs and in 1855 the much larger East Bute Dock was opened amid a fanfare and the entry of the *William Jones* of Sunderland. According to the Halls, the docks were 'busy, large and admirably-constructed' that began to rival Liverpool and London and 'its railways are night and day thronged with huge waggons bearing to the quays the dark produce of the hills'. There was an obvious hive of activity. Yet, less than twenty years later (1874), the next stage in the growth of the port occurred in the form of the opening of the Roath Basin, further followed, in 1887, by the construction of the Roath Dock. Then, in 1907, came the final piece of work that culminated in the reclamation of a huge part of the sea and resulted in the opening of the

Cardiff Docks, *c.*1900.

Queen Alexandra Docks. It was this reclamation work that produced the arm of land to the east of the Penarth Flats which ultimately allowed the construction of the much-opposed Cardiff Bay Barrage and the subsequent flooding of the Flats.

When one studies the trade figures for Cardiff, it becomes clear just how considerable the status of the port was. In 1893 almost 7.5 million tons of coal and coke was exported through it while the grand total of Cardiff-registered shipping cleared outward to foreign and British possessions overseas in 1890 amounted to some 5.5 million tons. Comparing these figures with other British ports we discover that Cardiff surmounted those shown by both London and Liverpool. Thus Cardiff was the principal port in terms of exported goods in the whole of Great Britain.

I wandered around the East Bute Dock, now called the Atlantic Wharf, absorbing these facts. Looking around, it was hard to imagine this place as the biggest hive of shipping activity in all of Britain! The West Dock has gone. County Hall seems to dwarf the area. Shipping occupied the Queen Alexandra Dock in the distance, now resigned to a small corner of the town as if it somehow brought disrepute to it, which seemed pretty unfair given Cardiff would have been nothing without it. Without a port, the population would never have jumped from about 1,000 inhabitants to 130,000 in the period of 1801 to 1893. Perhaps Swansea would have become home to the Welsh Assembly! I walked down to the Norwegian church, inside of which is an arts centre. I remember doing a 'herring exhibition' here some years ago when some unsuspecting passer-by called the fire brigade one evening while I was out in the pub. He'd seen smoke emanating from the smokehouse and the firemen had to cut the lock off only to find 150 part-smoked kippers! I was confused on my return to find a new padlock and was busy trying to understand this when someone arrived with the key to open it while recounting the tale to me. So much for inquisitive passers-by!

Boats bobbed about over the once prolific breeding grounds for various birds that so infuriated the environmentalists in the public debate before the Barrage's construction. Modernity was a word that came to mind, part of a phrase thrown carelessly about by Prime Minister Blair. Change is good, but not for change's sake and sometimes projects such as this barrage are exactly that – change for change's sake, the destruction of generations of heritage on the road to progression and profit. Even the dog wasn't keen: he didn't seem to be pulling at his lead! We found the van and drove over the new bridge that spans the mouth of the Taff, onto the Penarth Moors, round a roundabout, over the Ely River and into Penarth. There was somebody much more interesting to see here, if we could find him, somebody belonging to the vernacular zone, which Cardiff Docks didn't. And it is at this point that we leave the route taken by the Halls, for they journeyed up the Taff Vale Railway to Pontypridd, returning to Cardiff, from where they travelled to Caerphilly before again heading west along the South Wales Railway to Bridgend, a route upon which they noted crossed the Ely River some sixteen times. The coastal rail route via Penarth, Barry and Llantwit Major was not used – possibly because it hadn't even been thought of in their day!

Penarth was to Cardiff what Margate was to London. It was the working person's bolthole to the sea on Sundays and holidays. Situated on the western side of the estuary of the three rivers mentioned, the actual town lies upon the head of land that is Penarth Head. Leland refers to it as 'an hille or foreland into the Severn Se'. However, it was the docks that initially brought prosperity to the town.

Penarth Docks were developed because of insufficient space in Cardiff. Coal exports were rocketing and nobody had envisaged such rapid growth and thus boats were wasting time waiting for access into Cardiff. The original harbour, on the north side of the river, was opened in 1859 and was tidal but it didn't prevent the export of 200,000 tons of coal annually within five years of opening. Keen to capitalise while Cardiff was standing still, the owners obtained the necessary powers to build a dock on the south side of the river which then opened in 1865, still ten years ahead of the Roath Dock. This was again tidal and a boat could arrive through the dock gate at high water, load up and leave on the next tide. The same year a chain ferry across the Ely was opened, connecting Penarth to Grangemouth, the area to the west of the Taff. The fare on this was one penny and it employed two men. Two decades later ferries worked from Cardiff Pier Head to Penarth Dock, running every twenty minutes. In summer these went to the beach, landing holidaymakers onto movable stages.

In 1884 an extension to the dock at Penarth was added, enabling over 3 million tons of coal to be shipped out. By 1912 this had increased to 4,179,506 tons and together Cardiff and Penarth handled in excess of 14 million tons the following year.

In early 1881 some twenty ships were put ashore in a storm between Lavernock and Penarth Head, many of which were refloated. A lifeboat house had been established in 1861 when the eight-crew pulling lifeboat *George Cay* was placed on station. Three years later a Coastguard watchtower was built. In 1868 a slightly larger ten-oared boat, under the same name, was brought in, until this was in turn replaced by another eight-oared lifeboat, the *Joseph Denham* in 1875. In 1881 another *Joseph Denham* arrived, this time a twelve-oared vessel and two years later a new boathouse and slip was opened near the docks. Yet another lifeboat with the same name followed in 1895 but, with more efficient boats coming on station in Barry and Weston-super-Mare, the station was closed in 1905.

My first stop was at the western side of the new barrage where a large car park allowed expensive parking. Dog and I walked along the stony beach below the crumbling cliff and over several groynes that had convenient steps over. The tide was down so the return would be no problem unless we lingered at the other end. The eastern end of the seafront was broken up, obviously by frequent storms and massive slabs of concrete, complete with graffiti, lay yards from where they should be. We walked to the pier that was opened in 1894. A wooden pavilion was added in 1907 giving fine views of the distant North Devon coast, but unfortunately this was destroyed by fire in 1931. Pictures I found showed the pier a hub of activity with Campbell's steamers calling to take passengers across to the far coast. These also show the beach in 1896 with bathing machines and throngs of holidaymakers enjoying the beach. This day, though, it was sadly almost deserted, even in the afternoon sun, although a few shops lined the landward side of the shop and one particular kiosk near to the pier entrance sold me an ice cream. Furthermore, as I walked past this entrance I heard the sound of singing emanating from inside, a sign that some group was using the Edwardian building. However, when many piers around the British coast were wholly dismantled during the Second World War when the threat of invasion was real, this one was perhaps lucky to survive. In 1947 the 7,000-ton cargo ship *Port Royal Park* rammed it, after which some of it was demolished. It opened two years later in its present length and retains the grand concrete 'Pier Pavilion' on the shore end.

We retraced our steps to the barrage, noting some apricot-coloured boulders lying on the beach close to the eastern end of the cliff and walked over to the dock, passing the Customs

House, which had been built in 1865 and more recently converted to a hotel. Again most of the remaining dock area had been turned over to housing, with new roads and speed bumps. A marina, mostly filled with plastic boats, utilises the water space, and, with bits of greenery scattered around, there was an air of tranquility about the place. Nevertheless, this is not a place in which I would wish to spend my days out! In the boatyard I asked about the 'blind boatbuilder' I'd been asked to interview. 'Roger, yeah you'll find him up in his yard Keel Hall'd', was the reply and it was described to me the way there, past the big supermarket, under the railway bridge, fork left at the church and 'you can't miss him on the right'. This was correct, I didn't, but unfortunately Roger was not in, out sailing in a boat as it later transpired, given the sunny afternoon. It was not 'till three days later, after returning to Penarth from my journey west, that I managed to meet this amazing man.

Roger Hall has been registered blind since he was seventeen. Now he's fifty-five, so that was thirty-eight years ago. As a child he was taken out to sea in a carrycot on his father's converted lifeboat *Fiddlers 3*. At the age of twelve he got his first boat, the jolly boat *Porpoise*, and four years later he and his friend Ray Palfrey bought a converted lifeboat on which, according to Roger they 'sorted the rig, fitted an engine and proceeded to win boyhood races' before selling it on. Since then he's had a number of boats for some years which he has then sold on.

In the early 1980s Roger was in Barry working on boats. Deciding to break away from the mould that most handicapped people were placed in at that time, he decided to learn how to build boats, helped on by Pete Rundle who, then, was running the Penarth Boatbuilding Company. In 1982 he repaired a compass-net boat (of which we shall learn more in a later chapter) belonging to the collection at the Welsh Folk Museum at nearby St Fagans. Two years later he secured an enterprise grant to help him open premises in the old Pump House at Penarth Dock. Over the next few years he took on a number of jobs including twice re-skinning a coracle at the museum that was destroyed by vandals. For some years he restored, repaired and repainted the rowing skiffs from Roath Park in Cardiff.

In 1990, at a time when construction on the barrage was beginning, the Cardiff Bay Development Corporation obtained a compulsory purchase order on the building. Thus Roger had to find new premises, which he did in the middle of Penarth, where I found him. Since then he's been busy restoring various boats from Barry and Cardiff docks and restoring many museum boats including the lifeboat *John & Naomi Beattie* in the Swansea Industrial and Maritime Museum. This job progressed over eighteen months and is the subject of a video presentation that can be seen in the museum. He's also rebuilt a number of boats including a Thames Slipper boat and the Aberystwyth herring boat *Jane*, as well as making up masts and has several ongoing projects such as the restoration of the Tresco launch *Soleil D'Or* which I had already seen down by Penarth Docks.

To be visually handicapped and a boatbuilder obviously demands the help of others. Sian Dorling is his support worker, his eyes. But when I met Roger in his boatshed it was obvious from the start that he didn't need 'eyes' there. He knew his way around. I asked how he coped with the blindness. 'I don't think about it', he said, 'and I only get angry when I hurt myself'. He thought a while and added, 'After all it's too easy to sit back and do nothing and every job has a way round it anyway.' Wise words from a skilled man.

His shed was filled to almost bursting by a boat that was obviously under construction, although the hull was almost completed. All the time I got the impression that Roger would rather we talked about this boat, the boat of his dreams. 'You be wanting to write about her', he said. 'No', I replied, 'I'd prefer to write about you, I'll write about the boat when it's launched!' But I was soon enticed upstairs because the only way into the hull was through stairs leading from above, there was so little clearance between building and the walls and roof of the shed. There was hardly 6in either end and 18in at one side, yet Roger passed through the gap with total ease whereas I had to squeeze myself through. Above, there was hardly the depth of a fluorescent light between deck and ceiling.

The boat, named *Lundy Gull*, was a Maurice Griffiths design. The timber is mostly pitch pine although the frames are of oak. This boat is the fulfillment of a lifelong dream of both Roger and Ray. It started back in the Pump House during tea breaks. Above their heads were two huge gantry beams holding the roof up. At 41ft long and 14 by 9in in section, they often imagined what they could do with them until the building was demolished and the beams purchased for £50 each. Thus the plans to build *Lundy Gull* were put in place. Work started in 1993 and the pair work on the boat at weekends and when their other work is quiet. Ray is a professional boatman in Cardiff docks but lives locally.

Most of Roger's work comes from the National Museums and Galleries of Wales but he spends time with the RYA Sailability, teaching visually handicapped kids to sail. He's represented Britain at the first World Blind Sailing Championships in New Zealand in 1992 and sailed to the Azores in 1995. He rafted, cycled and climbed his way around Borneo in 2000 to raise money for the 'Sunshine Homes' charity and again cycled a tandem around Southern Ireland in 2002. On top of that he plays guitar and sings in the local pub. He is, in fact, quite a guy and I felt considerably small after spending a couple of hours talking to him.

The time was ticking on and I wanted to get passed Barry that night, and so we progressed by road, following the route of an old dismantled railway track from Penarth to Barry. We passed Lavernock from where Guglielmo Marconi transmitted the first radio signal over water. Thomas William's 'Lavernock Farm', where Marconi made his base, is near the church. His assistant was Cardiff Post Office engineer George Kemp and both stayed at the farm while making trips over to Flat Holm to set up the kite aerial there. On 11 May 1897 the message 'ARE YOU READY' was transmitted in Morse code from the aerial at Lavernock to Flat Holm. Seven days later the letter 'V' was sent from Brean Down to Lavernock. Thus the age of radio transmissions began.

Flat Holm was a Scandinavian base. Later there was an Augustinian chapel belonging to the Abbot of St Augustines in Bristol. Documentary evidence shows that there were forty she-goats and two cows on the island in 1291. In the eighteenth century it was primarily a smugglers' haunt although a light was first placed there in 1738. In 1766 it was acquired by the Lordships of Cardiff and, along with Sully Island, used for tented cholera hospitals. A battery was built there in 1869 after an 1860 Parliamentary Committee recommended the provision on forts at Lavernock, Flat Holm, Steep Holm and Brean Down to protect the Severn Estuary.

St Mary's Well Bay was once popular with beach lovers who thought Penarth was too busy and commercialised. There's a caravan site above on the cliff that is situated on the site of the Lavernock battery. Past Lavernock lies the beach of Swanbridge. In the seventeenth century this beach was one of a number of small ports along this coast. Limestone seems to have been the main export, although corn, and butter according to

Defoe were also sent to Bristol and Uphill. Once the larger ports were built these smaller ports ceased as harbours and in the nineteenth century the railway brought in day-trippers to the beach. Today caravans and 'The Captain's Wife' dominate the place. Parking costs £1 for four hours and £3 all day with a £1 voucher redeemable against the purchase of food in the pub, so I presume the pub owns the car park! However, at the end of the nineteenth and beginning of the twentieth centuries, Swanbridge was renowned for its, presumably white, wines. The Marquis of Bute, on his estate here, produced so-called French novelty wines in his vineyards mostly for the London market although it must have been a fairly short-lived enterprise for production had ceased by 1920.

The foreshore is crown property a sign informs us, and another notes that many people have been drowned while attempting to visit Sully Island, which lies just off Swanbridge. 'The causeway is a deathtrap – please take great care' it proclaims whilst another declares: 'WARNING – if a boat is called out to return you to the mainland – you may be expected to reimburse the cost thereof'. We'd better not wander over to the island, I surmised. In fact I was pretty glad to get out of Swanbridge.

The port of Sully is said to be just to the east of what is now the entrance to Barry. In 1542 Leland found 'a praty Havenet or Socour for shippes'. In the eighteenth century it was still an operating harbour from where 'cattle, sheep and Hoggs' were sent to Bristol and Uphill. In the nineteenth century the Bristol to Swansea packet service called here, being able to gain shelter in the lee of the island to set down passengers for Cardiff.

However, there does seem to be some past confusion between Swanbridge and Sully, given that what is today regarded as Swanbridge is actually in the lee of Sully Island, and the harbour of Sully used to lie some two miles west at the extreme of Sully Bay. Thus some of the above must be read with caution.

A ship ran on Sully Island in 1712 with a load of wine and brandy aboard and armed locals tried to get their hands on the booze. They were driven away by the intervention of the king's officers. However, as we shall see in the next chapter, smuggling, piracy, wrecking and looting was rife along these shores up to the end of the eighteenth century. Even as far back as the sixteenth century one of Wales's most notorious pirates was at work. Callice, originally a haberdasher's apprentice in Tintern, commenced his harassment of shipping in 1574 with the capture of a Portuguese boat laden with sugar. This he sold and bought himself a ship, the *Olyphant*. He soon headed a gang of pirates and attacked and looted vessels all along the west coast from the Scilly Islands to Scotland and, according to one source, as far as East Anglia and Catholic France. He supposedly had lairs at Lulworth Cove and Poole. In 1576 he brought a captured Breton ship loaded with Newfoundland cod in to Penarth Roads which was one of two main haunts of Welsh sea-rovers. According to a Haverfordwest Justice of the Peace in a letter to Sir John Perrot when writing of the Penarth Roads, 'Cardiff is the general resort of pirates and these are sheltered and protected'. However, it was not the roads that were protected, but the pirates themselves who sold goods cheaper than honest traders to the locals of Cardiff, Penarth, Lavernock, Sully and Cogan. Sounds familiar and similar to Britain's tobacco trade in the twenty-first century! Suspicion fell on one particular sheriff of Glamorganshire, Nicholas Harbert, that he was an accomplice and that the boats could anchor in Penarth Roads with being molested by the authorities. On another occasion he was blown off course and ended up across the Atlantic, but he managed to raid the French fishing fleet off Newfoundland and returned with a shipful of cod!

Trading Boats of the Welsh Coast

Severn Trows

The trows were the coastal working craft of the river Severn in that they carried goods anywhere between Pool Quay, near Welshpool, to the Somerset and South Wales coast. Developed from traditional flat-bottomed barges, they were mostly double-ended and rounded in the fifteen century and later adopted a transom stern that remained with them throughout their remaining working era. In the seventeenth century a longer afterdeck was added with accommodation for the crew below.

By 1760 there were two types of trow – the smaller 'barges' up to 40 tons and the larger 60ft, 80-ton boats that were only referred to as trows. It has been estimated that there were some 370 craft of both sizes working the waters of the Severn and Bristol Channel. At the time these were square rigged until they adopted the sloop rig in the nineteenth century. Most trows were built in small yards that lined the riverside, and carried almost everything imaginable – coal from the Forest of Dean, iron from the Severn valley, grain, hay, manure and other agricultural goods, bricks, stone, sand and other building materials, as well as household items, timber and oak bark.

North Devon Polaccas

The polacca rig consisted of two masts, the pole foremast carrying only two yards for squaresails and no gaff-sail, the mizzen mast a large gaff and topsail, with staysails between the masts. These craft were employed in carrying limestone and coal over from South Wales to Devon and Cornwall, chiefly around Bideford. These were the smallest of the British square-rigged merchant sailing vessels, although some sailed as far as the Iberian peninsular, the Mediterranean and even over to the eastern seaboard of Canada.

Smaller barges worked in the estuaries of the rivers Taw and Torridge, carrying clay from Fremington Pill to Bideford and Barnstaple, as well as lightering timber into the same ports from deep-sea sailing boats anchored off.

Mersey Flats

Flats were the sailing barges of the rivers Mersey and Dee. They were flat-bottomed, massively built to withstand constant beaching yet, unlike most other British barges, were round-bilged and had a short entry to the water to counteract the fact they had no leeboards to stabilize them in rough seas. 'Outside' flats that worked outside of the river estuaries (often referred to as sloops) were larger than the 'inside' flats of the rivers with bowsprit and square sail. They also had bulwarks, unlike the smaller barges, and many were owned along the North Wales coast.

Like many of our vernacular craft, they changed from a square rig to the sloop rig in the eighteenth century, which allowed them a greater range. Some adopted the ketch rig and became known as 'jigger' flats, working with auxiliary engines up to the 1940s.

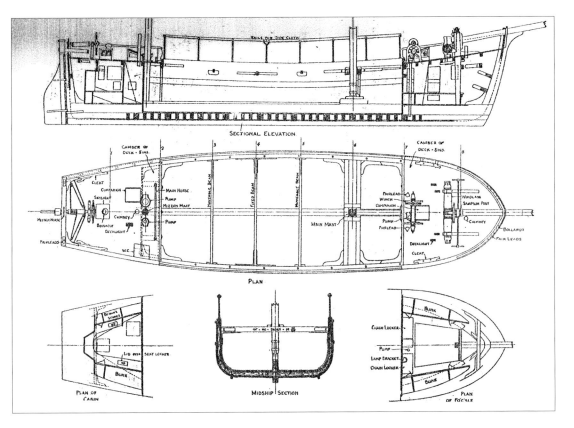

Plan of a Severn trow.

Welsh Sloops

A sloop is generally regarded as being a single-masted vessel with a fixed bowsprit with single foresail. The generic term seemed to fade out of use in the mid-nineteenth century in favour of the 'smack', although much of the time the two were indistinguishable. To further complicate the matter, a 'cutter' was very often called a sloop.

Sloops worked right along the western seaboard of Britain. Scottish smacks, built in Cornwall, fished in the Clyde and up the western coast. Smacks also fished in Manx waters. Thus it likely that Welsh sloops, as they've been termed, were similar in shape to these other boats, yet were small enough to navigate the narrow rivers of Wales. However, given that many sailed over to Ireland, Cornwall and Lancashire, and as far away as mainland Europe, they had to be strong enough to cope with heavy seas. Whether these Welsh sloops differed much beyond their English counterparts is, as yet, unclear.

Callice was eventually caught and imprisoned in the Tower of London in 1577 but he managed to be granted a pardon after pleading with Queen Elizabeth to be allowed to help them in their fight against piracy. 'I know their haunts, roads and maintainers', he urged. 'I can do more therein than if she sent ships abroad and spent twenty thousand pounds'. He was freed on the payment of a £50 surety. However, nobody seems to know what became of him after he gained his freedom although some of his associates were caught and hanged, probably through his informing.

The development of Barry Docks is due largely to one man's foresight – that of topsawyer and coalowner David Davies of Llandinam. Prior to 1880 the town of Barry did not exist and all that did were the agricultural parishes of Cadoxton, Merthyr Dyfan and Barry – a hamlet of seventeen houses – and Barry Island. Although a scheme for turning Barry into a resort by building a railway from the mainline had been mooted in 1867, nothing materialised.

We've already seen that there was considerable discontentment with the facilities at Cardiff. Davies and his associates had already considered the Ogmore River for the siting of a dock, and at Newport, but in 1882 they decided on the building of a railway to Barry and the building of the dock. However, one look at today's map will show just how many lines there were zigzagging the countryside in Glamorganshire, which helps to illustrate the huge amount of movement of coal in these South Wales valleys in the nineteenth century and into the next.

Davies' port opened in 1889 and was the largest coal exporting dock in the world. Most of the construction was contracted out to T.A. Walker, who had built the Severn Tunnel and the Manchester Ship Canal. He began by building hundreds of houses for his workers and newspapers reported that 'houses being built at Walker's Town were being erected at American speed'. Ships brought in building material and timber was supplied by Meggit & Jones who later became one of the biggest timber merchants in Wales. The new railway from the Rhondda Valley enabled the collieries there to increase output while some collieries built brickworks adjacent to the mines. Thus bricks and coal flooded into Barry so that another dock was added and opened in 1898. By the turn of the century Barry's exports dwarfed those of Cardiff and Penarth. Again 1913 was the peak year of trade with over 10½ million tons of coal being exported as well as a million tons of other commodities. However, again in line with the other ports, there was a reduction by almost half in the first half of the twentieth century and a total collapse in the second half in coal exports, although the docks are still pretty busy today.

We drove over Barry Island to the lifeboat slip. Barry has had a lifeboat stationed there since 1901 although ideas for a lifeboat at this 'perfect location' were discussed in 1893. The first boat was the ten-oared, two-masted, lug-rigged boat *John Wesley*. It seems a steam tug was always available to tow the lifeboat out through the breakwaters of the port into deep water. In 1922 the station received what was the first motor driven lifeboat in South Wales in the form of the 40ft Watson class *Prince David*. The station remains open with the *Margaret Francis Love*.

Alongside the lifeboat quayside lie the pilot boats. However, in the late nineteenth century this was the home of the Barry sailing pilot boats. Perhaps the best known of the Barry pilot boats is the *Kindly Light* that was for some time in the Cardiff Maritime Museum before being saved and restored by an enthusiastic owner. Today's pilot boats,

Captain Scott's *Terra Nova* leaving Cardiff on route to Antartica in 1910.

although purpose-built, are a far cry from those sailing cutters, as, of course, are the modern lifeboats in comparison to the sailing and oared craft.

By this time dusk was beginning to fall. I drove back to a spot I'd noticed where there were no 'no overnight parking' signs. Dog and I went for a walk along Whitmore Beach, a fine expanse of sand overlooked by the sprawling holiday camp. There's a sign saying 'No Dogs' from 1 May to 30 September! At the western end of the beach, at Friar's Point, there was once a short pier, locally called Treharne's Pier, although the reason is not known given for it was built by Francis Crawshay. It was subsequently demolished after being considered unsafe. Once trippers had thronged this beach in their masses, entertained by donkey rides and the boats that made trips around the bay, but it was quiet at this time. Music drifted over from the buildings behind. We walked over to the point. The old watchtower in Water House Bay was across the water, built in 1865 and where a lifesaving boat, not belonging to the RNLI, was kept for some years, at a time when there were fewer than 100 people inhabiting Barry. Once the lifeboat station at the entrance to the docks was opened, this watchtower ceased to be of any use and was converted into tearooms. We cut across Little Island, dog sniffing rabbits in the grass, until returning to the van and falling asleep to the sound of waves thrashing against the sand.

DAY FOUR
BARRY TO PORTHCAWL

Thomas Knight made Barry Island his main base for his smuggling operations in 1783. Previously Lundy Island had been home to his ship and forty-odd crew. However, he only managed to stay here four years before the Customs officers and men forced him out off the island and back to Lundy Island. Lundy had been the main base for smuggling in the Bristol Channel since the thirteenth century but there was always a need for suitable mainland haunts into which to run the illicit goods. Barry Island was obviously a perfect haunt for such activities, given its position away from habitation, because Knight's place was taken over by a Captain Arthur in 1788 until he, too, was also forced off by the officers. Three years later the *John of Combe* operated briefly from the island, after which the documented evidence suggests smuggling ceased.

We were up late. The sun was shining and the inside of the van was like a furnace. The beach was filling up and I noticed a young woman taking her dog along the sands. The loudspeaker issued a warning, 'No dogs allowed on the beach please.' She put hers on a lead and disappeared quickly. More orders barked out, 'Will visitors please only swim in the middle part of the beach.' It was almost worse than standing on a station platform listening to muffled messages about delayed trains! These beach-goers were at least meant to be enjoying themselves. How regimented even our spare time is fast becoming!

Carefully avoiding the beach, I took the dog over to where we'd been the evening before. One of the pilot boats was heading out to an approaching ship. Barry is base for the Severn pilots. Several anglers sat on the rocks at Friar's Point, lines out from long rods. I asked one what he caught. The reply was, 'Everything really, tope, doggie, all sorts really.' He seemed pretty vague! 'Any bass?', I asked. 'Yeah, that too,' he said, obviously not wishing to impart too much information to a total stranger! Angling is, as many of us know, the most popular hobby in Britain. More people fish than watch football, and that's saying something. It's the same in countries like Spain and Italy when every harbour pier and available rock is lined with a row of anglers.

In the September of 1935 a French schooner, the *Goeland*, was driven onto the rocks here in a storm. Her cargo consisted of a load of French onions, which were washed ashore and collected by the locals. The lifeboat *Prince David* managed to get the crew off prior to the vessel grounding, a rescue for which they were awarded RNLI medals.

An aeroplane came in low over the sea in its line-up for Cardiff Airport, which is a bit to the west of Barry. It reminded me of landing on Greek islands where the plane almost lands in the sea before touchdown. The sun was even hotter now, so that too prompted more thoughts of Greece, and screams from the beach! Below this grassy point there used to be a paddling pool at the beginning of the twentieth century. The idea of building a place to paddle physically alongside the sea's edge seems a bit bizarre to us now, but remember this was in the era of bathing machines. When queues formed awaiting the use of these machines, bathers were allowed to swim although the local 'Inspector of Bathing Costumes' had to check and approve the suitability of the swimwear. Imagine that now, some council inspector not approving some young woman's bikini if she showed off a bit too much! A century before these bathing machines were introduced the swimmers were quite happy to strip off and swim naked.

From Friar's Point we walked over the grass and along a path to Barry Harbour, the tidal bit between Friar's Point and Cold Knap Point. At the start of the breakwater there's a mosaic with the words 'Waverley' and 'Balmoral' so presumably these boats pick up and discharge here during their summertime trips from Penarth Pier, along the Welsh coast and over to Devon. It was these summer tours that were responsible for the growth in resorts such as Barry Island.

In the harbour lies the wreck of an Admiralty MFV and several other assorted craft lay at anchor. Across, the limestone kilns are close to Storehouse Point. We drove to the car park on the Pebble Beach and walked along to Cold Knap Point, past the Ford Fiesta that had been driven into the surf and abandoned, around to Watch House Bay where people were sunbathing by the watchtower. Rowing regattas often took place in this bay, run by the Barry Rowing Club, one of the oldest sporting clubs in the town. Today there's a slipway where boats can be launched. Beyond there's a boating lake full of swans surrounded by some beautiful and colourful gardens. Back to the beach (dogs now OK), but we couldn't walk to Porthkerry because of the bulk of Bullcliff Rocks that blocked the way unless we swam, and I didn't fancy that. So we had to drive round.

We parked up by the church at Porthkerry and walked down through the woods onto the golf course. Above, the 100ft high Railway Viaduct carried the Vale of Glamorgan Railway between Barry and Bridgend. Work to construct the viaduct began in 1894 and was completed three years later, although one of the piers collapsed, delaying the opening by a year. Another collapse closed it again, but by 1900 it was fully functioning. This was almost fifty years after the Halls embarked on their journey across South Wales and explains why we had drifted away from their route. They had to take the inland railway to Bridgend and only made incursions upon the south Glamorgan coast from that town. We would be able to follow in their footsteps once we reached Swansea Bay.

Porthkerry was, according to Moelwyn Williams, an ancient seaport of Siluria and it continued to be a landing place into medieval times. It is said that the remains of some of the stone buildings associated with this can still be seen, although we failed to find them. The harbour here, along with the castle, was wiped out by a storm in 1584. Limestone pebbles from the beach were at times collected and taken to Tenby where they were burned into lime.

There are three quarries marked on the Ordnance Survey map between Porthkerry and Rhoose, all having produced limestone in their time. Fontygary beach at Rhoose was said to be a beach frequented by those wanting a beach without shops and amusement arcades, thus preventing the kids spending their hard-earned money. The inference is that only the poor came here. However, with a holiday and leisure park atop the cliff, I doubt this is the case any more. The steel ship *Verajean*, launched in 1891 in Dumbarton, was blown ashore at Rhoose Point while on route from Cardiff to Peru in August 1908.

Aberthaw is noted as a port in 1577 and has a long association with shipping since before the Normans came here. The Saxons are supposed to have landed here in 1032.

Leland found that 'at the mouth of the Thawan Shipple-lettes may cum ynto the haven mouth' and he also noted that this was the nearest part of Wales to Minehead. There are references to a landing place known as 'the Mud' where smuggler's boats unloaded. It's situated on the estuary of two rivers – the Thaw and the Kenson – that drain parts of the vale of Glamorgan. The estuary used to be some three miles wide and ships traded from here to Somerset and Devon and some even traded as far as La Rochelle for salt and wine and the West Indies for sugar. In the eighteenth and nineteenth centuries this was the most important port in Glamorgan and is reflected in the fact that the postal address of Cardiff at the time was 'Cardiff, Aberthaw'.

The 'Blue Anchor Inn', a thatched fourteenth-century pub, was worth visiting for a swift pint. Its low doorways, and the only two-centred medieval timber doorway in Glamorgan, all point to it having been unchanged in centuries. It is said there was an inn on this site previous to this building. Its name is interesting for, due south, across the Bristol Channel, in northern Somerset, lies Blue Anchor Bay where there's another inn of the same name. I'd been there coincidentally a few weeks beforehand, camping overnight in the field behind the pub. According to John Gilman, the name came from the lias – a kind of limestone – which leached its blue colour into the clay. Originally the place was called Bradley Gate, a place where coal from across the water was landed. Vessels lay off the inn and found their anchors covered in the blue clay when they hauled them up. Thus the name stuck and presumably for the same reason, or simply because of the cross-channel trade, the inn in Aberthaw was given its name. There's a belief, in line with many of the smuggling stories, that a tunnel runs from the Aberthaw Blue Anchor Inn to the beach. In Cornwall, however, many of the so-called smuggling tales have been exaggerated to enhance the 'touristability' of the place, and I wonder how much of this has rubbed off in South Wales. Stories of cattle being let loose with lighted lanterns on their horns are well told in many parts of the principality, as are secret tunnels and illicit brandy! A few are well founded but many embellished.

The ancient port of Aberthaw today is completely overrun by a power station, this being the second such station on the site in almost fifty years. With its construction came a complete transformation of the foreshore. The old harbour area known as Pleasant Harbour lies to the east of the power station, where the limestone buildings still exist. Parts of the old harbour can also still just be seen although storms are said to have caused havoc here over centuries. Swans have settled on the remaining pools on the Leys.

Aberthaw became famous for its limestone after James Smeaton decided that it was best for the construction of the Eddystone Lighthouse in 1759. The lias limestone was found to set harder as a mortar than any other when underwater and was taken from the foreshore as 3 or 4in pebbles. It is said that the constant washing of the pebbles by the sea gave it its properties. It was used in the underpinning of the third lighthouse on the Eddystone Rocks and lasted until 1877 when cracks were found in the rock upon which it was set. Vessels had 'to lye upon the open shore' until 1813 when a new pier was built so that as many as twenty vessels might be waiting to load up at any given time. Demand for this limestone meant that the little port survived up to 1900.

We walked from the car park on the beach at Gileston around the footpath along the concrete seawall that circumnavigates the power station. Since power stations have been privatised, this one now belongs to Innogy plc and signs all around warn of the danger of trying to climb over the high fence. There's a huge area where the anthracite is stored and we watched a train loaded with the coal arrive. These are capable of carrying a thousand tons, I'm told. Further to the east there's a bridge across the river Thaw. The river has been re-directed some couple of hundred yards or so west of its natural route and to its east is 'the Leys' which is now a huge 'ash disposal site – unstable ground', according to the signs. In other words, it's toxic waste. Offshore, there's a concrete caisson that was built for the power station. When this was constructed, the contractors began to fill what was the famous 'mullet pool' until the locals objected, leaving the pool with a pile of rocks in its centre. It's still popular for its grey mullet. As we walked back along the seawall, some anglers asked me the way to 'the fishtrap' and I supposed this was what they were looking for so pointed in its direction. Breaksea Point, where it is situated, is, by the way, the most southerly point of Wales at low tide. Rhoose Point has that honour at high water. It's said that twenty ships were wrecked in one night on Breaksea Point in fog and a lightship was later stationed just offshore marking the sandbank.

Aberthaw must have been one of the most remarkable little ports of Wales in its heyday, although whether the port itself was the remarkable thing or the fact that evidence of it has almost been totally destroyed by twentieth-century advancement, I'm not sure. Power stations are indeed ugly and dirty – the Hinkley Point nuclear station is visible across the channel and is a nasty reminder of the alternative – but society has this increasing need to light up as much as it can. Whilst the demand is there it has to be realised that the generating capability has to come from somewhere. The only answer is to switch off the millions of streetlights, heating systems and unnecessary electrical items that consumers are led to believe they cannot survive without. We're all guilty, of course. I write this on a computer and have a lamp on to see, although it's the middle of a bright sunny day. But we live in a society of instant gratification so that, whether it's instant relief, knowledge or excitement, only we can make that decision to switch off and contribute to the overall reduction in pollution, be it that of carbon dioxide or light.

Wreck off Rhoose Point – SS *Verajean*.

Pilot Boats

One of the least documented areas of maritime history is the work of those who aid ships as they enter ports. Although pilotage became a respected occupation, that of serving ships as they lay at anchor waiting to enter is perhaps less identifiable, largely because this need was supplied by fishermen and others who have sometimes been labelled as salvagers. In general, especially off the Welsh coast, the small open boats used to take supplies out to waiting vessels were the same used for fishing and serving the holiday masses in summer. Thus it is impossible to categorise these craft. Pilotage, on the other hand, developed through a licensing system within the large ports. For the smaller harbours, again it was the local seafarers who undertook the task of leading vessels into the confined waters. An example typifying this could have been found at Llanddwyn, on the southwest tip of Anglesey where a pilot station was established to serve shipping entering the Menai Strait to reach Caernarfon (or sail through the Strait). These pilots also crewed the lifeboat at times, and spent other times fishing. Their craft were typical then of other craft in use around Anglesey at the time.

In the south, Newport, Cardiff, Barry, Swansea and Llanelli all had their own fleets of pilot boats serving the shipping. These vessels took the pilot out to incoming vessels, drew alongside the vessel to transfer the pilot aboard and sailed back to harbour or on to find another incoming ship. Competition was often fierce so that the fastest boat reached the ship first to get his pilot aboard and thus receive the fee.

The sailing pilots of the Bristol Channel have been well documented by Peter Stuckey in his 1977 book of the same name, and updated in a revised edition in 1999. He chronicles the development of the pilotage service that dates back to the late 1700s although there is evidence of its existence well before that. The Bristol Channel pilot cutter has become synonymous with the occupation and many such restored craft still sail, albeit for pleasure. Such craft were commonplace in many of the South Wales ports.

In Swansea, however, a different type of vessel was adopted. In an article on the Swansea Bay Pilot Boats (*The Mariner's Mirror*, vol. 29, 1943), J.F. Coates identifies what he calls a Swansea Bay crabber. This he depicts as a transom-sterned clinker vessel, probably about 20ft long with two masts. These, I would suggest, were similar to the oyster skiffs. It is possible that the Swansea Bay Pilot Schooners were first built on the lines of these early crabbers for they display a number of characteristics in the hull shape and positioning of the masts. Late eighteenth-century evidence suggests perhaps a lug rig, but this is doubtful. Later iconographical evidence shows the pilot boats as being 21–30ft long, clinker-built and two-masted with a schooner-rig. The gaffs were short, showing a certain similitude to the Aberystwyth three-masted beach boats, although, as we've seen, the Irish Sea was full of similarly rigged craft. The loose-footed main was boomed, and both sails were laced to the masts, no hoops being employed. The forward mast was stepped well into the eyes of the boat and no foresails were set. 1791 regulations from the Harbour Trust stipulated that a pilot boat must be at least 'twenty-one feet stowage, six and a half feet wide and not less than two feet seven inches to the gunwall, fitted complete, with six oars…'

These small vessels were renowned as good sea boats, necessary for working in Swansea Bay in most conditions when the job was to secure the pilotage of ships running for shelter. The bay was commonly packed with shipping, with gale force south-westerly winds blowing for days on end, waiting to enter the tidal dock.

The bluff-bowed boats became heavier in the mid-nineteenth century, so that a jib was added for speed. It is said that one reason the boats had such short gaffs was to reduce weight

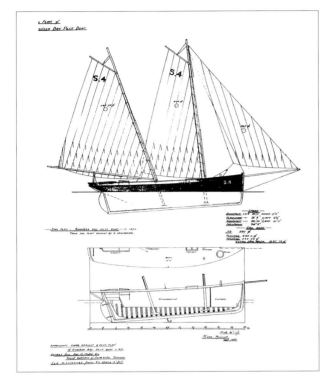

A plan of a Swansea Bay Pilot Boat, drawn by P.J. Oke in 1936. (Courtesy of the Science Museum)

aloft whilst coming alongside a ship to put the pilot aboard. It was sometime around this time they developed their unique rig in that the masts were raked back, the main's rake being far more exaggerated than that of the foremast. Neither was supported by standing rigging. It has been suggested that William Linnard, a pilot/mariner from Holland, introduced this rig to Swansea after he married a Welsh girl and settled in the town in 1784. However, with a similar rig in use prior to this date throughout the Irish Sea upon the wherries and other craft such as the Whitehaven Shallop, this seems doubtful.

Up to 1860 there were ten pilot boats in use but when the South Dock was opened the following year, the port attracted larger craft. This, in turn, necessitated sailing further westward to the approaches of the Bristol Channel. Thus larger decked vessels were adopted, up to 50ft in length and similar in shape to the Bristol Channel Pilot Cutters, although they retained their schooner rig and the unsupported, heavily raked mainmast. Eleven such craft worked, mostly built in Swansea by builders such as Philip Bevan, until a steam pilot cutter, the *Beaufort*, was introduced in 1898. It is said that when these schooners raced alongside the other Bristol Channel Pilot cutters in the regattas, they were able to equal the cutters in all weathers except light airs.

On the north coast, Liverpool pilot boats worked from a station off Port Lynas, on the northeastern tip of Anglesey. These cutters, after the service was introduced in the late 1760s, were sloop-rigged vessels of up to 50ft in length. It is said that several cutters were sent out to scout around for French troops at the time of the Fishguard invasion of 1797. After 1852 much larger schooner-rigged vessels began replacing the smaller cutters with later boats reaching 100ft. One such vessel, the 80ft *Mersey No. 11* was built by William Thomas of Amlwch in 1875. She sank ten years later after a collision with SS *Landana*. However, these schooners were themselves superceded by technology when the first steam pilot was introduced to Liverpool in 1896.

The story of Aberthaw is told well by Terry Breverton in *The Secret Vale of Glamorgan*. He obviously has a genuine love of the area and is active in inducing the owners of the power station to rectify past mistakes. It seems that when the station was originally built by the then CEGB in the 1950s, and I quote from Breverton's book, 'medieval wells, ancient footpaths, the Leys Pool, two inns, houses, a farm, boathouse, golf course, Iron Age tumulus and the last castle built in Wales' were all destroyed. That's quite a catalogue of destruction. He's also keen in seeing an extension made to the Heritage Coastline of Glamorgan that presently stretches from Porthcawl to Gileston.

Locals used to work seine-nets on the beach just west of the car park. Presumably there were tales of fish in the Limpert Inn, the shell of which stands by the car park. The hinterland is fertile for this is the Vale of Glamorgan, which is renowned as being the 'Larder of Wales'. Seaweed used to be collected here to make laverbread, of which we will hear much more later. From here it's a short walk along the edge of the beach, past the concrete tank blocks preventing wartime invasion, to Summerhouse Point where, like Breaksea, there's a watch house. Today it's the home of a Christian Conference Centre and before that, a convalescent home for miners suffering from silicosis. Like most of the headlands along this Glamorgan coast, there's an Iron Age fort here dating from the period between 700 BC and AD 76, when the Romans arrived. These forts were built to protect the Silures from, first, Irish invaders and, later, the Romans. There was a pier here until it was destroyed in the 1930s and is another of these lost landing places along this coast.

The next of these landing places is at Col-Huw where Leland found a place where 'hither cummith syntyme Bootes and Shippletes for socour'. The pier was said to have been in ruin by 1590 and the port abandoned by 1607 on account of a huge storm that carried away whatever was left of the pier. This place was the natural harbour for Llantwit Major (Llanilltyd Fawr), is where St Illtyd came in the fifth century to establish his church, spreading the word throughout the southwest and Brittany. At low tide there's a lovely sandy beach and, the afternoon being extremely hot, it was full of beach-goers, but alas, no dogs allowed, so the poor overheated pet had to rely upon a lie in the stream to cool off! In the 1930s there were chalets, a tennis court and café here but these had disappeared by the 1950s, to be replaced today by a café and nearby Surf Life Saving Association building. I sat on a bench overlooking the bay, atop the westerly hill. This was dedicated to the ex-Royal Naval man largely responsible for the founding of the association. I forgot to write down his name, for which I apologise. However, it was a tranquil place to gaze out over the Bristol Channel to England. The domes of Butlins at Minehead glinted in the bright sun. The view of the coast from Steepholm with the Mendip Hills beyond to almost Ilfracombe was wide although not particularly clear in the heat haze. I tried picking out individual places while the dog sniffed around the gorse bushes. Their yellow flowers still remind me of childhood days in Anglesey and fill me with memories of picking off caterpillars amongst the sand dunes. This was a place to linger although the screams of joy from the beach below brought me back to life after minutes of dosing. At the easterly end of the bay there are information signs showing three choices of paths to walk along – the westerly walk to Tresilian, the northerly to Llantwit and the easterly to Stout Point. Judging by the groups of folk along the northerly and easterly routes, these were popular. It must have been chance that led me to the westerly one, upon which I didn't see a soul!

At Tresilian Bay there's a cave – Reynard's cave – where it is said the infamous Breton pirate Colyn Dolphin was buried up to his neck in the sand to await the incoming tide. Dolphin, like the rest of his ilk, had a base at Lundy and when he captured Sir Harry Stradling while Stradling was crossing from his estates in Somerset to nearby St Donat's, Dolphin extracted a ransom of £1,400 for his release. When Stradling's men later captured the esteemed pirate, he wasn't so in need of the money and extracted what in his mind was a much fairer deal by so burying the ruffian and leaving him to his watery fate. Such was the justice of the day.

Stradling's St Donat's Castle was bought by the American newspaper magnate William Randolph Hearst in 1925 and it was he who renovated it for it had fallen into disrepair. In 1962 it became the United World College of the Atlantic and is now known as Atlantic College. The college helped develop the new breed of inshore inflatable lifeboats in conjunction with the RNLI and has an inshore rescue boat (IRB) based there.

The next beach of any consequence is at Marcross. Nash Point lies on the west point of the bay although the Nash Point lighthouse lies a few hundred yards east of the other side. Two lighthouses were built here after the wrecking of the passenger paddle steamer *Frolic* in 1832. This wooden hulled two-masted boat, owned by the General Steam Navigation Company of Bristol, was operating as a steam packet between Bristol and the Welsh ports including Carmarthen where it first served in 1830. After the ship went aground on the Nash Point sandbank and up to seventy-eight people were drowned, there was a public outcry, presumably because many of those lost where locals. The two resultant lighthouses were set 1,000 yards apart to enable ships steaming up channel to navigate safely clear of the offshore shoals by keeping the two lights in line. Today, though, only the easterly of the two lights work and between is a foghorn station. Peering through the window into a room with gleaming machinery, I noted the compressor for the horns were run by Gardner engines which anyone connected with the sea will know are the Rolls-Royce of small boat engines.

There's another Iron Age fort at Nash Point. Car parking at Marcross costs one pound all day yet wasn't anywhere nearly as busy as other parts of the coastline that charge more. Perhaps, I thought, as I walked around the lighthouse grounds, it was due to the lack of a good beach. The cliffs are quite dramatic – limestone in 9in or so thick layers with soft shale between. The shale weathers more quickly and falls out, leading to collapses in the cliff-face which are all too apparent on the beach below. Once this is washed away, wave platforms are left, smoothed by the sea's action. It did look as if the edge of the cliff was moving towards the lighthouse. Directly below lies the remains of the wreck of the *B.P. Driver* a coastal tanker that was blown by an unexpected squall ashore in 1962. The pub at Marcross, the suitably named 'Lighthouse Inn', was heaving with customers as we drove past, which might explain the dearth of visitors at Marcross beach.

Northeast of Marcross there are three relatively inaccessible sandy beaches, according to the map, although, judging by the cars parked along the narrow road, they are popular with the locals. Each involves a trek across fields. Nearby Wick is said to have been the base of the villainous 'Wreckers of Wick' who terrorised the local shipping by lighting beacons on the cliff tops. Dunraven Bay, on the other hand, was simply heaving with swimmers and sunbathers alike, and a dog ban. The little shop was doing a roaring business with people swathed in beach towels – you know a beach towel by the pattern and amass of bright colours! There are countless references to smuggling activities at Dunraven and it is also renowned as having the worst reputation for wrecking on the Glamorgan coast. Walter Vaughan was ostensibly the local lord in the sixteenth century who wasn't averse to a spot of wrecking to supplement his income. According to Terry Breverton, Vaughan's accomplice was 'Matt the Iron Hand', who secretly blamed Vaughan for the loss of his limb. After years of luring ships, Matt eventually got the boat he'd wanted for years to lure upon the rocks. He went back to Vaughan who asked him whether there were survivors. 'Only one', declared the pirate, 'a Welshman from Dunraven', and at that, with a laugh, he thrust a severed hand with a ring belonging to Vaughan's only son into his face. Matt was shot dead and Vaughan sold up and fled the area.

Another story tells how Vaughan had two sons – it isn't clear whether one of them is the same as the one in the story above. These two sailed out onto a nearby offshore rocky ledge and were stranded after their boat broke loose. With no other boat available and an incoming tide, the distraught parents could only watch as the two boys were drowned. This, the teller says, was Vaughan's judgment. Perhaps he had three sons, all lost to the sea.

The Glamorgan Coast Heritage Centre was closed, although I must admit I did arrive after five o'clock. Cars were being prevented from entering the Dunraven Park by a uniformed security guard that I found a bit bizarre in such surroundings. However, they must have their reasons. The park is open all day until the evening and I'd have liked to walk along the coast to the Pillow Mounds on Trwyn y Witch (Witches Nose) but time was pressing if I was to make it past Porthcawl that evening.

Ogmore-by-Sea (*Aberogwr*) lies on the southern side of the estuary of the river Ogmore that was another of the ports mentioned in 1577. Offshore lies the Tuskar Rock that has overwhelmed the occasional vessel. These days Ogmore-by-Sea is more likely to be home to a band of surfers rather than a sailing ship. Across the other side of the estuary, Newton was described as a 'Station or Haven for Shippes' in 1542 and 'a creke for small vessels' twenty years later. In 1577 'Newton and Ogmore' had three deputies assigned for her Majesty's service. Prior to that, before the young Henry Tudor landed at Milford Haven and claimed the Crown of England for the Tudors, early documents refer to 'the Weare at Newton'. In the seventeenth century fourteen ships traded from here, the largest being *The Three Brothers* at 30 tons which sailed to Minehead in 1695 with '24 chalders of coales, 2 fardles of stockings and 20 sheep'. The knitting of stockings, it seemed, was a thriving cottage industry around the farms of the Vale of Glamorgan at this time. According to the Revd J. Evans, in his 1803 tour of South Wales, the locals were also employed in blowing up the cliffs for limestone, which was shipped across the Bristol Channel. It sold for a shilling a ton, the owner of the land getting three shillings in the pound.

What is obvious from walking on the beach at Ogmore-by-Sea (dogs are allowed!) is the unnavigability of the river. However, two 1802 Estate maps mark a port along the road from the church towards Newton Point, one simply labelling it as 'Port of Newton'. Thomas Wyndham of Dunraven recorded that a consignment of port came by sea from Bristol to Newton in 1794 and was carried overland to Dunraven. He also mentions a 'packet boat' operating between the two ports, which tends to imply a regular service. I wonder whether this was the passenger steamer *Frolic*?

Porthcawl is an amalgamation of Nottage and Newton and some new growth towards the point known as Porth-y-Cawl, which translates literally to 'port of the broth', which has been taken to be a poetic reference to the often turbulent seas that are open to the southwest prevailing winds. A seventeenth-century survey calls it 'Port Call', obviously an English rendering of the name of the point. There was absolutely no intent on building a harbour here until the beginning of the nineteenth century when local businessmen examined the possibility of exporting coal and iron ore through a harbour on the Ogmore River. By that time, though, there was 'a well-established port' at Newton and subsequent plans made for a port to be built under Porth Cawl Point.

We do know that the Vikings came over from bases in Ireland and colonised all along the South Wales coast. Nearby Sker – Norse for 'jagged reef' – points to a settlement there. It is said that they used flat-bottomed boats that were able to penetrate deep into the hinterland to explore and raid. Newton is said to have been laid out defensively by the Vikings to confuse any would-be raiders. Later on, the Normans arrived to build a township. It is said that herring were once landed here.

However, as with the other dockyard developments along this coast, it was the coal and mineral deposits that led to the programme of port building. In 1825 construction of a tramway from the Llynfi valley to 'Pwll Cawl' was commenced and opened three years later. Meanwhile a small tidal harbour was built on the eastern extremity of the point although it was soon realised that this was open to the fierce Atlantic seas that swept into this shore. If only they had understood the etymology of the name of the point of land in the first place! Even after the addition of a short breakwater the little harbour could only be used in the summer months, and it wasn't until almost twenty years later that the facilities were enlarged as the collieries and ironworks developed. The tramway was converted to a railroad and in 1845 some 35,000 tons of coal and 21,000 tons of iron passed through the port. This led to a further expansion of the dock in the 1860s so that the coal export had risen to 165,000 tons by 1871. In 1874, 700 vessels berthed there. By 1892 this had risen again to 800 mainly steam-driven vessels and a record of 225,000 tons of coal was exported. However, there was one weakness for the tidal dock in that almost all the vessels returned empty, so that when the Port Talbot and Barry docks opened in 1892, trade was almost comprehensively directed to those ports. Even so, a further development was planned until it was realised that whatever was built, a tidal harbour just simply could not compete with docks that were accessible in all states of the tide and one without outlying reefs to catch the unwary vessel. By 1906 the port had all but closed except for the odd vessel carrying bricks from Bridgwater. Captured German shipping was broken up for a time after the First World War. The large inner dock was eventually filled in and became a car park after the Second World War.

However, during the town's development as a port, many modernisations had improved the quality of life for the inhabitants. Housing had been built and such innovations as gas lighting and a sewerage system had been installed. This encouraged the growth of the town as a seaside resort. The pier allowed steamers from along the coast to call and the train line brought in roves of holidaymakers. Hotels sprung up as did caravan parks to satisfy demand. Within a few years of the end of hostilities in 1945, Porthcawl, as it was by then known, was set upon a course to become one of Wales' premier seaside towns, serving the population of the industrial centres of Port Talbot, Bridgend, Swansea and Cardiff, as well as the valleys. Today it is just that, with developments on all sides, including Coney Beach on its eastern side and the quieter Rest Bay to the north. As we drove through on a Sunday evening of what had been a beautifully sunny day, it was apparent that Porthcawl had in one way lost its charm in the twenty-first century. The streets and promenade simply teemed with hordes of visitors. We didn't need to linger long!

Kenfig, a few miles north, has an altogether different story. In the eleventh century this place was described as a 'city' and as a market town. However, its positioning on the sands around the estuary of the river Kenfig (*Afon Cynffig*) were its downfall. Or, perhaps more precisely, its swallowing up, for the shifting sands and a series of storms around the beginning of the fourteenth century gradually buried the city in the sand. When John Leland arrived, it was nothing more than a little village on the 'est side of the Kenfik and a castel both in ruine and shokid and devoured with the Sandes that the Severn See there castith up'. What remains is Kenfig Pool, said to have been the largest stretch of freshwater in Glamorgan where a whirlpool would lure the unwary swimmer to his death. It's been used for sailing since 1958, although the larger Eglwys Nunydd reservoir, slightly to the north, would seem more suitable today.

As we drove north out of Porthcawl it was hard to notice that Kenfig existed, given the scarcity of buildings although a car park allowed access onto the expanse of sands. We stopped at the Angel Inn on the edge of Mawdlam, a thirteenth-century pub which was thatched until the 1950s, and it was pleasant sitting outside with a pint talking the day's activities over to the, distinctly uninterested, dog. Those that don't know me presumably think me mad, but forgive me if I hasten to reassure you, I do know he doesn't listen. He is a real friend, though! After a hasty meal, for me anyway, and in the receding light, we ventured over to view the remains of Kenfig Castle before retreating over the grassy dunes to find a somewhat noisy parking place close to the overpass carrying the M4. We did seem to sleep soundly amongst the forgotten ghosts of the city that was once Kenfig.

DAY FIVE

PORTHCAWL TO RHOSSILI

A change of plan on this bright and sunny morning. I like them – the changes of plan, that is – although sunny mornings are just as delightful! I decided to re-trace the road back to Porthcawl. I knew there was a museum there and decided a looksee would be a good idea. Unfortunately, though, when I arrived outside the building that used to be the police station and now houses both museum and tourist information, I found the former closed until 2.30 p.m. I wasn't waiting that long. The woman behind the counter at tourist information, when I could get her off the phone, gave me a number to contact as she knew nothing about the place.

Once outside again, I walked down to the harbour just in time to see the *Balmoral* moor alongside to pick up a queue of waiting trippers. The little pier was almost over-crowded with the number of folk, and the little ship – described as a 'traditional pleasure cruise ship' – looked distinctly small against the high outer wall of the quay and this massive throng of people. From the timetable I obtained, I see she was off across the Bristol Channel to Ilfracombe and Minehead, and had started from Swansea. During the summer both the *Balmoral* and the *Waverley* offer cruises throughout the week all around these waters – from Lydney at one end to Lundy at the other. Both of these ships have had re-fits, the *Waverley* – she's the last sea-going paddle steamer in the world – having been restored to her original condition, and the *Balmoral* having been given new engines.

In the harbour there were three gill-net fishing boats and an assortment of other craft. It was quiet; the only activity seemed to be the observing of the *Balmoral*. The lifeboat station was empty. Porthcawl's first lifeboat, the *Good Deliverance*, arrived in 1860 although a coastguard station had been established in 1834. The old lifeboat house, now a restaurant, housed the boat which was taken by carriage to the water. In 1878 a slipway was built and a new boat, the *Speedwell*, stationed in a new boathouse next-door. The service was withdrawn in 1902 because of the decline in the harbour's fortunes.

I sat drinking coffee on the promenade, purchasing the said hot liquid from a kiosk that turned out to be a mock-Victorian kiosk built in the mid-1990s. A road-train rattled past, almost devoid of tourists. Below me, on the seawall, a painted sign declared 'No Bathing'. A dog barked on the beach, which was good, and I did overhear the conversation on the next table, in which it seemed they liked the idea of the barking animal. The officer from Swansea City Council told me later that they have placed dog bans on most of their beaches because of public pressure. Yes, I agree that beaches are perhaps not the best place for dogs when it's extremely hot, unless they like to swim. Mine does. But neither is the back of the car. Do we have to always bring in bylaws and regulations? Why a blanket ban on dogs on every beach? If only owners became more responsible for their animals then there wouldn't be a problem. I usually carry a plastic bag to clean up, which seems simple enough to me.

Still, where were we? On the promenade observing how the population seemed to be quite aged. The conversation from the two old dears next-door continued about tablets. 'I always take mine when I get up and before my rest in the afternoon,' I heard. I guess I'm not far off that situation in life, I thought. We all get there for certain. It was time to move on. Nevertheless, the local library held me up for a couple of hours as the staff were unable to find one book I was after even though their computer told them it was there. It seemed somebody had stolen it. I ended up driving to Bridgend to find a copy and then spending time there reading other books. The downside of this was I didn't extract myself until well into the afternoon. Dog was desperate for a walk and a swim!

We'd eventually caught up with the Halls on their journey westwards. They alighted from their train at Bridgend and made excursions upon the south coast from their base at Bridgend. Moving towards the coast, they visited Ogmore, Ewenny, Dunraven, St Donat's and Llantwit Major. Of Dunraven they recount a different story in that Walter Vaughan was responsible for the death of both his children who were merchant seamen who were both wrecked on this coast through 'their father's hand having guided the light that guiled their vessel amongst the breakers'. No mention of the evil Matt the Iron Hand.

As the Halls were carried towards Neath they noted the 'coking works of Messrs Ford and Sons', the Maesteg Iron Works and described this as 'the region of copper works, the railway passing through one of these very money-making, but smoke-producing, establishments belonging to H.H. Vivian Esq., MP'. That gives a good picture indeed of this part of the coastline – from Maesteg to beyond Swansea – where riches were indeed made at the expense of the population who had some, but little, profit from it. They also mention C.R.M. Talbot, Esq., MP whose seat was Margam Abbey.

This was, of course, the Talbot whose name lives on forever in Port Talbot. He was born in 1803 into a Glamorgan dominated by the landed gentry. By 1830 he had almost but inherited the parliamentary seat from Sir Christopher Cole, the second husband of Mary Lucy Talbot. Glamorgan was a dichotomy at that time. In the Vale agriculture flourished on the fertile land. In the valleys, though, the Industrial Revolution was just beginning to wind up into second gear. By the 1850s most of the Glamorgan landowners were taking an interest in these industrial matters.

The Monks of Margam Abbey may have exported coal 800 years ago. So, too, might Roman soldiers have landed close by during their occupation of South Wales. Legends also prevail of Spanish treasure from ships of the Armada, although any wrecks are more likely to have been from trading boats as there is no evidence of any Armada ship coming this way. Coal was definitely exported from Taibach in 1696–97 from the Margam collieries and the first documented mention of a wharf is in 1715. John Cartwright and Isaac Newton leased land from the Talbots in about 1757 and began building a copper-smelting works. It appears that a ship, the *Betsy*, was first to bring in a load of timber in 1770 although she sank on the Old Bar at the entrance to the quay and became a wreck – hence 'Betsy Pool'. Shipbuilding started up about this time with the launch of a new vessel in 1773 although there is a mention of ship repairing at Taibach twenty years earlier.

Workers arrived in the 1770s and collieries opened as the copper-smelting plant started work, demanding coal. The old harbour at Aberavan was considered to be a major obstacle to industrial growth in the area by the time Talbot became involved. This implies there was more than just a quay by this time. He then became the main force behind the establishing of the Aberafan Harbour Company, which gained an Act of Parliament in 1834. 'I find we have a greater depth of water than exists at either Swansea or Neath. I have no doubt if the plan can be executed the place will drive a large coal-trade in a few years,' wrote Talbot in 1833, supposedly four years before the new floating dock opened. Talbot's father had, incidentally, been one of those responsible for the Porthcawl dock. In 1838 he bought the Taibach copper works from the English Copper Co. although he later sold that out to Vivian & Sons. But by 1840 the traders using the port wanted customs facilities and shortly afterwards the dock became known as Port Talbot. Josiah Mansfield of Clarence House, Aberafan, had a yard at the docks building vessels up to 50 tons and launched the *Prince Albert* in 1843 and later the *Gulliver* for Talbot himself. By 1868 Vivian's Wharf's export trade had peaked at 65,287 tons of coal. Talbot died in 1890. Between 1894 and 1898 the docks were extended. With these much improved deepwater facilities, and those at Barry, trade at Porthcawl almost dried up and eventually closed, as we've seen. The Margam steelworks were built during the First World War and still overshadow the town today, both with their physical appearance and the threat of closure in the global market in which they say they cannot compete. Perhaps they shouldn't pay the executives so much! In 1962 the coal export was switched to Swansea to allow the Port Talbot docks to concentrate on the iron and steel trade. However, now that Britain has to import the majority of its coal, thanks to Margaret Thatcher and her desire for revenge upon the miners, coal is imported into both ports. This idea of cheap imports might, on paper, seem financially viable, but if pensions, dole payments and redundancy pay are all taken in account, along with the country's balance of payments, the cost of closing down the pits, the social element of redundancy and all the other aspects of the equation, the policy seems crazy. Still, that's what is currently happening to the steel industry. What's next? I ask. The fishing industry has all but been handed over to other European Union countries, most notably Spain. Shipbuilding is almost non-existent so one wonders what component of the maritime field Britain has remaining, although we still rely heavily upon sea trade for these imports.

Sometimes it's easy to forget that industrial sprawlings such as this were once simply countryside. The Afan River was once a good salmon river, and fish weirs operated in both the tidal section and the non-tidal part. The latter usually involved setting some sort of basket trap or chest into which the fish would swim in through a hinged flap but be unable to escape. Their use was banned in the 1860s legislation. However, on the tidal part of the rivers, and especially around the estuaries, fish weirs proliferated in the Middle Ages and one such structure was briefly excavated in the sand of Margam Moors during the building of the steel works. This was a wooden weir, the rights of which belonged to Margam Abbey. It is presumed that a tidal wave that hit the Bristol Channel in 1607 wiped out much of the archaeology of this coast – at least it would be of archaeological interest now. Whole villages disappeared including Hawton in Carmarthenshire and 500 were killed. Fish weirs, as we shall see, were built and operated all along the Welsh coast between here and the north coast. Another stone and wattle weir operated into the twentieth century at the north end of Aberafan beach on the edge of the river Neath.

According to Revd Evans who passed through in 1803, a tame salmon inhabited these parts, and each Christmas Day he 'exhibits himself in the river', and would be so docile that folk could handle him. If anyone tried to take him, that 'wicked' person would instantly receive a divine judgment. However, he does add that many 'motley swarms of stories' abound in the 'feculent waters of superstition'.

We walked along Aberafan beach, a great expanse of sand stretching from Port Talbot docks to the river Neath (*Afon Nedd*). Britain was undergoing a heatwave so the beach was crowded with swimmers, surfers and sunbathers enjoying the heat's intensity, even if the trains weren't and the rails were buckling under the heat. A new housing development was taking shape at the southern end. The Hollywood Park leisure complex seemed busy. Dogs played on the part of the beach where there was no ban in force. In the distance, Swansea sat before a grey haze. The Gower peninsular formed the other edge of the massive sweep of Swansea Bay. It was a fine sight, watching a para-surfer against this fine backdrop and I became mesmerised for some time before moving on to Briton Ferry. The air was also, as I've said, hot!

Briton Ferry (*Llansawel* in Welsh) gets its name from the Normans who referred to the Welsh as 'Britons' and thus the Neath River crossing as 'La Brittonne'. However, from a trade point of view, the town didn't gain any significance until the Neath (*Nedd*) Canal was opened in stages in the 1790s, using parts of a disused canal at Melincryddan that dated from the 1690s and another 1790-canal to Penrhiwtyn. By 1798 the Neath Canal ran in its entire length of 10½ miles from Glyn Neath down to its terminus at Giant's Grave on the Neath River. However, part of the Act permitting the canal's construction insisted that no houses could be built within half a mile of Giant's Grave, thus safeguarding Neath's command of the area. The town's elders feared a rival town might be built. Yet when the Neath Abbey Iron Works built their mill close to the port, which Giant's Grave became, houses were built for the workforce. Thus the town of Briton Ferry sprang up. On the opposite bank to Giant's Grave is the Red Jacket Pill where the Clawdd y Saeson canal terminated. Edward Elton built this 'ditch' in the 1780s to send coal across the Crymlyn Bog from his colliery at Glan-y-Wern to emerge on the Neath River at what was then called Trowman's Hole, indicating trows worked this far west. Copper works then appeared at Red Jacket Pill, increasing trade. The Halls mention 'the tall masts of many colliers indicating the prosperity of its quays'.

By 1818 George Tennant had built a canal along some of the route of Elton's canal and onto Port Tennant at what is now Swansea's eastern edge. His idea was to bring coal down from the Vale of Neath by barge to Briton Ferry, cross the Neath River, and continue on to Swansea where it could be loaded onto ships. The advantage was that the ships were much larger than those that could enter the Neath. However, his plan failed because of tides in the river, so, by 1824, he had extended his Tennant Canal along the western side of the river to Aberdulais, crossing it by viaduct and joining the Neath Canal. But as the blooming railways soon outdated the canals, and as ships became larger, the need for a dock at Briton Ferry became apparent. This eventually was opened ten years later, although the riverside wharves continued in use. Another floating dock building scheme, this one to be called the Neath Harbour, was commenced at Red Jacket Pill in the late 1870s, although this was abandoned in the 1880s when high tides destroyed parts of the unfinished walls. The Briton Ferry Dock handled 2,398 vessels in 1870 but its use soon declined as Swansea developed. By the 1940s it had closed and the dock gates removed. At one point it was going to be filled but today stands empty and abandoned. A list of companies in the town in the 1970s illustrates the variety of industry back then: Briton Ferry Ironworks, Vernon Tinplate Works, Taylor's Foundry, The

Briton Ferry Pipe & Brick Works, The Victoria Works of Villiers Tinplate Co., The Wern Tinplate Co., The Gwalia Tinplate Co., Baglan Bay Tinplate Works, Baglan Engineering, Briton Ferry Steelworks, Albion Steelworks, Whitford Sheet Steel & Galvanising Works and Ward Shipbreakers & Scrap. The latter, opened by Thomas Ward in 1906, has broken up many a famous ship.

Neath Abbey Wharf continued to export coal – 600 vessels carried away 300,000 tons in 1906 – and copper and other goods continued to leave via the river. Copper smelting had, by the way, first started here in 1564. The collapse in the iron industry due to the introduction of the Bessemer process and the importation of high-grade ore from Spain affected many of these companies throughout South Wales and had a knock-on effect in dock traffic.

In 1884 the steamer *Westbury*, 411 tons, was advertised as operating between the Neath River and Antwerp, leaving Neath every ten days. According to the Halls, who paused in Neath after sensing 'the dense cloud' over the town, and continued on by describing it as busy and prosperous although it was 'a town of smoke'. At this point they detoured up the Vale of Neath before proceeding on to Swansea as did many travellers to the area. The Vale was renowned for its 'picturesque beauty and luxurious vegetation' and the upper reaches still remain popular, studded as they are with waterfalls, hills and magnificent views. At this point I must admit some failure and I apologise for this. My initial intention to follow in their footsteps has been not been wholly successful, although some of my onward route to Milford Haven will still mirror theirs.

The ferry across to Earls Wood ran over from a point halfway between Giant's Grave and the dock and only ceased operation when the first bridge was opened in 1955, although Thomas Telford had suggested a suspension bridge at the start of the nineteenth century. Before the ferry, cattle were taken across a ford that was said to be on firm ground. The last boatman was Harry Harris whose final customers were the builders of the bridge. In more recent times the M4 has been carried across with a new bridge so that many travellers into West Wales hardly know that Briton Ferry even exists, such is the height of the bridge above the town. However, on a more pleasant note, the wharves are still in use and rarely do I cross this bridge and not catch a glimpse of one ship or another berthed alongside. On the other bank, a little downstream is, according to the map, a marina, which is owned by the Monkstone Sailing Club. The very pronounced 'private' signs put me off entering when I detoured off the main road for a look!

Swansea's development as a port mirrors those of the rest of South Wales and I'm beginning to feel repetitive in this cataloguing of dates and events that all stemmed from the exporting of, in the main, coal, copper and iron. The most comprehensive book I've found on the subject is W.H. Jones' *History of the Port of Swansea*, first published in 1922 by Messrs Spurell of Carmarthen but now more widely available as a 1995 facsimile reprint, published to commemorate Swansea's Year of Literature. However, I feel I must put down the more salient points leading to the town's rise in fortunes.

The river Tawe has been crossed since at least the Romans were here. Their road – the Via Julia – joined Caerleon to Leucarium (Loughor), crossing the river by a ford. Later ferries operated and the lower one of these continued in use until a bridge was built in 1771. The Vikings came here, a fact known because the name 'Swansea' is Old Norse and comes from 'Sweyn's eie' meaning 'Sweyn's island'. Sweyn the Forkbeard was a Danish pirate who made the river estuary his base and the island referred to is assumed to be a tract of sand within the river's estuary. The Welsh name for the city is *Abertawe*.

Piers

Piers were a quintessential part of the British seaside and the embodiment of the Victorian penchant for ornate and glitzy structures and at the same time were purposeful. In an age of a growing desire to enjoy the benefits of holidays or days out by the sea, a pier became both a symbol of the affluence of a town, with its minarets and domes, and a means by which the visitors could be brought into that town. Although the first piers in Britain were built as early as 1800, the peak of their building was in the late nineteenth century. In many cases they became an extension of the prom.

Today there are some fifty remaining piers in Britain yet only seven of these are in Wales. These are at Penarth, Mumbles, Aberystwyth, Bangor, Beaumaris, Llandudno and Colwyn Bay. Unlike many of the other British piers though, all are in a good state of repair and are open to the public. There were others such as Tenby, which have since been demolished by councils unwilling to spend money to maintain their upkeep. Rhyl pier, opened amongst much festivity in 1867, was ultimately demolished almost a century later in 1965, after several collisions with ships had shortened it from the original 780 yards to only 145 yards. Continual battering from winter storms hadn't helped it. Rhos-on-Sea pier was unusual in that it was second-hand when erected by William Horton in 1896. It was originally from Douglas, Isle of Man, and was 1,240 yards long when positioned at Rhos Fynach. Again due to its poor state, and a fire a few years earlier, it was demolished in 1954, although the entrance survives as a museum, shop and restaurant.

Piers in most cases enabled steamers to call at the resorts at all states of the tide. Once the advent of the railway had superceded the passenger steamer as the most convenient mode of travel to transport these trippers, and later with the appearance of the charabanc, owners of the piers had to seek other means to continue with the financing for their upkeep. Thus arrived the neon-lit amusement arcades, music, theatre and dance halls, children's' fun shows and then bingo halls to entice the holidaymakers of all ages to part with their money. Promenaders were encouraged along their timber-decked lengths, having to pay an entrance fee for the pleasure, and ice-cream stalls and kiosks selling anything from a plastic bucket to a postcard were so positioned to attract a bit more of their money. In the words of Cyril Bainbridge 'pleasure piers were creations of the slightly shocking era of cockles and whelks, of mild permissiveness and of the uninhibited wearing of 'kiss me quick' hats and dancing in the open air before breakfast and after dinner'.

Today's piers survive through a mixture of grants and private enterprise. Storms and expensive maintenance bills continue to put pressure onto their existence. However, piers still manage to attract fishermen and holidaymakers, as well as tripping boats in some cases. The feeling of being at sea from a structure fixed to the seabed still grips many with pleasure.

Aberystwyth pier, 2003.

Penarth pier, 2003.

Coal production can be traced back to at least the fourteenth century and the probability is that mines were being worked before that. The first copper smelters were established in 1717 due of the harbour's proximity to Cornish ore and local collieries. More soon followed and later on this was expanded to include the production of tinplate, zinc, lead, nickel and other metals including even gold and silver.

Prior to the first Harbour Act being passed in 1791, little was done to improve the facilities for industry. A new quay was said to have been built in 1616 but those running the town preferred to look upon it as a seaside resort rather than an industrial centre. What harbour there was lay on the western bank of the river. But after 1791 steps were taken to widen and deepen the approach channel to the river as well as building two breakwaters and a lighthouse at Mumbles Head to aid navigation. This allowed boats of 300 tons to enter. Wharves were also built along with slipways and a graving dock. By 1800 it was being described as 'a well-built seaport... resorted to during the summer months. The machines for bathing are kept about half a mile from the town...'. Presumably these were situated along the bay towards the Mumbles and it would appear that both tourism and industry were the prime occupations of the inhabitants. Richard Ayton described it as 'the most considerable seaport in Wales' exclusively involved in the copper trade.

In the early seventeenth century barques and pinnaces were being built in the Strand at Swansea. In 1652 the building of these vessels here and at the new quay were causing a nuisance by obstructing shipping in and out of the port. Shipbuilding had obviously been practised for quite some time for, between 1558 and 1640, thirty-seven local ships worked out of Swansea and Mumbles and most were locally built. The Corporation eventually prohibited it on its quay, although records tell us that canvas, tar, pitch and oakum continued to be imported.

The Swansea Canal was authorised in 1794 and on completion four years later ran from Hen Neuadd near Abercraf to Brewery bank in Swansea, a distance of sixteen miles. A much shorter canal, the Smith Canal, running from Glandŵr to Llansamlet, opened in 1803 upon the route of a previous tramway. Both were to run iron ore and coal into Swansea. The following year saw the inauguration of the Mumbles tramway to open up the limestone quarries in the vicinity. An extension ran up the Clyne valley to serve the coalmines there, although Clyne coal had previously been shipped out from a quay by Black Pill. A 1794 chart shows this quay with a possible track across the sands. Within another decade a myriad of tramways brought ores and coal down to Swansea. However it was not until 1852 that the North Dock was constructed and opened by diverting the river along the New Cut. It must have just opened at the time of the Halls' visit. The streets were bustling and the quays crowded with forests of masts, 'large and small ships are unloading or unloading, and smart sailors are everywhere active'. The population was 50,000 and the Halls felt that the place had a general atmosphere associated with thriving maritime trade.

The North Dock was followed by the construction of the South Dock in 1859, the Prince of Wales Dock in 1881, the King's Dock in 1909 and, finally, the Queen's Dock in 1920. As can be seen by this dock building programme, Swansea's fortunes did not end in the 1880s when the copper-smelting trade declined due to cheap imports. Coal and anthracite ensured a continuation of brisk business in the docks well into the twentieth century. Indeed, the docks on the east side of the river still see a flurry of activity even if the coal trade is gone. A ferry service operates to Ireland and the *Waverley* and *Balmoral* operate trips during the summer.

Today the North Dock has gone and the South Dock has been modified as a marina with waterfront 'trendy' housing. The nearby Industrial and Maritime Museum has recently closed and work has begun on a £31 million development which will house the new 'National Waterfront Museum', due to open in 2006. This will display much of the artefacts from the Cardiff museum including many of the boats that Roger Hall has restored. Some of those from the original Swansea museum will also be combined into an exhibition that will, hopefully, make a major impact on the awareness of Wales' maritime history. The overall theme is to be the story of industry and innovation in Wales so how much importance is to be given to the maritime field we have to wait and see. Reading the various press articles it does seem that the image given out is one of 'slickness' in the world of corporate developing with the proverbial interactive displays and cameos that all too often dumb down the real historical facts through over-simplification. Added to this are the usual promises of hundreds of jobs and a huge boost to the local economy, pledges that all often fail to materialise as we've seen in a host of national projects funded, in part, by the lottery. I listened to a recent Radio 4 programme in which it was debated whether these so-called heritage centres distorted history. The general consensus agreed with the motion by a large majority. The danger, the proposers insisted, is of sanitising the past and thus overlooking the vernacular in favour of more tangible history that is easier to interpret. All too often, the people brought in to construct and run these places are business people without much of an understanding for the subject at hand. Let's hope this one is different. As regards the normal calls that Cardiff should house the museum, I feel that Swansea is the rightful location considering it is the heartland of the roots of Industrial Wales. Cardiff, as we've seen, was slow on the uptake. Overall, then, the project has to be welcomed and supported.

Swansea's fishing fleet is also based close to the marina although in 1901 the whole of the South Dock housed the fleet. Over forty deep-sea trawlers, most of which belonged to the Consolidated Fisheries Limited, landed here and a large fish market, curing house and ice factory were erected on the quay. It was said that the port was one of the six leading ports in the country although I find this an exaggeration of its importance. Today the majority of the South Wales fleet is own by Spanish companies – the so-called quota-hopping – so that little fish is landed. Such was the Spanish hold on the industry that when I spoke to one fisherman, he told me that he was being prevented from joining the local Producer's Organisation because he wasn't Spanish. A few local boats still manage to earn a living inshore but, in line with the rest of the UK, it is close to extinction. As to the antiquity of the fishing here, in 1553 the customs of Swansea charged a penny on every barrel of cured herring entering the port. Much of this came from across the Bristol Channel although some was possibly local fish because the 1878 'Report of the Sea Fisheries of England and Wales' mentions herrings being taken in the bay during September but that pollution from the smelters is said to have ensured this didn't happen too often.

In the early thirteenth century the rights to fishing in the river belonged to the Lord of Gouher who granted two fisheries to the Monks of Neath Abbey – one 'near Swansea Castle and the other at Horegrove, where the Memroth stream falls into the Tawy'. Records show other further upstream. In the sixteenth century many of the houses in

Swansea and Mumbles had, as appurtenances, a weir or weirs in the bay with the right for the householder to catch fish. A century later and there were at least thirteen weirs in the bay between the port and Mumbles. The 1864 Royal Commission on Deep Sea Fisheries visited Swansea and noted complaints between the oyster fishermen and the weir fishermen. The weirs, said the former, damaged the fish stocks. William Benson leased two weirs from the Duke of Beaufort at an annual rent of £1 each. The cost of building such a weir, he said, was £30. Edward Duncan's seascape of the bay, dated 1847, illustrates one such weir. It appears to be built of a low stone wall with a wattling on wooden stakes inserted into the stonework. Baskets are set at the apex of the weirs to capture fish. In the nineteenth century it seems that stake nets were preferred to wattled weirs. Today the remains of these wooden stakes can be seen below Blackpill down by the low water mark. I had a quick glimpse as I passed through, checking an earlier survey. The dog was happy to be free again splashing in the water, although I'm not sure whether he was meant to be on the beach or not!

The Halls met a group of mussel gatherers bound for the beach at Swansea. 'Mussels', they wrote, 'form staple articles of food with poor families along shore. And in proper season, mussels are not unpalatable – much superior to the cockle, and inferior only to the oyster.' All three are collected in the area. One local fisherman who lived at 12 Fleet Street, Swansea, was blind from birth. Every day he walked the few miles to Mumbles, and back. Furthermore, it is said he was one of the finest fishermen, knew exactly where the fish were and never lost a net.

The Halls also met one of the oyster women from the Gower, on her way to Swansea market with oysters and prawns. These women, with their Flemish descendancy, were unique to Wales, they say; women of Teutonic physique and a thorough Welshness. However, the Halls do seem to be more preoccupied by fairies rather than fishing folk!

'The Mumbles is famous for its oyster fishery, but no other fish' declare the Halls on their arrival at Oystermouth, which is, to be exact, the town under Mumbles Head. Today they have been fused into one as 'the Mumbles', and the town is a popular tourist haven. Offshore, boats lie at anchor and throngs of holidaymakers and workers from Swansea share the promenade, beach, and pubs and shops. I love this place for the atmosphere seems so unpretentious, unlike so many other supposedly quaint fishing villages. There's no harbour as such, just a quay, and the well being of the town doesn't seem to rely upon a somewhat embellished past. It's just a pretty place with a good sheltered beach, especially on a hot summer's evening. As to quays – the old quay previously mentioned, Black Pill, could perhaps have served Mumbles for the 1650 'Survey of Gower' states that Mumbles had 'builded a kay for that purpose [passage to England]' and this might well be it. A later wooden jetty was built in the 1890s near the lifeboat station for the use of the oyster boats but this has long decayed and gone.

Oysters were what the seaward side of the town was about, although the limestone industry was of the same importance to those on the landward side. They were merely two industries that co-existed. Indeed, many fishermen out of season worked in the quarries and vice-versa. They fished the abundant supplies of oysters that lay off the south of the Gower peninsular and into Swansea Bay. When the Duke of Beaufort visited Swansea in 1684 he noted that 'Oystermouth could boast the best bed of oysters in Britain'.

The original fishing skiffs were heavy open boats and, for some obscure reason, were sometimes referred to as Oystermouth lug boats. For those that were rigged with sails –

Print of early Swansea Bay Pilot boats.

and many were simply rowed – they were rigged with a shallop rig in the same way as the Swansea pilot boats. Some thirty boats worked the oyster beds although more came from Swansea, Porthcawl and from Port Eynon, around the corner. Each fisherman has his own 'perch' where he kept his landings of oysters just above the low water mark until they were sold. But word reached out and an influx of English dredgers caused resentment amongst the local fishermen who had happily maintained a sustainable fishery until their arrival. The worst offenders were the Essex men, renowned for their plundering of oyster stock throughout Britain and even over to Holland. In the words of Essex historian Hervey Benham, in *Essex Gold*, 'the rich Swansea grounds were dredged out to re-stock Essex and Kentish beds by a fleet of smacks up to 200 strong, provoking the Mayor of Swansea to voice the usual ineffective call for conservation and control as long ago as 1844'. However, so impressed were the Mumbles fishermen that a group of them travelled to Colneside in 1855 and ordered several smacks of 12 tons to replace their smaller skiffs. The first of these was the *Seven Sisters* and many more followed. These became known collectively as the Mumbles oyster boats, in contrast to what had previously been known as oyster skiffs. Many more new boats arrived from the shipyards of Appledore, across the Bristol Channel. Others, like the 1865-built *Emmeline*, 14SA, came from the Cornish yard of William Paynter of St Ives. Paynter was well known throughout the west coast for his vessels, his luggers being ordered as far away as Campbeltown for mackerel and herring drifting on the Clyde and off Kinsale on the coast of Southern Ireland. So popular were these smacks that they were imitated in a smaller class of Brixham cutters that became known as the Mumble Bees.

Once these bigger boats were introduced the numbers of vessels increased dramatically so that by 1871 there were 188 locally owned smacks from around Swansea Bay and Port Eynon. Some still retained the two-crew smaller skiffs while the majority were the larger boats crewed by three men. The fishery peaked that year when over 16 million oysters worth £50,000 were landed, employing 600 people. This exceeded the Colne fishery by a factor of three! Two years later the landings had halved though and the fishery was by then doomed due to over-fishing, so that ten years later the fleet had been reduced to forty-seven boats. Vessels that had originally cost between £200 and £250 were being sold off for no more than £40. Many were bought for firewood and others turned upside down and used as fishermen's stores. By 1914 this had fallen further to fourteen boats. The last surviving boat was the *Emmeline*, which was measured by P.J. Oke in the 1930s, and his plan of the vessel is the only one known to exist.

The Mumbles lifeboat station is attached to the pier, which lies at the very southern tip of the bay. This pier was completed in 1898 and the slipway opened in 1916 although the lifeboat house wasn't added until 1922 so that the lifeboat of the time, the *Charlie Medland*, had to be covered with a tarpaulin.

There's been a lifeboat stationed in Mumbles since 1866 although its original stationing here was not without argument. It seems that a new boat did first arrive in 1835 but was never put into service for it was moved to Swansea six years later. The boat appeared to lack money being spent on her, although just why a new boat needed sums of money spending on it isn't clear. It was eventually replaced by a ten-oared pulling boat that was kept in the South Dock but this boat only made one active service. A replacement was again provided in 1863, this being an identical vessel which had previously been stationed in Drogheda. By this time it had been decided to move the station to Mumbles but it took another three years to complete the boathouse which lies along the shore from the present station. The *Martha & Anne* eventually arrived there in 1866 and an oyster fisherman, Jenkin Jenkins, was appointed coxswain. A few months later a new boat was installed and since then a whole succession of vessels have made numerous rescues. Three disasters have occurred that have resulted in lifeboats capsizing and members of the crew being drowned. Two of these were in a storm of 1883 and another gale in 1903. However, in April 1947, the entire crew of the lifeboat *Edward, Prince of Wales* was lost while attempting to rescue the crew of the 7,000-ton ship *Samtampa*. Both vessels were ultimately wrecked on Sker Point, the lifeboat being found over-turned the next day. All thirty of the ship's crew were drowned, as were the eight lifeboatmen. In total, eighteen of the Mumbles lifeboat crew have been lost while on active service. The current lifeboat was sitting on the ramp of the station, outside of her shed, where visitors were able to view.

The Mumbles Head lighthouse lies right at the tip of Mumbles Head, already mentioned. Beyond is Bracelet Bay, a rocky beach that was swarming with people. The headland above, between here and Limeslade Bay, is the Tutt where there is a coastguard station. Coastguard operations stem from a will to stamp out smuggling in the early part of the nineteenth century and it became an official body under the control of the Board of Customs in 1822. By the 1850s smuggling was not so profitable and a much riskier venture, punishable by hanging. Coastguard stations, or Watch-Houses as they were called, were erected around the coast and one such being on Mumbles Hill in the 1850s. This one stands adjacent to the 1921 station and has magnificent views over towards the English coast so that a thorough watch can be maintained.

Limeslade Bay, where an iron ore mine was worked since Romans times up to its closure in 1890, was as busy as Bracelet. Both have dog bans in force as do the vast

Unknown woman with salmon
on the Gower.

majority of the beaches along the south coast of the Gower. I visited each beach that was
easily accessible – Langland, Caswell, Threecliff, Oxwich and Port Eynon. The dog had
to stay in the van! Each was as busy as the last, even though the sun's heat was losing its
intensity. Caravans and camping sites dominate parts of the landscape and the smell of
barbecues emanated from the beaches and parks. The roads of the Gower are narrow in
extreme so that at one point we had to wait in a queue of vehicles for almost half an hour
while some old dear reversed into a parking spot to allow vehicles to pass.

According to the Halls all these beaches were frequented for sea bathing in favour of
the Mumbles where there were 'neither sand, shelter, nor bathing machines'. There were
no houses near the coves, although there was one 'very neat and comfortable hotel in
Caswell Bay'. Oxwich Bay was a place for the Polaccas, the typical mid-nineteenth-
century sailing vessels from North Devon (primarily the Taw and Torridge rivers), to
come over and load limestone directly from the beach.

Both Oxwich Bay and Port Eynon had its own fleets of oyster skiffs although they
were very few in number at the former. Port Eynon, on the other hand, had a small quay
called Crowder's Quay from where limestone was exported across to North Devon.
Oysters were also landed here. It is known that a quay was in existence here in 1552 and
probably before that. At the end of the row of cottages stands the lifeboat house where
a boat was briefly placed on station from 1884 after the disaster in Mumbles to 1916. The
station was prematurely closed after the lifeboat *Jane* capsized and three of its crew were
lost on New Year's Day, 1916. The building is now a Youth Hostel. Beyond the remains
of the quay is the famous Salt House, which was home to the Lucas family in the
seventeenth century. Prior to that it was, as its name implies, just that: a place to make
salt by heating up seawater using local coal.

Evidence now suggests that not only does this salt house date from the sixteenth
century, but that the technology used to evaporate the water was extremely innovative
and possibly based on German ideas in the field. It seems that it is the only surviving

example of saltworks from this era in Wales. Salt was shipped from Port Eynon to Aberthaw in the late sixteenth century and in 1598 the Salt House and field were leased to the Gribble family for the annual sum of ten shillings. A 1697 survey of Gower notes a saltworks there forty years prior to that date. A survey and excavation by the Glamorgan-Gwent Archaeological Trust began in 1986 and much of the facts here are thanks to their thorough findings and conclusions.

The water was collected in a reservoir upon the foreshore and, by means of wooden pumps, pumped into shallow metal pans, which had fires beneath. Salt was used for all manner of things, most especially curing meat and fish. Herring, it is said, were landed here at one time. Presumably it was shipped out from the quay, from which the village obtained its name. Then, sometime about the middle of the seventeenth century, the reservoir was infilled with sand and the panhouse demolished to enable the Lucas family to build their house.

The siting of the saltworks at Port Eynon was no accident. The Gower peninsular has a relatively low rainfall when compared to much of the South Wales coast and thus the sea has a higher salinity, further increased by the lack of outflowing rivers in the immediate vicinity. It is also said that the water achieves an even higher salinity because salt crystalizes on the large rocks on the foreshore when the tide ebbs, which is again taken into solution on the flood, adding more salt into the water. Low-grade coal was mined locally and used to heat the pans. The possible existence of a quay may have also contributed to the decision to site the workings here.

John Lucas was the seventh-generation family member. According to one eighteenth century source, he 'possessed much wealth in moneys and did buy skiffes at Swainsey and Bristol to bear ye painte mineral away, to number five, from near Ye Salte House which was his forefather's, across the Sea unto Apeldor, and to coasts upon the high seas to Britain Very, Ogmore, and Nash and Kardiffe and even unto Bristol'. The 'painte mineral' came from the grinding of the iron-stained shales of millstone grit and was used to make paint. Lucas is also supposed to have been an active smuggler at a time when Port Eynon was the centre of the free trading. The cellar in the house was a store for brandy and there's rumour of a tunnel from it to the nearby Culvert Hole. Another leads from Stout House, where the family lived in the fifteenth century, to the Salt House – a distance of three miles, so that seems pretty unlikely. No one's ever found either tunnel though, so I guess these are just more stories. Brandy Cove, just west of Casewell Bay, probably supports the evidence that illicit brandy was brought in under cover of dark, probably from the great storehouse on Lundy Island. Lucas, however, died in 1703, purportedly from a broken heart shortly after a great storm that flooded the Salt House had destroyed his entire fleet of boats anchored off. The Salt House then became two oyster fishermen's cottages, and these were occupied until the 1880s.

Eight excise men with a Revenue boat were based in the little village to stamp out smuggling. They even had a watch-house. Once the practise had diminished somewhat, it simply moved its centre to nearby Rhossili. For from Port Eynon it's a short hop to Rhossili and Worms Head, which is the most westerly point of the Gower, whether you go by sea or land.

Leland describes how he had observed waves dashing over the top of the 200ft precipice below the footpath from Rhossili to the Head. Its name comes from the old English 'wurm' for dragon for they likened it to a sleeping dragon. We walked along the well-trodden path amongst a host of other walkers most of which were returning to the campsites and local pub. The sun was beginning to fall away and I watched its gradual decline into the sea as the dog chased rabbits. Below the expanse of the sands of Rhossili Bay spread north and I observed the last of the day's swimmers enjoying an evening swim. I was even tempted to climb down the rocks and copy them, but it seemed so much easier to observe the incredible sunset. The sea looked as still and peaceful as ever. Bit by bit the shadow of what was some sort of visitor centre lengthened and the tide ingressed over the rocks below Kitchen Corner. Worms Head is accessible some two hours either side of high water yet folk still get trapped and have to wait several hours before being able to return. Only once the sun had finally dipped below the surface of the silvery sea did we return to the van, a feeling of absolute calm engulfing my body at the end of a good day. It really seemed that we'd been to the end of the world!

Worms Head in the evening.

DAY SIX
RHOSSILI TO CARMARTHEN

The road from south to north across the western end of the Gower peninsular meanders its way around back from the coast, thus necessitating some amount of back tracking. At one point it passes through Llandewi, where one particular local wrecker, Mansel of Henllys, once lived. He was supposedly the leader of a gang of wreckers who ransacked the wreck of the Spanish vessel *El Dorado*, known locally as the *Dollar Ship*. He disappeared that very same night, towards the end of the seventeenth century, and to this day no one knows whether he fled with the treasure from the ship or was murdered. His ghost, some say, still races across the sand on a black coach drawn by four grey mares. Other stories abound of wrecks and wreckers. In Llangennith, Janet Ace, known as Jennie Grove for some obscure reason, used to tell how, after the great 1883 gale, her employer, a Mr Bevan, returned to the farm carrying a huge bag of gold coins which he'd found on the beach at low tide in Bluepool Bay. What proportion of these stories are anecdotal and what, if any, evidence there is I do not know. I could recount a few more tales but point the reader to *The Story of Gower* by Wendy Hughes, which has a fair rendering of many of them.

Llanrhidian Sands are vast, stretching at low water the whole length of the northern coast of the Gower – from the northeastern tip of Berges Island to the narrows of the river Loughor (*Afon Llwchwr*). This expanse of mud and sand is renowned for its cockles. Between the coast and the Sands is a significant area of marsh with veins of pills draining the land. To the casual visitor these not places to wander. The road follows parallel to the coast and offers good views over the estuary. It soon arrives at Penclawdd.

Fishing nets used to be set in the bay. These 'field nets' were strung between posts in the sand and proved very effective in catching an assortment of fish. *Will a Chwaer* was the only herring fisherman who set similar nets, although the net was fixed to the top of the poles. His catch was said to be quite a sight on a moonlit night when the glistening fish reflected against the silvery shimmering light. Just why these fish, once called the 'potato of the middle ages', are better known as 'silver darlings' becomes apparent. For they do not merely create wealth for the lucky fisherman, they really do become silvery in the moonlight. However, here upon the sands, it was from the cockles and not the silver darlings that any pretence at wealth was gleaned. Well, not wealth as such, but an income.

Cockles are to Penclawdd as prawns are to prawn cocktail. So much so that it is very difficult indeed to go anywhere in the village and not find a cockleshell. They are in the hedgerows, the chicken runs, the graveyards and gardens. They lie about in heaps and you crunch upon them on parts of the beach. They are everywhere and, according to the evidence, they've been there for centuries. Prehistoric man was cockle gathering on the sands long before the Celts or the Romans arrived here.

Left: The Cockle
Woman.

Below: Cockling at
Ferryside.

The unique factor about the Penclawdd cockle fishery is that the women of the village undertake it almost exclusively. Or at least it was until 'cockling', as it's known, became quite an industry and a convenient source of income for those officially unemployed. Whilst their menfolk worked in the nearby coal mines, metal factories or limestone quarries, the women would go out upon the sands when the tide was right and pick. The only men working on the sands in those days were those who had been injured in the mines or factories. For both partners in the household work was physically arduous but it's said that they never was much poverty in the village.

The Halls had met in Swansea some mussel girls and an oyster woman but nobody connected with the cockle fishing. However, they may have just been unlucky for these women were renowned for walking the nine-odd miles from Penclawdd to the Swansea market to sell their catch. Saturday was the main market day. Some were sold fresh in their shells and some boiled in vats upon the beach. Tradition has it that these hardy women carried a basket upon each arm and one on their head. They walked the first seven miles to Olchfa barefoot before donning their boots after washing their feet in the stream. They then reversed the procedure on their homeward journey carrying their baskets filled with provisions for the family. Only when the railway from Swansea to Penclawdd via the Clyne valley was opened in 1863 was their life made a little easier.

Cockle woman sieving her catch.

There was a Saturday-only passenger service for the railway was constructed primarily for coal which was brought down to the sea for export to, in the main, Ireland and Cornwall.

H.V. Morton thought the old cockle women looked like they were 'waiting for Rembrandt to come and paint them'. He went out onto the Penclawdd sands with a young maiden called Miriam who sang Welsh songs and 'was young and salted as a Bismarck herring'. However, though impressed with their exhausting, back-aching work the women did without complaint, he found he was unable 'to feel any pity under the sky, with the gulls wheeling and the clean wind blowing and Miriam singing in a loud voice about something that happened in Wales long ago'!

Nevertheless, the gathering of the little bi-valves was not much fun, especially in the extreme freezing, cold winter conditions they had to endure. To collect the shellfish they used a small knife, called a *scrap*, to expose the cockle and then a home-made rake, called a *cram*, to gather them up in little piles before they are sieved and washed in a nearby beach pool and sacked ready to be carried across the sands. Each woman usually had a donkey to load up with two sacks until carts were used in later times. Not only was it cold work, it was also backbreaking.

Numbers of cockle gatherers varied from about 500 in 1885 to between 200 and 250 in 1910. The latter figure depended on the time of year. Women from other Gower villages were also drawn down to the sands to participate. Once legislation was brought in to control stocks as they declined because of over-fishing, these numbers also fell. A minimum size was enforced and a maximum amount each could gather. Concerns on public health ensured tight controls were enforced upon their purification and boiling. Cockles were regularly tested to ensure pollution wasn't affecting their quality. However, very recently, this has caused an outcry for the fishery has been closed because of a poison scare. The Food Standards Agency have found traces of diarrhetic shellfish poisoning (DSP) in the cockles and have thus stopped all cockle fishing throughout England and Wales. It seems that the test involves injecting three mice with a solution of liquid taken from the cockle and if one mouse dies that's OK but if two or all of the unlucky creatures die, then a ban is enforced. This test, known as the mouse bioassay test (MBA), is subject to differences in opinion as to its usefulness to detect DSP. The industry maintains that the test is killing the mice and not any toxin, according to *Fishing News*. Furthermore, they claim that the Scottish Food Standards Agency refuse to use it. The Food Standards Agency makes contradictory claims. And so the two sides battle it out and research is commissioned. Meanwhile, those who's living depend on the cockle are left to await the outcome.

The Penclawdd Shellfish Processors Ltd have premises close by the sands. As well as processing cockles, they also prepare laverbread, the delicacy seaweed traditionally served in South Wales. The seaweed 'laver' (*Porphyra umbilicalis*) is found on many a British West Coast where it grows on beaches where rocks are embedded in the sand. It is a very nutritious plant, rich in protein, low in calories, and contains vitamins and iodine. Once collected it is thoroughly washed and cooked by boiling until it is soft and jelly-like. Traditionally it was cooked over a coal fire but today's technology and regulations ensure it is boiled over gas in modern pans. Once thus cooked, it is either sold fresh or tinned. The traditional Welsh way of eating it was with fried cockles, bacon, mushrooms and eggs, but it can also be made into Laver Cakes or a delicious Laver and Cockle Paté, or simply spread on toast and topped with tomato, bacon, cockles or whatever takes the fancy. It really is lovely stuff. I sometimes buy it fresh from the stall on the indoor market in Carmarthen.

Penclawdd also once briefly had its own canal. When coal was being mined in the late 1790s it was shipped out from a deepened pill near Berth-lwyd, which is the biggest of the pills about a mile east of the village. A few years later John Vivian, who founded the Penclawdd copperworks, built a small dock at Penclawdd. Both weren't suitable for bigger craft so in 1811 an Act of Parliament was obtained to build the Penclawdd Canal from the village to Kingsbridge, where the old Swansea Road crosses the Lliw River just outside of Gorseinon. The canal was just over 3½ miles in length and had two locks. It opened for business about 1814 and was still usable in 1825 although the copperworks had closed but within a generation all signs of it had disappeared, as much of the route was adapted for the railway.

The road and rail cross the river Loughor at Loughor Bridge, from where it's a short drive to Llanelli. Again good seams of coal in the locality were the main driving force behind the development of the area. The Llanelly Copperworks Company, established in 1805 by, amongst others, the Englishman Charles Neville, was one of the significant industries that all but had a monopoly on Llanelli coal in the nineteenth century. It has been said that it was his son, Richard Janion Neville, who made the Copperworks successful and that the Copperworks in turn made Llanelli into West Wales' premier industrial town. Before either of them, though, Alexander Raby had been another English entrepreneur who, beginning in 1796, invested significant sums of money into the local coal and iron industries – although twenty-seven years later he'd lost most of his investment. The Halls, arriving after the initial developments, found Llanelli to be thriving and described it as 'a town of coal foundries and smoke'.

When we look at the coastline of today, it is sometimes very easy to overlook particular areas of the vernacular zone where activity has in the past left little signs. I guess this was one of the main purposes of this tour in the first place. Llangennech Quay is one such place. Originally the Llangennech Pill, the point where the Mwrwg brook flows into the river Loughor, was a shipping place where vessels could load and discharge. In the 1770s a canal was built to ship coal out of the nearby mines, this being lengthened in the 1790s to the newly built Llangennech Quay. By 1825 this dock 'consisted of three quay walls enclosing two dock basins with rail tracks', according to *The Industrial and Maritime History of Llanelli and Burry Port 1750 to 2000*, a significant work on the area. By 1834, with a new railway available to move coal out, the quay fell out of use. Now only parts of the stone walls are visible so that it is normally forgotten about. In the marshy area a little further upstream, a shipping place on Llangennech Marsh is thought to predate this. A plan of about 1825 refers to it as a 'Site of old Shipping Place'.

In actuality there were several short canals in use. The Baccas and Yspitty canals both exited at a point just west of the narrows in the Loughor River, at Pill y Cefn and Townsend's Pill respectively. The Wern Canal (also called the Pen-y-Fan Canal) meanwhile served the Llanelly Copperworks and the Trostre Canal brought coal down to shipping places in the Dafen River and is thought to be the oldest of the lot. Other canals in the immediate vicinity were the Hopkins Canal and the Vauxhall Canal, the latter leading into the river Lliedi. Although all these appear to have been constructed before 1800, it appears that by 1810 they had all fallen into disuse, thus having a short useful life. Another even older canal was said to have been built by Thomas Bowen to ship coal from his colliery at Pen-y-Fan back in 1750. If so, this would be the oldest canal in Wales but unfortunately there is absolutely no evidence at present – including no Act of Parliament – to support it ever existing. Other landing places in the area were at Pencoed, the mouth of the Lliedr River and Pwll Quay. Little remains of any of these sites.

What must be remembered is that as the Industrial Revolution progressed and technology improved, different phases for different developments occurred. Thus a canal, cutting technology in the very late 1700s, might have been filled in a few years later to build a railway. As vessels grew larger, deeper dock systems were necessary, often smothering previous systems. Then, as we've seen all along the coast so far, dock systems themselves were filled in once they had become superfluous and more developments covering the site.

The period of the 1830s and 1840s was one of a dramatic increase in trade in Llanelli, which in turn led to an expansion of the dock system. Several shipbuilders established yards there, some drawn to the area by this massive extension to the coal and later tinplate industries which led to the town being nicknamed *Tinopolis*. However, decline set in, adding to navigational problems on the shifting sands of the Burry Inlet, so that trade collapsed after the Second World War. The North Dock, built in 1903 as a centrepiece showcase for the harbour, finally closed in 1951.

Some few months prior to this visit to Llanelli, I spent almost a whole day with two friends surveying the docks and studying a nineteenth-century map to orientate the position of the systems that had been either filled in or altered. Thus we found the sites of Pemberton's Dock and the Copperworks Dock and could almost trace the track of the Wern Canal. Today all that remains are the North Dock, recently restored, parts of the Carmarthenshire Dock and the New Dock.

Between Llanelli and Burry Port is Pwll Quay, where it has been mentioned there was a landing place. Bathing machines were once a common sight on the sands in the mid-nineteenth century. One hotel at Burry Port was advertised in 1868 as a 'family and commercial boarding house, the sands are unequalled for their extent and beauty for Sea Bathing'. Again we find that tourism and industry survive side by side. Offshore, the remains of several fish weirs have been swallowed up by the sands.

Burry Port's Dock has recently received a grant for the construction of a tidal gate at its entrance to keep it partially flooded at all states of the tide. This is all part of the Millennium Coastal Park that has provided an amenity to the coast between Pembrey and Llanelli, with cycle paths and footpaths, providing landscaping and clean beaches as part of a scheme to regenerate a depressed area. In much earlier times, though, Burry Port was the major port for the export of coal in the whole of Carmarthenshire.

Lifeboats were established here in the nineteenth century. Llanelli had the first one after a series of wrecks on the Burry Bar. The station was opened in 1852 but closed in 1863 because it soon was obvious that it should be positioned at Pembrey. This opened the same year that the Llanelli station closed but by 1887 had been transferred to Burry Port. In the meantime, a station was re-established at Llanelli between 1869-1871, after a disaster when the Pembrey lifeboat could not launch. Finally, in 1914, this station ceased operations.

In the eighteenth century much of the local coal was exported through nearby Kidwelly (*Cydweli*). A canal briefly linked Pembrey with Pill Towyn on the south bank of the Gwendraeth Fawr. This was built about 1796 and extended 1799-1801 but doesn't seem to have survived for much after that. A new commercial harbour at Pembrey was built in 1819, which was soon followed by the Pembrey Canal in 1824 to bring down anthracite and iron ore. Another harbour – initially called the New Pembrey Harbour – was built at Burry Port and opened in 1832. By the middle of that century virtually all the coal from the Gwendraeth Valley was passing through these two ports. The Burry Port and Gwendraeth Valley Railway was opened in 1869, much of the track utilising the bed of the Kidwelly & Llanelly Canal. With a flourishing trade and the discovery of new seams of coal, the Burry Port dock was extended with the construction of the West Dock in 1888. Declining trade added to the problems of silting up, as was the case at Llanelli, so that Pembrey's harbour was the first to fall into disuse, followed a couple of decades later by Burry Port so that all commercial trade had ceased here by 1942. Today, happily, the downward trend is in reversal, or so they hope, for this harbour now is only one of a very few in the immediate area – perhaps the only one in Carmarthenshire – where pleasure craft can lie continually afloat.

Burry Port also has a cockle and laverbread processing works and some cockles are picked from the sands. West of Pembrey harbour is Pembrey Country Park, with a dry ski slope, visitor centre, miniature railway and forest and beach walks. It is littered with the remains of an Army shooting range, including the bed of old railways along which ammunition was delivered into camouflaged buildings which can be fun to investigate. This area is where the infamous 'Hatchet Men of Pembrey' operated, luring ships onto the Cefn Sidan sands. It seems they liked to carry small hatchets with them as they wandered about the sands looking out for either new victims or the wrecks of those vessels fallen prey to their false lights. The niece of Napoleon Bonaparte's lover Josephine lies buried in the small churchyard after the wrecking of the *Jeune Emma* in 1828.

Kidwelly has a much longer history associated with the sea and its port can be traced back to at least 1229 when permission was given for the garrison to trade with Gascony, exchanging wool and hides for French wine. The Norman castle dates from the beginning of the twelfth century. It drew the bulk of its earnings from agriculture although cloth making was being manufactured and exported in the fifteenth century. Other imports included salt fish, wheat, barley, beans, flour, salt and ale. Leland found a 'pretily waullid' town on the point of confluence of the Gwendraeth Fawr and Fach rivers where 'ther lieth on eche side of Wendreth Vaur Pittes, wher Menne digge Se Cole'. However, it seems that coal mining wasn't of any significant importance. Smuggling and piracy seemed to be more profitable and Kidwelly is said to have been the centre of these activities in Carmarthen Bay. It wasn't until the second half of the eighteenth century that Thomas Kymer started coal mining nearby, thus beginning an industry that was foremost in the town's development. More importantly perhaps, it was Kymer who was responsible for the first canal to be built in Wales, to bring coal down to what was the developing 'ancient port' at the time. Opened by 1768, this three-mile-long canal also carried limestone down from the quarries at Pwllyllygod as well as culm to burn it in the kilns that had been erected a century earlier. Kymer's previous attempts to float barges down the river proved unsuccessful due to changes in the watercourse and an erratic lack of depth. There were no locks along its route, several bridges across it and two passing places at Muddlescwm and Morfa. Where it emerged at the seaward end Kidwelly Docks was built. It was later extended as part of the Kidwelly & Llanelly Canal until the advent of the railway, which saw much of the route of the canal being built upon Burry Port and Gwendraeth Railway. However, Kidwelly Docks were still used and two other dock systems were in existence further upstream, although there are no visible remains today. One, Kymer's Quay, on the Gwendraeth Fach, was located close to the road bridge below the castle and Coney Quay, the other, on the Gwendraeth Fawr above Commissioner's Bridge. It is said that at times there were twenty or more vessels lying in the river awaiting loading. However, a decline in the port's fortunes can probably be attributed to the silting up of the Gwendraeth estuary which, it seems, was a perpetual obstacle. This was noted back in 1586 and shipping movements do seem to have fluctuated over the centuries because of the danger to vessels of the estuary.

William Raynor was a local shipbuilder who built barges for the canal. In the first two decades of the eighteenth century he built ships of up to 163 tons, the latter being the brig *Margaret* in 1814. Later industries included tinplate manufacture, begun in 1737 (which makes it only second to Pontypool in manufacturing tinplate in Britain), the Kidwelly Ironworks, several brickworks and, in the twentieth century, two tarmacadam plants. Much of the tinplate was exported to America until President McKinley levied a tax on imported tinplate to discourage these imports. The ironworks, on the northern outskirts of the town, houses the Kidwelly Industrial Museum, which has fantastic displays on the tinplate and coal industry, the history of Kidwelly and some fine relics of the machinery sued in the tinplating.

From Kidwelly it's a lovely train ride along the very edge of the river Towy (*Afon Tywi*) up to Carmarthen. Living in Carmarthen, I've travelled along this route many a time and the ever-changing scene of the river life never ceases to fascinate each time. But this time we are driving along the road which runs parallel to the railway all the way to Ferryside. We stopped at St Ishmael's close to a little caravan site – not the Carmarthen Bay Holiday Centre, mind, but a little site further along the road. Its owner said we could park there while we went out over the sands. For the tide was low and half a mile out is the Salmon Point Scar upon which are the remains of an ancient fish weir.

I'd read about this weir and surveyed it last year. It was described as having a 'stone wall of large grounders sitting on a stone scar… turning… as far as the edge of the scar.' A gap in between was supposedly completed in timber. As there are historical references of medieval traps belonging to Whitland Abbey, it is possible that this weir is of great antiquity. Recent research suggests several weirs were operational hereabout at one time.

It's easy to find and I checked on a few details I'd been uncertain of. For there's some confusion for the records concerning this weir are entitled 'Pastoun Scar'. This one is on Salmon Point Scar and the description definitely seems to relate to this one. It runs south and then east, which agrees with the record. The remains of the walls are obvious and timber posts still protrude. The shape is almost semi-circular although not in one clean arc. At its eastern end there's evidence of a crew – where the stonework forms an acute angle to the main wall so that fish become trapped there once the tide recedes. The gap referred to above is also obvious. Inside the weir is the remains of a mussel breeding structure, which was supposedly used in the 1980s, according to the caravan site owner.

Coastal Footpaths

The Welsh coast is blessed with a good amount of coastal footpaths that hug and zigzag the contours of the shoreline. The best known of these is the Pembrokeshire Coast Path that stretches from the border with Carmarthenshire at Amroth to the Cardiganshire border the other end at St Dogmael's. The designated length is just under 175 miles but this doesn't include various stretches through built-up areas, the odd detour and diversions necessary at high tide. The total length walked then becomes almost 193 miles.

Although the National Park was established in 1952, the coastal path wasn't opened until 1970 when it became the first long-distance footpath in Wales. It's a well-trodden route and can easily be walked in short increments as one-day walks, or completed in one assault. Guide books and maps (Ordnance Survey Outdoor Leisure sheets 35 and 36 cover it) are available in most bookshops and local stores. I have a Constable guide to the Pembrokeshire Coast Path by Christopher John Wright (London, 1986 and reprinted second edition in 1993) which has served me well during various sojourns onto the path.

However, much of the coast is accessible along public footpaths. At the Chepstow end of the coast it's difficult to get onto the coast until Black Rock although it is possible to cut across and make St Pierre Pill. From Black Rock it's easy to get to Goldcliff although the path isn't necessarily a public right of way. It is always up to the walker to check this for himself. Between Newport and Cardiff any path is intermittent and roads have to be used. From Penarth it is possible to walk all the way to Porthcawl although a detour has to be made at Barry. The path from Gileston to Porthcawl is the Glamorgan Coast Heritage Path within a conservation area. From there a path takes the walker to Margam but from thereon there's no path until the other side of Swansea although Aberafan beach is pleasant to walk upon. Most of the southern coast of Gower (The Gower is designated an Area of Outstanding Beauty) has a public footpath but on the north it's a different question, partly because of the nature of the foreshore. There's a Millennium Coast Park along the north part of the Burry Inlet, which leads onto the Pembrey Park. At this point the walker has arrived at the estuary of the rivers Gwendraeth, Towy and Taf, which, combined with firing ranges and danger areas, makes walking almost impossible although it is possible to walk over the cliffs from Pendine Sands to the start of the Pembrokeshire Coast Path.

At the Cardigan end of the Coast Path the coast becomes more difficult to walk upon. From the Teifi to the Dyfi much of the coast was designated a Heritage Coast in 1982. To walk to Aberporth means using some lanes due to the lack of paths and the fact that there's a RAF station on the headland west of Aberporth. From there to Newquay has a path in areas and others without. It seems straightforward between there and Aberaeron and possible to get to the river Dyfi with some road detours. The best book I've seen detailing the complete walk from Cardigan to Borth is Liz Allan's *Walking the Cardigan Bay Coast* (Kittiwake, Machynlleth, 2000). There's no way to cross the river estuary to Aberdyfi without a boat or a bus ride. From Aberdyfi the map shows that it is possible to walk on paths and the road to Fairbourne to catch the ferry (summer only – check availability) to Barmouth and continue north on the same basis. A word of warning, though: when walking along the foreshore be aware of the tide so that you don't get caught out or, worse still, trapped by it.

From Barmouth to Porthmadog it's a bit hit and miss because of the expanse of sand and several river estuaries. However from Porthmadog there's a path most of the way to Pwllheli

The coast formation at Lystep.

with the odd road detour around the holiday camp and a river. There is of course another alternative between Aberystwyth and Pwllheli and that's the train. It's a wonderful ride along the coast via Machynlleth and Porthmadog! The rest of the Lleyn peninsular is not too well provided with paths although sections are walkable. Several books cover these footpaths that often do not follow the coast, thus necessitating using the narrow lanes. All along the north coast of the country paths are fewer and far between. Something like 75 per cent of the Anglesey coast is attainable, except in the built-up areas and along the Menai Strait, which is not good for walking on both its sides due to the ownership of private estates and houses. My book *Anglesey and its Coastal Tradition* (Llanrwst, 2000) covers much of the coast of the island as do other books. The county council, who administer the coastal footpath, state that the 'path allows users to walk most of Anglesey's 125-mile coastline'.

There's a path from Bangor eastwards, although this fades out once the coastal road is reached. However, the beauty of the Welsh coast is behind the walker at this point. The coast from here on is a constant mass of seaside resorts – Llandudno, Colwyn Bay, Rhyl, Prestatyn etc. and is not well covered with paths although large sections of the beach are accessible when the tides are right. Once at the Point of Ayr, the Dee estuary is perhaps not the best place to walk beside because of the tide and moving sands, although a path does follow much of it. Best perhaps to veer off at Prestatyn and walk the 180-odd miles southward along the Offa's Dyke Path to re-emerge along the eastern bank of the river Wye, near Chepstow and be able to declare that you really have walked around Wales!

Salmon Point Scar is less than half a mile west of Pastoun Scar and we walked over to it. Here we found another weir in the shape of a straight wall across a shallow pool. There was no turning in the wall at all, and no signs of a gap although the wall was breached. I decided that at some time these two weirs had been transposed in the record. Still the tide was flooding, the beach altering in shape by the minute and the dog sopping wet so it seemed time to return to the road.

On the left-hand side of the road through Ferryside there's a sign outside a little shed advertising fresh fish. 'Yeah, it's all fresh', I was told in the shop when I enquired, 'all caught locally. ' I wondered exactly how local 'locally' was, given that I doubted some of the fish advertised ever reached the river. Ferryside lies right upon the east bank of the river and here a ferry operated over to Llansteffan. It is said that the ferry would always wait for the train. Now that's an integrated transport system if there ever was one. We could learn a lot today. Just recently a friend came from Cork to Swansea. The ferry was delayed because of fog three days earlier (?) and then, once it had arrived at Swansea, they found the tide had gone out. Was there a train awaiting desperate travellers when it finally docked at 3 a.m.? No, of course not!

There's a short jetty for pleasure boats. Before the railway came, a ferryboat plied between here at Carmarthen, calling in at Llansteffan. The steamboat *Lilly*, the last vessel built at Carmarthen in 1865, plied a route from here to Tenby. The Revd Evans found that the cocklers of Llansteffan used the ferry to ship bags of their pickings up to Carmarthen, carrying as much as they could for the fare of 2*d* per person. Once they had reached home, they had managed to earn something like 6*d* per bushel. It's worth mentioning that Evans crossed over from St Ishmael's, not Ferryside, to Llansteffan before catching a boat upstream to Carmarthen. The river, he says, was full of pairs of coracles, meeting the 'fish with their trawls on the turning tide'.

Although now replaced with an inshore boat, there had been a lifeboat station here since it was established in 1860 although records of the Corporation of Carmarthen note that the Corporation had 'ordered… a lifeboat should be established at the Ferry Side' in 1834. The RNLI records show that this first lifeboat was stationed at Laugharne and that they labelled her as the 'Carmarthen Bay Life-boat'. The Ferryside station was eventually closed in 1960.

It was estimated that there were 150 cockle gatherers working from Ferryside in 1910 and today it is a public fishery – part of the Three Rivers – regulated by the South Wales Sea Fishing Committee. Only twelve people worked the beds at Llansteffan in 1910. Like its neighbour across the river, Llansteffan has a few pleasure boats and a good beach (no dogs during the summer months), and the additional benefit from tourism through the Norman castle on the hill dating from about 1138 and overlooking the estuary. With superb views across the Bristol Channel and over as far as Lundy Island, it is easy to see why this castle was sited in such a prominent position. The Halls, echoing Dr Beattie, tell us that it is one of the oldest castles in Wales, which suggests it was built a bit earlier.

Carmarthen was the first crossing point of the Towy in Roman times. It is the oldest town in Wales and coracle fishing for salmon and sewin (sea trout) is said to be its oldest industry. This, it is claimed, dates back to the early Britons who were using such craft before the Romans arrived. It's an occupation that continues today (more of that later).

The Normans built their castle upon Castle Hill in 1093 and later a walled town emerged. The port grew up from the need to trade wool and hide as at Kidwelly. Again wine, as well as iron, was brought back to the port. Leland found 'Smaul Balinggers' coming up the river and below the cliffs at Green Castle, a couple of miles downstream of Carmarthen, ships lying at anchor. This is believed to be the point at which vessels were unloaded and the cargo transferred to barges for bringing upstream for silting up was problematic here as well. A ballinger, by the way, was the term applied, in the fifteenth and sixteenth centuries, to a small and light sea-going vessel, a kind of sloop with a forecastle. The word itself comes from the old French 'baleine' for 'whale' and was formerly regarded as being a whaleship. Evans also noted vessels waiting at 'Green haven' before taking the tide over the bar.

In 1547 the mayor of Carmarthen was given the added title of 'Admiral of the River Towy'. When Defoe came, he found 'an Antient but not Decay'd Town, pleasantly situated on the River Towy' with moderately sized vessels. He also noted that he thought it, and the surrounding country, the 'most fruitful' part of all Wales.

The port grew in importance as trade flourished with coal, salt, wine and tar coming in and cereals and wool out. Coal was also exported, as was lead ore from mines to the north. Iron, tin and silver briefly played a part in the town's industries. The local inhabitants were also famed for their baskets and matting, which Evans considered equal in appearance to Indian imports. Vessels regularly traded with Pickle Herring Wharf in London and cured herring was sold direct from the ships upon the quay. The locals could buy any amount they chose – from a couple of herring to a whole barrel. By 1831 fifty-one Carmarthen-registered vessels, thirteen foreign vessels and 420 coasters had entered the port, providing £3,000 to the port custom's coffers. One local reported seeing thirteen American brigs in the river at the same time. Several ships were built alongside the river, some up to 330 tons (as was the *Princess Royal* which was launched in 1841). A Mr Bedford had come from Pembrokeshire in the early 1800s to start up a yard that became known as the Bedford Yard. The quay was extended right up to the bridge between 1808–09.

The *Frolic*, already mentioned for being wrecked off Nash Point, began a packet service to Bristol in 1830. It took until 1834 for a replacement service to be introduced with the arrival of the *County of Pembroke*. With the railway eventually reaching Carmarthen in 1852 and branch lines fanning out into the county, the port suffered the same decline seen all over industrial Wales. The launch of the *Lilly* saw an end to shipbuilding but, even with silting up problems, vessels still ventured up river into the twentieth century, although by 1930s they were only five vessels visiting, on average. By the end of the decade all seaborne trade had ceased.

Coracle fishing hasn't, though, although there may be a certain amount of truth in that certain authorities wish it had. There are those who would like to abolish coracle fishing entirely in the name of conservation, although these so-called conservatives are all too often members of the rod-and-line brigade. It was the very same folk who accused the coracle fishermen of almost sweeping the river clean of fish by using a net that stretched from one bank to the other and down to the riverbed. Of course, this was rubbish as the net was only 40ft long and 36ins deep, and the riparian landowners knew it, but it served as a distraction. All too often the pleasures of the so-called hierarchy take precedent over the necessities of the working proletariat. However, until the first Salmon Fishery Act of 1861 details of the salmon fishing are very slight because of the lack of legislation but we do have plenty of evidence of the use of the coracle.

A coracle is a small vessel made from a wooden framework with animal hide wrapped around its outside. Willow or ash is the traditional timber, either of which is easily bent to shape. The Romans noted the existence of these vessels, although from the various descriptions it is believed that it was the Irish curraghs – of a similar construction but much larger – that impressed Caesar and Pliny. This little craft impressed Giraldus Cambrensis and his description almost holds true today. 'For fishing and crossing rivers' he wrote, 'they make coracles out of withies. These are not oblong but rounded, and they are pointed in front, rather in the shape of a triangle. They are left bare inside, but are covered outside with untanned animal-skins. When a salmon is landed inside one of these coracles, the fish sometimes strikes the boat so hard with its tail that it is turned over, to the great danger of the man who is fishing. When fishermen are on their way to the river, or going home, they have the primitive habit of carrying their coracles on their backs.'

Today's coracles remain almost the same as Giraldus must have found them except for the fact that the outer animal-skin has been replaced by calico. These days this is coated in tar or paint as a waterproof layer. Coracles are endemic to most of the main rivers of Wales – and indeed some of those in Ireland, Scotland and the river Severn in England. Each river's coracle has subtle differences in construction and shape. Thus a Towy coracle and one from the river Taf are different in shape although these rivers are adjacent to each other, both emerging into Carmarthen Bay.

Coracle nets are only used in the Towy and Teifi rivers and are suspended between two coracles as they drift now downstream with the current. Each fisherman holds one end of the net, feeling for vibrations from a fish becoming entangled. Stories of multiple numbers of salmon being caught in one sweep are generally untrue, as rarely do they catch more than one at a time. Again these are red herrings often attributed to those against commercial fishing.

One aspect of the salmon fishing is the secrecy with which it is practised. The skill is in the predicting of the time to fish and the weights needed on the net to suit the tidal conditions and strength of the stream. These finer points have been handed down for centuries from father to son. Another tradition is that coracles are burnt once they have exceeded their useful life. When asked why, one coracleman simply told the questioner, 'Because my father, my grand-father, and my great-grandfather did so.'

In the very beginning of the nineteenth century, the Corporation of Carmarthen attempted to prohibit fishing from Carmarthen Bridge and insisted all coracles to be numbered. At that time there was no limit to their numbers and it is said that up to forty-eight pairs worked the river. The Corporation's intention was to purchase boats and tackle 'for procuring fish for supplying this town.' A man was sent to Brixham to obtain a fishing smack but this obviously didn't prove successful for the boat, the *Flying Fish*, was later hired out. Any fish caught was landed at Ferryside and sent up to the Wednesday Carmarthen market. Carmarthen still holds its market on that day and has a magnificent indoor market hall. Unfortunately, the current Carmarthenshire Council wants to pull this down, against the wishes of the townsfolk, so that some department store or other can be enticed to the site. But they don't want yet another bland department store and they don't want the market moved to another site. They don't believe the promises of jobs, many of which will be part-time jobs and badly paid. Many people are gainfully employed already in the market, thanks very much, so why should they lose their livelihood just because these council bods want their way? And no doubt some financial incentives too.

Still, that's getting us away from the river. Time to get a decent night's sleep at home in the green-painted house.

DAY SEVEN
CARMARTHEN TO TENBY

'See, to be good on the river you have to understand the *clefwcwr*. That's hard to put into English. It's a time, not fixed, see, but moving.' Like the river, the edge of which I was standing with Raymond Rees, coracle fisherman and fishmonger of the town, where he and his ancestors had been fishing for generations.

'Back to 1710 they were here on this bit of the river'. He pointed to the water, gently flowing under the bridge that was built in the 1950s to replace the earlier one, the first road crossing over the river. 'Two miles upstream and seven down, that's where we can fish'.

I asked him to try and explain *clefwcwr*. As far as I could understand it is the time between dusk and the moment in time when the river stops flowing, when the flood equals its normal stream. Sometimes this lasts half an hour and at other times maybe four hours. Dusk, he said, is, by agreement, the time when seven stars are visible in the sky. Assuming there's no cloud, that is. I didn't ask what happened then!

One thing that became clear after spending a couple of hours with Raymond in his shed alongside the river was that coracle fishing wasn't easy. There might now be a resurgence of coracle building around Wales – and further afield for that matter – but using them was altogether a different skill.

'Success is down to reading the river', he continued. 'Don't get it right and you might as well fish in the bath'. He pointed to a block in the nearby bridge and told me how he watches that. From the height of the water, and the pattern of flow around the base, he can tell the time and place to fish.

Three men work the nets. The three men bit is worked out as being twice the number of men needed to work the net minus one. Since 1934 there have been twelve licensed fishermen on the river, although this year only five took their licences up. Such is the dismal state of the catches of salmon and sewin.

Traditionally, these three were made up of father, son and grandfather. 'Now they've ruined that; ruined the traditional way of fishing, see. ' For before, each generation taught the next how to fish, but now, with new regulations from the Environment Agency, the licensee, often the elder who often stayed at home, has to be present. That, effectively, has put an end to the handing down of the skill. In 2001, the Foot and Mouth crisis meant that the season was delayed, and so Raymond didn't take up his licence. His son works in a bank in Bristol, so he's given up altogether. Not worth it, he reckons, to pay the £399 annual fee plus all the other expenses. With the season lasting from 1 March to 31 July (salmon can only be taken after 1 June) the financial incentives have disappeared.

We went into his workshop, a mix of woodworking equipment, strips of timber, netting and various pots of whatever. He pointed into the roof. 'Built by my grandfather over fifty years ago', he said of a coracle. We pulled it down. 'Now our coracle building here on the Tywi is truly a work of art. We call it *eielgody*, meaning to resurrect'. He expanded on this by showing me how the coracle consisted of seven horizontal, seven vertical and two diagonal strips of ash. The gunwale consisted of several rows of bent hazel – or willow, he added – the first one starting on the left side, the second on the right, around the front of the boat. Next they come around the tail – the stern - of the boat, and so on, building up a series of plaits. Then the calico shell had been laced on. Above this, a final plait of four strands of hazel formed the top of the gunwale. As this is the first part of the vessel to rot, it can easily be removed and replaced - resurrected so to speak. 'Innovation', he said. 'No other coracle has that. That's what sets us coracle men apart of others.'

Fitting the priest – or *cnocer* – into its leather strap, he lifted the coracle onto his back, suspending it over his shoulders with another leather strap. This, he assured me, was another difference, as normally this strap would be made from several strands of hazel. To walk with the coracle, the paddle was used as a lever under the arm to lift it away from the back of the legs. 'This ensures the legs don't get wet'. Another innovation. And another was the fish box beneath the seat. Below this was the *orlais* – a sort of bulkhead, to support the seat (*astell*). It had added advantages of preventing the fish slithering to the

Raymond Rees with one of
his coracles on his back 2003.

tail of the coracle where it was possible one might jump out. When carrying the craft, it served as a box to retain the fish for the walk home. The technique of lowering the coracle back to the ground was also exacting to ensure the fish remained in the coracle and not being dumped onto the ground.

'Yeah', he continued, 'we coracle fishermen evolved our coracles much more than upon any of the other rivers. Not only that, we were the early warners of any peculiarities on the river. ' In that he meant they were the eyes of the bailiffs, informing them of any alteration in the river's behaviour or pattern. A pollution incident of oil, or even milk from the creamery, or a change in temperature, ulcers on the fish – as once happened a few years ago – and they would immediately inform the authorities. Yet nothing else was volunteered such as the number of fish caught. Never lied when asked, but never given if not. And neither did they ever let on to other fishermen if a catch had been good in a certain spot, because otherwise that spot would be taken up on the next day before they arrived.

The individual community of fishers was close-knit. When the licences were introduced in 1934, the Towy Coracle Fishermen's Association was formed, enabling the fishermen to agree on unwritten, informal rules, such as what constitutes dusk. Raymond was secretary for a time. It was agreed that no one would fish within 200 yards of another, and there was to be no interference. Competition was fierce but amiable. They caught only what they could sell and were always mindful of the fact that stocks were not limitless, thus ensuring continuity in supply – supply they don't have today, for other reasons that are well known.

Raymond indicated how they'd set a net in the river. They'd paddle out and shoot it across the river and drift with the remnants of the tide. Holding the paddle in one hand, they'd use their head as leverage – another innovation with an extra-long paddle – while holding the net in the other. Here the vibrations can be instantly recognised, whether it is the net running over the bottom, or a snagged branch, an eel, a sewin, or salmon, each is recognisable. Feelings, he said, translate to sounds in the head as they become second nature. Deaf hand was the description when there was no feeling at all. He and his brother often fished by the railway bridge over the river, and the vibrations of a crossing train were enough to make his brother go deaf in both hands. In other words, he lost his concentration until the train was gone.

Of course, the fish heard you coming and would turn away, but sometimes turned back on themselves and into the net. Other times a shoal sent a pilot ahead, which, when caught, alerted the others who dispersed. All too often the net was simply empty.

Raymond took me into his other padlocked shed. The net, he emphasized, was the important piece. At each fishing, the net was prepared to suit the conditions of that time. It's a single wall trammel net, with two curtains, one with a large mesh and the outer a smaller mesh weighing little over 1½lbs. Very light. It worked by opening and closing 'like a purse'. Tiny strips of lead weighted it down. 'Now if the river is flowing you need to add more of these strips. Always single strips to the outside of the mesh so's you know in the dark. If you start with three groups of three weights, then always, because three plus three are six, you have six groups of two, followed by eight of one, and then one to the centre…' Even with a degree in naval architecture I was confused. 'Three here, then two, see…' I eventually understood what he meant. But, to the coracle fisherman, this was essential stuff to prevent too much weight causing the net to snag, or not enough so you were wasting time.

The nets were self-made. Raymond recalled how he used to go to the 'Hide & Skin Depot' down the road and ask for the cow's tails. These were pulled apart, weighted down in a pan and, by pulling and twisting, formed into ropes. He showed me, the resulting rope of two or three braids being strong. Tough enough for the work, but not so strong that it won't break when snagged on the bottom, thus preventing further damage to the net. Corks were used as floats with a piece of cow horn inside to protect the cork. Sometime alder was used for this.

Raymond spends his time either working in his fish shop in the indoor market hall or making the odd coracle. Fibreglass ones, he admitted, are favoured these days, although a couple of willow ones were still in use. It's all right playing with the real thing, he said, but when you are working, well, fibreglass is so much easier.

The Twyi fishermen were simply the best, he assured me. So I asked what about the Teifi coracle men. He was dismissive. Fishing there was free until the 1990s. Most of the Teifi coracles were built by one man in Cenarth, an ex-miner called Tomas whereas all the fishermen on the Twyi built their own. 'Their coracles haven't really evolved like ours have because the tradition isn't there. Because here the ones that use them build them we've been able to adapt to the needs of the river. As I said, see, success comes from an understanding of the river.' Yes, I could see that as he stood by its flowing streams. Here was a man who had grown up with the river, probably from his first steps, a man for whom the river was still a mystery; yet few know it better. A man, short in stature but strong in understanding every eddy, every ripple from a lifetime gazing into its ever-changing depths. Sadly, though, the last in his long line.

In the Carmarthen library I found a whole host of references to the salmon fishing. In 1809, I discovered, the Corporation had ordered that tariffs were put upon all fish sold in the market. 'For every 100lbs weight of turbott, brett, sole and john dory; and so in proportion for every 25lbs weight of such fish so brought and sold in the publick market, the sum of 15*s*. For every 100lbs weight of flat fish, commonly called Plais, 4*s*.' Those that were detected of forestalling (buying provisions before they are offered in market, with intent to sell them at higher prices, or to evade paying the market tolls) or regrating (purchasing provisions and selling them in the same market) were to be prosecuted.

In 1844 Thomas Jenkins of Llandilo-fawr built a coracle for fishing at Llygad Llwchor which could be taken to pieces and re-assembled and which cost 10*s* 6*d*. He returned there in 1855 and found his coracle 'all decayed'. Sir Joseph Banks, during a tour in 1767, said of the salmon fishing:

> ... boats used in the Fishery are perhaps the most ancient and least artificial of any used in the Island, perhaps in the world, as all the canoes I have seen, even in the most unpolished Indians, are made with infinitely more art than these. They are called CORACLES, their shape is almost round, at least very tubish, for a boat. That which I measured was 4 feet 6 inches by 3 feet 3 inches. Their edges are wattled together with small rods, such as baskets are made of; in these are interlaced split sticks, such as hoops are made of, seven or eight of which cross the bottom. Over these is put a piece of flannel dipped in tar, which is sewed to the watlings. The bench is of deal, pretty strong and goes across the middle of the boat. These, which are just capable of holding a man, are guided by a small paddle, consisting of a blade and handle, just like the Indians ones; with this the man moves the boat by putting

it in before him and moving it to him. Two of them will haul a salmon net of a very large size, and draw any pool in Towy.

There are records of actions being brought against fishermen for fishing the waters of the Towy between Carmarthen Bridge and the Bar in 1817 as well a note of the scarcity of fish in 1806. It seems that a form of licensing was introduced briefly then and that the fishermen refused to comply. Thus there was no salmon at market and other fish were reaching exorbitant prices!

Further along from Raymond's workshop is the Carmarthen Heritage Centre on the aptly named 'Coracle Way'. Here the story of the coraclemen is told with artefacts and pictures but unfortunately the council are about to turn the centre into a literacy and numeracy centre and transfer the exhibition to the library, a site that many say is unsuitable. If anything, the coraclemen want a bigger space to be able to display more of their heritage, not a smaller, more confined space. According to Michael Ellis, one of the few surviving fisherman who's fished for thirty-seven years, since he was fifteen, they've asked for another property but the council say they can't give them one.

It was time to leave Carmarthen and to continue westwards. I would soon be leaving for good as I was in the midst of selling my house. I decided to go to Laugharne because it's a good place for dog to have a swim.

Laugharne has changed a lot since I was here in the spring drizzle. Then the cafés were under re-decoration and shops darkened without lights. They were waiting for the tourists to come, perhaps fearful that they might not materialise. They didn't need to worry. As is my own tradition, I visited Corran Books, a good second-hand bookshop that always draws me in. We went down to the beach, down below the castle. Up some steps under the garage where Dylan Thomas wrote *Under Milk Wood* and a peer through the window. Where's the flue to the chimney? I wondered. The paintwork was pristine and somehow I couldn't imagine the unhappy Dylan seated on the shiny chair, pen in hand. The view, though, is spectacular across the Taff estuary. A few boats dot the banks, a far cry from 1566 when ships from here traded with Bristol, Dublin and La Rochelle. Some even went upstream as far as St Clears. Cistercian monks came up the estuary around 1140 and built an abbey at Tref Garn and later moved on to Whitland Abbey. In the early nineteenth century, Alfred John Kempe observed that the lower parts of the village were sometimes subjected to severe flooding at which time they had 'to stop the crevices of their doors with clay'.

It's hard to imagine that Laugharne was, during the time of Queen Elizabeth I, one of six chief Welsh towns, bigger even than Carmarthen. Having only ninety houses then (there aren't so many more now) means that there were something in the region of 600 houses in the main population centres in Wales. Something doesn't add up here!

Of course, in common with many other of the seaside communities we've visited, this was a haven for pirates. Today, though, it's the haunt of ghosts. Did the boats riding on the 'dewgrazed stir of the black, dab-filled sea' have names like '*Arethusa, Curlew, Skylark, Zanzibar, Rhiannon*, the *Rover*', I wondered. The New Three Mariners is the 'cheeriest pub in Laugharne', according to the signboard on its exterior wall. Brown's Hotel, Dylan's favourite bar, dates from 1752 or so its plate says, with 1938 below it. Presumably, by its look, it was last decorated then or is it some forgotten stage prop for the Sailors Arms in Llareggub? Is the pink house the 'germ free guest house'?

Laugharne from the Castle Wall.

The horse being led down the street didn't deflect me away from nineteenth-century imaginations.

We walked along to the boathouse Dylan and Caithlin shared from 1949 to 1953, his 'sea-shaken house on a breakneck of rocks'. It was the fiftieth anniversary of his death so Laugharne was holding an extended festival to mark the occasion. That evening, and for the next two, the Swansea Little Theatre were playing on *Under Milk Wood* while I noted that if I stayed till Sunday I could experience the extravaganza of 'Cockles in the Castle'. Various other events filled almost a month of celebratory tributes to the great man. For Laugharne really does have to rely upon its literary heritage for its health.

Again a recent lick of paint on the boathouse portrayed a false impression of its appearance all those fifty or more years ago. I went into the bookshop, tying dog up outside, avoiding paying the £2.95 to view the museum part of the building. Don't, though, overstep the fine line between hanging pictures for sale and those on display or the wrath of the woman behind the counter will send you flying back up the steps without a purchase. Back along the grass, the dog crapping in the grass and me trying to poop-a-scoop within sight of the proverbial sign showing a dog standing over a red turd! I wonder just what this red blob represents – danger or blood? To the tea-room, last time under re-decoration, and away, away up Llareggub Hill, leaving behind the sleeping fishers (and cockle gatherers presumably, of which there were fifty here in 1910) and the rest of Captain Cat's villagers to bugger all!

It was somehow more refreshing to reach Pendine, although this seems unfair to poor old Laugharne. Pendine Sands stretch for several miles although much of the beach is part of a military danger area. Land speed records have been broken on this expanse and a tiny museum tells the story. At the western end of Pendine lies Gilman Point between there are Ragwen Point is a small, almost hidden bay, said to be the home of the Ragwen Wreckers.

Lifeboats

The origins of the first Welsh lifeboats, other than it is known they stemmed from experimental craft in England, are as obscure as those of its neighbour. Three men are generally acclaimed to have been responsible for the design of early lifeboats: Lionel Lunkin, Willie Wouldhave and Henry Greathead. Lunkin patented his 'Unimmergible Boat' in 1785 after converting a Norwegian yawl and the following year he converted a Northumberland coble, after which he built five other boats. Wouldhave, along with Greathead, submitted models of lifeboats in 1789 to a group of Tyneside dignitaries calling themselves 'The Gentlemen of the Lawe House'. Neither design was adopted although Greathead went on the following year to design and build a specific vessel to use for lifesaving at South Shields. Named the Original, this is accredited as being the first such purpose-built vessel.

However, the first documented boat used as a lifeboat was at Formby, Liverpool, where the Liverpool Dock Commissioners established and financed a lifeboat in 1776. Details of the boat are unknown and others may have followed in other parts of the country. Greathead went on to produce more of his lifeboats over twenty years so that by 1810 there were some thirty-five lifeboats on station in Britain either built by him or based on his design. Although most of these were concentrated upon the East Coast, especially around Greathead's home on the Tyne, none were based in Wales.

Fishguard was to be the first harbour in Wales where it can be said with certainty that a lifeboat was established in 1822. The Trustees of Liverpool Docks Committee were known to have operated a lifeboat at Hoylake in 1803 and it is thought possible that one was established at Point of Ayr although records only existed from 1835. There is a mention of a lifeboat arriving at Holyhead at the end of 1808, but no further details have been forthcoming. Similar hints of a lifeboat at Barmouth in 1813 are equally sparse.

The Fishguard lifeboat was designed and largely financed by local man Thomas Evans and built locally. At 25ft in length, 8ft in beam and 3ft in depth, and costing £95, it is assumed that it was of the Greathead type. Llanddwyn was next to have a boat, in 1826, with another Greathead boat presumed to have been stationed there.

By the 1820s another three men were commanding the expertise in the field of design: George Palmer, MP, and James and Edward Pellew-Plenty. By 1826 designs of all three men had been built for the Royal National Institution for the Preservation of Life from Shipwreck which had been established two years earlier (this became what we now know as the RNLI in 1854). With the opening of stations at Barmouth, Holyhead and Cemlyn in 1828, all three had Palmer-type vessels. Over the next twenty-odd years, another eight stations were opened and kitted out with mainly the same Palmer-type boats.

In 1851 the Duke of Northumberland, the Institution's president, offered a prize of 100 guineas for the best new design of lifeboat. There were 282 entries and the winner was declared as being Great Yarmouth boatbuilder James Beeching. Palmer and the Pellew-Plenty's all submitted designs. However it was left to James Peake, Master Shipwright of the Royal Naval Dockyard, Woolwich to modify and improve Beeching's 36ft design and the standard 'self-righting' lifeboat appeared. This model of boat was built in varying sizes to suit the local conditions and many were brought on station about Wales.

However, another design submitted in 1851 was the 33ft Tubular lifeboat designed by Henry Richardson of Bala. The first of his iron-hulled boats, the *Morgan*, was stationed at Rhyl in 1856 and deemed ideal for the shallow waters. Another, the *Caroline Richardson*,

Beamaris lifeboat station, *c.*1960. Note fish weir in the foreground. (Courtesy Bridget Dempsey)

named after his wife, was stationed at Pwllheli in 1891, but, with different sea conditions, it was found to be unsuitable and transferred to Rhyl in 1893 to replace the first Tubular lifeboat. A third Tubular boat replaced the earlier one at Rhyl in 1897 and this vessel, the last of the type, remained in service until 1939.

In 1887 George Lennox Watson, principal of G.L.Watson & Co. became the RNLI's consulting naval architect and he soon began producing 'Watson' type pulling and sailing lifeboats, of which several came to Wales. Although non-self-righting, this was regarded as less likely to capsize and has been described as 'rather sophisticated compared to the smaller self-righting lifeboats'. In 1888 steam lifeboats arrived on the scene and the only one of these to serve in Wales was the *James Stevens No. 3* at Angle between 1908 and 1915.

Watson himself died in 1904 and his successor was James Barnett. Then along came the petrol driven engine so that these units were added to lifeboats. The first new boat with an engine was brought on station in 1908 on the East Coast of Scotland. In 1913 the first motorised 'Watson-type' was introduced, a 45ft-long vessel fitted with a Taylor 60hp petrol/paraffin engine which made the lifeboat capable of 8.2 knots. Within ten years the 60ft Barnett, with twin engines and twin propellers, arrived with no masts or sails. However, like Watson before him, Barnett believed in achieving greater stability rather than building boats as self-righting. Barnett's death in 1950 and his replacement by Richard Oakley coincided with several tragedies where lifeboats and their crew were lost. The first of these was at Mumbles with the loss of the motorised 'Watson-type' *Edward, Prince of Wales* in 1947. In the 1950s the 37ft 'Oakley twin-screw self-righting motor boat' entered service, a type that heralded a new era of lifeboat design. Several versions were produced so that by 1969 they were over 48ft in length. These were soon followed by the 44-foot 'Waveney' class and the 50ft 'Thames' class, both of which were 'fast' boats. With the adoption of the 52ft 'Arun' class in the 1970s, and the subsequent 47ft 'Tyne' and 12m 'Mersey' classes were introduced in 1982 and 1988 respectively. More recently, modern improvements in materials and technology have resulted in the 14m 'Trent' and 17m 'Severn' classes, both of which are capable of speeds up to 25 knots. In Wales, many of the lifeboat stations have these latter types of boats on station.

There's a tale that a farmer and his wife used to supplement their income by a spot of wrecking, hanging out lanterns to lure ships onto the sands. Their son went off to sea, the story goes, and after one particular storm, when the couple were searching for washed-up cargo, they found a body, face down in the sand. 'He's alive,' declared the old woman but the husband, picking up a rock and smashed his skull, replying that dead men tell no tales. When they turned the body over, they found that it was their long-lost son!

Between Ragwen Point and Telpyn Point lie the Marros Sands where there was 'Marrosse a landing place' in 1566 with two fishing boats called *Sondaye* and *Marye*, both 'two tonnes a peece', owned by David Bealt and John Hoddyn and both used for 'fysshing nere the shore'. A further note in the *Welsh Port Books* adds that there were no licences here for the 'lack of shyppes and vessels'. At Telpyn there is a big cave known as Telpyn church because it appears to house galleries, windows and a pulpit.

We drove over the hill and back to the coast at Amroth, where, at The Water's Edge, Pembrokeshire's coastal footpath begins. 'Earweare' is the site of a castle and the old name for the place. It probably means 'the weir of the sand or gravel bank' from *eyrr* and *ver* meaning respectively 'sandbank' and 'weir' in old Norse. There was a toll of fish here in the Middle Ages. In 1814 Richard Ayton described this border hamlet of 'New Inn' as being of 'a most perfidious name', and consisting of a few fishermen's cottages. Thirty years later Samuel Lewis noted that 'this part of the bay is celebrated for Salmon, Cod and Flat-fish, which are taken in abundance, and of which considerable quantities are sent for the supply of the market at Tenby.' In recent memory fishing has not been commercially exploited to any extent. Other historical facts include a woollen mill producing cloth in 1841, a limestone kiln at the junction near the Amroth Arms, a medieval mill in decay by 1481 and a corn mill by the castle. Traditionally there was a fair here the week after the Narberth Horse Fair, which fitted in between haymaking and the corn harvest. Such was the demands of rural life, which surely explains why the sea was never exploited. If you have fertile ground around you, why suffer the pain of a life at sea!

Further along from Amroth is Wiseman's Bridge. Between 22 July and 5 August 1943 a full-scale secret rehearsal for the D-Day Normandy landings, code-named 'Exercise Jantzen', was held, utilising the whole coast from Pendine Burrows to Saundersfoot. A huge assortment of craft landed some 16,000 tons of stores in preparation for the real assault and Eisenhower, Churchill and Montgomery all came along to view the progress of the exercises. All sorts of lessons were learnt, including the fact that the concrete barges designed to carry fuel leaked, all of which went to make the eventual Operation Overlord a success in 1944. During the exercises, Saundersfoot was deemed to be an enemy harbour whilst movement of the local population was carefully monitored and a curfew put in place in Tenby. The use of cameras and binoculars was prohibited and one test spy was quickly uncovered and caught.

From our point of view, however, we are back in a coal-producing area where the industrial nineteenth century has again left its marks on the coast. The remains of the old tramway that brought anthracite down from the Stepaside Colliery to Saundersfoot harbour runs along the edge, between sea and hill and a wonderful detour along Pleasant Valley made the dog happy. This passes the ironworks at Stepaside which were opened in 1849 by the Pembrokeshire Iron & Coal Company. Local anthracite was used to extract the iron from the ore that was mined in the cliffs between Wiseman's Bridge and

Coppet Hall Point where the tramway tunnels beneath. Inland a few miles is the once-important coal village of Kilgetty. The construction of a canal was commenced in about 1792 to carry coal down to the sea. However, it appears that it was never completed as there is no evidence of it ever being used. Much of the coal was taken down to nearby Tenby prior to the sixteenth century. Subsequent laying of tramways down to Saundersfoot opened up a harbour there in 1829.

Saundersfoot, when it did open, although tidal, was considered to be a state of the art harbour with specially built staithes to tip the coal directly from the trams into the vessels lying alongside. In 1856 a visitor observed 'its small but strong harbour built of solid masonry. Several schooners were lying in it and an air of bustle and trade prevailed... tramroads lead to the harbour by which the culm and anthracite are brought down, whence they are emptied into the vessels alongside the wharves through large wooden chutes'.

In the 1840s some 20,000 tons of coal was being exported from one pit alone. Mixing the anthracite with clay to make it burn more intensely produced culm. This was particularly good for limestone burning. The anthracite itself was regarded as being high grade and was shipped to East Anglia, Kent and over to the Guinness Brewery in Dublin. Much of the local iron passed through the harbour. However, the local collieries closed in the first two decades of the twentieth century so that the port lost its purpose and gradually was overtaken by tourism so that today the village was host to hordes of holidaymakers. The harbour has a few working boats but in the main pleasure boats sit upon the sand at low water. Parking, though, can be a problem, and, not finding anywhere in the vicinity of the harbour, and with the evening beginning its descent, I decided to push on to Tenby, just around the corner. Parking was easier there and thus, because dogs are allowed on the beach after six o'clock, or so I was informed although the signs didn't tell me this, we went for a walk and swim along the South Beach. Tenby is one of my favourite places in Wales, so I was happy to linger here and soak up some of the atmosphere that makes the town what it is – that is one of the most popular of resorts of its ilk and one that has benefited from tourism for many generations.

DAY EIGHT

TENBY INCLUDING CALDEY ISLAND

Tenby in the early morning is more wonderful than the night before. It's dead quiet except for the odd dog-walker enjoying the sands before the daytime ban comes into force. The sun began its steady climb from the grey motionless sea, and orange, yellow and grey mixtures of colour danced upon its surface. Britain was sizzling in sky-high record-breaking temperatures, which were exciting weathermen and media alike. And while the majority was just keen to enjoy a proper August summer, there were of course those who complained that it was too hot!

'Fair and fashionable Tenby' declared the Halls with gusto, 'is one of the prettiest, pleasantest, quietest and in all respects most attractive of the sea bathing towns that adorn the coasts of England and Wales'. How right they were. Two hundred years ago Tenby was fast gaining a reputation as a handsome resort, a reputation that has survived today. However, prior to that, things were very different.

The Welsh name for Tenby reflects its roots: *Dinbych-y-pysgod* literally means 'little fort of the fishes'. In the fourteenth century the town was one of the principal herring ports of South and West Wales. Its first quay was built in 1328 after Edward III gave the 'good men of Teneby' the rights to raise money for its construction by levying charges – 'quayage' – upon its use. Tithes upon herrings and oysters were paid by the fishermen for mass to be said on their behalf in the tiny quayside St Julian's chapel. Prior to the building of the quay visiting vessels had to draw up the river Ritec (*Afon Rhydeg*) into Pill Lake, at the back of the town and beach in the mud. Boats were said to be able to reach as far up as St Florence. In 1375, 10-ton ships traded with Brittany and Spain, exchanging hides, wool and coal for pitch, iron, salt, wine, wine vinegar and oil. 22,000 gallons of wine were imported on average in a year. It is said that the names of the seamen were a mixture of English, French, Welsh and Flemish.

Its geographical position and available shelter made the harbour a thriving place of trade so that it was not just the fisheries that led to its development. Over the centuries it's had its fair share of travellers keen to jot down their opinions of the town. To Leland 'Tinby ys a walled Towne hard on the Severn Se yn Penbrokeshire. Ther is a *Sinus* and a Peere made for Shyppes'. John Bassett, the Commissioner appointed by Edward VI to report on Charity land in 1548, found a place 'where the inhabitants of the saide Towne haithe beildyd a fare peire for the saifegard of shippes whereoute there is greitt repare of straingers', referring to traders from Cornwall, Devon, France and Ireland. Woollen cloth, Welsh flannel, butter, coal, malt, salted herring and corn were amongst the exports while dried fruit, timber, flax, cattle and wine was brought in, mainly from Ireland and France. In 1566 the first recorded cargo of oranges in Wales arrived from Aveiro in Northern Portugal.

By 1662, according to the geologist and botanist John Ray, it was 'a place strongly situated and well walled. It hath a very pretty safe harbour made by an artificial pier of

A 1900s postcard view of Tenby.

stone. Great variety of fish are taken near this town'. George Owen of Henllys noted that Tenby and Caldey Roads were rich in fish and that Tenby was one of three market towns in Pembrokeshire. Defoe came across 'the most agreeable Town on all the Sea Coast of South Wales, except Pembroke, being a very good Road for Shipping, and well frequented: Here is a great Fishery for Herring in its season, a great Colliery, or rather export of Coals, and they also drive a very considerable Trade to Ireland'. There's not a lot more, then, that could be said to describe the harbour up to the middle of the eighteenth century. After that, the town seems to have slipped into decline.

Much of this has been credited to a decrease in the herring fishing all along the Pembrokeshire coast. Whereas a century before George Owen had found the coast 'enclosed with a hedge of herring' and 'these kinde of fishe is taken on the shores of this Countrey in great abundance', after 1750 there was a substantial lack of landings. Local myths account for this. One story is that a local by the unlikely name of Leekie Porridge beat up and very nearly killed a deaf and dumb beggar who was falsely accused of spying for a pirate. As the poor man staggered out of the town he cursed it, and from that very day the herring deserted. Another tale tells of the fishermen's greed in that they used to fish over an exceptionally rich bank called Will's Mark. As they grew rich they began to forget the landmarks that enabled them to pinpoint the bank's position. In years the fishery was lost altogether. When they realised the error of their ways they tried to relocate it but without success. However, another, perhaps more realistic, reason for the decline in landings was that the fishermen were too poor to build larger boats. Once the larger boats from Brixham arrived in the eighteenth and nineteenth centuries, the evidence supports this. However, by then, the fishermen had discovered other means of earning a bob or two.

Sea bathing became fashionable in the late eighteenth century and St Julian's chapel became a bathhouse in 1781 (and later a blacksmiths forge before being destroyed in

Above: Tenby North Sands, from a postcard.

Left: Excursions from Tenby in 1915.

EXCURSIONS
FROM TENBY
(UNTIL FURTHER NOTICE).

By the STEAMSHIP " FIREFLY "

(Wind, weather and other circumstances permitting).

EACH DAY
(SUNDAYS EXCEPTED),

The Steamer will leave the Royal Victoria Pier, Tenby, at 2.15 p.m. sharp, for the

ISLE
OF
CALDEY

Returning from Caldey at 5 p.m.

FARE.—ISLE OF CALDEY (Return), 2s., including
   Landing Permit and Official Guide, giving a
   Map and History of the Island. Tea can be
   obtained at the Tea House on the Island.
   TICKETS TO BE OBTAINED ON BOARD STEAMER.

For further particulars apply to the
ESTATE AGENT, ISLE OF CALDEY.
August, 1915.

PRINTED BY J. LEACH, "TENBY AND COUNTY NEWS," TENBY.

1842). The wealthy London banker Sir William Paxton was first to recognise the town's potential due, in the main, to its wonderful beaches and cliff-top setting. In 1810 he built a bath house which burned down weeks after opening. Not to be thwarted, he built another – the present-day Laston House ('Laston' comes from *lastage*, the loading dues paid by ships). Houses for the rich to reside in were built and a new road down to the harbour constructed over arches which, when the road plan was altered, were utilised as stores for the fishermen. By 1809 a visitor noted that 'two swimming baths are provided for ladies and gentlemen, with dressing rooms to each and four private cold baths for single persons. Several warm and vapor baths, with dressing rooms tempered with warm air and a cupping room fitted with the latest improvements. Bedrooms are provided in the bathhouse for invalids'. In the 'cupping room' warm glasses were applied to the body to increase the blood flow and thus help constitutional ailments. It appears that refreshments were provided, as was 'a spacious vestibule for servants to wait in, with mixing with the Company'. The baths were designed solely for the wealthy. Costs were 2*s* 6*d* for a warm bath, 1*s* 6*d* for a hot shower and 9*d* for swimming and these were considered high enough to put the baths out of reach of the locals.   Doctors were also recommending that seawater be drunk with port or milk to taste as a cure for gout, scurvy and jaundice. Yet the beaches were also popular. In 1856 George Eliot arrived, finding that 'the air is delicious – soft but not sultry – and the sands and bathing such as are to be found nowhere else'.

There was no lack of scandal. When Horatio Nelson arrived with Sir William Hamilton and his wife Lady Emma Hamilton in 1802, Nelson was seen to walk with Emma 'evidently in vain of each other, while poor Sir William, wretched but not abashed, followed at a short distance', according to a visitor named Gore. By the mid-1800s byelaws were introduced controlling bathing. No nakedness was allowed on the South Sands and no bathing was allowed except from bathing machines between the hours of 8 a.m. and 9 p.m. Bathing machines, wooden huts on wheels and horse-drawn, had first appeared in Scarborough in 1736 and later versions included Benjamin Beale's model which had modesty hoods so that ladies could shelter while climbing down the ladders. They must have been introduced to Tenby by 1767 for Peggy Davies, the most renowned of the town's bathing attendants, worked from then until 1809. About that time the cost to hire one was a shilling including a towel.

In 1857 the mayor suggested that 'the police should be instructed to proceed against any man bathing without drawers within a hundred yards of a dwelling house'. Licences could be withdrawn if any proprietor permitted male bathing without 'drawers' from a machine. Furthermore, a gentleman could not swim from a bathing machine that was less than fifty yards from any ladies. It seems that if anyone did want to swim in the nude then they had to hire a boat and 'row seawards to the distance of two hundred yards from any of the promenades or beaches' before stripping off and swimming!

Surprisingly, these bathing machines were still in use in 1932 although visitors were not compelled to use them. According to the *Corporation Guide to Tenby* for that year they were permitted to bathe at all times from tents and from the shelter of cliffs. Mixed bathing, it continues, has been the rule in Tenby for many years. One wonders what the Victorians would have made of Tenby today when it's not unusual to see topless sunbathing on the beach during the day and, likely as not, to stumble across a copulating couple upon it in the dark after the town's nightclubs have closed!

Welsh Lighthouses

The dominant influence for the building of lighthouses on the Welsh coast was primarily the growth of Liverpool as a port, seconded by the port of Bristol in the western trade routes of Britain. From a glimpse of any map of the coast it is easy to see why the Smalls and the Skerries were the two lighthouses to receive the highest light dues in the mid-nineteenth century. However, they weren't the first lights to be sited upon a naturally dangerous coast. St Ann's Head is generally regarded as having the first light exhibited in 1662 although there are suggestions of Roman beacons at Flint and Holyhead. A purpose-built light was later established on St Ann's Head in 1713 to replace the older light although several additions account for today's lighthouse structure.

However, the Skerries light is generally regarded as being the first permanent light built upon both the West Coast of England and Wales. Rumblings of discontent about the danger of these rocks on the direct route between Liverpool and Dublin first surfaced in 1658. Henry Hascard, a private speculator, appealed to Oliver Cromwell's Council of State to build a beacon but Trinity House opposed his application on the grounds that they retained sole rights to such structures. Again, in 1705, 140 merchants signed a petition drawn up by Captain John Davison and again Trinity House opposed this, agreeing only to a beacon if these merchants contributed to the cost. But the Attorney General disagreed and recommended that Davison's offer of construction be granted although it was never taken up. William Trench then obtained his 99-year lease in 1713 and built his coal-burning light which was 'about 150ft higher than ye sea about it and on ye 4th November a fire kindled therein and ever since supported'. It had cost him £3,000, consumed over 100 tons of coal a year to keep alight and ultimately produced a tidy annual profit. The lighthouse standing today, though, has been altered and added to on various occasions since its base was built about 1759.

The Flatholm light, erected in 1738 to serve ships entering and leaving Bristol, is said to be one of Wales' oldest surviving lights, although it, too, has been altered. In the 1770s the Port of Ayr, the Smalls and the Port Lynas light, on Anglesey, were built. Over the next two decades a pattern of lighthouse building developed, specifically serving the shipping to both ports – Mumbles, South Stack, Bardsey and South Bishop – but some attention began to be paid to the developing ports of South Wales. Thus the West Usk, Caldy and Nash Point lights were constructed. The Penmon Point (Trwyn-du) and Llanddwyn lighthouses aided navigation of the Menai Strait in 1838 and 1846 respectively. The stone-built Smalls light was finished by 1861, replacing the earlier timber structure. The Great Orme (1862) and St Tudwals (1877) followed. The last light in the chain – excepting harbour lights – was the illuminating of the Strumble Head light in 1909.

The early lighthouses of Wales were fantastic feats of engineering in anyone's book. The Smalls light, for example, is Wales' only light built upon a totally wave-washed rock although Whitford Point and Penmon Point are wave-washed but not at low water. The builders of the original timber structure of the Smalls had to sail out from Solva in small boats, often being unable to land on more than two consecutive days, owing to the state of the sea over the reef. If the sea was calm, it was unlikely there would have been enough wind to fill the sails of the boats. Work was nigh on impossible during the winter. When the stone-built lighthouse was later constructed, the same problems thwarted the builders, although they had the benefit of a steam tug to tow the barges containing the dressed stone to the reef. Similar problems were presumably encountered in the building of the lighthouses on rocky islets such as the Skerries and South Bishop. To a lesser degree, building the Bardsey light must have had its share of access problems.

Wales still retains lighthouses that are unique today. The Whitford Point light is the only surviving cast-iron tower on a wave-swept coast while the Mumbles light was the last coal-fuelled open-fire light built in Britain. The Point Lynas and Orme Head lights have the unusual layout of having the lantern at ground level and thus have no tower. The Port of Ayr light still utilises one of the earliest lanterns in Wales while the South Bishop has the earliest completely unaltered lanterns in England and Wales. Bardsey has the highest square tower of any lighthouse in Britain. The Skokholm lighthouse is the last stone-built tower to be built in Britain.

By 1875 three light-vessels were once stationed in Welsh waters in Caernarfon Bay, off Cardigan and off Worms Head while in more recent times three others were still stationed off South Wales – off Port Talbot, on the Helwick Bank and off St Govan's Head. The Helwick can be seen in the marina at Swansea and presumably will become part of the new National Waterfront Museum.

Today all the lighthouses in Britain, Wales included, are automated. Many can be visited exteriorly, but the interior may not be open to the public. For a full account of Welsh lighthouses, the reader is urged to read Douglas Hague's *Lighthouses of Wales*.

Above left: Nash Point lighthouse.

Above right: Strumble Head lighthouse.

One inhabitant of the town for which it owes a great deal is Charles Norris who lived in the town between 1805 and 1820 and closeby until his death in 1858. It's not that he really contributed much to its development but, through his work as an artist, much knowledge of the visual appearance of the town before the advent of photography has been learnt. It is estimated that some 1,200 of his works survive in public collections throughout Wales, and some 200 of these are in the collection of the Tenby Museum and Art Gallery. A visit was a timely interlude, both physically and historically, after a swim on the busy Castle Beach.

Some years ago, while I was researching for my book *The Herring Fishers of Wales*, the museum was extremely helpful in searching out photographs of the harbour and allowing me to reproduce some of these in that book and a subsequent one – *Traditional Fishing Boats of Britain and Ireland*. This is in direct contrast to certain museums, most notably the Ulster Folk and Transport Museum, who charged what I regard to be an unreasonable fee for reproduction. In their case it was £30 an image, which meant that we could only use three, whereas I'd have liked to include more. Considering they also charge for the original copy of the photo, and the fact that they probably were donated in the first place, it leaves you with a slightly bitter taste in your mouth. I've never forgotten the generosity of the Tenby museum and always like to visit when I'm in Tenby. Theirs is a great museum and any visitor to the town should ensure they walk up Castle Hill and have a look in. It's an independent community museum with displays on the local archaeology, natural history and heritage with important collections in the art galleries.

Opposite the museum is St Catherine's Island, so named because of a chapel there dedicated to St Catherine, patron saint of weavers and spinners. A fort was built there in the late 1860s as part of a string of coastal defences built to protect the new royal dockyard at nearby Pembroke Dock. There was once a footbridge across from Castle Hill until it collapsed. It was eventually sold into private hands and became a summer residence for the Windsor-Richards family until they sold it in 1940. Today it is still privately owned and deserted, although numerous bathers seemed to swim over across the short channel and climb up below the 'No Access' signs. At low tide it is joined to the beach by a sandy isthmus. Returning to Castle Beach for another swim – dogs are allowed on the eastern extremity of the beach – I did exactly that and climbed up to the steel gate that prevents entry up the steps. It seems its only residences today are seagulls.

I decided to wander the streets, peering into cafés buzzing with activity and passing the pubs filled with the lunchtime trade. Hidden down a narrow passageway I found a second-hand bookshop that just happened to have all nine volumes of the 1770-edition of *The Itinerary of John Leland the Antiquarian* for £100. Needless to say, I made the purchase and left the shop glowing with excitement. Other shop tills rang out and, up the road, the old market was thronged with more people for whom the beach was too hot. Or so I surmised, for I could not think of any other reason why the holidaymakers were wandering around just like I was, unless they were after bargains. I noted the market tolls of 1892 – fish baskets: 1*d*; each or per stone: 1*d*; cod or ling when sold above 1*s*: 1*s* 2*d* each; same when sold at 1*s* or less: 1*s* 4*d* each; hakes per dozen: 1*d*. No mention of oysters although there were rich beds some two miles north of Caldey Island and near Stackpole and these had been exported since 1582. By the beginning of the nineteenth century oyster fishing was the chief winter fishing but over-fishing resulted in a collapse by the end of the century because there was no re-stocking of the beds. Throughout the century it seems that an average 2,000-3,000 oysters appeared at any one time in the market. Once the quay was rebuilt in 1842 after its destruction (at the same time that the chapel was destroyed) and the railway arrived in 1870 – the Halls had come by road from Narberth Road station – markets across South Wales opened and more boats came to land fish here. Thus there was a revival in the harbour's fortunes. Brixham- and Dartmouth-registered boats especially landed for the Bristol market.

The Tenby fishers did develop their own specific boat – the Tenby lugger. Charles Norris gives us evidence for these shallow-keeled open boats. Built primarily for oyster dredging, they were used off-season for long-lining, trawling, mackerel and herring drifting and also for going alongside vessels waiting in Caldey Roads. Some allegedly smuggled goods in to places such as Penally. They were about 20ft long, were clinker-built and had two square sails and resembled many other craft that undoubtedly evolved through Viking influence. By the end of the nineteenth century they were larger, with the biggest built being the *Eileen* in 1891 at 27ft overall and 25ft on the keel. In fact, any boat under 20ft in keel length became to be referred to as a 'punt'. Thus the luggers were built with little overhang, a slightly raked transom stern and upright stem and little forefoot. A short foredeck was added with a cuddy below and the construction, once carvel build had been adopted, was heavy for their small size. The transition from square to lug sail began in Britain around 1800 and later that century all the Tenby luggers set a dipping lug main and small spritsail sheeted to an outrigger on the mizzenmast.

In 1891 there were forty-nine luggers in Tenby and rarely did their numbers exceed that. Thomas George was the last of a family of renowned builders and he was succeeded by Palmer Wickland. Some fishermen owned more than one boat while others brought smacks in from Brixham and these became known as Tenby cutters. A few had engines

Tenby luggers dried out in the harbour.

added but the luggers soon disappeared altogether as the fishing declined. Today I only know of two luggers that have survived. The *Lilac*, built at Appledore in the 1920s, belongs to the Swansea Industrial and Maritime Museum (soon to be the National Waterfront Museum) and the National Museums and Galleries of Wales owns what is probably *La Mascot*, built in Tenby in 1896. Both await restoration.

The luggers were often used to take trippers around the bay or out to Caldey Island. Thus I thought it a good idea, seeing how pleasant the afternoon was, to take a trip out their myself. Leaving the dog with some friends who had come to Tenby for an afternoon on the beach, I paid my £8 and found the Weymouth-built *Isle of Caldey* waiting at the end of the pier. Only two other passengers joined the vessel for the thirty-minute trip across so I was able to spend most of the journey speaking to Clive Thomas who helped out aboard the boat. Nine ferryboats operate during the season that lasts from the beginning of July to September, he told me as he lit a cigarette. Clive himself was a merchant seaman although he was off sick due to some rare disease that was causing him problems with his fingers. He showed them to me, all curled up and unable to be straightened. He was wearing a straw hat and an open shirt, which didn't hide much of his red and hairy chest. He had what I call a welcoming face and didn't seem suspicious when I began asking lots of questions. 'Fishing,' he said, 'is mostly whelks now although some good bass is got over by those buoys'. He pointed to two buoys in the distance, off St. Margaret's, the bird sanctuary island off the northern tip of Caldey. Some herring was still being caught in the winter season and mackerel in summer. In addition, three boats were working lobster pots. 'Sundays,' he replied when I asked, 'No, no boats on a Sunday cos the monks don't want a load of visitors, they want peace one day a week!' Good thing I hadn't arrived on the Sabbath then, I thought.

We landed at the little pier by the wonderful beach. I walked up through the trees – the southern part of the island is wooded in direct contrast to the open, cropped northern end – to the village and found the tiny museum inside the Post Office that Clive had suggested I visit. I asked the woman behind the counter her opening hours. 'Six days a week, 9 to 5, during the season and just a couple of hours a day during the winter'.

Monks from various orders have lived here for over 1,500 years. The island's Welsh name *Ynys Byr*, the Island of Pyro, refers to the first Abbot in the sixth century. Caldey derives from the Norse *keld* and *eye*, meaning 'cold' and 'island' respectively. I could imagine it being cold here almost all year round, except during the occasional heat wave, of course! However, although this etymology of the name suggests a Viking influence, no archaeological evidence of the Viking's presence on the island has been discovered to date.

The current Cistercian Order of monks arrived here in 1925 after purchasing the island from the Benedictines and gained full possession four years later. Since then, they have combined a life of prayer and self-denial with more economic necessities such as making chocolate, fudge, ice-cream, yoghurt, perfumes and other goods to sell as well as tending the soil.

For almost two hundred years limestone quarrying was the main source of income for the owners of Caldey. In 1792 Thomas Kynaston of Pembroke bought the island and lived in a mansion adjoining the medieval priory. When he died in 1814 his son Cabot took over and developed the limestone quarries on both the island and St Margaret's.

Emblem of the Caldey
Island Monks.

These quarries were all positioned close to the coast to enable ships to come alongside
the actual workings to load up, thus doing away with the need for costly double
handling. Much of the stone was shipped over to West Wales for use upon the roads,
which were using huge amounts of crushed stone to build. Some found its way into the
dozens of limestone kilns that dot the coast, including that at St Philomena's, on the
island. Small boats were said to be able to sail right up to the steps below this kiln. Some
one hundred people, mostly miners, were said to have lived on the island when quarrying
reached its peak output in the first half of the nineteenth century, after which the island
reverted to agriculture after Cabot's death in 1866 and its subsequent sale to James
Wilson Hawksley.

Seine-nets were set on the beach in the eighteenth century, depicted by a print that I
saw in the museum. It's probable that oysters were landed given their abundance close by,
and other fish such as herring would have formed part of the staple diet of the monks.

I walked across the island to the lighthouse that sits on the southernmost Chapel Point,
which is also one of the highest spots on the island. This, I later read, was built in 1829
at a cost of £4,460 by Joseph Nelson and was only electrified in 1997. I clambered down
the grassy bank below the lighthouse to view the rocks at the water's edge. Several
angling boats bobbed up and down and one of the excursion boats from Tenby that takes
visitors around Caldey to view the seals passed by. One angler was persevering on the
rocks. I then had the first of three strange encounters with wild life that day. Well,
perhaps 'encounter' does not rightfully describe this first sighting of a seal attempting to
climb onto the rocks, but it was weirdly strange. The seal, a big one at that, spent some
ten minutes trying to come ashore but at each attempt he was thwarted by the surge of
the swell. He swam from rock to rock trying to get out but all to no avail. Eventually he
gave up and dived under the surface so that I didn't see him again.

The second encounter occurred on the walk back to the ferry. As I followed a group
of perhaps six people along the path, a duck wandered across in front from a short flight
of steps. Behind were seven of the tiniest ducklings I'd seen since keeping ducks twenty
years ago. They must have only hatched within a couple of days. The ducklings were

Castle Beach, Tenby, with bathing machines, *c*.1890.

jumping up the steps, some having to take several attempts while one managed to reach the top only to fall back and roll back down again. Still it got up again onto its feet and tried again. It was fascinating watching until mother decided to retrace her path back down the steps, followed by her seven-strong brood.

The return boat – the *Polar Star* – was much more crowded for the last ferry left at five o'clock. Half the junior population of Tenby was jumping off the end of the quay into the sea. Once back on dry land I counted at least fifteen mackerel that one fisherman had caught off the outer edge. He landed another as I peered over the shoulders of the surrounding group of on-lookers. Several anglers were fishing from the rails of the lifeboat station.

The fishermen and boatmen of Tenby often had to venture out in stormy weather to save lives. Caldey Roads were notorious death traps in sudden changes of wind when vessels would get driven ashore. During the 1830s and '40s several vessels were so wrecked and a life-saving apparatus, a 24lb Manby mortar, was supplied. This, according to several sources, including Charles Norris who depicted the mortar in his etching of the wreck of the collier brig *Durham*, was pretty useless and didn't do much to save lives. Thus a lifeboat was established in 1852, based in Penniless Cove, in the harbour. In 1862 a boathouse was built on Castle Beach, which today survives as a surf shop. Various boats were put on station, mostly self-righting types of ten oars, until a new boathouse and slipway was built on Castle Hill, and a new Watson-class boat, the *William and Mary Devey* in the first decade of the twentieth century. The first motor boat, the *John R. Web*, was installed in 1923, and was replaced seven years later by the *John R. Web II*, a 45ft twin-engined Watson. The present boat dates from 1986 and is kept afloat.

The Royal Victoria Pier was built in 1897 to commemorate the Diamond Jubilee of Queen Victoria and was extended two years later. Jutting out from Castle Hill into North Bay and accessible at all states of the tide, this became a stopping off point for excursion steamers from Swansea and Ilfracombe. Its heavy metal construction with graceful arches and ornamental ironwork was considered to be amongst the best

Tenby's lifeboat *Annie Collin* in 1896.

examples in pier building in Britain. However, facing heavy repair bills in the 1950s, the Borough Council decided on demolishing the structure in 1953.

And so I returned to Castle Beach to swim and find my friends. Here I had my third strange encounter, this time with a fish. Swimming between the beach and the island, I saw a fish's snout sticking out of the water. It was moving around and kept coming up to the surface as if to breathe. But fishes don't breathe air, I thought, I looked closer. Getting within a couple of yards, I identified the fish as a mackerel. Both fish and I were drifting westwards with the ebb, and I soon touched bottom upon the shallow sandy isthmus. However, the fish drifted closer so that, after two attempts, I was able to grab him. He was a small mackerel, but with a nasty gash on the back of his head which was the obvious reason for his disorientation. People on the beach couldn't believe I'd caught the mackerel with my own bare hands! It seemed best to give him the priest treatment to put him out of his misery and let the others take him home to eat. Presumably the man on the pier had hooked him, but he'd escaped with the deep wound. It was a very bizarre encounter indeed!

I sat on the beach as people began their early evening migration back to their hotels and apartments. From a beach that was earlier dense with sun-worshippers and where hardly a grain of sand was visible, the transition to an empty solace was sudden. Within a couple of hours the town would re-awaken again as the pubs and restaurants busied to cope with the demand. However, Tenby still retains its charm when so many resorts do not. The beaches are natural and without the confounded theme parks. Here, too, there is no pedestrianised street, simply a road that is temporarily shut down to traffic during shopping hours. Somehow this makes so much sense, a reduction in traffic that still retains the charm of a town with narrow streets. I hate these pedestrianised areas, not for their lack of traffic, which is great, but for the fact they contribute so much to removing of individualism, to the making of British high streets all exactly identical. So many are fast becoming characterless places of excessive corporate sameness. The Tenby fathers must have great insight, even if it's not intentional! Seeing Tenby so hectic made me love it even more.

It doesn't take too much imagination though to visualise the beach in Victorian times, an era of much technological innovation but little social development. You can almost see the ladies with their flowing swimwear climbing down rickety ladders into the sea, their giraffe-like necks stretched to prevent wetting their over-sensitive heads. The peasantry, pushed towards the rocky parts of the beach, might briefly look over in awe as Lord Bighead, adorned in knee-length shorts and full shirt, genteelly steps into the waves and gingerly takes his first few breaststrokes, but they weren't fooled by the pretence of it all. They must have smiled before some beach attendant came running to tell them to look away. Thank God, I say, Margaret Thatcher wasn't able to return us to the Victorian values she held in such great esteem. If history teaches us one thing, it should be the errors of past ways. Mind you, the present lot should take heed because inequality lies at the root of many of our society's problems and nobody ever tries much to pull the extremes of the social divide together.

The magical hour had arrived. I could walk with dog along the South Beach, aided by the fact that the tide had ebbed around the rocks beneath the cliffs. We walked up to the railway line where it crosses the Ritec Marshes. Sir John Owen was the first to build an embankment across the entrance of the Ritec River between 1811–1820. The idea was to enable travellers to take the direct route rather than detouring upstream. Owen, though, ran out of money and sold the marshes to Charles Mathias. He continued the project until the wall was breached in 1826 by a southeasterly gale – winds from this direction still are feared in Tenby – so that it wasn't until the railway line was built in the early 1860s that the present higher embankment was constructed.

When the railway was finally completed between Paddington and Tenby in 1864, it is said that a change in the social class of visitors occurred. Suddenly the workers from the capital and towns along its route could come, wanting ice-cream carts instead of bathing machines. Swindon Trip Week, the first week in July, became an institution with trippers pouring in from the town. Judging by the numbers of caravans at Kiln Park, the other side of the line, they were still coming. Ahead lay a rifle range and danger area, but I note from the guide book that the Coastal Footpath around the south of the danger area is open even when the range is in use. However, it wasn't the bullets I was worried about, but the golf-balls flying around the course and the fact that every rabbit in the area was out playing and dog was going crazy chasing them. Time to double back across the sands up into the town, and find a place to eat some fish.

DAY NINE

TENBY TO MILFORD HAVEN

Before we proceed along the Pembrokeshire coast, a word from George Owen of Henllys. Owen was, as were many of his contemporary antiquarians, a country gentleman and he was also lord of the barony of Cemais. His book, originally entitled *Description of Penbrokeshire* and published in manuscript form in 1603, is a seminal account of the daily life and customs of this corner of Elizabethan Britain, and thus gives us a brilliant insight into Pembrokeshire society of four hundred years ago. In it he includes a whole chapter on the fisheries of the county. Incidentally, his spelling reflects the Welsh name of the cantref of *Penfro* prior to the 1536 Act of Union.

Herrings and oysters were among the chief commodities that Pembrokeshire yielded to its population. Corn, cattle, wool, butter, pigs and sheep appear to have been the major exports above fish and shellfish, whilst sea-coal, hides, tallow and sheepskins were of a lesser importance. By fish, he listed the following, omitting herring which he'd already described as hedging in the coast: 'turbot, halibut, burt, sole, plaice, fluke, flounder, ling, millwell otherwise called cod, hake, mullet, bass, which breeds twice a year as says Rondelet, conger, gurnet, grey and red, whiting, haddock, shad, the friar, bowman, sea smelt, sea bream, the cow, swordfish, sprat or sandeel, the earl or needle, whose fins grow forward contrary to the nature of all fish, rough hounds, smooth hounds, thornback ray, shark, and many other kind of sea fish which I cannot remember'. Other fish included salmon, sewin and trout, eels and lamphreys, and pilchards and mackerel. Shellfish included oysters, lobsters, crabs, shrimps and 'mussels, limpins, crevisses, sheath or haft fish, cockles, flemings, whelks, periwinkles, hens and divers other fish'. He added that seals, porpoises and thornpoles were sometimes caught in the herring nets as these fed on the shoals. Mussels were fished principally for their pearls and in the rivers they could grow up to seven or eight inches long, the meat inside being rejected as rank.

Eels and lamphreys were caught in every river. In the Cleddau eels were caught in August in weirs, wattled wheels and nets. They were then salted. Herrings were taken all around the coast but chiefly at Fishguard – where the inhabitants were referred to as *sgadan Abergwaun* ('Fishguard herrings') into the twentieth century – Newport, Dinas, Goultrop Roads, Martin's Haven, Broad Haven, Hopgain, St Bride's, Tenby, Milford Haven etc, all the way to Earewere, 'so that it seemed they had laid siege by sea to the county, so greatly has God bestowed his blessing this way upon this poor county, the Lord make us thankful therefor'. The herring season lasted from August to Christmas and sometimes twenty meises of herrings were taken by each boat, a meise being either 600 or 620 herrings, depending on the tallying.

Chief amongst the shellfish was the oyster, which was shipped to Bristol or the Forest of Dean and from there exported all over Shropshire, Worcestershire, Gloucestershire,

Somerset and Wiltshire as well as being carried by landed throughout South Wales. The Cleddau River, within the Milford Haven, Caldey and Stackpole were the main dredging grounds. As to the dredging itself, he describes the process thus:

> ...a kind of iron made with bars, having a piece of horse or bullock skin sewn to it like a bag, in such sort as that it fastened to a rope's end, is cast into the bottom of Milford at eight or ten fathoms deep, and is dragged at a boat's end by two rowers which row up and down the channel, and so the bag of leather, being made apt to scrape up all manner of things lying in the bottom, gathers up the oysters that breed there over certain known beds, which bag being filled they draw up and empty their oysters into their boat, applying their labours so all day, and when they have done they row to some appointed place near the shore at full sea and there cast out the oysters in a great heap, which they call beds, where every tide overflows them, and so are kept for lading boats to Bristol and other places.

These sentences may be mouthfuls, but the book is superb reading. Its publication is due in the main to another of Pembrokeshire's sons, Richard Fenton, who discovered the manuscript and included it in *The Cambrian Register* in 1795–6. Fenton then published his own *Historical Tour through Pembrokeshire* in 1811, making much use of Owen's work. We, in turn, shall make use of both of these works during our tour!

The road from Tenby passes rows of Nissan huts at Penally Training Camp. Military installations are to be a thing for the next stage of the tour. I parked briefly at Lydstep Palace, a building dating from AD 1350-1500. 'Pirates, bishops, barons and judges have all by tradition been associated with Lydstep Palace, though there is no supporting proof'. The Halls came here to examine the old ruin they called 'The Palace'. Beyond is the narrow road to Lydstep Head where a National Trust car park enables access. We walked down to the holiday camp and then up through the woods and along to the Point. Limestone quarrying has left its mark on the landscape with several deep recessed holes in the cliffs on the north side, and below this is the 'step' into the water where 130-ton vessels were able to lie alongside to load up. A tramway carried the stone to the edge and a device lowered it into the waiting vessels. Quarrying was said to have been a summer occupation and smuggling in winter! However, the view was impressive. Below us, the Lystep House and the Haven and its lovely, albeit stoney, beach with dozens of nearby caravans – obviously up-market for most had timber decking outside. These contrasted with excellent views over to St Margaret's Island, which seemed almost close enough to step onto. Behind St Margaret's was Caldey and beyond that Carmarthen Bay and the Gower stood out. The coast of Devon was just visible and to the south I got my first glimpse of Lundy.

The rock formation was impressive. An easy ten-minute walk, past a picnic site, and we arrived at steps above Skrinkle Haven. Beyond here, the danger area of the Royal Artillery Range, based at Manorbier Camp, prohibits access to the Iron Age fort on Old Castle Head. Below Lydstep caverns are accessible on its western end including the famous 'Smuggler's Cave' although most can only be reached at low water. The existence of this latter cave had led to several local myths concerning illicit trading hereabout. Whether there is any truth in them or not is unclear.

We retraced back to the van and drove to Manorbier (*Maenorbyr*), a couple of miles further west. The beach here is below the castle and is sandy and dog-territory. Giraldus

Stackpole Quay with vessel being loaded, *c.*1890.

Cambrenus – his real name was Gerald de Barri by the way – was born in this castle in 1146. He described Maenor Pirr as the 'pleasantest spot in Wales'. Well, he would, wouldn't he, living in this wonderful spot. The Halls thought it a charming place too. But there are many places as pleasant and some more pleasant, I think.

Freshwater East is a lovely sheltered beach surrounded by a monstrous housing development. One description is of 'a chaotic shambles' and 'the visual squalor produced by shack development...' Stackpole Quay, in absolute contrast, is a tiny quay within a small creek of glorious turquoise water, said to be the smallest harbour in Britain. In 1566 there were twelve households. It was built for the exclusive export of limestone from the nearby quarries, although in later centuries imports included coal. It is said there were also one or two fishing boats working from here. Seemingly to support this, there were two modern boats indeed anchored off.

The name comes from the Norse – *stac*, a rock and *pollr*, a small inlet – and seems to originate from the eleventh-century castle built here. This was replaced by a mansion and later by Stackpole Court, which was demolished in the 1960s.

There's a fine limestone kiln alongside the road to the car park that is in the old quarry. It's National Trust property and the charge of £2 seemed a bit steep to enable me to take one photograph. This portion of the coastpath between Freshwater Bay and Barafundle Bay was the first one I ever walked many years ago. I remember the hike well, across the Lily Ponds to find the road and the walk back along it to Freshwater East. That was in winter and the Boathouse tearooms were closed.

The road to St Govan's chapel passes through Bosherton where there's a coastguard centre. The portion from there crosses the Castlemartin Royal Artillery Range and was open. On arrival in the free car park and opening the door, we were confronted with the sound of the clatter of automatic fire from the nearby range. These were followed by explosions, and rifle fire, and more clattering. A fellow visitor remarked how bizarre it was to hear the shooting. Still, this was Ministry of Defence land, and I suppose they have to play their war games somewhere if we wish to invade more countries like Iraq!

The chapel itself is most remarkable, wedged as it is down the cliff between two huge rocks. St Govan is thought to have been St Gobham, Abbot of Dairinis in County Wexford, who, tradition has, was pursued to the cliff by a gang of pirates. A cleft in the rock miraculously opened up for the poor abbot to hide in until the thugs had left. Thus he stayed on for the rest of his life, preaching right up to his death in AD 586. The chapel itself dates to the eleventh century, and perhaps had been founded in the sixth. St Govan is said to have been buried under the altar, although this seems to contradict the building date of the chapel. The water in the well was said to cure skin and eye complaints and rheumatism.

Another story concerns pirates. St Govan's silver bell was stolen by these marauders and their ship was subsequently sunk in a storm, whether by God's grace or not isn't clear. However, a troopsie of angels carried it back here and entombed it close to the chapel. When tapped by St Govan, it rang out a note a thousand times louder than the original bell. I wondered why those people were tapping the rocks!

Slightly east of the chapel is St Govan's Head with New Quay on its eastern side. Here clay was shipped out from the pits at Flimston. It was supposedly a popular smugglers' landing so that two coastguards were stationed here between the 1840s and 1880s.

The coast path west of here was closed due to the firing. I'd wanted to walk over to the Huntsman's Leap where a nineteenth-century huntsman was said to have leaped over the vertical fissure in the rock and died of fright when he'd looked back. Silly bugger! And I don't mean the slouched, headphoned man in the little army box telling us we couldn't go through to see it. Well... maybe.

The road to Stack Rocks was likewise closed. I spent five minutes watching tanks firing at the targets in the Spectators enclosure at Castlemartin with another four cars. I was surprised the army encouraged us to see the spectacle. The shock waves from the explosions were quite real upon my ears, even at the distance of half a mile.

Freshwater West is another large sweep of sand, albeit exposed to the west and considered dangerous to swimmers. At the southern end of the bay there's a seaweed collector's reed-thatched hut which was used to dry the edible seaweed prior to its boiling into laverbread. There were once twenty of these huts in the 1920s, and this one, the only surviving one in Wales, I'm told, was restored by the Pembrokeshire National Park Authority.

I was disappointed with Angle, which is probably unfair. Perhaps I was just shell-shocked! Leland called it 'a pore Village'. Evans described 'the Nangle' as small with 'miserable accommodations for numerous passengers to and from Ireland'. Developing from a small fishermen's community, it seems that more modern housing developments have superceded the quaint single-storey Welsh cottages. One I saw was derelict and roofless with a pretty hideous dwelling almost abutting it. Depressing! Ironic, really, because Angle was renowned for its brick-making. Angle Bay is the largest bay in the Milford Haven waterway and is busy with yachts and boats that dry at low water. The local seadogs say the best anchorage in the bay is so close to the Point House pub that the clock in the hall can be read through the front door!

Just around the northwestern tip of the bay – Angle Point – is the old lifeboat slip where a lifeboat was stationed in 1868. This was known as the Milford lifeboat until 1892 when the more accurate Angle was used. In 1908 the steam lifeboat *James Stevens No.3* was stationed experimentally here so that two boats were on station until 1910. Four years later she torn from her deepwater mooring and stranded ashore, holed and battered. She briefly came back to Angle after substantial repairs before being sent to the Isle of Wight. When she was sold in 1928, she was the last of six steam lifeboats commissioned by the RNLI. The present boathouse was built in 1928.

The Angle lifeboat played a part in one of the most infamous wrecks in the waterway, saving thirty-three lives in the process. The *Loch Shiel* was on route from Glasgow to Australia with a full cargo of, amongst other items, whisky and beer when she hit rocks off Angle. Although the Customs Officers arrived pretty promptly, the locals managed to hide away much of the 7,500 cases of whisky (and 7,000 of beer) in their own *Whisky Galore* episode and it was reported that between fifty and 100 persons were seen drinking on the beach. Whereas all the crew of the ship were rescued by the lifeboat, three locals died in either attempting to collect some of the bottles or, as in the case of a young man, from exposure after collapsing in a drunken state on the beach at night. Divers from Swansea recovered seven bottles in 1999.

It's about half an hour's walk from the slipway to West Angle Bay, past the Chapel Bay Fort and Thorn Island where there used to be a Victorian battery. Today there's a summer hotel where boats from West Angle can be taken out to reach it. But we didn't walk this part of the coast path, choosing to take the short hike over to 'the bluff summit of a rocky cliff' upon which sit the remains of the East Blockhouse. Jelinger Symons, according to the Halls, describes the view from here as 'one of those magnificent scenes of which one carries the image through life'.

The Milford Haven waterway has been described as a perfect waterway by dozens of eminent visitors. Defoe referred to it as 'one of the greatest and best Inlets of Water in Britain' while Nelson called it 'one of the finest possible stations for a British Fleet...' Thus, when the Admiralty decided to set up a dockyard at Milford, later switched to Paterchurch, they also built a system of coastal defences to protect these installations from a seaborne attack. Thus, in the nineteenth century, batteries were built at numerous sites – West Blockhouse Point, Dale Point, South Hook Point, Stack Rock, Hubberston, Scoveston, Pembroke Dock, Popton Point, Chapel Bay, Thorn Island and the East Blockhouse Point. The fort at St Catherine's Island, Tenby, we've already discovered was part of the defences. However, all around the waterway, other fortifications dating back to the sixteenth century were built to protect it from seaward attacks. Both the West and East Blockhouse date from 1580 while plans were drawn up fifteen years later by George Owen – he was Deputy Lord Lieutenant and Deputy Vice-Admiral of Pembrokeshire at the time – to build defences at Thorn Island, Dale Point and Stack Rock. Pill Fort was built in 1643 to protect Castle Pill. Still, we haven't reached Pembroke Dock yet.

From Angle we drove back past the Rocket Cart House, the old coastguard watch tower that I later saw on the market for £225,000. Across the Kilpaison Burrows we went, intending to visit Hundleton and Monkton, although we took a wrong turning because of some roadworks, and ended up in Pembroke, parking up by the Tourist Information Centre. Inside there's a small display on the history of the town.

Pembroke grew out of the castle, which Arnulph de Montgomery built upon the high promontory in 1105, soon after the Normans arrived here. Later on, King Henry VII was to be born here. Such was the importance of this strategic centre that the king created the

Postcard of Pembroke Castle.

Earldom of Pembroke in 1138, installing Gilbert de Clare as the first earl. Merchants arrived and a town emerged alongside the Pembroke River after the earl decreed that all vessels in the Haven waterway had to load and set down at Pembroke Bridge.

The castle was built over Wogan's Cave which, it has been suggested, was used as a boathouse with space for boats up to 70ft long and 11ft in beam – such as would be the Viking galleys. The town prospered under this monopoly for many years, even after Haverfordwest and Tenby became themselves trading centres in their own rights, albeit with limited seaward access up the shallow river.

According to Leland, the town was well walled but 'it is totally yn Ruine' which suggests a decline in its fortunes in the early sixteenth century. However, in 1566 there were two boats, the *Ann* (12 tons) and *Katheryne of Pembroke* (7 tons), locally owned, trading with Ireland and going 'upp Severne afishinge'. Nearly two centuries later, though, Defoe found the largest and richest town in South Wales with 'a great many English Merchants, and some of them Men of good Business; and they told us, there were near 200 Sail of Ships belong'd to the Town'. The Halls thought the castle 'inexpressibly grand'.

Exports included salt herring, wool, hides and butter. Corn was milled in the tidal mill on the bridge below the castle since 1199 and the last of these mills – a five-storey building – was spectacularly burned down in 1955, although the tidal pond is still flooded.

However, by the nineteenth century the port of Pembroke was largely redundant save for a few vessels. This was largely due to the emerging more favourable harbours on the waterway, to which was added the arrival of the railway in 1863, so that Pembroke declined as other places thrived. Walking around the footpath across the river from the castle, and later up through the town, I was struck with a feeling that this was a misunderstood town in some way. One contemporary guidebook described the place as dull. Yet it is undoubtedly pretty, although it has that air of not quite belonging to the present. By comparison to some of its contemporaries its position alone should warrant much more interest in its future and the fact that it has a fine castle which itself is wrapped in history should ensure a rekindling of its due dividend from tourism. Its transition from one of the richest towns in Wales to one of ruin seemed abrupt, but I can only hope that another transition from its present state to a future major place of desirability is not far off. For, this is, as far as I am concerned, one of the loveliest places in this part of Wales.

Crossing the mill bridge takes you almost immediately into Pembroke Dock. My first port of call was the Royal Dockyard, which is now a cross between an industrial estate and a ferry port. Stopping to photograph some of the buildings, I was accosted by a boy of about eight on a quad bike telling me not to photograph otherwise he would run me over. He seemed to have emerged from the gypsy camp across the road because that was where he returned to. I told him where to stuff his instructions, adding I'd a fierce dog in the van, but his interjection into my business didn't impress the joys of this town upon me. On previous visits to Pembroke Dock I'd come to the conclusion that, without the dockyard, the place seemed to be redundant on the map. This little brat simply increased this aspersion. The Halls obviously weren't impressed as they only wrote a few sentences on the place!

The Admiralty was helped in its convincing of the sense in the construction of their dockyard here instead of at Milford by the natural formation of the shoreline. By the time Milford ceased operations in 1814, five vessels were already under construction here. Houses were built for workers in Front Street, which was then known as Thomas Street after Sir Thomas Meyrick. The following year it was formerly established as a Royal Dockyard, the only such establishment in Wales.

The first of these ships were launched in 1816 – the *Ariadne* and *Valorous*. At the same time fortifications were built to protect the dockyard itself. Some have already been mentioned. The Defensible Barracks overlooked the growing town while two Martello towers were built between 1849-1851, one at Front Street and the other on the western approaches. The former is now open as the Gun Tower Museum in which exhibitions explain the dockyards, its defence, the Garrison town and the twentieth-century flying boats that operated out of the dockyard after its closure in 1926. Over that period some 260 ships and four Royal Yachts were built here, and at its peak it was regarded as the premier shipyard in the world.

At the end of Front Street are the workshops of the West Wales Maritime Heritage Society, a group set up in 1984 to record and preserve the area's maritime heritage. They have various wooden vessels in varying states of repair. The Yorkshire coble *Quest* and the coal-fired steam harbour launch *HSL296* are amongst these. Several years ago I took the lines off *Agnes*, a Dale gig they have on permanent loan from the Scolton Manor Museum. This 17ft two-masted boat was built in 1906 by an unknown local boatbuilder for a local lad called Frank Knights and named after his mother. The extraordinary thing was that Frank was only fourteen years old at the time. He used the boat 'to make his living as an inshore fisherman, within the confines of the Haven' with 'long-lines, nets and pots for shellfish'. During the war *Agnes* was used to ferry people across the lock pits at Milford Haven. Frank Knights retired soon after the war and the boat was subsequently solely used for pleasure purposes.

Hobbs Quay is an interesting place. Named after Nicholas Hobbs who once owned the land before the Government bought it in 1758, the pier was built between 1830–32 to enable ships to lie alongside whilst they were being fitted out. It also served as a quay to ferry troops and stores out to awaiting vessels, and as a landing stage for the local people. A ferry across to Neyland had run since 1858 and a regular steam service began in 1902 with the wooden twin-screwed *Menai*. This was joined by the *Amy* and *Pioneer* the following year and the service changed ownership in 1933 when two car ferries – the *Lady Magdalene* and the *Alumchine* – were introduced. By 1947 there were financial difficulties so that the Pembrokeshire County Council commissioned the *Cleddau Queen*, the last of the paddle steamers to be built in Britain for service, followed by the *Cleddau King* in 1965. The service ceased in 1975 with the opening of the Cleddau Bridge.

The two 30lb cannons that line the quay today were cast in Sweden for the Royal Dutch Navy. During the Napoleonic Wars they were captured by the British and eventually ended up as bollards on the quay until being re-instated in their present position.

Llangwm fish wife.

Another ferry operated from the Ferry Inn at Pembroke Ferry (almost below the bridge) to the Jolly sailor at Burton Ferry. Known locally as 'The Passage', this was said to have been the busiest ferry on the waterway. In 1832 the cost was 1*s* 2*d* for foot passengers and 1*d* for a man and horse and 1*d* for each wheel on a cart. Ferrymen are also said to have rowed across children to their school in Pembroke Dock and on Tuesdays and Fridays the Llangwm fisherwomen crossed over to sell their catch at market, leaving their donkeys and carts in the adjacent fields. This ferry survived until the 1950s.

One of the reasons for the demise of shipbuilding at Pembroke Dock was the advent of ironclad warships. The local workforce was unskilled in working with iron and the raw materials were said not to be in supply although considering the amount of coal mined in Pembrokeshire, I find this surprising. However, being at the end of the line, so to speak, the yard was some distant from the major ironworks. Composite vessels continued to be built.

One of the best known of the ironclad ships was the *Warrior*, the first iron-built warship in the world launched in the Thames in 1860. She saw little service until the First World War but by then she was out-dated. For many years she was used as a floating pontoon for the Admiralty oil tanks at Llanion until she was moved to become a rotting hulk, only to be later saved, restored and taken to Portsmouth where she remains as a major tourist attraction.

It was time to circumnavigate the Cleddau River, an area rich in mining, quarrying, milling, shipbuilding and fishing history. At Cosheston shipbuilding flourished using local oak. At Carew (*Caeriw*), famous for its fine oysters, I visited the Carew Tidal Mill, which lies below the castle. The existence of a mill on this site dates from the early sixteenth century at a time when Pembrokeshire was 'the corn county of Wales' with a quarter of all its exported corn going to North Wales, Bristol, Barnstable and Ilfracombe. At the time most mills were owned by monasteries or the local manor and 'soke rights' enabled the lord to demand that his tenants use his mill so that he could take a percentage of the corn as a toll. By the end of the century exports to Cardigan Bay had increased and by 1617 it was being taken to London, Somerset, South Devon and Dorset. By the 1740s some 160,000 bushels of corn, malt and oatmeal were being exported from the waterway annually. The present mill dates from the early nineteenth century and has recently been restored. The millpond covers an area of 23 acres. Open to the public, the mill features various exhibitions on the process of milling and much of the machinery can be viewed close up.

We stopped for a quick drink at the waterside Cresswell Arms at Cresswell Quay (*Cei Cresswell*). Inside I found an original 'Capstan strength' cigarette advert in colour portraying a steam trawler. These are sought after, and although the publican declared he'd got another, he was unwilling to part with either! The three quays that were once here were used to load and export culm and coal from the nearby mines. In 1566 it was mentioned as a landing place with one household. Out of forty vessels registered locally in 1795, twenty-one were said to have been associated with Cresswell Quay. However, the coal trade had ceased by 1850 although some river traffic continued using the quay into the twentieth century.

At the same time nearby Lawrenny had twelve households. During the period 1780–1860 over sixty vessels were built making it only second in importance to Milford Haven. Limestone quarrying and coal mining thrived hereabout and barges carried both commodities to the quay for loading onto ships. The oysters from hereabout were once found in 'great abundance and conveyed principally to the London markets in boats from Chatham and Rochester'. They were regarded as being the 'fattest, whitest and sweetest' and were also sent to Bristol and elsewhere about South Wales. A ferry once plied between here and Cosheston until the last ferryman, Tom, died in the 1960s. Today, though, Lawrenny is a haven for yachtsmen. A sign on the chandlery door reads, 'When chandlery closed please make all enquiries at the hotel'. Does this suggest the same ownership or that the proprietor is always propping up the bar?

Another ferry crossed from Landshipping Quay to Picton Point until its closure in the 1930s. In 1800 over 6,000 tons of coal and culm was also shipped out. Remains of the railway and weighbridge can still be seen, as can a limekiln. Around from the quay is a memorial to those killed in Pembrokeshire's worst mining disaster when the incoming tide broke through the roof of the garden pits mine and flooded it in 1844. Forty mine workers drowned including three eleven year olds and 'miner John' (a child).

It's quite a drive around the northern end of the East and West Cleddau rivers. We stopped briefly at the Blackpool mill, once an iron forge and later a corn mill and now a visitor centre. I was tempted to call in at Picton Castle but didn't for the dog had received enough exercise on each of the foreshores we'd visited as they were all dog friendly. At Haverfordwest (*Hwlffordd*) we paused again briefly. The name is Norse from the Haefer's west fjord. George Owen describes the town 'the greatest and plentifullest markett of the shire… And for fishes it passeth all others in Wales, without anie comparison, both for plenti and varitie'. To Defoe, Haverford (the west was added in 1409 but presumably he hadn't heard) was a better town than he'd expected and was 'Strong, well Built, Clean and Populous'. The first castle was founded in about 1110 by the Fleming Tancred. Although trade flourished in Elizabethan times, by 1616 the quay was in such a state that no vessel could use it. Things must have improved for by the early nineteenth century vessels of up to 200 tons were frequently calling at the Gasworks Quay with timber, bricks and limestone blocks. Much of the timber was used for shipbuilding that seemed to have thrived. Again it was the coming of the railway that precipitated a decline in river traffic, although coal and culm continued to be brought upstream by barge from Hook. By the middle of the twentieth century the river was all but quiet of commercial traffic.

But it wasn't just commercial traffic that worked upon the upper reaches of the Cleddau. The area is also renowned for 'compass-net' fishing, a method very similar to the stop-netting of the Severn. Indeed it is said that two men from the Forest of Dean, Ormond and Edwards, introduced the method into the Cleddau after they had come to work in the Landshipping Quarry in the early 1800s.

Fishermen from the two villages of Hook and Llangwm – pronounced Langum – competed with each other in the fishery. The main fishing grounds lay in the river at Little Milford below Hook yet the Llangwm men believe the rights to the fishing are their birthright as they've been at it for much longer. The Hook men were employed in the local anthracite mine until its closure in 1947 and say that anyway the fishing grounds are geographically closest to their village.

Like the stop-net, a compass-net consists of a bag net suspended between two larch poles, seasoned in the salty mud of the river and formed in a 'V'. The boat, a small 14ft boat tarred inside and out, is moored in the river between a post driven into the

Fisherman with his family at Black Tar Point, Llangwm.

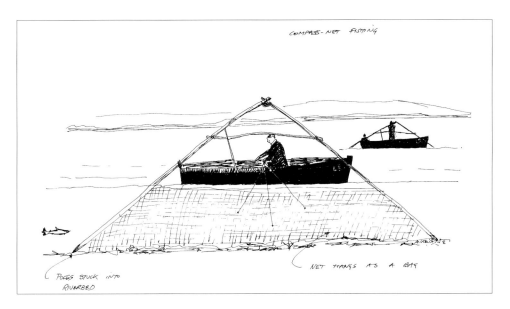

Drawing of compass-net fishing.

riverbank and an anchor so that it lies across the tide. The net, with feeling strings are attached at strategic points, is set by rocking the boat back and forth until the momentum take the whole device over the side so that the bag net streams out below the boat. Weights, normally stones, tied to the apex of the 'V', act to both hold it down and counterbalance it. When a fish is felt, the apex is drawn down and the net springs up into the horizontal position.

As elsewhere, the salmon season lasts from June to August and fishing is best on tides of 6.3m two and half hours below low water. Night-time fishing was always said to be best, although fishing between 6 a.m. on Saturdays and noon on Mondays is prohibited. Cynics say that the reason the boats are painted black is to avoid detection at night! Until the 1866 Commission into the Salmon Fisheries, some 100 boats were said to fish. Today this is restricted to eight licences, although some are not taken up. We found three boats out on the river. In 1869, and again in 1939, temporary bans were put in place to help stocks of salmon revive.

Some years ago I'd come here to measure up one of the small compass-net boats. Even then I had difficulty finding more than five of the wooden boats. Today I found only two. One fisherman I spoke to by chance told me that only one person fished with a wooden boat. He, it later transpired, was Alun Lewis from Landshipping Quay. The remainder use fibreglass versions of the traditional boats.

We drove down to Blacktar Point, the place probably where the boats were tarred up, and walked along the shore to Llangwm. One wooden boat lay in a dilapidated state outside its owner's home, who informed me that he'd never part with it. He was happier to see it fall apart, a sentiment I'd found in many fishing communities who were often suspicious of outsiders. The people of Llangwm were essentially of Norse and Flemish ascendancy. Many of them worked in Pembroke Dock and it is said they carried the timber back with which they built their stout oak boats. The women were equally enterprising and were renowned for their black pointed bonnets, flowing aprons, short petticoats and baskets of fish slung over their backs. They often walked miles as they hawked salmon, sewin, herring and oysters, and many other kinds of fish. The androminous herring was caught in drift-nets when the fish swam upriver in the autumn, using the same little boats. Nineteenth-century writers alike were so impressed with these women that they are well documented. One particular woman, Mary Palmer, was even featured in the *Daily Mail*.

The road from Llangwm back to the northern end of the Cleddau Bridge passes through Burton Ferry, of which we have already heard. Alongside the old ferry slipway is the Trinity Pier, an impressive structure built in 1861 as a depot for lightships and lighthouses. The wooden jetty provided a landing stage with plenty of storage in its underslung rooms. The ship *Siren* carried relief crews and lamp oil out to the light stations and was often moored offshore. The crews stayed in the cottages at Trinity Terrace. However, when operations were transferred to Swansea in 1926, the depot closed and pier and house were sold off to private owners.

From Burton Ferry we arrived at Neyland, the town that owes much of its existence, certainly in its modern context, to that most innovative of British engineers, Isambard Kingdom Brunel. Aptly, the first place we visited was Brunel Quay, the site of the terminus to the Great Western Railway that brought fortune to the town. Today neither the terminus nor the railway installations are visible as these were demolished in the 1960s. Neither does any sign of the floating pontoon attached to the land by the 'tube', a great covered walkway, remain for this is a grassy park with information boards relating to the history of the port. The handrails around the edge are made from Brunel's original railway.

Brunel (1806-1859) was an exceptional man and began designing the Clifton Suspension Bridge when he was only twenty-three (it was completed in 1864 as a memorial to him). In 1833 he was appointed the engineer to the Great Western Railway to design and build all the various tunnels, bridges and viaducts for the route between London and South Wales. Brunel's original idea had been to take the railway to Fishguard to create an Irish ferry link but the potato famine in Ireland brought those plans to a halt. He then proposed diverting the line to Abermawr but this scheme was abandoned and the railway taken south to Haverfordwest and reaching the terminus at Neyland in 1856. The ferry service to Ireland commenced the same year. It's ironic that it did reach here, for twelve years earlier Brunel had surveyed Neyland and favoured the tiny hamlet alongside the Westfield Pill as his first choice for an international port in South Wales.

Brunel, as is widely accepted, was a man of vision and his desire was to connect steamers to the railway. His first steamship was the *Great Western*, which was the first to operate transatlantic. In 1843 he designed the *Great Britain*, the first iron and screw-driven steamer. Finally, he designed the largest and longest ship of her day, the 692ft *Great Eastern*, a monstrous creation that was ultimately to consume him. Built at the shipyard of naval architect John Scott Russell on the river Thames and owned by the Eastern Navigation Company, she took several years to build, was four times over budget and was beset with problems all along. Just as construction was about to begin in 1853 a fire broke out at the yard, delaying this for five months. Then Russell was almost forced into bankruptcy after financial problems, further delaying the project another five months. A riveter was killed at one point. Then, when 100,000 people turned up to the launch even though Brunel had wanted a quiet affair, the ship wouldn't go into the water after jamming on the ways and killing a worker in the process. It finally took ninety days to launch her with Brunel feeling publicly humiliated. The owners almost changed the ship's name prior to launching. Brunel, with an incurable kidney disease, fell ill and the vessel was fitted out while he was recuperating. Then just as he was about to depart on the maiden voyage eighteen months later, he collapsed. The vessel proceeded on her maiden voyage to Holyhead but an explosion off Hastings killed five of the crew. Brunel heard this news and died soon afterwards. He was only fifty-three. In reality, his dream vessel was a financial disaster even if she was an engineering wonder – although she was probably built fifty years before her time. Some say Brunel was more interested in glory than profit, which would explain why he pushed the project.

The *Great Eastern* visited Neyland twice, on both occasions to undergo repairs on the only grid that could accommodate her. Sadly, the boat that never became a success even if she could carry 4,000 passengers was sold and used to lay the first transatlantic cable in 1865/6. Later that same year she ended up in the Hubberston Pill at Milford Haven where she sat for twelve years before being eventually scrapped in 1888. When the double-skinned iron hull was pulled apart by the breakers, they found the skeletons of two workers who had become trapped during the construction. Some say this was why the vessel was jinxed from its very beginning.

Westfield Pill, now home to a modern marina, was once the site of Scurlock's yard where ships of up to 100 tons were built. As far back as 1758 a survey had recommended this pill as suitable for shipbuilding. Shipping brought timber in, and later sugar which required the building of a Customs House in 1870 (duty was previously paid at Pembroke). Neyland had also been a herring port since the eighteenth century when, according to the 1758 report on the British Fisheries, some 100,000 herrings were annually landed. When the Irish ferry was moved to Fishguard in 1906, the GWR formed the Neyland Trawling & Fishing Company and established a fishmarket alongside the Westfield Pill. For several years the fish landing flourished although the enterprise was short-lived. By 1914 they found they were unable to compete with Milford Haven.

Limekilns

The purpose of a limekiln is to burn limestone so as to manufacture lime. Lime had a number of uses. Early builders relied upon it as a mortar for the stone walls, for plastering and waterproofing these and painting them with lime-wash. It was an integral part of the process of tanning hides and bleaching paper, and was even taken as a medicine as limewater. In many parts of the country the dead were buried in lime. In agriculture lime was necessary to balance the pH of the land while it was also used to purify water and treat effluent. To satiate this demand for lime, hundreds of limekilns were built at one time or other close to the supply of limestone. As in many rural parts of the country this limestone had to be brought in by boat, the limekilns were positioned close to a suitable beach or quay. Coal also had to be imported in the same way. In the case of big buildings, a kiln would normally be built nearby.

Lime burning is no modern invention. One limekiln dating from around 2450 BC was excavated in Mesopotamia and the Minoans are known to have used it in Crete in about 1800 BC. The Egyptians, Greeks and Romans used it, the latter realizing its benefit upon the land. In Britain, the remains of limekilns have been found in castles while records tell of timber being burnt to operate them. In more recent times, records of limestone importation into Pembrokeshire date back to 1385. George Owen has one of the earliest descriptions of the building of a limekiln in *A Description of Pembrokeshire*.

Pembrokeshire has plentiful supplies of limestone so many a kiln was built close by a quarry. Owen wrote, 'This limestone, being dug in a quarry in great stones, is hewn lesser to the bigness of a man's fist… and being hewn small the same is put into a kiln made of a wall six foot high, four or five foot broad at the brim but growing narrower to the bottom, having two loop holes in the bottom which they call the kiln eyes. In this kiln first is made a fire of coal, or rather culm… the kiln is then filled with these small hewed pieces of limestone, and then the fire being given, the same burns…and makes the limestone become mere red fiery coals… the lime so burnt is suffered to cool in the kiln, and then is drawn forth through these kiln eyes…' This lime was destined for spreading on the land, a habit that began in Britain in the fifteenth century.

Various kinds of limekiln existed, fired and cleared of lime on an almost continual fashion. Some kilns were an integral part of a village life. Indeed, a watercolour by J.M.W. Turner, dating from about 1824, depicts a woman drying her washing on the rim of a kiln in Devon. Some were single, small kilns while others were built blocks of several kilns alongside each other. One of the finest sets of these kilns can be seen at Llanrhystud, just north of Aberaeron, upon the coast of Cardigan Bay. The remains of a quay can still be seen below, on the beach, from where the limestone was landed. The coast of Pembrokeshire still has one of the highest concentrations of coastal limekilns. Details of these can be found in Peter Davies' *Pembrokeshire Limekilns*.

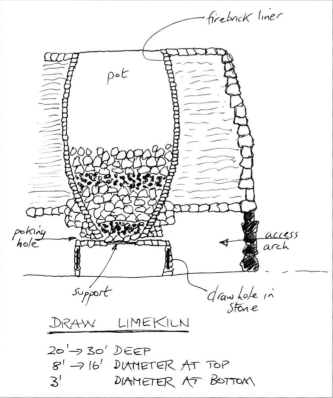

Above: Photograph of limekiln at Stackpole quay.

Left: Sketch of limekiln.

firebrick liner

pot

poking hole

access arch

support

draw hole in stone

DRAW LIMEKILN

20' → 30' DEEP
8' → 16' DIAMETER AT TOP
3'   DIAMETER AT BOTTOM

The ice works remained open until the late 1930s. Today I saw two fishing boats tied up to the pontoons alongside the quay.

We stopped briefly at Llanstadwell, close to the site of Warlow's yard where ships were built in the nineteenth century. Here was a small port with its own stone quay that was thriving throughout the seventeenth, eighteenth and nineteenth centuries with imports of coal, culm, grain and limestone. Further along the coast is Wear Point, sometimes referred to as Weir Point, presumably denoting the existence of a fish weir. However, asking around, I found no answer. I'd intended walking along the coastpath, but time was short and I wanted to get into the museum at Milford Haven before it closed at five. For from there it's a short journey into Milford Haven.

I was only just in time. Raymond Harding, the administrator with the black cap, introduced me to what they had on show. Housed in an old store – some say it was the Customs House but Raymond assured me this was not true – the museum follows the growth of the port from a tiny settlement to the west coast's largest fishing port, to today's harbour with its marina and Spanish and Belgium fishing boats. Raymond himself has forty years' experience working on deepsea trawlers.

The first settlers, in 1792, were Nantucket whalers who were keen to develop the market for whale oil to light the streets of London. Prior to that there was only a chapel and two farms. Nearby Hubberston and Hakin were thriving with shipbuilding and fishing. The mail packets sailed over to Waterford from here. These Quaker whalers, loyal to the king, found they were hounded by the Americans after Independence. At the same time, William Hamilton had inherited the substantial Pembrokeshire estate from his wife Catherine Barlow who had recently died. He appointed his nephew Charles Grenville to run and develop the estate. Rumour has it that, in return, Grenville gave Hamilton his mistress, young Emma Hart, whom he later married to become the second Lady Hamilton, and soon after, became Nelson's mistress.

In the early years of the nineteenth-century, plans to build a town and port were dragging. There was an unsuccessful attempt to launch a Newfoundland fishery from here. In 1805 an Act was passed 'to regulate the oyster, sole and salmon fisheries within the harbour of Milford and the rivers running into it' (46 Geo III c.19). A shipyard was opened about the same time, which was leased on an annual arrangement to the Admiralty to build warships. However, by 1814, these operations had been transferred to Paterchurch. Several ships did use the facilities. The *Frolic* ran between Bristol and Tenby, Milford Haven, Pembroke and Haverfordwest and it set out on its final voyage at 7 a.m. on Tuesday, 15 March 1831. Some time that night she was wrecked at Nash Point, as described in an earlier chapter. A month later another paddle steamer, the *George IV*, continued the service.

Although Milford was a hub of activity by way of a maritime trade, they were keen to attract the transatlantic business. Piers had been built and a huge scheme to build docks abandoned in 1860s. But plans for the Hubberston Pill docks resurfaced in the 1870s and work commenced on the project, albeit behind schedule. When the new docks were opened, far from attracting transatlantic liners, the first boat in was the steam trawler *Sybil*, LT77, on 27 September 1888. Within a few years some fifty-five steam trawlers and 200 sailing smacks – mostly from Brixham – were based here. At the turn of the century the port gained its first steam drifters with the arrival of *Girl Daisy*, *Boy Fred*, *Cato* and *Favo*, owned locally, and within another year there were forty such vessels. By

1904 this had amazingly increased to 200 drifters. The first smokehouse was built in 1908, with four more coming after the impending war. By 1925 Milford Haven was the premier herring station in England and Wales, surpassing even Lowestoft, with 124,000 barrels being landed the previous year, 4,000 of which were even sent to the East Coast. In terms of landings, the port peaked in 1946 when some 59,000 tons were landed. Its fortunes declined thereafter except for a brief revival in 1963 when Scots boats landed 45,656 hundredweight of herring.

We walked along the harbourside, past the marina and the several building projects that were intended to breathe some life into the port. Several Belgium fishing boats were moored around the harbour, perhaps the remains of a link from when twenty-four Belgian trawlers worked from here after the German invasion of 1914. The Halls, before boarding a train back to London, their journey done, thought Milford 'is now in decay', but would be revived. And, as I sat upon a wall overlooking the waterway, with its oil refineries and tankers tied alongside jetties, and fishing boats in the harbour, I realised it was as if Nelson, Brunel, Grenville and those Nantucket Quakers, and the rest of those pioneers who invested in the town's future have been cast adrift from memory. I remembered the words of H.V. Morton when speaking of Nelson's memory being kept alive in Milford by a relic of the French battleship *L'Orient* that blew up at the Battle of the Nile: 'But Milford, generally speaking, cares less for this than for getting kippers to London in time for breakfast.' For no fishing port in Britain could 'turn a herring into a kipper quicker than at Milford Haven'!

DAY TEN

MILFORD HAVEN TO FISHGUARD

So it was goodbye to the Halls, as we lost them after they returned to London from Milford Haven. We were on our own then, dog and I – for now. We'd proceeded west of Milford Haven, past the former Esso refinery, construction of which had begun in 1952 but which closed in 1983, and on to Sandy Haven where Pembrokeshire's last seafaring family based their operations. It was here in the car park that I awoke that next morning, bright and early to blue skies and calm seas. After a quick brew up of coffee, dog and I headed down to the beach. There's another nice example of a limekiln here, which undoubtedly burned limestone from the nearby quarry. Crossing the stepping stones – and getting wet footpaws – we walked along the coastpath to Great Castle Head, passing Sleeping (which seemed like a good place to spend an afternoon in the sun), Butts and Longoar Bays. Across the water west of us was Watch House Point, upon which is a folly built about 1860 by a serving officer in the Crimean War. In the distance, Dale Fort Field Centre stood out clear.

Looking at Dale today, it's hard to imagine that this was once another of Pembrokeshire's busiest sea trading ports. It's been said it was comparable to Fishguard. Three vessels were based here in 1566 – the *Sondaie* and *Mary Motton*, both of eight tons, and a third nine-ton boat with no name given. All traded with Ireland and North Wales and went 'upp Severne afishinge'. This seemed to be the general pattern for the vast majority of boats listed in the 1566 report entitled 'Ports and Creeks of Wales in the Sixteenth Century'. Dale, at the time, had twenty households. Lewis Morris described the place as a 'ready Outlet for small Vessels'.

Piracy affected this coast as elsewhere and in 1609 the Lundy-based Thomas Salkeld raided Dale, making off with two laden ships. Oyster fishing supplemented an income for some Dale folk, and in 1810 there were seven small fishing boats between 13–18ft long. Boatbuilding must have been practised to supply these boats and in the 1850s two vessels of a total tonnage of 43 tons were built. In 1851 the census shows nine shipwrights and six apprentices. Dale's most notable export was, however, ale which was brewed under the name of Runwae and was in great demand in Bristol and as far away as London. However, all forms of trade seemed to die off in the eighteenth century for in 1748 the pier was described as having fallen into disrepair. By 1801 the village was almost deserted and ruinous, but today survives as a popular holiday and boating centre.

A couple of miles south of Dale is Mill Bay where Henry Tudor came ashore with his band of men in 1485 and fifteen days later triumphed at Bosworth to gain the crown by killing Richard III of York, thus beginning a dynasty that lasted up to the death of Elizabeth I in 1603. It has been suggested that in recognition of his victory he had a chapel built near Mill Bay at St Ann's Head. Permission for the first lighthouse to be built here was given in 1662 and it is thought that the tower of the chapel was used, making this the first medieval lighthouse in Wales. Charts published in 1663 show either one or two lights. In 1713 Joseph Allen, the landowner, was granted a ninety-nine-year lease to erect a tower and to levy dues on passing vessels, and later that century there were two towers upon which coal fires were lit and which served as leading lights. By 1800 two new towers had been built each with oil lamps, the lower of which was rebuilt in 1844, the basis of the present lighthouse. The high light remains standing, although it is now crowned with an observation box, which is used as a coastguard lookout station.

Any part of the coast is susceptible to oil pollution in these days of moving tankers around with shortened crews. Near refineries the risk is obviously increased as the vessel closes upon the shore. The result can be catastrophic. Although the area has seen numerous wrecks upon its coast, the one of February 1996 is fresh in many memories. The *Sea Empress*, with a cargo of 6,000 tons of crude oil, hit rocks below the West Blockhouse Point, spurting oil out into the sea. The damage done by emulsified crude oil affected the fishing industry for several years, not to mention tourism and bird life.

A few months before this tour I had walked with a friend along the coastpath from Dale to Marloes. The rock formation of Marloes Sands was incredible, especially the Three Chimneys where alternate layers of sandstone and mudstone stand vertically. There used to be a mill working closeby many years ago.

Today we drove to Martin's Haven, the base for the Marloes fishermen and from where the Skomer ferry departs. We'd missed the last twelve o'clock sailing by minutes. Instead dog and I walked over to the old coastguard lookout in the Deer Park. The island, the largest of the Pembrokeshire islands, lies a mile offshore and the clearness of the day gave us a fine view. Skokholm lies about two miles south of Skomer, which, too, was pretty clear, and out in the distance somewhere, seven miles west of Skomer, was Grassholm. Further out beyond Grassholm are the twin reefs of the Hats and Barrels and beyond that the most westerly point of Wales. This, sixteen miles out from Skomer, is the tiny rock of the Smalls, with James Walker's graceful lighthouse that dates from 1861. This is Wales' tallest lighthouse. However, the previous lighthouse on the site, built between 1775–77 by Henry Whiteside, is considered to be the first example of a piled-light in the world, certainly in Britain. The remarkable feature of this lighthouse – it's been described as bucolic – survived until 1861, at which time it was demolished when the new light became operational. Whiteside used the small village of Solva to assemble his light before sailing to the Smalls in 1775 with eight Cornish miners, a blacksmith and two labourers to erect it. They travelled back and forth each day until the structure, which contained living accommodation for three keepers and stores as well as the lantern, was complete. The new lighthouse, built from Cornish granite, which was dressed at Solva before being towed out to the Smalls on barges, was another amazing feat of engineering by James Nicholas Douglas.

Skokholm also has a lighthouse on its southwestern tip, which was first operational in 1915. This was the last tower of traditional construction to be built in Britain.

It had most definitely been my intention to catch the ferry out to Skomer although I later discovered dogs were not allowed there, as they aren't on any of these islands. I felt I ought to land on one of these outlying nineteenth-century communities, even if, from a maritime perspective, they are not particularly relevant; farming has been the traditional source of income for the families leasing them, with the exception of Grassholm which was never inhabited. It is said the only people who stayed out there were the Marloes fishermen when they went out lobster fishing and might camp on the island for a night or two.

The islands' names are Norse although it appears the Vikings only used them as navigational marks. The Normans weren't interested in them either. It seems that it was not until the nineteenth century that people realised they could grow and graze upon them. Not that they have ever been renowned for their over-fertile land, though! All the islands are now bird sanctuaries and part of the Pembrokeshire National Park. Skomer and Skokholm have farmhouses where visitors can stay although, presumably, one has to book in advance. I read somewhere that they limit numbers on Skomer to 100 at any time up to the end of July except for the spring Bank Holiday weekend. Skokholm can only be visited on a weekly basis and only one boat is allowed on Grassholm with day-trippers. These limitations are to protect the bird life, especially during breeding seasons.

Martin's Haven once had twenty fishermen working from its beach landing. It's a sheltered bay with a shingle beach but is exposed to the north. Much of the fishing has disappeared. Up the path from the beach is an old boat shed, now converted to an information centre, which was open and sold guide books and gifts.

St Brides Haven is a couple of miles along the coast and is a delightful place. Indeed, now that we are away from the populous areas of the coast, I find that all the little havens and villages are both tranquil and picturesque, especially after the summer crowds of southern Pembrokeshire. In 1566 there were estimated to be six households between here and the Goultrop Roads. In 1707 there was an 'Olde Cellar or Fishouse' and nearby a house built 'for the purpose of making fish and cellaring and keeping of goods'. Fenton tells us that:

> There was in former days a great fishery of herrings; and close on the shore a little raised above the beach stood a small chapel where the fishermen were used to put up their prayers for their successes and averting the dangers of the sea... out of the ruins of the chapel a salt-house for the convenience and use of the fishery was erected, and from that time the fishery failed, which occasioned the following distich:

> When St Brides Chapel a salt-house was made,
> St Brides lost the herring trade.

But an earlier chapel on the site was said to have been swept away by a storm. It was sited close to the remains of the limekiln. Lobsters and crabs were also fished due to their abundance all around the rocky coast.

Little Haven had a lifeboat station established in 1882 and the boat was kept afloat in a sheltered spot under Borough Head in the Goultrop Roads. A storehouse was built on the shore. In 1903 a new lifeboat house was opened complete with slipway on the eastern facing side off Borough Head. However, owing to the difficulty in obtaining a crew for the boat, the decline in inshore traffic and the fact that the St David's and Angle boats provided enough coverage, the station was closed in 1922. Today there's a Little & Broad Haven D-class inshore lifeboat on station housed in the car park in Little Haven.

Although all of St Bride's Bay abounds with smuggling stories, rarely is there ever any tangible evidence to support these. But on the beach known as The Settlands, which lies

Inkwell lobster pots at St Bride's Bay.

View of Little Haven, *c.*1910.

between Little and Broad Havens, and which is only accessible at low water, there's a hole in the rock. This is said to be the bottom of a passageway that leads up to the Haven Fort Hotel on the headland above the bay. This, it is said, was the route the smugglers used to carry their contraband away from the beach. The existence of a passageway – the entrance of which I entered – surely supports the possibility.

Invasion at Fishguard

The Norman invasion of 1066 is generally regarded as the date of the last incursion onto these islands. Prior to that came the Vikings, Saxons, Romans and Celts. The Spanish tried it in 1588 and the Germans contemplated it in 1941. Otherwise, to many Britons, nobody else has tried it, except perhaps the bureaucrats of Brussels. How wrong they are.

We all love to hate the French, our nearest neighbours. In 1789 the French Revolution instilled fear around the parliaments of many European capital; it also inspired movements towards the hatching of a dastardly plan between an Irishman, Theobald Wolfe Tone, and the French, represented by General Louis Lazarre Hoche. The plan, essentially, was for a French invasion of Ireland to free it from its British bonds, and then a full invasion of Britain could then be launched from the free Ireland. Once Ireland had been taken after landings on the West Coast, a two-pronged attack on Britain would be made. One group would land on the Northumberland coast and the other at Bristol. Once that town was ransacked, the marchers would move through Wales, freeing that country, before attacking Liverpool. If a landing in Bristol was impossible, then the French were to land anywhere along the Welsh coast. By mid-February all was ready.

But the Irish assault failed before it had started due to weather and argument. The Northumberland invasion was equally cut short by the weather. On the West Side, the French fleet of four ships was under the command of American adventurer General William Tate. Due to the weather Tate decided on a Welsh landing and on 22 February arrived off Fishguard, finally anchoring off Carreg Wastad Point on the Pencaer Peninsular, two miles from the town. That evening the troops began landing ashore. The last invasion of Britain had commenced.

The local militia was caught off guard and bewildered by an invading force of unknown force and calibre. The populace fled inland, leaving property and possessions. Most thought the French had sent their crack troops when rumour announced their arrival. This, though, was far from the truth.

By daybreak panic had gripped the area. Over half the French invaders had been busy looting open farmhouses, finding supplies of Portuguese wine that had previously come from a wreck a few weeks earlier. Hungry marauders, mostly convicts, got drunk or gorged themselves from local larders. Several were shot, as were a few of the militia. One local woman, Jemima Nicholas, the town cobbler who was immensely strong, captured twelve Frenchmen single-handedly. For this she was later granted a pension of £50 per annum until her death thirty years later. Mary William of Caerlem, on the other hand, was shot in the leg and raped by a party of Frenchmen. She was subsequently granted a pension of £40.

Because of their behaviour, no Welshman turned to aid the French who were either totally confused, drunk or out of the control of Tate – or perhaps all three. By the end of the day the locals had become defiant instead of fleeing. They were hell bent on joining the British to repel the invaders or capture them. Thus the French ships, with their plan in tatters, weighed anchor and cleared out, fully aware that British warships would be on their way to intercept them. But over a thousand French troops were left behind, frightened and with no means of escape, no plan and no back up. And probably a hangover!

Tate, who was on shore, sent in his second-in-command to negotiate with Earl Cawdor, who insisted on a full unconditional surrender. Thus the French agreed on any terms, on the morning of the second day after the invasion. The invasion was over. The invaders were

Photograph of the dog at the memorial stone to the invasion at Carreg Wasted.

marched off to captivity in Haverfordwest while the forty-five officers were taken to the Ivy Bush Hotel in Carmarthen, which is only yards from where I write this.

Witch-hunts attempted to find scapegoats amongst the local population such as those who dissented against English rule. Nothing was ultimately proven and the only outcome of the invasion was a full reappraisal of British defences. One effect was the opening of the Milford dockyard to increase the size of the navy. More recently, some historians are inferring that the truth of the invasion has been heavily exaggerated.

One final note. It has been suggested that because of the invasion there was a rush on the Bank of England whose cash reserves were low. Payments were stopped on Monday 27 February, four days after the invasion. One pound notes were introduced for the first time as a consequence.

In the eighteenth century Lewis Morris suggested a twenty-yard-long pier be built under Borough Head to assist the loading of coal boats. Nothing was ever done, though, and coal continued to be exported from the beach to Ireland, southwest England and other parts of Wales. Some was even exported to America. The pier, he also noted, could help vessels in distress due to the lack of any other shelter in this part of the bay.

The bishop of St David's (*Tyddewî*) wrote in 1595 that 'the sea-coasts nere about it [Milford Haven] yeld plenty of fish' in reference to the abundance of fish in these parts. Other than fishing, and smuggling and the coal export, tourism seems to have been the other occupation. With fine sweeping sandy beaches resorts such as Little Haven, Broad Haven and Newgale developed in the nineteenth century. Broad Haven was developed as a Baptist temperance resort. Given the fine weather of my visit, it wasn't surprising to find the beach almost overcrowded and the narrow roads congested.

Fenton tells us that, in 1810, the air at Broad Haven is 'remarkably salubrious, coming laden with salts wafted over St Brides Bay, and the sea being quite pure and unmixed'. Bathing machines could be hired on the fine hard sands although swimming from the 'retired coves under the romantic and high cliffs of Drewson' was just as desirable. Drewston was the local name for Druidston Haven, coming from Alfred Drue or Drew who settled here in the twelfth century, hence Drew's town. Two ambiguities, then, for there never has been a town here nor any Druid connection! Some 'gentleman' who came here year after year sailed their yachts around the bay and caught 'fish, turbots, soles, and doreys' for their tables, selling the surplus for 6*d* per lb. Today the place appears overwhelmed by a big hotel near to the beach.

Further up the coast is the tiny cove of Nolton Haven, described as a colliery portlet. To the east are the culm pits that appear to date to the sixteenth century which were simple holes dug down to the seams of anthracite and which were then enlarged. To the north of Nolton Haven the mines were at Trefane, close to the coast. A myriad of tramways brought the coal down by horse to boats waiting on the beach. Pembrokeshire's anthracite was reputed to be amongst the best in the world but the main reason for many of the mines being abandoned was the constant threat from flooding, especially as some of the workings were under the sea. The Trefane Cliff colliery remained working until 1905 and signs of the tramways and of the other mines can be seen in many parts. The nearby hamlet of Nolton whose stone, according to George Owen, was excellent for making grindstones and mustard mills, as well as windows, doors, arches, chimneys and other building uses because its ability to be hewn easily.

Newgale sands extended from Trefane to the northeastern corner of St Bride's Bay, a distance of over two miles. I took the dog out onto the sands at the southern extremity, away from any 'no dogs' signs. He swam while I threw sticks into the calm sea. But it is not always calm. Giraldus Cambrensis came along this beach on Thursday, 24 March 1172, during a storm that denuded the beach of sand exposing tree-trunks from centuries before which he described as being like ebony. The sea was so vicious that conger eels and many other sea fish were being driven up onto the rocks and collected by the locals. Leland notes the fresh water in the creek.

Ships also have floundered on this beach, sometimes helped along by those on shore. In 1690 the ship *Resolution* was wrecked here after being blown ashore and robbed 'by the more unmerciful people of the neighbourhood'. In 1754 the Dublin-registered *Margaret* came ashore and the customs stationed thirty men to protect the wreck from the local 'populace who appeared in good numbers with hatchets and other instruments of destruction'. Another vessel wrecked here was the *Prince* from Bordeaux on route to the West Indies with brandy and wine aboard. She was attacked by the British privateer *Liverpool* and somehow the *Prince* became lost in fog off Skomer. They anchored in St Brides Bay but a gale drove her inshore where she was deliberately beached at the southern end of Newgale sands. The brandy and wine was, it seems, shared out locally.

Solva (*Solfach*) is another of those treasured places that are almost best being kept secret. Says Leland, '4 Miles from Newgal upward on the Shore is Solvach, otherwise Solverach, a smaul Creke for Ballingers and Fischar Botes and hither resortith a little Fresch Water'. Leland also notes 'other litle Crekittes' between Newgale and St David's Head. Presumably a 'Crekitte' is the diminutive of his 'Creke', which sounds Spanish to me. In 1566, however, it is listed as having no households and yet was a port trading with Ireland. The first documented trade was in 1602 when the *Guift of Solvaugh* took a cargo of wheat and malt to Ireland, returning with timber, cloth and oar blades. Subsequent visitors all noted the sheltered harbour, although Lewis Morris thought it should be mended, presumably implying it was in a ruinous state in the 1740s. He also suggested the building of a marker on the headland to aid vessels with identifying the creek within the rocky coastline. This was one of many pieces of advice he propounded but which, it seems, were mostly ignored. Fenton notes the remains of an old pier, further substantiating Leland's claim.

By 1756 the town had its own prospering Trading Company with seven vessels which had increased to more than thirty by the beginning of the nineteenth century. The 'Trinity Quay' reflects the town's links with the Smalls lighthouse, as has previously been discussed. In 1814 Ayton described it as 'a small town, but in a very romantic situation, at the bottom of a deep, narrow, and serpentine valley opening at a distance of half a mile into the sea, which at high-water flows up to the town'. In 1869 a lifeboat house was built on the quay and the *Charles and Mary Egerton* placed on station. This lifeboat remained on station until the station's closure in 1887 when it was deemed that the entrance was too difficult to navigate during adverse weather. The boat was also unable to launch at low water, further aggravating delays in putting to sea so that the St David's boat would tend to reach a casualty first. The Little Haven boat, remember, was also on station at that time.

Smuggling was a popular pastime with salt being brought over from Ireland to escape the salt tax. Much of the activity was centred on *Ogof Tobacco*, a cave behind a little cove a little west of Solva. Here wine, brandy, perfumes, and spices, as well as salt, were brought in under cover of darkness. It is said that one of the local magistrates was sympathetic to this cause and often warned the smugglers prior to his inspection of their craft. The salinity of the water in Solva was significantly increased immediately before one of his visits. Probably he benefited from the odd case of brandy on his doorstep! Some of the salt was undoubtedly used to salt herring that was landed here at times, though the fishing fleet was always tiny in comparison to other havens along the coast.

Thus Solva's fortunes declined in the middle of the nineteenth century as the coastal trading business gave way to the railways, although the nearest station was several miles away. The warehouses fell empty and the sailing ships gradually disappeared, as did any passing fishing smack. Only a few small boats work lobster and crab pots otherwise they take out anglers on day trips. It's also a boating centre used by dinghy sailors and cruising boats.

The harbour at Porthclais, St David's.

Porthclais is another of these hidden coves. Built as the harbour to the religious community of St David's with its cathedral, a small fleet of herring boats was once based here. The harbour wall is reputedly Roman-built and in 1566 the harbour had a couple of boats of some 8 tons, with four crew members, that traded with Ireland and North Wales as well as fishing up the Severn. Timber was imported with corn, malt and wool leaving. Limestone was burnt here as early as 1384, with Pembrokeshire coal being used, probably from across the bay. Incidentally, I learned in Solva that there were once over 260 limekilns around the Pembrokeshire coast, Solva itself having eight in 1908. No wonder the fields of the county were so productive with so much lime being produced, even if it wasn't all spread about – the wind must surely have carried a fair amount over the land.

The island of Ramsey can be visited from Porthstinian – known locally as St Justinian's – when occasional summer trips take place at the discretion of the owner. Fenton crossed over from here in the very early 1800s. However, some say the best way of seeing the island is to take the daily boat trip around the island that sails from the lifeboat slip in the summer. Enquiries must be made prior to any intended trip from an information centre. Don't rely upon my information because it might change at any time. Ramsey was fairly productive, agriculturally speaking, when butter, cheese, corn, sheep and wool were brought over to the mainland until the last farmer left in 1968. Since then it's been left to the birds, which is why visitors are not encouraged.

Three miles beyond Ramsey lies South Bishop, the most southerly of the Bishops and Clerks, a collection of eight rocks that extend four miles north to the North Bishop. South Bishop has a lighthouse that dates from 1838 and is renowned as being Britain's longest serving unaltered lantern.

Porthstinian has been the home of the St David's lifeboat since just after the 32ft *Augusta* was first brought on station in 1869. To begin with, the boat was kept at St David's while the new boathouse was being built, and then it was moved to Porthlysgi where a temporary boathouse was built until the new Porthstinian came into use. This lifeboat station must surely be situated in one of the wildest and most secluded – and exposed – spots in all of Britain. Ramsey Sound is renowned for its reefs, especially the Bitches and the Whelps, and the area is full of shipwrecks. The *Gem*, the second boat, was itself wrecked on the Bitches in 1910 when it was launched to rescue the crew of the *Democrat*, which was in danger of striking the reef. Three of the lifeboat crew lost their lives although the three crew of the ship were saved. In 1936 the 46ft Watson lifeboat *Swn Y Mor* was brought on station and during its 27 year tenure, it was responsible for saving 108 lives, although one lifeboatman was sadly swept overboard and lost in 1956. The *Swn Y Mor* was eventually purchased by Warren Scott in 1980 and he and his wife subsequently, after a couple of years of preparation, sailed the boat 60,000 miles on a circumnavigation around the globe, visiting South America, the Caribbean, the East Coast of the United States, Chicago, through the Panama Canal to British Columbia and Alaska, across the Pacific to Australia, and back to Britain via the Suez Canal and the rivers of Europe. Some years ago I was lucky to be able to cover a lifeboat 'do' in Beaumaris from aboard this fine craft. She really is a lovely vessel, fitted out in every way possible for extended living with a feeling of safety inbuilt into a boat that really has faced all the perils of the sea – from operating in atrocious weather off the Welsh coast to travelling the seven oceans. I was hoping to visit the Scotts later on in this trip but subsequently heard that they had literally just sailed off again on a year's voyage to the Mediterranean and across the Atlantic and into the Pacific back to their favourite haunt – British Columbia.

From Porthstinian with its impressive lifeboat house – this was built in 1911 – and equally tantalising views over Ramsey Isle, we drove to Whitesands Bay (*Porth Mawr*), a magical expanse of sand just south of St David's Head. Several ships have been driven ashore here and the remains of the *Bolina*, wrecked in a storm in 1833 with two other vessels in the vicinity and the paddle steamer *Guiding Star*, blown ashore in 1882, can both be seen if the tide is right and the sand levels are down. We didn't linger on the beach because of a dog ban, much to his disappointment!

Moving north again we turned the corner of St David's Head and at last entered Cardigan Bay. The only way to the headland to view the fort, caves and burial chamber is by foot. Instead we drove to Abereiddi. This is an old slate quarrying settlement that was abandoned in 1904 when the sea broke through into the quarry. What remained was a 'blue lagoon' where several fishing boats are still based, although the entrance needs local skill in navigation. Remains of the quarry buildings and worker's cottages can still be seen.

Two miles north along the coast path is another hamlet that derives existence from slate quarrying. Porthgain, although originally a simple cove with a few fishing boats and the 'Sloop Inn' that dates from 1743, was developed after a lease to extract slate was granted in 1837. Stone was also crushed at a time when Britain's road building program was at its peak, with upwards of 40,000 tons being produced annually. The Company owning the rights – this changed many times – built the hoppers, tramways and housing for the workers so that the whole place, except the pub, was a 'Company' village. The

Porthgain Industries, early 1900s. (Courtesy Mervyn Jones)

slate was not of the best quality and much of the waste was made into bricks. The harbour was built around the middle of the nineteenth century and extended in the first few years of the twentieth. The whole enterprise was short-lived, however, and production ceased about 1931. The buildings fell into disrepair and would have been demolished if the Welsh Office had not scheduled them as worthy of preservation. Today Porthgain is a popular tourist destination with a pub, café, harbour, housing and various other amenities. I was reminded of a visit one wet winter's day, some months earlier, during filming aboard Scott Metcalfe's *Vilma*, a man and his boat that we shall come across in due time. But, as usual, we were in a rush for the day was progressing too fast and I wanted to get to Fishguard before dark. The dog sneezed as I started the engine!

Our next port of call was Abercastle where a pretty little cove was once 'a harbour for small vessels', according to Ayton, and home to its own fleet of limestone and slate carrying boats and where ships were built on the beach. In 1566 nearby Trefin had six households and in 1851 the census lists eight seamen, six seamen's widows and three wives of seamen away. Between 1790 and 1820 three vessels between 25–30 tons are recorded as having been built here. For such a small community it seems that it produced more than its fair quantity of seafarers who sailed worldwide in the eighteenth and nineteenth centuries. Coal was imported as elsewhere and locally made bricks were exported. Today, like all the other similar old havens along the coast, the beach is quiet to the sound of flapping sails, the caulker's mallet and the cry of men as they set out to sea. The shrill of the gulls is all that remains, save for the odd tourist, and the dog barking at his stick, of course!

We drove north again and parked up, almost into a hedge the roads were so narrow, and walked along some woods to the beach at Abermawr, the point that Brunel chose for his Irish ferry port after Fishguard was abandoned. How different this place would be today if he had proceeded. There would be none of this peace and solitude. Brunel's plan included the building of two breakwaters, a short one in the north extending westwards and a longer one from the promontory of Penmorfa extending over half of the bay. Inside of this was to be another pier for the vessels to load directly from the railway. Some of the visual remains of Brunel's work can still be found amongst the undergrowth.

From there we went north to Strumble Head, where the lighthouse sits on Ynys Meicel. This light, built in 1980–09, replaced an earlier lightship that was anchored in the south of Cardigan Bay. The pedestrian bridge over to the island was closed to the public so we motored eastwards to Llawnda, where we parked by a little chapel and walked over several fields to Carreg Wastad Point to have a look at the memorial to the last invasion of Britain. The Fishguard Bay Hotel was built before the railway arrived here and commands startling views over the bay from its high up position.

Goodwick was a tiny fishing harbour with an equally tiny stone quay until the railway arrived in the 1890s, albeit fifty years after Brunel had first planned to bring his railway here. This pier, according to Fenton, was built by two brothers from Devonshire (I've also read that the town was Barnstaple) by the name of Rogers, They built an oil-mill on the pier which was used more as a cover for illicit smuggling than for milling oil. But by 1906 the rail line had been improved, as it had previously been unable to cope with anything but slow trains, so that the Irish ferry terminal was transferred from Neyland, Fishguard being only fifty-four miles from Ireland. The old pier, then, and the mill were demolished to make way for the new deep-water harbour, the building of which

Goodwick pier and supposed smuggling shed.

involved the blasting of the cliff-face to create 27 acres of land, this rock then being used for one of the two piers and the new quay. The first three ships in service were all brand new – the *St George*, *St Patrick* and *St David*, the first built by Cammell Laird on the river Mersey and the other two by John Brown on the river Clyde. *St Andrew* arrived two years later. The port was officially opened on 30 August 1906. Because there was a twenty-five-minute time difference between Ireland and Britain, the sailing schedule had to differ by these twenty-five minutes, although this was equalised in 1914. There were two sailings daily to Rosslare, and two in the opposite direction. For a brief period transatlantic liners called in at the port, until the First World War destroyed any dreams the town's fathers had of becoming a major port. Today, along with Swansea, Pembroke Dock and Holyhead, it remains one of the main departure points for Ireland.

The Fishguard lifeboat is housed in Goodwick, at the far end beyond the ferry terminal. First stationed here in 1822, Fishguard is the oldest remaining lifeboat station in Wales. The 25ft-long, ten-oared boat was paid for by Lloyds of London (£50) and Thomas Evans, a retired Royal Navy Lieutenant and local Lloyds Agent. Not much is known about the boat, although there are various mentions of its launchings. By 1846 it had been withdrawn from service. An effort to purchase a new lifeboat was made in 1854 after many of the town's inhabitants watched a schooner being washed onto rocks under Dinas Head in a storm. In the following year the RNLI put on station a new Beeching-Peake lifeboat and built a lifeboat house at the top of Goodwick Bay. This has since been demolished but it was situated close to the anchor at the entrance to the ferry port. A No.2 lifeboat was opened in 1869 and a new lifeboat house built the following year. By 1908 the No.1 station had closed and another new lifeboat house and slipway built at Pen Cw. This was moved again in 1911 and in 1930, but subsequently remained until the present boat was moored afloat. One notable rescue of this lifeboat was in October 1910 when the *Gem* from St David's was lost. The *Charterhouse* set out in horrific seas to Ramsey Sound, sixteen miles away, 'to help their comrades'.

In Welsh, Fishguard is *Abergwaun*, 'the estuary of the river Gwaun', but it gets its anglicised name from the Scandinavian *fiskrgard*, literally translating to 'fish yard' and inferring a 'fish weir'. The remains of this can be seen just south of the new Goodwick Quay, and is clearly marked on the Outdoor Leisure Ordnance Survey Map as it was on Lewis Morris's map of 1748. Luckily the tide was down so I was able to follow the line of stones in the water. As I sloshed around for several minutes in the water, dog enjoying the chance for a swim, I suddenly realised that the evening was upon us and my stomach was starting to rumble and grumble. And so, with that in mind, we headed to Fishguard and the Bennett Navy Tavern for refreshment where there's 'entertainment every Friday at 9 p.m.', although I chose it not for this, but because of the model of the Fishguard lifeboat *Howard Marryat* in the window. Well, at least I went to the pub – wet dog stayed in the van!

DAY ELEVEN

FISHGUARD TO NEWQUAY

The quay at Lower Fishguard is a great place to wake up, especially on a Sunday morning and with the sun already climbed above the hill. I didn't note the time but I know it was late for the church bells were ringing. It was certainly hot inside the van again with the sun beating down and I reminded myself that exactly a week before I had been in Barry waking up late in an overheated van. Although Barry and Fishguard are less than a 100 miles apart, I mused that we certainly had covered some ground in a week. But I wanted to reach the river Dee by the end of the following week so I thought I'd better get my skates on. No lingering about in bed on a Sunday morning, even if, according to Morton, 'on the seventh day a hush falls over Wales'. He reckoned it was 'so deep and significant that you can feel it even in the country'. In these days of Sunday opening, his hush has turned into more of a loud din and dash to the shops!

Lower Fishguard was an important herring fishing station in the Elizabethan era. Leland described it as 'a little Haven, havynge a Resort of Shippis'. The port trade increased in the eighteenth century when the population grew to 2,000, many of these being listed as mariners and fishermen. Corn, butter, slates and cured herrings and pilchards were amongst the principal exports in 1792 when fifty coasting vessels were said to have been based here. Shipbuilding peaked during the period 1810–19 with one main shipyard famous for its schooners and square-rigged vessels.

Ayton noted that 'the fishermen have a small harbour for their boats, defended by a small pier'. Of the herring fishery he noted that its success 'is of the utmost importance to the people, for herrings form a material part of their subsistence throughout the year. On the first appearance of a shoal the interest of the county round is immediately alarmed, and on the morning of the first night of adventure, the returning boats are hailed by an impatient crowd on the Strand, and the number of herrings caught by John Morgan's or William Jones' boat are noised about the country with as much eagerness as the news of an Extraordinary Gazette'.

Richard Fenton attributes much of the development of Fishguard to his uncle, Samuel Fenton, merchant and shipowner. He had 'energetically raised Fishguard from a poor fishing village to a port whose shipping and trade were larger than any other South Walian port'. Part of this Richard Fenton accounts to his uncle having discovered that sardines and *Schadyn* were the same species and that *Schadyn* were not herrings although the Welsh for herring is *sgadan*. Presumably these fish were pilchards – or mature sardines – for Uncle Sam introduced to Fishguard 'the business of preparing these fish, and their fry or sprats, in the same way as the Spaniards did, and export[ed] them to Italy, N. Africa and other western lands' as well as, it seems, to the Baltic. The fish were also caught off the Irish coast where large fishing companies were formed. Fenton was the only person

Lower Fishguard from an old postcard.

to prepare them in the Mediterranean way. He built a tall, four-storied warehouse with cellars and racks for curing both herrings and pilchards. This is still standing by the road bridge and is used by the Sea Scouts as their headquarters under the name of 'Skirmisher'. Uncle Sam was also responsible for the pier at the entrance of the inner tidal harbour 'at his own cost'. However, some historians question the accuracy of Fenton's work and suggest he exaggerates his family's involvement in the development of Fishguard. Samuel Fenton died in 1796, at which time Richard inherited.

We walked to the fort at Castle Point, which was built in 1781 after the privateer vessel *Black Prince* had captured a local ship and demanded a ransom of £1,000 for its release. When the town refused, the privateer bombarded it, damaging St Mary's church and some houses. The fort became the headquarters of the Fishguard Fencibles, who fired alarm guns at the invasion but were then withdrawn. The fort was abandoned after the Napoleonic Wars and fell into disrepair. The view across towards the ferry harbour and the Irish coast (sometimes visible, I'm told) is superb.

Next we visited Dinas Island, a National Trust promontory with Pwllgwaelod, a sandy beach at the western side of the isthmus, and Cwm-yr-eglwys at the other. The pub at Pwllgwaelod, the Sailors' Safety Inn, dates from 1593 and always displayed a light to help vessels navigate across Fishguard bay. Herrings were landed at Cwm-yr-eglwys up to the nineteenth century. A lease of the island, dated 1825, demands, as well as £170 a year and '6 fat hens at Shrovetide', all the customs of herring landed by the fishermen. In return, the fishermen were able to erect 'poles for the drying of nets' on the foreshore 'as is the usual custom'. Slates were also shipped out from this once thriving cove. A huge section of the chapel that once stood by the shore was washed away in a great storm in October 1859 during which a total of 114 ships were wrecked off the Welsh coast. Only a tiny portion of it remains standing today. Between here at Newport are several sandy coves including Aber Rhigian, where Lewis Morris notes the presence of slate quarrying.

Parrog is the maritime hamlet of Newport (*Trefdraeth*) although both the bay and the sandy beach take its name from the latter. Both lie on the estuary of the river Nevern (*Afon Nyfer*), although the town of Newport, with the remains of its castle that date from 1191, is itself some way off the sea. In his *Report on the Harbours and Customs Administration of Wales under Edward VI* (1547–53), Thomas Phaer wrote that the estuary was a 'barred haven to serve a small ship with a westerly or northerly wind upon a string'. By 1566 it must have been a substantial port for there were twenty households, as many as Fishguard, yet only one boat was trading from the Nevern – the 6-ton *Savyour* owned and mastered by Owen Picton, who, with his three crew, traded with the now-familiar Ireland and North Wales and 'upp Severne afishinge'. Defoe found a good harbour with an active trade with Ireland. A cloth and woollen manufacturing trade was thriving in the sixteenth century.

Newport has been famed for its herring industry amongst other trades. In 1594 it was reported that this yielded 'greate commodite to the inhabitants of the towne and countreye thereabowtes'. In 1611 one John Owen complained in court that James Lewis had reneged on an agreement to 'supply five nets for herring fishing and to place them in the boat of Rees Lloyd, gent'. It seems that Owen and Lloyd were to fish together. Lewis Morris noted that, amongst the natural production of the town, herrings and other fish were, like corn and butter, in plenty and he added that between Fishguard and Newport 'they cure Yearly about a Thousand Barrels of Herrings'. By the beginning of the nineteenth century the fishing was in decline and by 1848, according to Samuel Lewis, 'a herring-fishery exists here but the demand is so inconsiderable that it is not productive of much benefit to the persons engaged in it'. Other than these items, slates appear to have been the other export of importance and Samuel Lewis added that this had become the principal trade by then. A quay was built at Parrog in 1825, even if the dangerous bar across the mouth of the river impeded its development. Imports, according to records, were bricks, coal, culm, limestone, tiles and manure. Shipbuilding, as elsewhere, was prolific from the eighteenth century onwards. According to Dillwyn Miles, in *The Ancient Borough of Newport*, John Havard and his son Levi were the most productive shipbuilders and, out of a list of fifty-four locally built vessels, all but ten were built by these two over a period from 1762 to 1842.

A lifeboat was stationed in a boathouse at Cwm, at the western extreme of the beach, but was abandoned by 1995 because of the difficulty in launching, which could only be done at high water. By the second half of the nineteenth century sea trade was well into decline and this gradually petered out with the last cargo arriving by sea in 1934. Although never served by a railway, its proximity to the line arriving in Fishguard in the later 1890s was largely responsible for this collapse.

Fishing for salmon and sewin using seine-nets was carried out in the estuary, where 19ft-long black-tarred boats were used with a net shelf at the transom. These were said to have all been built by the Aberystwyth boatbuilder David Williams, of whom we shall learn more later, and a seine was operated by five men. Several fishing stations (*ergyd*) were licenced along the beach and the nets were shot in a similar manner to those we set in the river Severn. It was said that the fishermen would not set out until Y Garreg Fach showed above an ebbing tide. In adverse weather some netting was practised on the river. Coracles were also working the river and the 1861 Special Commission allowed four coracles to continue, although these men were regarded as troublesome.

Northwards from Newport the coast is outstanding with splendid views and precipitous cliffs, occasional coves and little signs of habitation. Sights such as Pwll-y-Wrach (the Witches' Cauldron) and Ceibwr Bay are impressive but are only accessible to the coast-path walker, although the road does pass close to Ceibwr. But we drove straight to Poppit Sands, at the southern entrance to the Afon Teifi, where the dog could run wild on the expanse of sand although there was a ban in force in the western end of the beach. Here, too, is the new 1998-built Cardigan Inshore Lifeboat Station, although the port of Cardigan (*Aberteifi*) itself lies about one and a half miles upstream.

The first lifeboat was put on station in 1849 at Cei Bach, Poppit, where Oliver Lloyd of Penrhyn Castle had built a breakwater to house his yacht. Between 1850 and 1863 this boat saved fourteen lives and was replaced the following year with another boat that saved fifty-three lives before itself being replaced in 1883 by the *Lizzie and Charles Lee Clare*. In 1876 a new lifeboat house and stone slipway were built on the same site and these were renovated in 1881 and again in 1905. The pier itself was rebuilt in 1886 and made 200ft long. After saving a total of 136 lives, the station was closed in 1932 until an inshore station was established in 1971. Two years after its closure, Cardigan saw the biggest ship ever to be wrecked in its vicinity. The liner SS *Herefordshire* was under tow when it broke loose and eventually ended up on rocks on Cardigan Island. The four men aboard the ship were rescued by breeches buoy and the contents of the wreck later salvaged. These were then auctioned in the town so that many living there today still own relics of this, Cardigan's most famous of wrecks.

The road from Poppit follows the south bank of the river. We walked a little on the salt marshes by the Webley Hotel, viewing the half dozen or so fishing boats moored in the river. Further along is the Ferry Inn where presumably a ferry once plied across to the other bank. Then, almost immediately, we were in St Dogmaels (*Llandudoch*) where much of Cardigan's maritime activity was centred.

The monastery of St Dogmaels was founded in the early twelfth century and survived until being sold in 1537 and eventually demolished. However, around it, a small town grew up with a separate identity to that of Cardigan, just across the river, although the development of both is intertwined by the sea. Thus, by 1566 there were twelve households in St Dogmaels and fifty-five in Cardigan. Yet, the report continues, 'we have no shippe belonging to eny of the sayed havons crikes or landing places or eny other bottes or vessels other then smale shyppinge bottes conteyinge 4 or 5 tonnes apice wich use to fyshe apon the cost of the sayed shire [Cardiganshire] and do use non other trad and that chifly heringe physshinge after Michelmas; in everi of the sayed bottes duringe the fysshinge tyme are continually six or seven persons all fysshermen and no mariners'. From this we deduce that these coasts were only home to herring fishermen and any coastal trade was operated from outside of the shire. But this was soon to change.

In St Dogmaels much of the maritime activity was in an area known at the Pinog. Here ships were built, fishermen went fishing, and much of the lifeboat crew was drawn from, as were the majority of the Teifi river pilots. It has been said that St Dogmaels' men had been fishermen for centuries. It seems that in the winter they fished extensively for whiting and then in summer they fished the salmon. Two fish weirs are known to have been worked, one between Cei Bach and Trwyn Garreg-ddu and another at Traethgwyn. The latter belonged to the monks of the monastery. Later on, several seine-

Coracle fisherman with his family in a coracle at Cenarth falls.

nets were operated in the river, similar to those at Newport, although these were worked in pools in the river itself, rather than from the beach.

Defoe noted that the Teifi was 'very noble' and 'famous for its plenty of the best and largest Salmon in Britain'. Two coracle communities developed at Cilgerran and Cenarth where they have been used for fishing since at least the Middle Ages, and probably earlier. In his *The Scenery, Antiquities, and Biography, of South Wales*, B.H. Malkin noted that, 'The salmon on the Tivy is esteemed the most excellent in Wales; the principal

Coracles on the river Teifi.

fishery and a very abundant one is between Kilgerran and Llechryd'. He also adds that there is scarcely a cottage close to the great river, which doesn't have a coracle hanging by the door. Today twelve licences allow coracles to work the tidal section of the river below the Llechryd bridge but none are issued any longer above the bridge. Incidentally at Cenarth, beside the falls, the National Coracle Centre is well worth a visit between Easter and the end of October. Here coracle-making can at times be viewed, as can coracles occasionally be seen on the river. We didn't make the detour because I'd been there before, so it's best to check out their details before making a visit.

At Cilgerran there has been a salmon weir directly below the castle since the Middle Ages. In 1314 permission was granted for its reconstruction after it had interfered with the carriage of stone and timber to Cardigan Castle during Edward I's time. George Owen referred to it as, 'the chiefest weare of all Wales… built of strong tymber frames and artificiallie wrought therein with stone, crossinge the whole ryver from side to side and having six slaughter places, wherein the fishe entringe remayne inclosed and are therein killed with an iron crooke proper for that use'. Owen added that 140 salmon were once caught in this weir in one day and that these were 'most excellent, and for fattenes and sweetenes exceeding those of other ryvers'.

Cardigan has always had a commanding position on the banks of the Teifi, recognised by the Normans in 1093. The word itself comes from Ceredigion, the land between the Dyfi and Teifi granted to Ceredig by the Roman Cunedda after he had driven out the Irish in about AD 450. This was shortened by the Normans to first Kerdigon, and then to today's version. The early settlement gave them access to the rich fertile hinterland, fish-rich seas, and a good river crossing point as well as a good access into the Irish Sea.

The first bridge across the river at this point was built about the same time, although an earlier bridge existed further upstream. But, while the St Dogmaels men succeeded in surviving from the sea, Cardigan stood still until the Act of Union in 1536 when the English realm began to develop Cardigan Bay. When a Customs House was opened Cardigan took its first tentative steps to becoming the 'gateway to Wales', a title it was soon to gain.

Lewis Morris noted the 'King's Weare of Kilgerran' and the fine salmon fishery, and the considerable amount of barley, wheat, malt, oats and oatmeal that is shipped out through the town – about 50,000 barrels. To improve facilities, he suggested the building of a pier at Pen yr Ergyd at the mouth of the river, where today there is a boatyard and caravan site – but no pier! By this time, the maritime trade was fast developing in the town with shipbuilding, sail and rope making and other trades ancillary to seafaring thriving. As well as at the Pinog, shipbuilding gained importance at the Netpool on the Cardigan side of the river where many small coasting vessels were built.

All of a sudden, it seems, a trade in salted herring expanded between 1678 and 1709, with timber for the barrels and salt being imported from Ireland. In 1702 some 1,734 barrels were exported to Dublin while ships sailed regularly to Pickle Herring Wharf in London with cargoes of salted herring. Others sailed to Bristol, Wexford and Waterford. The same shipbuilders building the coasting vessels also produced the boats for the herring fishermen – 25–30ft open, clinker-built boats that displaced up to 20 tons and which were capable of carrying ten men and were either rowed or sailed. The most common method of catching was the drift-net although nets anchored in specific places were sometimes resorted to. Fishing was generally practised at night. The catch was then brought back and barrelled, although later it was either smoked or sold fresh around Cardigan or St Dogmaels, with the women of St Dogmaels acting in a similar way to the Penclawdd or Llangwm fisherwives in hawking the fresh fish, carried in baskets on their backs. In 1872 'Nansy Sgadan' and 'Nel Sgadan' were recognised sellers outside of Shire Hall. On average, a herring sold for ½d. Unfortunately for Cardigan, though, St Dogmaels completely took control of the herring fishery leaving Cardigan to thrive from the coasting trade.

The usual commodities were imported – coal, culm, timber, limestone and other requisites of the shipbuilding and fishing industries. As well as herring, slate and oak bark was exported. Several emigrant ships called in during the first half of the nineteenth century on their way across to America, taking locals with them. By the mid-century there were seventy-eight vessels employing over 400 men based in Cardigan.

But it was again the railway that was to bring about the fundamental change in transporting goods around Wales. Although several different plans had surfaced since 1845 to build a line, including one to take the railway across the Teifi to St Dogmaels and a new pier in a new deepwater port, a branch line running from Whitland was finally completed in 1885 and officially opened the following year. Sea trade declined accordingly although an attempt was made in the 1920s to revive its fortunes by the formation of the Teifi Steamship Company which survived for twenty years.

Our first port of call in Cardigan was at the Cardigan Heritage Centre on the Teifi Wharf. Moored in the river outside the centre is the Rye-built, Lowestoft-based sailing trawler *Keywaydin*, owned by Paul Welch, whom I'd met before, and his partner Jo. Luckily they were aboard when I arrived so I was able to share a cup of tea and a chat.

Fish Weirs

Early hunter-gatherer man probably first began to realize the benefit of fish as a resource for food by finding stranded fish in rock pools once the tide had receded. After that, all he had to do quite simply was wait and remove them. The obvious development from this was for man to add boulders from the vicinity around the pool to increase the catchment area. Next came the damming of the mouths of rivers. F.M. Davis, in *An Account of the Fishing Gear of England and Wales*, suggested that the earliest way of collecting fish was by 'stopping the mouths of narrow tidal creeks with brushwood or stones, through which the water would run off on the ebb tide, leaving the fish inside the barrier high and dry'. However, to encourage the fish to enter the weir, man next mastered the siting of the structures to take advantage of the current to force the fish inside and, secondly, to prevent their escape. Once he'd mastered this, all he had to do was increase the size of the structure, both in area and height, using timber poles bedded into low stone walls for the latter. Woven into this was wattle fencing made from hazel wood.

In Wales, these weirs are *gored* or *goreddau*. In Scotland, which has many examples of weirs remaining today, they are referred variably as *yair*, *yare*, *cairidh*, *doach* or *cruive*, the latter being lingistically close to what Davis refers to as the 'crew' of a trap – the catchment area that remains flooded on the ebb.

Documented evidence on the early use of fish traps is scarce but their antiquity is certain. Three traps excavated at the Late Kongemose site Agerod V in southern Sweden date to being older than 6,000 years. Danish finds have been dated to belonging to the Mesolithic and Neolithic times. In Britain, various fishing baskets and fish traps at Goldcliff have been observed in the minerogenic sediments and date around 4000–5000 BC. Another in Lough Beg, Northern Ireland, dates to before 1000 BC. In Britain, the first documented one is from an Anglo-Saxon charter for Tidenham on the Severn estuary and is described as a 'haccwer or hedge weir'. Excavations around the site of the second Severn Bridge have found evidence of hurdles belonging to weirs from the eighth century.

The oldest weir in Wales is thought by some to be the Gored Beuno, which has been recently dated to the thirteenth century. Others maintain that the Rhosfynach weir at Rhos-on-Sea is, being built by the Cisterian monks of Aberconwy in the late twelfth century. Some forty weirs in total have been identified in North Wales, and probably the same number in South and West Wales. Furthermore, a considerable number of river weirs once existed in the country. But for the sake of our classification of fish weirs, we shall confine this to saltwater weirs.

The first weirs were thought to be passive and 'v' shaped, although some at Whitstable, in Kent – the Snowt Weirs – were 'u' shaped. Usually a set of these weirs was built in a line, as in Swansea, with a basket at the apex to catch the fish. However, taking into account that weirs developed from rock pools, it follows that the earliest form was in a semi-circular form of stones with its ends turned towards the shore, thus forming a tidal pool where the fish gather in a cluster. Thus these passive weirs work simply by the twice-daily ebb and flood of the tide. In Scotland such structures were deemed to be the 'simplest and cheapest mode of fishing that can be devised', according to the Old Statistical Account of the late eighteenth century. They also seem to be the most common type from surviving examples throughout England, Scotland and Wales. Sometimes the shape is altered because of certain topographical elements, but the theory is the same.

Active weirs, by their very nature, have to be designed with the flow of the current in mind and the earliest seem to be rectilinear in shape. However, many Welsh examples exhibit a different shape, such as those on the Menai Strait. Two weirs on Ynys Gored Coch rely simply on the tide rushing straight through the weir and are almost 'v' shaped.

Estuarine weirs, such as the Gorad Alaw, are sometimes built parallel to the river and work by the tendency of the fish to swim towards the shore when running downstream.

The final group, semi-permanent weirs, come in all sorts of shapes and sizes. In Germany, a weir on the Schei fiord is still worked. Every year posts are driven into the seabed from a barge to form a shallow 'v', with a hoop-net attached at the openings. Willow is used to form the barrier, and the whole structure is removed at the end of the season. Davis notes in 1936 that an old man 'within the memory of the present generation…used to build small temporary stone weirs at Aberdaron'.

Today fish weirs are banned from use, due to their tendency to be extremely unselective in what they catch. In fact they used to land all sorts of fish, from herring and whitebait to salmon and bass. The only one in working order is one on Ynys Gored Coch, although the gratings have been removed to allow the fish to escape. However, the remains of them can be seen all around the coast. Locating them and understanding the way they worked gives an interesting insight in the way coastal folk used to live. It is to be recommended.

Remains of weir at Goldcliff.

The weir at Ynys Gorad Coch, Menai Strait, with Stephenson's Britannia Bridge behind.

They'd bought the boat in Malta several years previously when she was not in too good a state. They'd eventually sailed her home, where, after a hell of a lot of work, time and energy (not to mention money) they'd got her into her present good state. During the summer they'd worked out of Brixham, from where several smacks of this size do charter work to earn their keep. Having just returned back, they were in the process of planning to lay her up as their winter home.

The Heritage Centre, with an entrance fee of £2, is well worth a visit for it tells the story of the port's growth in much more detail than I've given. W.J. Lewis's *The Gateway to Wales* is the definitive publication on the town and, I noted, was on sale at £5.50. Shame I already had a copy because it is worth every penny. Sensing an opportunity for a good photograph, I walked over the bridge for a shot of boat and centre, and, unwittingly, stepped into Ceredigion without realising it. A brief walk around the town followed before returning to the van and driving out to Gwbert. Here the Cliff Hotel was built in the desire to harness a tourist industry but the scheme failed to develop Gwbert into a bustling centre with planned promenade and all the other trappings of tourism. Today it remains a quiet spot with fantastic views, several bungalows, the hotel and campsite and a certain amount of real peace. Cardigan Island itself is owned by the West Wales Wildlife Trust and, as such, access is prohibited and it is inhabited solely by a flock of wild Soay sheep – and some birds, I'm sure. On rocks below the nearby Farm Park, a colony of Atlantic Grey Seals breed in the caves, while offshore sometimes Bottle-nosed Dolphins can be seen, for Cardigan Bay is home to the only resident population of these mammals in English and Welsh waters. West of here there's a fine beach at Mwnt where limestone was once burnt. East of here the coast is pretty inaccessible and impossible once the Ministry of Defence radar station on the outskirts of Aberporth is reached. Cribach Bay, according to Lewis Morris, was 'much frequented by French Privateers in Queen Anne's war' and, as such, he advised the building of a small pier

Seine-net fishermen at Gwbert.

'with a very inconsiderable Expence', which would be of great use to the Herring-fishery'. Nothing ever came of his advice.

Aberporth is another extremely pleasant village nestling on a bay of the same name. In actuality it consists of two sandy bays (*Traeth y Plas* and *Traeth y Llongau*) with an expanse of sand at low tide, the westerly beach being dog-free while they were free to run on the other. And dog did just that, running with two other black dogs into the surf, chasing sticks and generally woofing around like dogs do, while I wandered over to photograph what appeared to be what is termed an Aberporth herring boat. Unfortunately it turned out to be a fibreglass boat, but I was sure the shape was so similar that it must have come from a mould made from the old wooden type so used by the fishermen of this place. In English this beach was the 'Ship Beach', because of its gentle shelving nature, and was the beach used for landing both goods and fish.

For Aberporth was once a place of seamen and fishermen. Back in 1566 it was identified as a 'crike' but the village never developed as a harbour. Boats always worked off the beach while the sea was wrapped up in the daily life of each and every of its inhabitants. It was quite common for a man to go to sea for nine months of the year and to return in the autumn for the herring fishery, such was the strength of this fishery. Some seamen worked locally which meant that the winter was a time to repair and fettle their craft, while others went deep-sea, travelling to all four corners of the globe aboard Welsh ships. Come September, and the excitement of the herring fishery would descend, as would the returning seadogs eager to supplement their annual income with three months fishing. Their herring nets were set in specific places, avoiding strong tides and rocky seabeds, and in many cases they fixed them to the seabed. These places had names such as *Fathgarreg*, *Cribach*, *Penpinfach* and *Pentraeth-bach* and this method of fishing was known as *tranio* or *setin* while drift-netting was *drifio*. The latter was usually carried out on the ebb so that they drifted as far as Cardigan Island, returning to Aberporth on the flood.

The boats were similar to those at Cardigan, 25–30ft long and strongly built to work directly off the shore. Later in the nineteenth century carvel construction gained favour. Boats were rigged either one or two lugsails although this was later altered on some boats, with a gaff main and sprit-rigged mizzen being preferred. Similar boats worked all along the coast from Fishguard in the south to Aberaeron, to the north. I was lucky to find several superb photographs of these boats, and other aspects of village life, in the Ship Inn. 'We found them in the attic and had them re-framed when we took over the pub', the woman behind the bar told me as she poured my pint. We sat a while, dog and I, at a table outside, overlooking the bay whilst I pondered on the various aspects of the maritime trade on this coast, while all around us the ever-present bustle of the summer trade continued. How complete opposites these small coastal communities are these days from their former seafaring times. Yes, I realise this is something that has been obvious from the moment this tour began, but somehow the metamorphosis of these tiny, inaccessible places is far more reaching, so more relevant, to the misled way we are leading out lives today. This place is far away from the excesses of the modern world – fat cats and football players earning ridiculous money – and it's a world apart from political spin and the unjust Iraqi war. It should be tranquillity at its best yet amongst the bustle there is an almost tangible sadness. It's as if a cloud hangs over, disguising the past as if there is some disgrace in it. If it wasn't for those pictures in the pub then the only

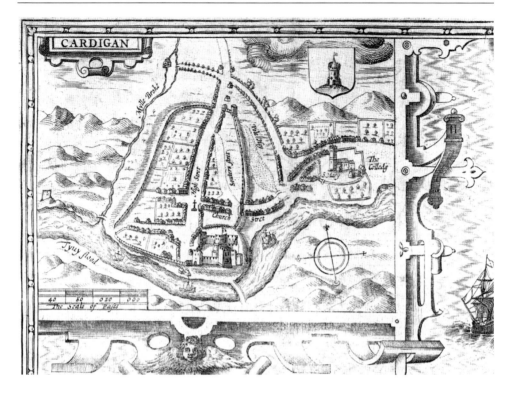

Postcard plan of Cardigan.

reminders that this beach was the busiest in Cardigan Bay by way of the herring trade
would be gone. Nobody really cares, let's face it. They are more interested in themselves
in this consumer-led society than in real people. I downed my pint before I depressed
myself too much. Dog looked at me with his peppercorn eyes as if to say, 'Don't worry,
I do take an interest in very real and valuable things such as rabbits and squirrels!'

   The beach of Tresaith is less than a mile to the east, and its past mirrors that of
Aberporth, although inhabitants were few. Practically all the residents were once involved
in the herring trade, helping with the landing, the net mending, boat hauling and the
carrying away of the booty. Each family salted down herring for their winter and spring
food. Some say it was a break from the monotony of salted meat and root vegetables. It
probably became a survival food for the poor months when the fields were naked. Then
came tourism and its one-time label of 'The Second Brighton'. It might have been
popular as a destination, but certainly not that popular! Today the beach is quiet except
for a several groups of sunbathers and swimmers, and a couple of folk in the Aberporth
Surf Life Saving Club. In a few days the annual Tresaith to Aberporth swimming race
was to be held and all were welcome. This was a tradition handed down, for the first
regattas were held in 1909 at Aberporth to create swimming races, boat races and other
seaside games after the advent of tourism. Offshore, the Cardigan Bay SAC (Special Area
of Conservation) was home to dolphins and porpoises, as was the Pen Llyn a'r Sarnau
SAC. Dogs were banned from the left side of the beach. At Penbryn they were banned
altogether. Yet still, three beaches once the most busiest and profitable of Wales' herring
fishery. It's just so bizarre, I thought!

Llangrannog is somehow different. Yes, of course, here was the proverbial partial dog ban on the beach and dozens of visitors milling aimlessly about, but Llangrannog retains an element of industry, unlike Aberporth, thus reflecting a portion of the past.

Herring reigned supreme here again in the autumn, with salt coming from Ireland and salted herring being exported all over. In the words of Geraint Jenkins, 'Llangrannog is a creation of the sea' for the youth of the village would help with the fishing so that they would soon go off to sea. The inhabitants looked towards the horizon for their living and not back up the valley. Thus, by the middle of the eighteenth century, a seafaring tradition had become firmly established in the village. Of course, there was the piracy so notorious on this coast, and the smuggling too. Howell Harris, the Methodist Revivalist, preached of 'the wickedness of stealing wrecks, cheating the King of things excised and their inhuman behaviour towards ship-wrecked sailors'. The latter I find hard to accept because it's rare to uncover a maritime people without respect for those brothers in trouble. But cheating the king – that's like cheating Gordon Brown, and by the way governments tax us, in my mind they are the cheats. Smuggled salt was the most common commodity after the price rose with the Salt Tax. In 1750 salt was costing 4*d* a pound in weight. The same salt cost just 1d across the water in Ireland. Why pay that when smuggled salt cost only 2*d*? That's the same as why pay £8.50 for a pouch of tobacco when it is just as easy to find it for £4? As I said, it's the Chancellor of the Exchequer who's the thief here, not us!

So the coastal trade developed as the list of Llangrannog ships grew. Some of the ships were built on the beach or on neighbouring beaches. Jenkins lists fourteen vessels built in the village between 1787 and 1859. Most were registered in Cardigan or Aberystwyth and traded over an area extended from Somerset, Devon and Cornwall up as far as

Vessels unloading on the beach at Llangrannog.

Lancashire and the river Mersey. Many sailed over to Ireland and a ferry service operated between the village and Dublin for many years. Limestone and culm were the principal imports into the village, along with goods such as slates, pottery, bricks and household items. Exports were few as a small village is largely without local produce. Any surplus butter or corn might be sold off, and in the herring season barrels of salt herring were shipped over to Ireland or South Wales.

But again, the decline in the maritime trade in the late nineteenth century affected Llangrannog as it has elsewhere. Gradually the fleet shrank as the railways took away their business. Most trade was directed to far off places aboard bigger ships, which resulted in the village people being away at sea for longer periods. Some left altogether, taking their families with them. The herring, too, disappeared in their droves. So, as the beach emptied, so did the houses, only to be filled with tourists. But, somehow the way Llangrannog straggles down the valley, the way the houses stand, some fronting the sea, some at right-angles, and the way the place retains an air of expertise, this small coastal village will continue to charm, yet at the same time act as a reminder of a lost way of life. The tradition might have died, but its memorials still stand.

Vessel being unloaded at the pier at Newquay, *c.*1890.

Cwmtydu is a tiny cove along the rocky coastline towards Newquay, yet it seems to have thrived on both the herring and smuggling, with French brandy being another of its main 'free-trade' goods. Limestone must have been imported for local use for there is a limekiln. Ships, too, were built in this inaccessible and uninhabited place. In 1784 the 35-ton sloop *Ledney* was built here, as was the equally sized *Hope*, which completed in 1814.

Newquay (*Ceinewydd*) was said to have been the centre of the smuggling trade along this coast. I guess it's got that typical smuggling air, so common in quaint Cornish villages. Sloping streets, narrow accesses, stone harbourside quays, a beach with steep steps and an out-of-the-way setting. It was busy when we arrived, very busy, with queues outside the ice-cream parlours and streams of people wandering along the harbour wall. The little beach just west of the pier was open to dogs so he went swimming while I watched. The smell of the sea was great, all seaweedy and damp. Brightly coloured housing lined the hill above. We walked back up the hill and down to the harbour, passing the Newquay Heritage Centre that was only open on Saturdays and Sundays, 12–4, which was unfortunate. Inside of the pier, lobster boats mixed with dozens of pleasure boats. Two vessels, the *Ermol 5* and *6*, were running trips lasting between twenty minutes and two hours out into Cardigan Bay. According to the blurb, Winston Evans 'started crewing for his father on the Ynys-Enlli' which was running similar trips back in the 1950s. And behind the inner quay is the present lifeboat house with its Mersey-class offshore boat and inflatable inshore lifeboat.

The lifeboat was first brought here in 1864, stationed in a boathouse above the main pier. This now houses the public toilets where I'd just been. In 1904 this lifeboat was moved across the harbour to its present site behind the small pier. The present building that accommodates both boats dates from 1991.

Few of the hordes, though, will realise how proud a maritime history this village has, especially if the heritage centre is rarely open! In early times herrings were landed here, and in 1795 it was described as a place of 'infamous notoriety' for giving shelter to vessels engaged in smuggling brandy and tobacco which was later disposed of at Lampeter and Tregaron. Evans described it as 'a shelter of a nest of smugglers, who have several vessels of burden here; indeed, the principal trade of this coast appears to be contraband or illicit'. But it is for shipbuilding that this place really gained its reputation in later times.

Although this trade did not begin here as early as other coastal sites, it did develop into one of the main shipbuilding centres in the southern part of Wales. At the beginning of the nineteenth century, the village was hardly more than a few thatched cottages, but the beach was sheltered enough to build a pier, which had been completed by the late 1830s. Within a few years ships were being built in three areas: at Newquay itself, on Traethgwyn, the small beach I'd been on and at nearby Ceibach. Up to 300 people were engaged in the industry and well over 200 ships were built over a period of about forty years. By the 1870s the bubble had burst. But what set Newquay ships apart from others from this coast was, other than the number of vessels built, the fact that some were large ocean-going ships as against coasting vessels. Furthermore, there were at least half a dozen blacksmiths, three sail lofts, three rope walks and a foundry, all engaged in the ancillary trades necessary to shipbuilding. Timber came from Cardiganshire, Carmarthenshire and Brecon, brought in on carriages drawn by up to eight horses. This was sawn in pits above the beach and the boats built close by. Today, though, it's nigh on impossible to imagine such activity: the sight of these large ships growing day by day, the sound of caulking mallets or the smell of freshly sawn timber. The inhabitants must surely have breathed the sea deep into their lungs, for their whole lives revolved around the sea. Even after shipbuilding ceased the majority of the male population went off to sea and Newquay men captained many ships around the world. Until that, too, came to an end. For a much more detailed and comprehensive report on the subject, the reader is pointed towards 'Shipbuilding at New Quay, Cardiganshire, 1779-1878' by Susan Campbell-Jones in *Ceredigion, the Journal of the Ceredigion Antiquarian Society*, vol. vii, 1974/75, No.¾.

Newquay appears as a sleepy coastal village, proud of its connection with Dylan and Caithlin Thomas who came to live here in 1944. Much of the influence for *Under Milk Wood* came from the village, so that we can possible transpose my previous comments of Laughaurne to Newquay. There were once twenty-four inns here catering for the hundreds of maritime workers. Today there are far less, but these serve the tourists, who largely keep this place alive, and the locals. The fishing boats thrive in a trade of lobsters and crabs, most of which is exported to continental Europe. In winter it's quiet, shrouded by the winter weather and emptiness, and a nicer place in my mind. Nevertheless, you can't beat the fresh smell of seaweed, the sight of brightly painted houses overlooking the sea and the sounds of history echoing around the cliffs that only summer can bring. I was glad to be staying the night here!

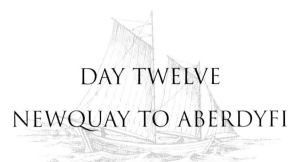

DAY TWELVE
NEWQUAY TO ABERDYFI

We drove to Ceibach for an early morning swim. The beach was deserted save for us, and the warm velvety water sparkled around me as I watched the sun climb over the hill. This was almost paradise I thought, as I swam naked, selfishly letting the water cleanse my mind and seduce my senses. After twelve days my mind and body were in need of a thorough purification from the dust and debris of both the historical data I'd gathered in my brain and the normal day-to-day life on the road. The water really did feel smooth and glossy as I dived into its murky green depths, taking its medicinal effect deep into my lungs. While I thrashed around enjoying these moments of freedom the dog stood knee-deep at the water's edge, refusing to come in until I was back out. Only then did he swim for his sticks while my every pore tingled in excitement as I stood by the sea, drying with an inadequate towel. Time to go for soon the visitors would be upon the beach.

At one time the 'new quay' was going to be built here until they chose Newquay. In 1566 'Lanina' was noted as being a creek and later herring were landed here. Shipbuilding, as we learned yesterday, thrived here, the earliest documented ship built being the *Betsy* in 1805 while the biggest was the three-masted barque *Syren* at 291 tons, built in 1887. Four limestone kilns once were worked close to the beach, serving the hinterland with lime for agricultural use. According to local folklore, a mermaid once lurked around Llanina Point, basking in the sun on the rocks. When once entangled in fishermen's nets, they freed her and she warned them of an impending storm. Seems an improbable story, not for her being a mermaid, but why she should warn the fishermen who obviously nearly killed her! We didn't stay too long, having parked illegally, and passed the Thomas' house on the way back towards the main road, then heading north once more.

Dylan Thomas also frequented the pubs in Aberaeron in the 1940s, during the time he and Caithlin lived at Tal-sarn. He once called the Aeron valley 'the most precious place in the world', presumably after one of the walks he was also known to enjoy.

The town of Aberaeron only dates back to the early nineteenth century, although previously it existed as a small settlement as far back as 1145. In 1551 Thomas Phaer found that this coast had 'no trade of merchandise but all full of rocks and dangers'. Yet fifteen years later there was 'a small Crike or landinge place at Aberayron within the lordshipe of Aberayron John Lloyd esquier, and Mathew ap Owen beinge coheyres and owners of the same'.

The coastal trade and the herring fishery rapidly developed here in the late seventeenth century. Lewis Morris noted a total of thirty-eight small sloops fishing from Aberdyfi, Borth, Aberaeron and Newquay. Two vessels, it is said, began the coastal trade from Aberaeron in 1698 – the *Lyon* and *Hopewell*, bringing in salt and coal. By 1750 grain, cured herrings and lead-ore from the mines at Llanfair Clydogau, near Lampeter, passed out through the creek. Thus the hamlet grew by the beginning of the nineteenth century with an inn run by a Mrs Felix and another, less salubrious, tavern frequented by herring fishermen. A local brewery supplied both with ale. When Richard Ayton arrived in 1814 with William Daniell, they found 'a very comfortable inn' which they reckoned was the only one along the coast between Cardigan and Aberystwyth. One can only suggest that Dylan Thomas would have been equally at home in them all!

The land surrounding the creek was owned by the Reverend Alban Thomas Jones Gwynne who obtained an Act of Parliament in 1807 to build two piers at the mouth of the river. Construction of the harbour, warehouses and the town followed. Most of the materials needed were brought in by sea – slates from North Wales, timber from Canada and the Baltic, limestone and culm from Pembrokeshire, pottery from Flintshire and general supplies from Bristol. By 1850 the Georgian town consisted of well-laid-out streets lined with uniform Regency-style houses, a new tidal harbour, an inner harbour (Pwll Cam) and a fleet of up to sixty herring boats. One report described how 'several hundred strange boats came for the fishing' during the autumn season. Shipbuilding, too, flourished during the latter half of the nineteenth century with at least sixty-seven vessels being built including thirty-five schooners.

But, again, it was the railway that resulted in the ultimate demise of the coastal trade. By 1867 the Cambrian Railway line from Aberystwyth to Carmarthen had been completed, with a stop at Lampeter, from where goods could be carried to and from. Even though the Aberayron Steam Navigation Company had been formed in 1863 to maintain a cargo run by sea, followed by the Aberayron Steam Packet Company in 1877, much of the trade was diverted to the railway. The *SS Ianthe*, and later the *Norseman*, continued the milkrun to Bristol, calling in at Newquay, Fishguard and Solva, and a subsequent service to Liverpool on the *SS Telephone* commenced in 1895. However, once the railway arrived in Aberaeron in 1911 none of these steamer services were able to compete. Seven years later the Steam Packet ceased so that only a handful of ships visited the port each year. With the sailing of the steamer *Drumlough* from the port in August 1934, centuries of sea trade were at an end. The harbour was left to the mercy of pleasure craft although some commercial fishing boats remained. Ironically, the railway itself was closed by the Beeching axe in 1963.

Today, though, the town was a bustle of activity with the gaily painted buildings shining in the bright sunlight. Visitors crowded the streets and sunbathers lay on the stony pebbles of the south beach. No dogs were allowed on this beach. The caravan sites heaved under the summer pressure. Even the second-hand bookshop I often call into was hectic. We walked around the harbour admiring its variously painted houses facing the dozens of pleasure boats sitting in the mud at low tide. Various establishments supplied the tourists – a sea aquarium, fish shop, information centre amongst these – while the former harbourmaster's building was now a hotel! Still, Aberaeron, changed as it is from its earlier grandeur, is a pleasant spot to wile away a few hours.

A mile north of here is Aberarth, a small village nestling on the banks of the mouth of the river Arth. This is one of the earliest settlements in Ceredigion. On the beach below the village are several examples of fish weirs. Over the years that I've been compiling my collection of fish weir surveys, I've found eight to date on the beach here but, according to Evelyn Lewes in *The Goredi near Llanddewi Aberarth, Cardiganshire* (in Arch. Camb. Series 7, 1924), there were twelve fish traps in use between the Aeron and the Arth in about 1860, only six of which were still being operated in 1896 and two by the 1920s. These, she continues, were the property of Rhys ap Gruffydd and were offered to the monastery of Strata Florida in 1184. In reality they probably existed centuries before that for, in *Hanes Taliesen*, a weir of the sixth century is mentioned thus: 'Ac yn yr amser hwnnw yr oedd Gored Wyddno yn y traeth rhwng Dyfi ac Aberystwyth'. Aberarth was known as the port for the monastery while, in the nineteenth century Evan Jones was building ships at the mouth of the Arth until a great flood wrecked his yard in 1846 and he subsequently moved to Aberaeron.

Two miles north-east of Aberarth are the remains of two further weirs at Llanon, at the mouth of the Afon Cledan. Just to the north, the Afon Peris emerges at Llansantffraed (named after the patron saint of milkmaids) where ships were built at the Peris Yard until its closure in 1865. Fifty-five vessels were built here, where there are also the remains of a wooden quay. In 1566 this was described as 'a landinge place'. A brewery, mill and limekiln were once working here. Nearby Llanrhystud – a village of mud-built cottages according to the Reverend Evans – lies approximately a mile upstream of the mouth of the Afon Wyre and is named in the 1566 report as a small village. Shipbuilding also flourished at this river mouth as well as there being four limekilns and a quay on the shore below the kilns.

Aberystwyth has been described variously as the 'Brighton of Wales', 'Biarritz of Wales', 'Athens of Wales' and even the 'St Andrews of Wales'. These all bear reference to its two greatest assets – its tourism and university. None of the descriptions, though, are in my mind valid. I spent two years studying at St Andrews and see no resemblance. I have a house in Greece and see no likeness to Athens. I've been to both Brighton and Biarritz, and see little comparison. Yet this is not to denigrate Aberystwyth for it has its

'Mixed bathing at Aberystwyth', 1911.

The beach at Aberystwyth during the summer season.

own charm and characteristics that do not warrant any such comparisons. The town is simply unique in that its great university happily sits alongside a thriving visitor trade, unlike elsewhere. After all, what scholar could refuse to study at a place sandwiched between a cool seascape and a dramatic landscape? Morton's double life of the town he refers to doesn't relate to its boarding houses, inadequate pier, railway posters, half-moon of blue shingle or its being the oldest university town in Wales, as he says. To me, its double life is quintessentially relative to its history.

Here, in the middle ages, was the very epicentre of the Welsh herring fishery. The Chronicle of the Princes (*Brut y Tywysogyon*), written about 1206, informs us 'that year Maelgwn ap Rhys built the castle of Abereinion. And then God gave an abundance of fish in the estuary of the Ystwyth, so much that there was not its like before that'. That's the 'Red Book of Hergest' version while the 'Peniarth MS20' version is slightly different: 'In that year there came to the estuary of the Ystwyth such an abundance of fish that their like was never heard of'. A subtle difference between each, maybe; both are from 1950s translations, but with the latter omits highlighting God's help.

In 1302 fines handed out to fishermen for selling herring below the high-water tideline are documented. The fishermen did this to escape paying market tolls. Others were fined for not having the requisite licences for their boats. The rights of the Crown had to be acknowledged by these fishermen whose normal arrangement was to pay five score herrings each time they went out to sea. This later became an annual payment of £1 10s (£1.50), and became known as a 'Pryse, or castle, maes of herring' – hence 'prisemes'. Later, when the Nanteos family held the lease, the first herrings caught in the bay each year were sent to the Nanteos estate which is about three miles southwest of the town. Later that century there were twenty boats of four or five tons working out of the creek.

In 1561 Thomas Phaer found 'a barred Haven of no Valewe, the Mayor of the town claymeth the port'. Five years later things hadn't altered much for the creek was still 'a havon or landinge place at Aberstwyth beinge a bard havon liinge within the jurisdiction… of the port towne… wherin shippes and vessels reparinge to the sayd port were acostomed to lad and unlad…'. Some three or four score households inhabited the place with an equal number of decayed dwellings. It appears that all those involved in making a living from the sea were fishermen and there were no mariners as such. The fact that I would call fishermen mariners is of no consequence it seems.

The town continued to be an important herring station throughout the seventeenth and eighteenth centuries, with herring tithes of about £1 being paid for each boat in the harbour. The list of tithes paid in September 1730 clearly states that there were twenty-four vessels that paid up. These boats had typical English names such as *Success*, *Maria*, *Hopewell*, *Providence*, and *Dove*. Eighteen years later Lewis Morris found fifty-nine sloops working out of the harbour, as well as the aforementioned thirty-eight from the neighbouring havens. Fishing lasted from September for three or four months. Throughout the rest of the year the men were employed in the coast and Irish trades, with larger sloops carrying lead ore, timber and bark. The fishermen obviously had become mariners in a short period! Most of this oak bark went to the Irish tanning industry.

The majority of the lead ore exported from Cardiganshire passed through the port. Both Leland and Defoe had noted this trade, Defoe describing the place as being 'enrich'd by the Coals and Lead which is found in its Neighbourhood, and is populous, but a very dirty, black, smoaky Place… however, they are Rich'. The chief factor delaying the expansion of the any trade within the harbour was the bar, which became more of a hindrance as the size of vessel grew. According to Morris it was 'often choaked up, so that the smallest of Vessel can neither pass nor repass; and all the Vessels in the Harbour are obliged to lie there, till a Land-flood from the rivers Rheidol and Ystwyth sets them at Liberty'. Furthermore he suggested that 'at least one half of the Season [for the herring fishing] is lost for want of a good Harbour'. Morris, who was originally from Anglesey and was working there when he produced his surveys of St George's Channel in 1748, subsequently moved to Cardigan in the 1760s and produced a host of surveys of the mining areas.

His figures for the herring fishing on the night of 5 October 1745 make interesting reading. Forty-seven boats of about 12 ton apiece – as many as could get out that evening because of a heavy sea running over the bar – caught 2,160 meises of herring, which at 126 herring to the Hundred, and five Hundreds to the meise, amounted to an incredible 1,360,800 herrings (total weight about 54 tons) which, he calculated, would take 1,111 barrels to cure. Such catches he reckoned would be sustainable with a convenient harbour being built.

A note about the way the fishermen measure their herring. The Hundred or Long Hundred was one of the most common measurements and not just within the fishing. It probably originated as ten dozens, but has acquired different meanings throughout Britain. In the case of the herring fishery one Hundred can represent a varied number of fish, depending on the region. In Cornwall it counts for 132 fish – thirty-three warps of four fish – while in the Isle of Man it counts for 124 fish – forty warps of three fish plus four tally fish, one for every ten warps. Here in Wales there are three possibilities.

In Aberystwyth one Hundred was counted thus: the fish were counted by the score, so that every second score an additional fish was tossed to one side as a warp. Every sixth score another fish was set aside into a different pile as the tally (*tale*). This, then, meant

Fishing smacks, Aberystwyth.

that for every six score – 120 fish – there were three warps and one tally, making a total of 124 fish. This method was generally used for counting out by the meise of five Hundred. However, when only a Hundred was being counted, the final tally was not thrown, thus the total would only be 123 fish. Lewis Morris notes that a Hundred was 126 fish, which only adds to the confusion. However, in 1908, the Cran Measures Act stipulated that a cran measurement was equivalent to 37½ imperial gallons or 28 stone by weight. Quarter cran baskets thus held seven stone of herring and were government branded to confirm they conformed to the Act. This became the standard measure adopted throughout Britain's fishing fleets.

The Aberystwyth fresh herrings were, according to Morris, carried off to supply 'the very middle of England'. Fresh herring, as against that salted down, accounted for almost half of that supplied. Shrewsbury was one place that records show as receiving herring from Aberystwyth. These records show that in 1702 some 1,734 barrels of cured fish had been shipped out to Ireland on both English and Irish ships. In 1789 between 2,000 and 3,000 barrels of Aberystwyth herring were left lying on the quay in the Isle of Man, awaiting shipment to the Mediterranean. Morris also noted that there were very few pilchards landed, observing philosophically that this showed that fish, as well as men, have their own particular countries allotted them. The pilchard fishery at Fishguard is proof of his error in judgment. He also noted that, during the herring season, there was a glut of cod, whiting, pollack, rays and other fish, to which they attached little value.

In 1759 a group calling themselves 'the Big Fourteen of Aberystwyth' petitioned Parliament to move the Customs House there. Four years later it was. In 1780 an Act of Parliament was obtained to 'repair, enlarge and preserve the harbour'. Yet, over the next fifty years, only a dribble of money was spent on the harbour. Various harbourmasters absconded with money and there was a general total lack of management on the part of the trustees. Eventually a well-known civil engineer, George Bush (no relation to the US president I hope), was employed to build two piers at the harbour entrance on similar lines to those suggested by Lewis Morris. These were successful in aiding the silting problem, although storms destroyed portions of the piers on occasions, necessitating costly repairs. With the arrival of the railway from Machynlleth to the town in 1864, the income from harbour dues that were financing these improvements fell sharply. Three years later the line to Carmarthen was opened, connecting north to south Wales. This did little to revive the decline. By the time the narrow-gauge Vale of Rheidol Railway arrived at the North Quay in 1902, purportedly to serve the lead mines inland, the lead mining industry was dying out, so that too had little effect. Not surprisingly, the harbour was described as a 'white elephant'.

Shipbuilding thrived, though, through these uncertain times in the fortunes of the harbour. Before the mid-eighteenth century these were small open boats used mostly for fishing. Pictorial evidence of the type of fishing boat in use in about 1830 comes from a drawing by E. Prys Owen in which a clinker-built of about 25ft in length is depicted. It has a bluff and transom stern, a tiny foredeck and transverse beam to divide the hull into two working sections. It was cutter-rigged with a mainsail, jib and staysail set on a long boom extending over the stern. On the starboard side is a beam trawl, which suggests it trawled out in the bay, presumably drifting for herring in the autumn. Around the middle of the century a three-masted boat was introduced into the town from, it is said, Borth, a few miles to the north (we shall visit here soon). These undecked boats were unique to Wales in that they set two boomless gaff sails and a spritsail mizzen. Built usually from yellow pine and larch below the waterline, they were ballasted with beach shingle. Being lightly built, their working lives were short. They were widely used as tripping boats, taking visitors around the bay on short outings.

Various shipbuilders worked from sites on both sides of the river, although most of the bigger vessels were constructed on the northern side. The best known of these was the Evans family with three generations spanning almost a century. David Williams began building fishing boats for use in the bay from his workshop in Queen's Street in the 1880s. Each of his herring boats was capable of carrying six or seven meise of fish. It has been said that these were based on the design of a whaler, double-ended (i.e. pointed at both ends) so they could be beached and launched with ease. In 1937 the family moved over to Trefechan on the south side of the river and built anything from local fishing boats and lifeboats to motor launches and Admiralty MFVs. With a lack of demand after the end of the war, they finally ceased business in 1959, ending an industry that had been practised for many centuries. The full story of shipbuilding, and indeed the port itself and its trade, is told in *Born on a Perilous Rock* by W.J. Lewis. William Troughton's *Aberystwyth Harbour*, although much briefer, has some excellent pictorial views of the ships.

The merchants of Liverpool and Hoylake brought a huge influence upon both the fishing itself and, to a lesser extent, the type of boat adopted by some fishermen for use further out to sea. Much of the herring caught passed through these merchants' hands so that they received the lion's share of the benefit. After the arrival of the railway, most of the fish was bought up and carried direct to the Liverpool market. Many of the fishers even came from the northwest of England for the season's fishing, bringing with them their Lancashire nobbies so favoured along the Lancashire and Cumbria coasts.

Early fishing boats

'I never saw a fishing-boat on the Welsh coast that was longer than a Thames wherry, or much better calculated to resist the force of a gale of wind at sea', wrote Richard Ayton whilst touring round the whole coast of Britain in the early 1800s with William Daniell. Whilst the Cornish, English Eastcoasters and Scottish were in the midst of developing larger sea-going craft to fish further offshore, between Wales and the Clyde, fishing boats seldom were larger than 25ft in overall length.

In the eighteenth century and before, the smuggling of goods from a central Irish Sea storehouse in the Isle of Man occupied a large proportion of seafarers in this part of Britain. For this they used wherry-rigged vessels that sported two masts of a similar length with two gaff sails, again of a similar size. Although not of a standard hull-form type, these wherries, as they were often called, usually had a transom stern, giving plenty of buoyancy aft and thus being, along with the wherry rig for speed, the most effective hull shape. In parts of the south of Cardigan Bay, boats with three masts followed a fashion familiar in the English Channel and on parts of the Irish coast.

In 1765 the English Crown took over responsibility for import duties and more resources were directed to making concerted efforts to stamp out smuggling from the Isle of Man into England, Scotland and Wales with a degree of success. Those who participated in smuggling were persuaded to the benefits of directing their energy into fishing. It's probable that the two occupations previously went side by side so that fishing was followed when it was advantageous and smuggling when it wasn't. However, after 1765, the same boats were used for it seems unlikely that a new vessel could have been afforded. Thus the same wherries were adapted for fishing so that, over a period, the rig was changed by removing one mast so that only one mast remained, with its gaff sail. Two masts in the main body of the boat would have wasted space, especially when shooting and hauling nets. Thus the smack rig came into being.

At the same time Scandinavian influences brought in double-ended hulls in many parts of Wales for the herring fishing. Others retained the transom, such as the fishermen of Tenby who were influenced by the Cornish, adopting the lug rig with a sprit-rigged small mizzen sail. Indeed, there is evidence to support the theory that the wherry rig was never adopted along the South Coast of Wales.

Pictorial evidence of the smack-rig comes from the drawings of E. Prys Jones of about 1820. Other evidence, such as that of William Daniell, suggests that small craft around West and North Wales were often fitted with a small sprit-rigged mizzen sail, similar to that of Tenby. Most craft, until the late nineteenth century, were clinker-built.

Another interesting depiction, from another aquatint of William Daniell, comes in the form of double-ended hulls on the East Coast of Anglesey, which supports earlier suggestions that double-ended hulls worked from some parts of the coast, especially for the herring fishery. The transom stern was adopted later for lobster potting.

The evolution of fishing boat design is not an exacting science for very different influences come about on differing areas. The three distinct avenues that dictate the particular type of hull and rig in use are the local customs, innovation and influences from outside the locality. This first group is governed by more factors: the type of fishing, the type of beach or harbour working from, the availability of timber and traditions that may have been handed down through generations. Thus there is often no obvious lineage of a particular type of vessel.

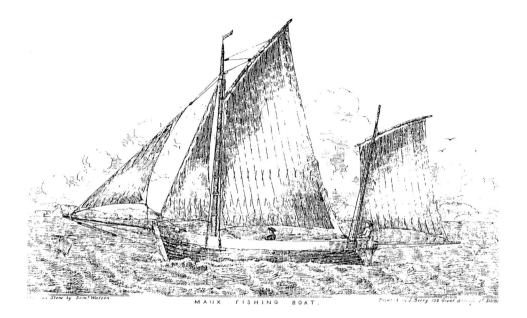

MANX FISHING BOAT.

Above: Manx fishing boat, similar to a fishing wherry.

Left: Fishing wherry.

What is clear is the ultimate fishing boats that worked these waters in the days of sail. Tenby luggers, Aberporth herring boats, Aberystwyth three-masted boats, herring gigs, Aberdaron boats, Welsh nobbies and Anglesey beach boats have been well documented and continued in use after the advent of motorisation. However this motorisation effectively succeeded the sailboats so that the ubiquitous motorised fishing boat soon replaced all the older boats. These MFVs, as they were known, were of Scottish designs, and were to be seen in all the main ports. With technology developing modern materials in the twentieth century, the GRP workboat soon became a common sight for inshore fishing. Steel workboats followed, while the older wooden MFVs too were outdated and replaced by modern steel fishing boats, bristling with electronic gear, larger and larger nets and more mechanisation. The only problem is that the fish soon disappeared as these much bigger boats soon over-fished the Welsh coast. Today, the ailing Welsh fishing industry is following the general European pattern of reduced European Union quotas and limits of fishing time. Stocks are well down and set to decline even further. The only hope on the horizon is a properly managed inshore sector that is able to sustain local stocks.

These carvel-built boats, with sloping sternposts, little sheer and cutter-rigged, of between 25 and 40ft in length, were perfect for the shallow northwestern waters, but somewhat alien to Cardigan Bay. Yet they performed well and were adopted into the town's fleet so that by 1872 there were eighty-three boats registered in Aberystwyth, eight of which were over 18ft. Nine years later the town was described as 'the most considerable fishing station in Cardigan Bay' with nine second-class boats totally over 60 tons in weight.

In contrast there were fifty-two small herring drifters working from the harbour, mainly of the three-masted type. Williams introduced his double-ended versions around the end of the 1880s, many of which were used to take trippers out around the bay during the summer. Their size decreased to 18ft in time and they were popular amongst the fishermen who often sailed them long distances with two crew and the ability to set six to eight nets. At the turn of the century there were 'a considerable number of them' in use. Herring gigs, mostly spritsailed with a few gaff-rigged, also worked from here as they did from many West Coast harbours, and have been subsequently raced. Throughout Wales, and indeed the West Country, gig racing has become well established over recent years, with regattas being held for the boats that are usually owned by community groups in many towns.

In 1878 Frank Buckland and Spencer Walpole came to the town when they were preparing their *Report of the Sea Fisheries of England and Wales*. They interviewed several fishermen; two of whom expressed a willingness to pay harbour dues for the sake of better facilities. At the time they were paying nothing. Thomas Cooper reckoned it wasn't a harbour of safety but merely a harbour of refuge. At Whitehaven he paid 10s a year and would be willing to pay the same here.

The same report gives a good insight into the late nineteenth-century fishing. One smack owner, Humphrey Owen, recognised the great herring fishery of thirty to forty years earlier but added that the old people believed there was curse on the herring because they had been used as manure at times of glut. However, this is an argument I've heard in many areas, especially in Scotland, so do not give much credence to it. It seems to be man's way to explain the erratic nature of the herring's migration. John Jones mentioned that fifty-three meise were caught by one boat with a fleet of sixteen 'old hemp nets' in 1831. He reckoned that the shoals deserted the area about 1840, due mainly to pollution in the rivers from the increased mining activity. These prevented them from spawning just outside the harbour. John Jones Attwood, solicitor for the Corporation, denied this. He lived at Aberaeron and believed that the herring had deserted the entire coastline. He remembered sixty meise of herring being brought there, selling at 5s a meise. He also thought that the shoals were beginning to return. John Gibson, editor of *The Cambrian News*, recalled seeing the water boiling with little fish like sprats and herring. He had watched them for five hours and mentioned large quantities being landed at Pwllheli.

We parked up on Harbour Quay, close to the inshore lifeboat station. The first lifeboat was put on station in 1843 and was kept on a carriage by the sea. This had disappeared by the time the RNLI established a lifeboat and new boathouse in Queen's Street in 1861. Another boathouse was built in 1875 on the same site, which housed a boat until its closure in 1960. Three years later an inshore lifeboat was put on station, housed in a former fisherman's shed on the quay until this present lifeboat house was constructed in 1994.

We walked along the promenade for part of the beach was dog friendly while on other parts a ban was in force. This seems a wholly acceptable approach. The promenade is 2.4km long and supposedly has the flags of fifty nations although I didn't count them! The castle, built by Edward I in 1277, captured by Owain Glyndwr in 1404 and recaptured by Henry V four year later, is in ruins. The War Memorial, commissioned in 1919, is the work of Professor Mario Rutelli and was unveiled in 1923. The figure at the top is supposed to represent 'Triumph' although I was told that this might otherwise have been 'Winged Victory'. The bottom figure has been interpreted to be 'mankind in chaos' while the base is undoubtedly 'humanity emerging from war' Quite why an academic from Palermo University produced this work is unclear but presumably he was a friend of somebody connected with the university. I cynically wondered whether it was this monument that gave the town its so-called connection with Athens.

People were swimming and swarming. The pier has become a variety of businesses – Pier Amusements, Pier Videos, Pier Pressure (Aberystwyth's premier nightspot), Pier Pavilion (bar & brasserie), Pizza Royal at the Inn on the Pier, Royal Pier Social & Snooker Club and an ice-cream parlour – presumably under the same ownership. The neck of the pier is inaccessible for fear of collapse and, judging by old picture postcards of the structure, its end has dropped off since its days of splendour. Marine Terrace extends around the edge of the bay and I remembered reading about one particular storm in 1938 that engulfed this area of the town causing severe flooding and structural damage.

One aspect that I've hardly touched is tourism, for this had a major impact on the town's growth. When exactly Aberystwyth first attracted that breed of Englishman rich enough to afford to dally by the seaside is not clear but it was first termed the 'Brighton of Wales' in 1797 so presumably it was already busy in season. When Revd Evans passed through he found it a 'fashionable resort for sea-bathing' and noted that the price of lodgings was as high as at Weymouth. Then there were six bathing machines and two pleasure boats but by 1826 there were twenty-one such machines operating on the beach north of the pier, ladies by the pier and men at the other end. However, 'natives of both sexes among the mountains are much addicted to sea bathing during the summer nights', according to an 1806 report. It seems they assembled by blowing horns and travelled down to the town from their mountain homes and stripped off before taking 'a promiscuous plunge without any ceremony'. This, the report stated, they only did on Saturday evenings so that they could rest on the Sabbath!

With the railway came an influx of more visitors. In 1865 the pier was opened and some 7,000 people paid to walk along its length the very next day. It was damaged the next year in a storm and not repaired and improved until 1872. The new Pier Pavilion was constructed in 1896, which remains. The following year the building of the Cliff Railway on Constitution Hill led to the construction of an entertainment centre atop the hill, with a camera obscura, laid out gardens, a pavilion, kiosks, a scenic railway and shelters. However, ironically the shelters were probably the most used bits as the wind and rain contributed to making the centre a financial disaster.

The beach was busy and couples paraded along the promenade, smiling at a dog with stick in his mouth as they passed by. The Ceredigion Museum & Art Gallery is just off the promenade, housed in a former theatre and cinema, and has displays relating to life in Victorian mid-Wales, farming and seafaring as well as contemporary and historic art. Some of the original works of Frank Worthington (1837–1927) are on display – the artist himself was from a family of fishermen – and show local boats at work. I spent some time inside before trailing the dog by lead for an hour, gazing into shops that resembled those on any British high street, then spent another hour reading the newspaper over some excellent coffee. After that, we walked down to the six-arched Trefechan Bridge, which had been built in 1887 after the previous one was swept away by a sudden swelling of the river. Evans had described it as 'handsome' and it undoubtedly has an air of grace. Then we were back to the harbour at Y Lanfa. What fishing boats remaining in the harbour fish for lobsters and crabs, and mackerel in season. The marina, constructed in the 1990s, now allows twenty-four-hour access to that part of the harbour, thus resulting in a place of shelter, accessible at any stage of the tide, between Holyhead in the north and Milford Haven in the south for the first time. The shame is that it took plans for a marina for the town's fathers to act whereas if they had had a bit more insight to create a harbour two hundred years before things in Aberystwyth might have been very different.

I left Aberystwyth with a heavy heart. Tourism, one half of Morton's Aberystwyth, was not operating at its optimum, even if the heat wave was continuing. The academic half was at home for the summer, although I did see some very obviously foreign students around town. The university, established in 1872, doesn't quite compare to St Andrews, established in 1411. If anywhere on this coast resembled St Andrews, I would have said that place was Aberaeron, with its neat streets and small harbour similar to the Scottish town. One benefit to Aberystwyth, though, is the National Library of Wales, one of the six copyright libraries in the UK, and one where it is easy to wile away many a happy day in its archive. For once this institution wasn't taken to Cardiff. However, overall, the town emitted an air of sadness so I was glad to be heading north once more.

To Clarach that was a tiny bay literally around Constitution Hill, although by road is a bit longer. This is a holiday place, with the Leisure Park, Barn Restaurant and Spar shop, and a landscape of caravans colouring the hinterland. The place's saving grace was the sign in the car park informing us that the 50 pence fee went to LATCH, a charity for children with cancer and leukaemia. I liked that, so paid up.

Coming over the hill you suddenly appear to almost fall onto Borth, but stop if possible because there's a fantastic view over the village, the Dyfi estuary and right along the coast and over hills of North Wales. Borth itself stretches along the pebbly beach for about a mile, a sort of coastal chain of protection for the marshland of Cors Fochno behind it. Equally, groynes along its length protect the beach. Offshore somewhere lies the Gored Wyddno that I've already mentioned. In 1566 a small landing place is documented as being here. I took a quick look on the beach as a sign declared that dogs are banned in summer on the southern part of the beach. We continued along the road, between the lines of houses each side, to the other end, by the golf course, where he was able to run into the water with waves breaking over him and bark when I didn't throw sticks. It was here that the nineteenth-century Borth – or *porth* (port) – was located at the point where the river Leri entered the sea, as depicted on Lewis Morris's plan of the Dyfi estuary. Here, too, was the maritime activity associated with the coastal trade and fisheries. With the railway came the re-routing of the river and the added 'bonus' of a decline in the need for trading smacks. At Ynys Las, North Wales seemed a stone's throw away across the Dyfi estuary, yet we had a journey of twenty miles or so to get to Aberdyfi. The ferry across here was said to have been one of the very first in Britain. The boat was kept across at Aberdyfi and was hailed by the ringing of a bell that hung on a post on the shore. A refuge tower, built on wooden piles at Cerrig Penrhyn, enabled waiting passengers to shelter from the weather and the incoming tide. Three ferries operated at one time – one for horses and coaches, another for horses, cattle and goods and an express service for foot passengers.

We stopped briefly at the bridge over the river where the 'Steelkit' boatyard is today situated, alongside of which several boats sat miserably in the river Leri in its present position. Presumably somewhere around here was the site of the 1566 landing place on the 'Divi'. At Glandyfi, the seine-net boat I've seen anchored in the river for many years was still there. We again stopped to photograph it. Two seine-nets still operate in this river. A couple of vessels were once built here. At Derwenlas, Cei Ward was the only port of Montgomery, used until 1863 when the railway eradicated the need for a port. However, thirty years previously, according to Samuel Lewis in *A Topographical Dictionary of Wales*, the annual exports from here included 500 tons of bark, 40,000ft of oak, 150,000 yards of oak poles for collieries, 100 tons of lead ore and 1,500 tons of slate. Wheat, coal, culm, limestone, hides and general goods were imported. Some ships were also built here until the majority of the sea trade moved to Penhelig, Aberdyfi. For us, then, it was on to Machynlleth and over the *Pont ar Ddyfi*, the 1805-built bridge that spans the Dyfi River – the traditional division between North and South Wales. And to sleep in a lay-by further along the road.

A rush-thatched farm house near Pontrhydfendigaid.

DAY THIRTEEN
ABERDYFI TO BARMOUTH

> Devye, being a Haven and havinge no habitacion, but only three houses whereunto there is
> no resorte: save only in the tyme of hearinge fishinge at which time of fishing there is a
> wonderfull great resorts of ffyshers assembled from all places within this Realme with
> Shippes Boottes and Vessells, and duringe there abidinge there, there is of the said cumpa-
> nye there assembled one chosen among themsellfes to be their Admirall. And there is nother
> Shippe nor vessell that belongeth to the same Haven otherwise then aforesaid, whereof we
> have deputed David ap Thomas ap Rutherche, and Thomas ap Humffrey beinge the sub-
> stanciallest and nerest to the same haven.

So reads the entry for Aberdyfi in *The Haven and Creeks of the County of Merioneth in Elizabethan Wales, 1565*. For fishing was the principal occupation at Aberdyfi in the sixteenth and seventeenth centuries, and, of course, herring was the chief catch. During the West Wales famine of 1649 Aberdyfi herring was sent to South Merionnydd and West Montgomery. In 1748 Lewis Morris noted the good herring fishery but suggested that the main commodities were timber and oak bark, the latter being exported mainly to Ireland for the tanning industry. The lead trade was mostly exhausted, although he did note the presence of smelting houses at Garreg. Things were much the same into the eighteenth century so that in 1834 Aberdyfi was still just a small, quiet fishing village with nets often drying on the foreshore, smacks on the beach and a plentiful supply of herring, salmon and mackerel, as well as mussels, lobsters and crabs.

Then came the effects of the Industrial Revolution in the nineteenth century and Aberdyfi saw a rapid growth in its port. By 1838, according to Samuel Lewis, the port possessed:

> ... a considerable share of coasting trade: the imports are coal, culm, groceries, limestone,
> bricks, timber, &c., and the exports, timber poles for the collieries, bark, lead ore, and slates.
> The harbour is excellent, but there is a bar on the north side of the entrance to it, which is
> said to have assumed its present position in consequence of the wind blowing frequently
> from the south.

Most of the slate came down from the quarries at Corris, Abergynolwyn and Aberllefenni. Smaller riverboats were largely used to transport this from the upper reaches of the navigable part of the river to Penhelig, Aberdyfi where the main loading quays were. However, as we've already seen, some smaller ships were able to sail upstream as far as Derwenlas, and some also loaded at Pennal. But Penhelig became the principal loading point when the larger vessels were unable to sail upriver. At the same time the building of the railway crossing of the Dyfi just upstream of Glandyfi also prevented

Drying sails of the Aberdyfi herring fleet, 1910. (Courtesy Hugh M. Lewis)

access upstream. Records of these river vessels is scarce, although it is known that *The Caernarfon and Denbigh Herald* reported the launching of the *Taliesin*, a large river vessel from the yard of Robert Edwards in 1857.

Shipbuilding began to flourish at the same time with at least seventy-nine vessels being built between 1840 and 1880. Prior to this, small sloops – referred by Mike Stammers as Welsh sloops – were being built on the river at various locations, including Garreg (Glandyfi), Derwenlas and Aberdyfi. Three men are said to have dominated the ship-building – John Jones, Roger Lewis and Thomas Richards, the latter dying in 1880 whilst he was overseeing the construction of Aberdyfi's last sea-going vessel, the *Olive Branch*. The 99-ton schooner was launched later that year, ending the shipbuilding tradition. Richard's sheds, surplus timber and tools were sold at auction soon after, and raised the meagre sum of £19 10s. That surely is a sign that the hey-day of shipbuilding was almost over.

Fishing smacks from Devon and Fleetwood are said to have unloaded fish at Aberdyfi, probably after the railway was opened in 1867. In 1882 a wharf and jetty were built around the point from Penhelig, enabling a faster loading of slates. The coastal trade eventually petered out, as we've seen, so that Aberdyfi was left to reflect over its past and continue to thrive from its tourism and fishing. Fishing was then undertaken in locally built transom-sterned skiffs or gaff-rigged nobby-type boats. One story tells of an open boat in Tremadoc Bay that took aboard an immense haul of herring so that it was so heavily laden that its 'oars floated out of the rowlocks'. It had to leave some of its nets behind, and just managed to make Pwllheli without sinking!

In the 1830s the town was 'rapidly rising in estimation as a bathing-place: the beach is highly favoured for bathing, being composed of hard firm sand, and several respectable houses and a commodious hotel have been erected of late years, for the accommodation of visitors', so Samuel Lewis tells us. Paddle steamers called in after the building of the quay, connecting Aberdyfi – as it did many of the Cardigan Bay ports – to Liverpool. One of these steamers, the *Telephone*, we've already come across in a past chapter. At one point, in the late 1890s, there was a plan to develop a route between Aberdyfi and Waterford to encourage traffic between Ireland and the Midlands, but this never came to fruition. By the end of the First World War, Aberdyfi's port was redundant, except for fishing and pleasure boats, the same vessels that use it today.

Regattas were held at Aberdyfi back in the 1840s including sailing and rowing races. The Wynne's of the Peniarth estate were partly responsible for the organisation of the event. From the same estate comes, from the Estate Books of 1770, a mention of the herring fishery:

> ... the first Herrings that came to the town was second week in September and all shotten; the slender supply continued in that state till October, about the middle of the month: then they became many full-roed, and delicious when taken at Nefyn in Caernarfonshire so late as the end of November, and have not altered these twenty six years, till the present, it being the 19th day of September and not a single fish arrived... On the 6th October the first herring were brought to market 1796, and sold at a penny each, but shotten, and again on 7th, 10th, 12th, 15th, 18th, 21st, 22nd, 23rd at the reduced price of a half penny from the 21st to the 29th October inclusive. But in the month of Dec 16, I bought three as fine full-roed fish for two-pence taken at Barmouth, as ever were eaten, and again on the 23rd the same number at the same price but one only soft-roed – In the memory of the oldest inhabitants there never were taken any at this time at Barmouth in such perfection; I consider it a blessing and as such insert it.

I'd been reading the work of Lewis Lloyd in his splendid *A Real Little Seaport*, which tells of the growth of the port and its people between 1565 and 1920, and I recommend this book to anyone who wishes to consider the port in any detail. Hugh M. Lewis, MBE, is another local author who kindly sent me a photograph to include in *The Herring Fishers of Wales*. In all, he has written a dozen books on the town that I know about and was obviously a prolific writer.

Dog and I arrived relatively early in the morning, after I'd spent the task of breakfasting in the lay-by overlooking the river Dyfi and mulling over the journey. One factor that I was increasingly becoming aware of was the reliance upon the written works of others, both in a historical context – i.e. such as Lewis Morris, Thomas Phaer, Fenton, Pennant to name a few – and the contemporary historian of the today. Without the works of people such as Lloyd and Lewis, I'd be pretty stymied for information unless I was willing to spend days, if not months, in one particular place. The tour then would probably last for years (highly impractical!) and is, as such, my excuse. My own academic studies lie in the roots of fishing vessel design upon the west coast of Scotland and therefore are irrelevant here. However, there are similarities in design in Irish Sea vessels for which I was on the lookout for, but so far had seen only a little of interest. I add this paragraph merely as an assurance to the reader that I am aware of using others' research.

The town was filling up with visitors, given the continuing fine weather, although the edge of the heat had now disappeared. Bright blue skies still emancipated the soul.

Gorgeous girls with seemingly endless legs paraded around in their ubiquitous short skirts and bare midriffs whilst on the beach skimpy triangles of glossy material covered little more than the bare necessities. How different it would have been a hundred years ago when the self-conscious Victorians were clad with more garments in the sea than out. Two hundred years ago they would have been happy to be naked and nobody would have cast a glimpse in their direction. Today, though, we were somewhere in between, both keen to wear little but at the same time highly conscious of our appearance in our tiny morsels of expensive designer ware! What slaves to peer pressure we've become.

Outside of the lifeboat station a group of these girls were twittering amongst themselves in a silly way, and it was these that made me consider this point in the first place. They certainly didn't look as if lifeboats had any interest for them. The station sits upon the quay and thus is central to where groups of folk gather. Perhaps the girls were interested in the group of young men in their wetsuits who looked like they'd just come in from a trip out at sea.

The lifeboat station houses an inshore Atlantic 21 lifeboat. However, the service in the town dates back to 1837 when the first open boat, the *Victoria*, was put on station at a new boathouse at Penhelig and managed by the Harbour Authorities. In 1853 the RNLI took over and five or six years later (the date seems uncertain) a new boathouse was built close by to the old one, and a new lifeboat brought on station. This boat appears to have been unnamed although, more likely, its name has been lost on record. It was replaced in 1865 with the *Royal Berkshire,* which cost £338, the money coming from collections in Berkshire. Yet another lifeboat house was built in 1886, again at Penhelig, and the *Thomas Nicolls Stratford* placed on station, costing £479. The 10-oared *William Brocksopp* (cost £865) arrived in 1904 and the *George and Margaret* (cost £888) in 1921. This latter boat was the last for the station finally closed in 1931 after ninety-four years of service, thirty-seven launches and seventy-five lives saved. In 1963 the first of six inshore boats was brought on station with the present boathouse being built in 1991, complete with a souvenir sales outlet where I was able to purchase a potted history entitled *Aberdyfi Lifeboat Station.* For some reason Henry Parry's book *Wreck and Rescue on the Coast of Wales, part 1 – The Lifeboats of Cardigan Bay and Anglesey*, doesn't include the Aberdyfi lifeboat and begins at Barmouth, neither does *part 2.*

Several fishing boats were at anchor, sporting big powerful engines. This reminded me that the Gwynedd River Authority, the body responsible for administering the fishing until recent times, prohibited the use of motor boats on all the county rivers. In the 1970s, according to Geraint Jenkins, there were six licensed boats, with another three working from Glandyfi, and these were between 12 and 14ft long. In the mid-nineteenth century there were coracle nets, salmon weirs and draft nets all in use on the river but suffered a great deal from pollution from the lead mines until their closure. It then became renowned as 'one of the finest salmon rivers in Wales', according to Jenkins.

The seine-net fishermen worked from the half flood to half ebb and, unlike most fishermen, believed that night fishing was best. Three men worked each boat, two crewing the vessel and one, the shoreman – *tantiwr* in Welsh – on the beach or riverbank. The net was carried upon a board across the transom of the boat. Once this method of fishing declined, as licences were lost in deference to the rod and line brigade, these men became part-time and only one man worked the boat and another onshore. Nets were once 200 yards long, four yards deep and a 2in mesh, although this decreased to 150 yards, and down to 100 yards long upstream. It was customary to spit on the net for luck at each shot much in the same way as many folk spit upon a ball or piece of wood for their particular good luck. Perhaps, I thought, that was why footballers were always spitting, believing themselves to be on hallowed ground! Today, so I was informed, only two seines are occasionally operated during the shortened fishing season.

From Aberdyfi it's a short hop to Tywyn, the next place along the A493 coast road north. According to Samuel Lewis:

> ... the town is beautifully situated at a distance of about a mile from the sea-coast, near the mouth of the river Dysynni in a small and pleasant vale, watered by that stream, and on the verge of a tract which once formed a very extensive morass, but which has lately been secured by an embankment from the inundation of the tide. The fine beach in front of the town, being remarkably convenient for sea-bathing, has made it the resort during the summer for numerous visiters [sic], chiefly from Llanidoes, Newtown, Montgomery, &c.

Two differences between the above description and Tywyn of today are immediately obvious. Firstly today's town has spread towards the coast so that it edges the shore rather than being a mile away and, secondly, the river Dysynni flows into the sea almost two miles northward, diverted by the embankment. However, Hucks, when he passed through in July 1794, also observed that the town lay a mile away from the shore. He added that 'there is nothing attractive in that place, or captivating to the eye of a stranger' which brings me to my third point. This difference is a matter of personal preference but I, too, found little of beauty in either its position or substance. Although we did venture out for a walk along the seafront, the beach is not particularly outstanding in comparison to others along this coast. The groynes, although necessary to prevent the beach marching away with the wind and current, are nevertheless ugly. The houses, caravans and the Morfa Camp do absolutely nothing for the town's appearance, save to contribute in rendering it characterless and without charm.

'Dessynny' was noted as 'beinge a Creke havinge noe habitacion nor resorte, and there is nother Shippe vessell or Boote that belongeth thereunto' in 1565 although there were two deputies, Lewys Gethyn and John ap Gruff' ap Harry, who were the nearest inhabitants to the river estuary. Although there is subsequently little mention of a sea trade from the river, several ships were built here in the early nineteenth century. Several mariners were said to live locally, but it seems that any maritime activity was centred upon Aberdyfi.

Revd Evans, in the early 1800s, noted the town as 'having a fine sandy beach, it is frequented during the summer season by numerous genteel families, for the purpose of sea-bathing'. Subsequent travellers seemed to disagree, finding it dull, secluded and poor. Although the Aberystwyth & Welsh Coast Railway arrived in 1863 from Aberdyfi, it was another four years before this stretch was connected to the national network. This, unfortunately, didn't seem to have much impact upon tourism.

High up in the hills above Tywyn, in the Gwernol valley, slate mines had been producing slate that was carried by packhorse over the mountains to the south and down to the river Dyfi near Pennal, from where it was taken to Aberdyfi. Encouraged by the opening of the railway to Aberdyfi, the new mine owners built a narrow gauge line down from the Gwernol valley, close by Abergynolwyn and thence to Tywyn, thus feeding slate down to the terminus alongside the main railway. The line opened in 1866 and was the first slate quarry railroad to terminate at a railhead, in contrast to a port. The slate was then carried down to Aberdyfi where it was loaded aboard the slate vessels.

This line had the added advantage of serving the communities it passed through, including an incline down to the village of Abergynolwyn, along which supplies were taken, including a supply of beer to the village pub! Annual passenger numbers reached 20,000 up to the 1920s and both the quarry and railway were subsidised by the local landowner Sir Haydn Jones. At his death in 1950 the railway was saved from inevitable closure by the formation of the Talyllyn Railway Preservation Society, the first such organisation in the world. Today the railway operates along its entire length throughout most of the year, although the service is heavily restricted in the winter months, due in part to the inclement weather. A museum at the Tywyn Wharf terminus tells the story of the line, a place we did not visit because I'm not much of a train buff.

Having said that, I did venture into the little museum at the terminus of the Fairbourne Railway, several miles further north along the coast road. The way this road and railway are squeezed together between shore and mountain only serves to clarify just why this part of the coast was largely ignored by travellers up to the nineteenth century. The place must have been pretty inaccessible before these routes were built.

The museum recounts the history of this narrow gauge line. When the main line was opened in 1865 there was no bridge across to Barmouth (*Abermaw*), thus passengers alighted at Barmouth Ferry station and took the ferry across to Barmouth, which was a fashionable resort for holidaymakers from NW England. However, the bridge was complete two years later and the station closed. The siding remained in use for a limited slate trade.

Barmouth, *c*.1910.

Commercial Fishing Methods

Fishing methods are either passive or active, much in the same way as we've already seen with fish weirs, which were one of the easiest and productive ways of catching fish.

Drifting-netting was the most common form of fishing up to the eighteenth century, and continued to be used for herring and mackerel into the twentieth. It basically consists of a curtain of net being laid in the water to hang on or near the surface so that herring – or other pelagic fish – get entrapped by their gills. Usually shot at night, it drifts with the boat it is attached to and is hauled in the next morning. In parts of the country the net is fixed at one end or both to the seabed so that the boats do not have to stay out with it all night. Technically it then becomes a gill-net, which are set at different depths to catch bottom-feeding fish.

Lines – lengths of cord with smaller lines (snoods) attached every three feet or so, having hooks at the other end – are set on the seabed to catch bottom feeding fish such as cod. Long-lines have upwards of 2,000 hooks whereas small-lines have much less and are consequently shorter, with smaller hooks.

Trawling is an active way of fishing whereby a net is trailed behind a boat to scoop up fish that swim across the entrance to the net. Two main methods of keeping the net open are using beam trawls (a beam is fixed across the mouth) or otter boards (one attached to each side which, due to the flow of water over them, have a tendency to exert pressure away from the net, therefore holding the mouth open). Whereas beam trawls usually travel over the seabed, otter boars allow the net to be set at any depth. The fish a forced into the bag of the fish – the cod end – which, when hauled up, is untied to allow the fish to drop onto the deck of the boat. Today's trawls are high-tech operations, consisting of single, twin or triple trawls, and have contributed more than any other way of fishing, to the decline in white fish.

Dredges are devices that are dragged across the seabed to gather up shellfish such as oysters and mussels. They are lowered from the side of the boat with a towrope and remain down for a short period before being hauled, emptied and reset. They are rarely more than a few feet across in size.

Baited lobster pots are placed on the seabed, attached with a line to a buoy, and are left until, usually, the next day before being hauled. Traditional pots were made were willow and called 'ink-well pots'. Nowadays they are largely steel framed and set in trains of ten or twenty pots, depending on the size of fishing boat.

Hand nets are used close inshore to gather shellfish, while hand picking of cockles is still common practice in parts of Wales. There are, of course, many other ways of catching fish, from seining (a Danish invention) and purse-seining for herring to fishing from the shore with a rod and line and spinning for mackerel. But these are either not used in Welsh waters or are non-commercial, so are not included in the above.

Bringing in a dredge of mussels aboard the *Tannie Christina* in 1997.

A full hold of mussels aboard a dredger belonging to Myti Mussels of Bangor.

When Arthur MacDougall of flour fame bought the Penrhyn Estate, he built a holiday resort and brought in visitors, mostly from the Midlands. To carry building materials from the sidings to his new resort he opened a horse drawn tramway in about 1897. Two years later the station re-opened on the mainline and was called Fairbourne. At the same time a passenger service was introduced on the narrow gauge line, enabling passengers to travel out to Penrhyn Point. *The Gossiping Guide to North Wales*, 1912, states, 'near the village of Friog a station called Fairbourne has been opened... A tramcar (fare 2*d*) runs in summer down to the shore of the estuary (opposite Barmouth) where there is a ferry... In wet weather the tram is sometimes stopped; a flag hoisted at Penrhyn Beacon, seen from Barmouth, shows when it is running. It is over a mile from the station to the ferry'. By 1916 steam had been adopted and this continues today. According to one of the drivers I met at the Penrhyn end as he was stoking up his boiler – we'd walked from the village, the dog and I – the railway is owned today by two associates from Salisbury who prop it up although it just about breaks even. Open from a week before Easter through to the end of October, the quiet times at either end of the season are the times that the serious enthusiasts come down to savour the railway in the off season. During the summer season the line is popular with the holidaymakers, as is the little museum and Nature Centre alongside it. It was free to get in and I probably would not have bothered if I had to pay! Walking back along the rails, I noted, lying on the beach, a lovely small open Norwegian fishing boat that, on close inspection, I saw had been built in Tresfjord.

From Fairbourne we drove to Penmaenpool, the point of the first road crossing of the river. Prior to the wooden bridge being built in 1879, this 'pool' was a thriving centre of maritime activity. Between 1770 and 1827 over 100 ships were built in several shipyards along the estuary, all from locally grown oak. The nearby small slate quarries brought their products down for loading and shipping out. Woollen webs, coarse flannel woven by the people in the Dolgellau area for which this area is renowned, were also exported while the usual commodities such as coal, limestone and general goods were imported.

The bridge was tolled; it still is. An agreement, drawn up between the Penmaenpool Bridge Company and the Barmouth Harbour Trust, amended the original plans of the bridge so that the bridge could be converted into a drawbridge to allow the sailing ships to pass through. However, given that the days of the coastal trade were numbered, it was never necessary.

The railway from Aberdyfi to Dolgellau passed between road and bridge, although this was another line to suffer the Beeching axe in the 1960s. The route of the track bed is still clear. The George III hotel, built in the 1650s, was used as a tavern for the estate workers of the Penmaen Uchaf estate and also housed ships' chandlers at one time.

We trundled over the bridge, wondering whether to turn left or right at the main road. A friend has some land at Llanelltyd and might be there. I'd read a reference to several ships being built at Llanelltyd, perhaps on his land by the river, but opted not to visit. Instead we turned left towards Barmouth until making another last-minute decision to head up into the hills, along a single-tracked road, to exercise dog away from the sea. If he was indeed getting fed up with sand and water, then so was I. The tranquility of the hills, and the splendid views over the Mawddach valley with Cader Idris in the distance, were superb. We came by accident across the remains of a mine but didn't take too much notice until arriving back at the van a couple of hours later. What I did then discover was that we'd unwittingly come across the Clogau mine. This mine, and the nearby Gwynfynydd mine, lie in the rich Merionnydd 'Gold Belt' and here the brilliant fine gold was dug by hand in the nineteenth century.

The day was passing before we'd got anywhere. It was very late into the afternoon before we arrived in Barmouth. So late, in fact, it was easy to park by the sea. The tiny museum housed on the first floor of Ty Gwyn was miraculously still open. The building was built by Gruffydd Fychan (Vaughan) in the 1460s to act as a landing place for secret meetings between the Lancastrian supporters during the Wars of the Roses. When Henry Tudor arrived near Dale in 1485 with his troops and marched through Wales, people such as Fychan supported him. The museum itself tells, not surprisingly, of the history the town. Ty Gwyn is not to be confused with Ty Crwn, a roundhouse gaol, which was built in 1834 to incarcerate drunks and petty offenders. It was built with two separate compartments, one for men and another for women. Barmouth, at the time, was noted for its many females who habitually caused disturbances – so said, probably, by the male element of the population!

I'm not going to enumerate in chronological order the events that created the history of the port as these are reflected in the other ports of the area, especially mirroring those of Aberdyfi. I'm fed up of doing that! Thus this potted history will be even briefer than before. There were only four houses in 1565 – Ty Gwyn must have been one of them – and there was 'nother Shipp nor vessell that belongeth to the said haven, But only towe litle Bootes that the said Res ap Res and Harry ap Eden' do use to cary men over that Passaige'. Not only did they own two of the houses but they were running the ferry. It's pretty likely that these two used their two little boats for doing a spot of herring fishing in the season.

When the ferry first began operation is unknown. In 1505 two brothers who had a duty station on Ynys y Brawd (Isle of Brothers) ran it. The island was much larger then, and the main channel ran between the island and Barmouth. The island now forms part of the breakwater. When Lewis Morris arrived, he found that the chief trade of the place was woollen manufacturing of white cloth and stockings, a good herring fishery, plenty of other fish such as salmon, cod, whiting pollack, mullet, most flatfish, sandeels and cockles, and other exports of butter, cheese, timber and oak bark. He also noted the presence of mineral veins.

In 1751 the ferry was being run by the Harbour Trust and let annually. It was obviously quite busy although those coming from the south had to leave their horses at Penrhyn Farm while they crossed to do their business. When it was leased to the Penrhyn Farm owners, a larger ferry was brought in that was capable of carrying horses. When the farm was sold, it was noted that carrying the mail over the river was the backbone of the business.

Past users of the ferry were: Baldwin, Archbishop of Canterbury in 1188; Adam of Usk, priest attached to the Court of Henry IV, in 1408; Shelley and his wife Harriet in 1812; William Wordsworth in 1824; Charles Darwin in 1828; and Gladstone and General Booth. Today it still runs, mainly for the benefit of the visitors, and is privately owned. Bad silting up of the harbour makes a full service difficult to maintain. It runs from April to September with some dates having no service. An adult single is £2, return £2.50 with reductions for under-16s; dogs are £1 and under-1s free. And all that information came from a notice on the door of the ferryman's hut.

Sorting the catch of
herring at Barmouth.

Ships were, of course, built here, as elsewhere. In 1729 some of the vessels registered
at Barmouth were *Hopewell*, *Speedwell*, *Elizabeth & Margaret* and *Catherine*. These were
mostly 6–20 ton vessels engaged in the coastal trade, carrying Llanelli coal in and oak and
corn out. Fifteen sloops were built up to 1770 but by 1790 130 vessels had been built –
117 sloops, fifteen brigs, four Brigantines, one Snow and one ship. Barmouth was then
known as the port of Merionnydd and was the second port of significance in the whole
of North Wales, dwarfed only by Conwy. The shipbuilding flourished until the 1860s,
at which time the railway arrived in 1866.

Fishing continued to contribute to the economy into the twentieth century. Slate was
brought down the Mawddach in lighters for shipping out. A small pier was erected in
1802 for this purpose while prior to that Aberamffra was the main quay. The other
principal means of earning a living was through tourism, which continues to thrive
today.

According to Samuel Lewis in the 1830s, the town had an appearance, when viewed
from seaward, of being peculiarly romantic, with the backdrop of the mountains and the
cluster of buildings around the shore. Joseph Hucks described the houses as 'whimsical'.
Lewis continued:

On the banks of the river is found a profusion of scurvy grass, the efficacy of which, in conjunction with the benefit of sea-bathing, is supposed to have originally made Barmouth a place
of resort for invalids; and the salubrity of the air, the fineness of the beach, the beauty of the

surrounding scenery, and the varied and interesting excursions which the environs afford, have
contributed to render it a place of fashionable resort during the summer months, and to raise
it to an eminent rank amongst the watering-places on this part of the coast.

Hucks, too, found a town which 'in season is full of company, who resort thither for the
purpose of bathing'. Furthermore, Lewis says that before the war with France, the
inhabitants 'carried on a commercial intercourse with Ireland, Spain, and Italy; but the
trade is now principally coastwise and consists chiefly in the exportation of timber, poles
for collieries, bark, copper and lead ore, black jack, manganese, turnery, webs, and slates;
and the importation of corn, flour and meal, coal, limestone, American and Baltic
timber, hides and grocery'.

I had a good meal in a pub across the road from the railway arches. Trains clattered
across in surprising frequency. Across the road was 'The Last Haul – *Y Llwyth Olaf*', a
sculpture denoting three fishermen hauling in a net. Underneath was the inscription:

In 1709 a 700-ton Genoese galleon was wrecked in a storm five miles north-west of this
point. Its precious cargo of 43 huge blocks of Carrara marble was en route from Italy to an

Herring boat
alongside the
quay at
Barmouth.

unknown destination. This two-ton piece was raised from the wreck by its finders, the Cae Nest Group of Divers, and donated to Barmouth. The community chose the design, and local sculptor Frank Cocksey was commissioned by the Town Council to create this unique work of art as a celebration of the new millennium.

Barmouth is also known as being the starting point for the 'Three Peaks Yacht Race'. This yachting/running premier challenge involves sailing from here to Fort William, stopping off at Caernarfon to run up Snowdon, Whitehaven for Scafell Pike and a final sprint Ben Nevis. First competed in 1977, it takes in 389 miles of sailing, twenty-nine miles of cycling and fifty-nine miles of running with a total ascent of 14,500ft. This year's race (2003) began on 21 June.

The lifeboat station is one of the oldest in Wales, dating from 1828 and first operated by the Harbour Trust until the RNLI took over its running in 1853. The chief reason for siting a station here was the large number of vessels being lost on St Patrick's Causeway (*Sarn Badrig*), the reef that extends for fourteen miles out into Cardigan Bay. The first lifeboat house was at the head of the quay but this was moved to the eastern end of the town, on the shore of the Mawddach estuary, in 1859, and the railway line was subsequently built over it. Some dozen lifeboats have been on station, and today both an all-weather boat and inshore boat are on duty.

I walked around the town, with the moon shining down creating fingering shadows. The Lobster Pound was firmly shut otherwise I'd have been able to buy a lobster. Several fishing boats were tied up alongside the quay, devoid of crew. The Sailor's Institute was

Carnavon Castle.

likewise closed and I peered through grimy windows, imagining the atmosphere when the old seadogs were chatting away. Several piles of magazines and some books sat on the long table and the walls were adorned with pictures. The RNLI museum was shut too. The harbourmaster had gone home. In fact, the whole place was shrouded in silence. I half-expected it to start raining, such was the fill of gloom. Mind you, I hadn't really expected them to be open at this hour. I picked up the dog from the van and walked along the concrete wall onto the Brothers' Island. Not surprisingly, a big sign said, 'No dogs on beach'. Dog smelt rabbits in the sand dunes and ran off. Offshore a big light flashed. I counted the interval between flashes – one flash every fifteen seconds. Even further off was another with a five second interval. This was Bardsey I presumed. Red lights directed vessels into safely over the bar into Barmouth. Well, they would have done if there were any vessels, but the sea was quiet tonight. The Llyn peninsular was just visible in the moonlight. Another train rattled over the town. The dog came back panting. We retraced to the van and I sat a while at the side door, gazing out, wondering about the world and just how perfect a place it could be. And what a wonderful coast I was cemented to. So much for the thirteenth day.

DAY FOURTEEN

BARMOUTH TO ABERDARON

Again it was exquisite to wake up to a view across the sands to the sea. The dog immediately jumped out when I opened the door and he ran out onto the forbidden territory of the beach. Although he cocked his leg, he didn't crap, so I felt vindicated in not calling him back straight away. There was no-one about anyway to smack our wrists. Instead, after brewing some coffee on the little stove, we left. It was too early for the cafes to serve breakfast, much too soon for museums to open their doors and too late to watch the fishing boats depart.

The next stop was at Llanbedr, a small village nestling on the banks of the river Artro. Again this was mentioned in the 1565 survey as 'a Creke havinge no habitacion nor resorte, and there is nother Shippe vessell or Boote that belongeth thereunto'. It's said that some of the stone for nearby Harlech Castle, built between 1286 and 1291 by 940 stonemasons, was brought in through here, as was food for the workers.

From there we drove alongside the RAF establishment and across the causeway to Shell Island or *Mochras*. The river used to flow out on the southern edge of the 'island' but when the Earl of Winchelsea cut a new entrance to the river on the north side in 1819, it really was an island, albeit briefly. Today the causeway floods at high water, preventing vehicles from arriving, but the 'island' is joined to the mainland by dunes. Mochras was farmed for many years and in the nineteenth century it was leased to John Lloyd. From the farmhouse (which is mentioned in the Doomsday Book) a tunnel leads off in the direction of Cors-y-Gedol Hall. Whether it reached the full three and a half miles is not known these days, but part of it has been excavated. Presumably a spot of free trading went on hereabout for Lloyd, who was once having difficulty paying the £95 annual rent, died leaving a fortune.

Six ships are known to have been built on the island between 1760 and 1790, the largest being the 50ft, 60-ton *True Love*. There's a small harbour, which was the dropping off point for tourists catching the ferry from Llandanwg after a short walk from Pensarn railway station. Tourism flourished after the 1880s, and collecting shells was of prime importance for those coming. It seems that St Patrick's Causeway, the reef that reaches out from Mochras, funnels shells upon the beaches here. Presumably several fishing boats once worked from here for there are reports of large catches of herring. These, along with lobsters, crabs and other fish, were sent by train to London during the Second World War. Today the island is run as a campsite and resort, so that I had to pay £1 just to have a quick look around. The attendant, though, was extremely apologetic for asking me to pay and told me I could stay all day if I liked. If I'd come in 1960 the charge would have been two shillings!

After visiting the 'island', we parked up on the edge of the shore of the mainland and walked in a northeasterly direction along an embankment that was built to retain the sea.

Several boats bobbed at moorings and I watched the tide rise. The quay of Mochras, busy too with boats, lay across the estuary. Eventually we arrived at the railway and were unable to proceed. Just across was Cei Pensarn, which had been built to export slate and stone from the Llanfair and Llanbedr quarries. This was brought down the river in flat-bottomed skiffs when the river was in flood. Indeed, the entrance cut through to the north of Mochras was to improve access to this wharf as it doubled up as a place to import necessary goods into the hinterland. Today the building on the wharf appeared to be an outdoor pursuit centre judging by the canoes outside.

From Llanbedr the road runs north, past the Pensarn and Llandanwg stations. The latter wasn't in existence in the 1880s so that the Victorian holidaymakers had to walk along the edge of the shore with their suitcases to get to their destination. From there it's a short hop to Harlech with its imposing castle that was captured by Owain Glyndwr in 1404. Joseph Cradock, in his *An Account of some of the most romantic parts of North Wales* (1777), wrote of Harlech 'there is a good harbour for ships, but no ships for the harbour'. I'm not sure to what he was referring, as Harlech has no harbour, although presumably he meant Llanbedr.

The road sped us north again until turning off to cross the *Pont Briwet*, the toll bridge that cuts some eight miles off the journey that would otherwise entail a drive along the Vale of Ffestiniog, through Maentwrog, and back along the other side of the river Dwyryd. In 1833 there were six quays on this river that connected with the Ffestiniog slate quarries, enabling something like fifty small slate barges to carry slate down to the sea for loading onto ships. The remains of the only known example of one of these barges were discovered in the river mouth in 1988. The flat-bottomed boat, some 26ft long and 10ft in beam, was built using a carvel bottom and clinker topside constructional method. According to oral evidence, these boats were built to a local traditional design and were said to have been well built.

At Minffordd there's a junction to Portmeirion, the Italianate 'folly on a mountain crag' according to its owner and architect Clough Williams Ellis. Deciding that the queue of cars turning off was a pretty good indication of probable delays, and wanting to make up some of the lost time from the previous day, I decided not to visit. Having been there several times, the thought of having to pay several pounds to enter seemed a poor alternative to a cup of coffee with Chris Partington.

Chris, who's been a friend since our college days, lives in one of the oldest houses in Porthmadog. 'The Oakeleys' was built in about 1820 as the slate wharf manager's office and home, just along from the first and main wharf – Oakeley Wharf – in the harbour. The name comes from what was then the largest slate mine in the world at Blaenau Ffestiniog, owned by the family of that name. 'It's an unusual spelling, Oakeley', he told me, but didn't know the reason why.

He bought the house after discovering it for sale while on an angling trip in the area. He'd been looking for suitable premises since 1981 for an angling museum and thought that this house, with its large garden, big house and proximity to both the harbour and main drag, would be perfect. I became involved in advising on a possible commercial fishing museum of Wales. When the plans were finally submitted to the local council, the proposed buildings were to house the two museums, an environmental centre, a Welsh language centre, a local TV station, bar and restaurant to finance the project and other spin-offs such as a public speaking platform in memory of Lloyd George and a rebuilt clocktower. The TV station idea came from his reading about how the Government was offering the opportunity to every town in Britain to set up community stations encouraging the making of local films. Having the acquaintance of a film cameraman, and knowing of a college in Pwllheli with a media studies department, he thought the Porthmadog community would jump at the chance of being involved.

However, the planning application was refused twice. An appeal to the Welsh Assembly was likewise turned down. He wasn't prepared to air his views on the planning committee but I could tell he was unhappy. 'It took two years to put the plan together with the help of twenty-five people. Two years, and the planning committee discussed it for exactly four minutes before refusing it. They've just got no vision. My first vision was simply for the angling and fishing museum, and we added different aspects of the social and environmental question.' He added that he had received a letter from the Ancient Monuments Society, a group advising on the utilisation of listed buildings ensuring the retention of character using traditional materials, that likened the finished architectural masterpiece to the Guggenheim Building in Bilbao and the Sydney Opera House. The sad thing is that, adjoining his garden, is one of the ugliest buildings in Porthmadog – the Canolfan – and the council seemed to have no problem allowing that to be built.

Another of Chris' projects was his purchase of a French fishing boat, which he had originally intended to convert into a half-sized Porthmadog schooner. If that had been successful he thought that maybe he could convert many more decommissioned fishing boats into the same and sell them. Unfortunately vandalism and thieving took their toll on the boat and, down-hearted, he then planned to turn the boat into a fifteenth-century galleon to commemorate Owain Glyndwr's capture of Harlech Castle. 'We could sail her over at night and mount a surprise attack on the town. The kids I asked thought it a great idea but only one bloke offered to volunteer with the conversion when it came down to it,' he told me, his voice edged with disappointment and desperation. I imagined the people of Harlech tucked up in their beds as cannon fire rained down and hordes of screaming kids roused the town! But nothing happened and so he advertised the boat on the internet for £1 – the engine is knackered – and received no offers so was contemplating scrapping the boat. 'The Oakeleys' itself has been sold, subject to contract, and he intends finding another suitable location. Although he's eccentric and relatively crazy, Porthmadog will be the loser from this man's moving on.

From personal experience, as I think I've said before, I think planning committees stink, are all too often manned by petty, insignificant, blinkered and brainless individuals, corrupt to the bone with their decisions and willingness to accept the odd back-hander, and thoroughly contemptible. A generalisation maybe, but all too often true. And it's called democracy!

Next door to his house is the maritime museum, and we wandered in. Rarely is this place busy but the displays are superb. We looked over his boat, which was moored in the harbour. Sometimes, in the summer when the tides are right, the seine fishermen set their nets in the harbour, watched by the throngs of holidaymakers that Porthmadog always seems to attract. Dog and I then walked to Borth-y-Gest and out along the shore – one of my favourite spots in the whole of Wales – where we were able to swim before doubling back to the harbour.

We've already discussed shipbuilding along the Welsh coast in some detail but, with regard to the vernacular zone, one harbour alone stands at the forefront of Welsh sail.

Shipbuilding at David Willams' yard at Porthmadog, *c.*1900.

That is Porthmadog. Here, two builders, David Jones and David Williams, produced what have been termed some of the finest vessels ever seen in British waters, both in beauty and efficiency. However, the origins of these goes back to 1824 when the smack *Two Brothers* was launched into the nearly-completed harbour being built by W. Alexander Maddocks in this remote northeastern part of Cardigan Bay to export slate from the Ffestiniog quarries. Although this was not the first boat to be built in the area, and the slates to leave the new Oakeley Wharf weren't the first to do so, this new smack marked the beginning of shipbuilding in what became known as Porth Madoc – in other words Maddock's port. Previously slates were brought down the Afon Dwyryd, as we've seen, in the slate barges and transhipped aboard ships anchored in the lee of Ynys Cyngar.

Henry Jones, joined later by his son William, built at least thirty sloops in the period from the opening of the harbour to 1860. Yet the volume of slate passing through the port increased rapidly and bigger ships were needed, so that they also were responsible for thirty-two larger vessels. More quays to load the slate were built by Samuel Holland, J.W.Greaves and the Welsh Slate Company. The narrow gauge railway from Ffestiniog was completed in 1836 and 4,275 tons of slate was brought down upon its carriages that year. In 1856 it was reported that there were 100 shipwrights and blacksmiths working in the various shipyards of the harbour.

The early boats built by people such as Henry Jones were described as 'short, bluff bowed, stout sterned and tub like vessels of a small size' by Owen Morris, as quoted in *Porthmadog Ships* by E. Hughes and A. Eames. Yet thirty years later, according to the same source, 'a more easy wedge-like overhanging shape was substituted for the bluff perpendicular bow, and a more gradual curvature was adopted for the stern – greater length given – and altogether vessels were modelled with greater regard to sailing and weatherly qualities than heretofore – stowage not being deemed the only essential quality constituting a good vessel'.

Evan Evans and Francis Roberts were building sloops and schooners from 1826 to the mid-1850s. Simon Jones worked from Borth-y-Gest and built the barque *Pride of Wales*

The Porthmadog-built brig *George Casson* entering the Bay of Naples 1868.

in the 1870s. This era was the height of the boom years for the shipbuilding industry in Porthmadog and it is said that the years 1877 and 1878 were the busiest years ever. In those two years eighteen boats were completed and the list of boatbuilders reads like a *Who's who* of Porthmadog: Simon Jones, Richard Jones, J & Eben Roberts, Hugh Williams, David Jones, Griffith Williams, Morris Owen and R. Ellis. Most of these vessels were schooners of a tonnage 93-141 tons, with four three-masted schooners of 165-186 tons, three brigs of 131-185 tons, two barquetines of about 250 tons each and a brigantine of 179 tons.

One of these, the *Olga Elkan*, was described in the *Cambrian News* as 'a finely built schooner… this fine vessel is eighty-two feet length of keel, twenty-two feet broad, and twelve feet two inches in depth of hold. By carpenters measure she is to carry two hundred and thirty-three tons and she is one hundred and thirty-nine registered tonnage', and was named after the wife of a Hamburg slate merchant.

The next two decades in the fortunes of the Porthmadog were depressed with only one boat being built, the *Richard Greaves*, coming from the yard of David Jones in 1885. Most of the work in the shipyards was confined to ship repairing. However, in 1891 building recommenced with David Jones launching the 129-ton *Blodwen* while David Williams completed the 142-ton *Dorothy*. Both of these vessels were three-masted schooners and were considered as keen rivals. For these two boats were the beginning of what became known as the Western Ocean Yachts for which these two builders became renowned. Ten or fifteen years of healthy orders followed, building almost entirely three-masted schooners, the biggest being the *Sydney Smith* in 1895.

As the twentieth century arrived, the demand for wooden ships dwindled yet the two shipyards managed to continue building their fine ships. However, with Porthmadog ships being almost the last to take to the seas around Wales, this must surely signify just how the ships were held in esteem by the seamen. Yet the overall size of the new vessels decreased and David Jones built his last ship, the *Elizabeth Pritchard* in 1909 and four years later David Williams launched his *Gestiana*, the last ship to come from these yards and the end of an era stretching back many generations. With war breaking out the following year, the maritime community of Porthmadog saw the demise of the German trade so important for their port and its survival.

The subsequent war resulted in the sinking of some of the Porthmadog ships, but some survived. But the *M.A. James*, built by 1900 by David Jones, was requisitioned in the Second World War into the barrage balloon service. She eventually became the sole remaining survivor until she ended her days at Appledore. The Porthmadog ships were all gone. Although these boats had sailed the world and were recognised in every ocean, little remains of them except their memory. Apart from the harbour itself, Cei Ballast, the island south of the harbour where empty vessels dropped their ballast before loading with slate, is one of the only visible evidences that this great age of sail ever existed. Sure, there are photographs and assortments of gear in the museum, but nothing of substance to remind us of this once fascinating place. The Ffestiniog railway continues to attract visitors on its little trains that chug seemingly endlessly up into the hills during the season – and some in winter, too. The ketch *Garlandstone*, a West Country vessel built in Devon and launched in 1909, was once moored in the harbour where she was to be restored as part of the maritime museum. This vessel could perhaps have invoked some of the old atmosphere of the harbour but, alas, the project never developed and the *Garlandstone* went off to be restored on the river Tamar, where she is based today. Porthmadog is left simply with its hopeless memories. And, of course, its councillors.

Porthmadog was, albeit briefly, home to a lifeboat station. The early history of this is unclear but it seems that an inefficient one was stationed before 1845 by the Harbour Trust. What is known is that the fifteen-man crew of the American vessel *Glendower* was rescued that year, and the likely candidate for this service was the lifeboat although it has been suggested that the pilot boat undertook the rescue. Seven years later the Shipwrecked Fishermen and Mariner's Benevolent Society were operating a lifeboat from the town. However, in 1854, the service was transferred to nearby Cricieth.

Porthmadog is also known as the 'gateway to the Lleyn peninsular' although the ancient 'hundred' of Lleyn doesn't begin for some miles. Nevertheless, after another while chatting in the kitchen of 'The Oakeleys', we took our farewells and returned to the road once again, keen to discover more of the Lleyn.

Cricieth was in fact our next destination, a small town west of Porthmadog with the ruins of a castle on a rocky outcrop overlooking both the town and sea. We could have walked along the sands from Porthmadog, past the holiday park of Morfa Bychan – I've done this before and enjoyed fine views of both mountains and sea – but decided time insisted on progression onwards. There's a tiny quay upon which a couple of small boats were moored. In the bay tiny dots flicked from side to side. These were windsurfers way out. The blue-painted and aptly named 'Blue China Teas' café was busy while next door the 'Peckish' café was quiet. Further along the seafront the dilapidated wooden sheds looked perfect in the maritime vernacular zone, and it occurred to me that examples of fishermen's sheds throughout Europe mirror these.

Cricieth, *c.*1900.

The castle was built in the late thirteenth century at a cost of £318 17*s* 4¾*d*. This was the cheapest of the North Wales castles. Here, under the castle, several clinker-built herring boats would have been found up, right to the First World War. These are depicted in another drawing by E. Prys Owen of 1831, being some 20–25ft long, having two masts and either sprit or gaff-rigged it seems, and a transom stern. One is shown with three masts. Cricieth herring were well known, but unfortunately they were generally regarded as inferior to the Nefyn herring, those from the north side of the peninsular being of a superior tasting. To add insult to injury, it was said that Cricieth herrings 'are cured in the village, but, I fear, with no great attention or skill than what are but too commonly bestowed upon them in the county' according to Edmund Hyde Hall in his *Description of Caernarvonshire 1809-1811*. He also noted that 'some trade in the export way is however carried on by the sale of herrings taken in the adjoining bays by half-decked vessels of scanty tonnage and limited number'.

As already mentioned, a lifeboat was brought on station in 1854, in preference to having to navigate the treacherous Porthmadog bar. Some say a boat was stationed here the year previous by the Shipwrecked Fishermen and Mariners Royal Benevolent Society, but it isn't totally clear whether it was the same vessel. The lifeboat house was built at Lon Felin, below the castle. In 1893 this was rebuilt on the same site and remained open until the service was withdrawn in 1931 after fifty-four launches had saved 133 lives. The building became a café and the town developed as a resort. However, after several fatalities, public outcry led to the reopening of the station in 1953, with the old boathouse being repurchased and the *Richard Silver Oliver* being put on station. The offshore boat was again withdrawn in 1968 and an inshore vessel remains on station, in the same boathouse, which has been rebuilt and modernised. Ironically for Cricieth, it seems that the station was always known as the Porthmadog lifeboat until 1892.

Leaving Cricieth westwards I was suddenly reminded of words once spoken to me by an item of news on the radio. This person, who shall remain nameless here, when decrying history, said there was no need to write history. 'You can just show some drawings or photographs and that tells it all'. I obviously disagreed otherwise I wouldn't be writing this. Photographs are all very well, I replied, and do tell a story, but that's all. Drawings are simply images of a human mind. Both are only a snapsnot of a moment in time, even if they do, in their preciseness, leave us with a greater scope of interpretation. They remind me of maritime excavations where archaeologists uncover wrecks, which are like looking through a time tunnel into a period of that ship's existence. Some call wrecks 'time capsules', where man's activities over a particular short period of time are unearthed and interpreted. All are, of course, valid tools for ethnologists but nevertheless only tell a fragment of the story. Photographs ignore change. Take a harbour, for instance, with its ever-changing fleet of vessels, its people and buildings, and its physical changes. Or a single boat with a varying crew. Most boats undergo alterations in their life. You could display a whole series of photographs depicting the life of the boat or the harbour, but the reality of that is unpractical. Thus we are left with the written account to complete the picture. 'How can you say a picture is enough yet you want the entire image?' I asked. Pouring himself a big glass of wine – we were at a party at the time – he then also poured out a pile of venom about history, its lack of value, its sense of negativity and his bombastic opinions of historians, much of which I wouldn't like to repeat. As it was, he turned out to be a computer programmer, although I refrained from adding my Luddite views to his sense of objectivity. Still, sometimes it makes me stop and think about whether what I am doing is a total waste of time and energy!

Dog and I were now well into the arm of the Lleyn. The narrow peninsular juts out into the Irish Sea from the main body of Wales as if it was grasping the harvest of the sea. It's a pretty inaccessible place, or at least it was before the motor car allowed entry. Stuck the 'wrong' side of the mountainous bulk of Snowdonia – some will rightly say the 'right' side – which confronted the traveller in his direct route, he had to circumvent the barrier, either north or south, to reach the rich, wonderful land of the Lleyn. Roads were unheard of until the twentieth century, so that man found it easier to arrive and depart by sea. And, although Lleyn man has always had his fertile lands to live by, it was the sea that he gazed upon when he had moments to pause. Ships have traded here for generations and hamlets have grown up all along the seaboard. Today, though, tourism plays as much a part in the economic life as does the sea and the land. Or perhaps it is the tourism that is the sea and land.

Two writers of Caernarfonshire – for that is the old name for the county that is now part of Gwynedd – stand out foremost in my mind. Edmund Hyde Hall has already been mentioned, and Wrexham-born Professor A.H. Dodd produced *A History of Caernarvonshire* in 1968, the other. Both are invaluable, although other writers such as Revd William Bingley, Revd John Evans, Joseph Cradock, E.D. Clarke and Thomas Pennant are worthy of a mention. Of course there are more. In contemporary times, Ian Skidmore's *Gwynedd* (1986) contains something that is relevant to the maritime zone.

We passed Llanystumdwy, on the banks of the river Dwyfor, famous for its fishing, according to Chris. This was the boyhood home of David Lloyd George – many think he was born here but he was, in fact, born in Lancashire – although his father was from Fishguard – which was where he received his only formal schooling, and now where a museum is dedicated to his life. Known as the 'Welsh Wizard' (*Y Dewin Cymreig*), he is famed for taxing the rich to help the poor, giving women the vote, leading the country during the First World War and trying to solve the Irish 'problem'. His grave is here, close by the river. The brown sign directing folk to the museum declares there's a 'Rabbit Farm' nearby, as well. This reminded of a quote by someone who reckoned that the Welsh coastal dwellers were more actively involved in rabbit catching rather than fishing and farming! Thomas Pennant contradicted this in his tours, noting that the Lleyn people ignored almost all other aspects of life in favour of the herring fishery. This preoccupation, more than the state of the roads, he blamed for the 'backwardness' in the peninsular.

According to a licensed fisherman I once met in Porthmadog, the fishermen occasionally operate a seine-net in a pool at the mouth of the river, although it seems that this is a very rare occurrence these days. Further on we passed the holiday camp with its own station of Penychain on the mainline railway where carriages must have spewed out hundreds of thousands on their way to holiday here! And after several more twists and turns in the road, we were in Pwllheli, which literally translates to 'Saltwater Pool'.

Today Pwllheli harbour appears at first to be just one forest of metallic masts. The channel in from the sea is home to North Wales' largest marina, and on both sides of the narrow waterway are lined with boatsheds. However the inner harbour 'pool' was almost empty. Yachts sailed up and down the river, in and out, crewed by young and old alike, many with the proverbial scantily clad beauties lying on the foredeck. Marinas to me are superficial – simply floating pontoons with plastic boats tied up alongside – and there's always a feeling that a puff of wind could blow the whole lot away. Like the boats themselves, there's no substance to a marina as against a stone harbour where large ships have lain to. Marinas of course reflect the general trend to the sea, where there's just a desire to play – and show off your wealth – with absolutely no thought of tradition or history. But Pwllheli wasn't always like that.

One of the first references to fishing is in 1293 when there were two boats in the harbour with five nets between them. Another seven families shared another twenty-two nets, which suggests seine-net operations wholly from the shore. Furthermore a mease of herring was paid as part-payment for a lease of land in the thirteenth century and presumably this was caught locally. Although in 1566 'Pullely' was 'a port or haven having a town… wherein are 36 householdes or cotages', none of the 'shippes barkes or vessells' belonged to the town. In seems that the port didn't get its own vessels until the turn of the next century when the *Elin* and *Philip* were named as small vessels plying Cardigan Bay and the Bristol Channel. There were of course the stories of piracy and wrecking, which we've seen were common along the entire coast. To thwart these activities, a Revenue cutter was stationed in the harbour from the 1820s.

At the beginning of the eighteenth century a considerable amount of salt was being landed into the harbour and salted herring being exported to Liverpool, Dublin, Milford Haven and Carlisle. Because of the high tax on salt much of this was smuggled over from Ireland thus Salt Officers were stationed at about the same time. The Salt Tax was regarded as a burden on poor fisherfolk throughout the country and the Lleyn fishers were no different. It wasn't until the repeal of the legislation in 1825 that the cured herring export could really develop into anything more than a cottage industry.

In 1748 Lewis Morris noted the healthy herring fishery and the supply of good oysters. Butter and cheese, though, were the principal commodities. In 1774 the will of a certain blacksmith showed that he owned 'two boats, a large net, four herring nets and a large rake to Harvest oysters'. Oysters were indeed plentiful but it is doubtful whether this trade benefited more than a handful of locals. In 1851 it was reported that seventeen boats were fishing up to a thousand oysters a day but much of the dredging was done by Essex and Jersey smacks. The locals were only able to retain exclusive fishing to the few oyster beds close to the shore, although one particular rich one, off Gimlet Rock, had been discovered in 1839.

Heavy catches of herring were reported around the mid-part of the nineteenth century when they sold for *2s 6d* per Hundred in 1844. On 2 December 1848 the *Caernarfon and Denbigh Herald* reported that 'on Wednesday last, upwards of 8000 fine herrings were netted and brought in here [Pwllheli] by the crew of the Fishing Boat *Wylan*, Owen Lewis, master'. Large catches of mackerel were also reported and these fetched high prices. In 1857 the Pwllheli market had plentiful supplies of herring, when it seems many of the fishermen were from the Wirral. During 1880 there were about 400 fishermen from the Isle of Man in residence in the town, participating in the autumn herring fishery. The Cheshire fishermen were there again in 1896 and from these came the fishing 'nobby' much as we saw in Aberystwyth against the traditional style of small herring boat we saw at Cricieth. Of course, there were the low years in the fortunes of the fishery as in 1878 when it completely failed so that a relief fund had to be set up for the penniless fishermen. In early 1879 £64 was raised through a house-to-house collection, and £40 of this was handed out in food to some fifty families. By October 1880 the *Caernarfon and Denbigh Herald* was again reporting large catches of herring, several wagon loads of which were barrelled and sent away. However, the autumnal herring fishery declined throughout the early twentieth century and lobster fishing became the only way to support full-time fishing, or something close to full-time. Today a few fishing boats were moored in the harbour, including one of the ugliest boats I've ever seen.

Ships were built in Pwllheli with timber being shipped over from Merionydd. In 1730 nine cargoes of timber arrived from Aberdyfi and Barmouth while Barmouth alone sent fifteen loads in 1808, suggesting an increase in the size of boats, if not the number being built. Many of these depended on the Porthmadog slate trade for business. Between 1782 and 1878 – almost a century – it has been estimated that 421 ships were built in the town, a figure that would mean there were more vessels built here than at any other North Wales port. Considering its position along the peninsular it is quite incredible. Yet again, it was the railway, arriving in 1867, causing the collapse in the coastal trade. At the same time iron ships began to command the export of slate overseas.

One building that stands out proud amongst the square-shaped yachting sheds on the south side of the river is the lifeboat station. Opened relatively late – in 1891 – the first boat was the tubular *Caroline Richardson*, which was soon transferred to Rhyl once it was found to be unsuited to the local conditions. A self-righting boat was introduced, launched from the boathouse. But this was changed in 1930 to a boat kept afloat until, following a tragedy off Cricieth, they changed back to a carriage launch from the boathouse. Although extended and modernised, the boathouse today houses a Mersey-class lifeboat and inshore boat. The next-door boatbuilding firm of Partington's is the oldest still in the yachting business in the town, although they appear to rely more on winter storage and repairs these days rather than boatbuilding.

We sped westwards towards the lowering sun. We passed Llanbedrog, described as 'a village of a few hovels, more mean and uncouth than I have yet had to mention' by Richard Ayton in the 1820s. Some months before I'd been on the beach looking for the remains of a fish weir that lies on the beach, but was unable to find it. The beach huts were all in a state of dilapidation. Boats used to set sail for the fishing grounds here not that long ago but these are long gone.

From here the road veers round the mass of Mynydd Tir-y-Cwmwd before returning towards the coast. Between road and sea lies the extensive chalet site known as 'The Warren'. Not unlike a township with trees, and reminding me of a rabbit warren, this site, I'm told, is the holiday playground of middle class Cheshire. The road from here leads into Abersoch, which was thronged with these people. Yachts joggle for space in the narrow river and a few boats lay against the small quay. Ayton noted that he 'saw a sloop there discharging a cargo of limestone, which constitutes the sole article of importation. A few fishing boats complete the wealth of the port'. Oh, how these people from wealthy Cheshire have transformed the place. Edmund Hyde Hall noted some shipbuilding with the timber, like Pwllheli, coming from Merionydd. We didn't linger for long.

Machroes lies at the western end of the 'Welsh Riviera' that begins at 'The Warren'. The sandy beach has a few colourful beach huts along its edge, and unsightly groynes fill the beach itself. A hard standing area is full of yachts in the winter. Car parking is free which meant it was busy although evening was upon us. The dog ran on the beach while I watched the last boats sail landward.

Here was the original Abersoch lifeboat, established in 1844 and closed eleven years later. In 1869 the RNLI opened at a station at Abersoch itself, housing the lifeboat in a boathouse alongside the river. In 1894 the service was switched again back to Penrhyn Du until its closure in 1931. This building has been converted into a dwelling, with the slipway still intact, while the original Abersoch one by the river was demolished. The present inshore lifeboat is housed in the boathouse to the north of the entrance to the river.

Around the tip of Penrhyn Du lie the islands of St Tudwal. In 1566 'Stydwalles' was 'a wyld rode and landyng place where divers shippes do repair'. Lewis Morris found the Roads here one of the best in Britain and noted that they would be capable of containing the entire 'Royal Navy of England'. Furthermore, he suggested the building of a quay at the point to produce a good drying harbour. Needless to say, it was never built. As to the local commodities, he found several veins of lead and copper ore, and 'a blackish heavy hard Stone, which is reckoned better than Brass for the Center Pins of light Engines to turn on'.

From Machroes we headed towards the tip of the Lleyn with the sandy expanse of Hell's Mouth (*Porth Neigwl*) on our left. Unfortunately the road was closed before Rhiw, which necessitated a detour to reach Aberdaron.

Aberdaron nestles in a small vale, a cluster of whitewashed houses and a few more substantial stone houses. Two hostelries serve the tourists and we were in time to sit on the balcony of the Ty Newydd Hotel, overlooking the beach with a pint, watching the last rays of the sun, itself already disappeared behind Mynydd Anelog.

The village has associations with the sea, its only neighbour, that stretch back far beyond anyone's memory. Fishing was paramount to their survival although piracy and smuggling seem to have dominated at various times. Ayton noted that there was an abundance of John Dory but that it was deemed too ugly to bother with. Herrings were their principal support and these were exported to Liverpool and the Irish markets by Irish wherries. Some even went as far as London. Some say it was the principal herring port of North Wales as far back as the fourteenth century. However, they were obviously ill equipped to fully exploit the fishery for Ayton continued 'they are not supplied with suitable boats and nets', and needed assistance to procure these. Ayton and Daniell were unable to reach Bardsey Island (in Welsh *Ynys Enlli* – island in the currents), lying around the corner off the tip of the peninsular, but several other travellers such as Pennant and Bingley did. The unfortunate thing was that I, too, was going to be unable to reach the island. Everything was against me – time, tide and the boat. Bardsey was one place I every intention of visiting so the realisation that this was not going to happen was extremely depressing. Thus I had another pint (or two).

The island, famed as a place of pilgrimage, has a strong tradition of fishing. Here, in 1800, Revd William Bingley wrote that, 'collecting lobsters and crabs occupies most of the time of the inhabitants'. Pennant, twenty years before, noted the abundance of fish and lobsters. The remainder of their time was spent working the land.

The typical 'Bardsey boat' in use was a double-ender, some 20–25ft in length and rigged with two spritsails and a tiny jib. Construction was clinker with softwood planking on oak frames and backbone. Together with potting, the boats were used for drifting for herring and for general transport to and from the island, with Aberdaron being their mainland terminus.

Aberdaron also used to have its own fleet of similar but smaller double-enders that worked two herring nets from *Porth Meudy* or Fishermen's Cove. However, as the herring fishing declined and work concentrated on potting for lobsters and crabs, the fishermen adopted the transom stern with a skeg, said to allow them to be rowed backwards onto a pot. Previously many boats had capsized while hauling in over the stern quarter. The boat that evolved was a 12–16ft clinker-built, at first lug-rigged until gaff was adopted around 1900. Today's boats – and a fleet of about twenty – sport a very high peaked gaff, or gunter rig, with a daggerboard for their weekly summer races. Some of these have local names such as *Anelog, Wennol, Awel, Cadl* and *Gwenlli*. Others are anglicised – *Jane, Swan, Lizzie* and *Betty*.

Two local boatbuilders were responsible for the majority of the Aberdaron fleet. Sion Tomos was born in Bardsey in 1880 where his father and grandfather had been building ships on the beach. After spending years at sea, he returned to nearby Rhiw where he commenced building the beach boats. He reportedly built over 100 until he ceased at the age of eighty-three in 1963. His father built the *Annie*, the oldest survivor of the type. My informant tells me that she was built in 1865, but others contradict this. Wil Jones, the other builder, built his boats without any tuck to the transom whereas Sion Tomos built in a degree of tuck to produce a wineglass shape. Douglas Jones of Pwllheli built a couple of the surviving boats, the *Anelog* and *Marian*.

Slate

Although slate was worked to some extent as far back as the Roman era, it wasn't until the eighteenth century that the beginnings of a slate industry could be said to have commenced in Wales. Slate occurs naturally in many parts of Britain – in North Wales, parts of Cardiganshire and Pembrokeshire, western Scotland (primarily around Ballachulish and Easdale), Cumbria and Cornwall. Around the world, Spanish, Brazilian and North African slate is available.

The word itself comes from the French *esclater* meaning 'to split', which became slat in old English and *ysglatus* in Welsh, later becoming *llech*. It is a metamorphic rock that has been under pressure and heat for millions of years, breaking down and becoming a reformed mineral with a defined bedding plane – the plane of cleavage – which gives it its unique splitting feature so suited to its use.

Its main use is as roofing slates, as any look upon the roofs of Britain makes obvious. However, it can also be found in many other uses such as gravestones, architectural products, floorings, a walling material, fencing posts, writing tablets, and as large slabs that have a thousand of uses such as water tanks and covers for septic tanks. Latter-day uses are for the base of pool tables.

By the late eighteenth century Wales was outstripping any other part of Britain in its annual output, with the quarries of North Wales producing the vast majority of Welsh slate. Here two principal varieties exist – the plum-coloured Cambrian slate from the Bethesda- Nantlle vein (500 million years old) and the blue-grey Ordovician veins of Ffestiniog and Corris (400 million years old).

Up to the eighteenth century, although slate was dug out of the mountainsides of Wales, it was only used locally. Transport was the chief factor preventing any major development for slate is a heavy material, even when split thinly. Methods to transport it about the quarry were essential for most of the dressing work was undertaken close to the quarry. Furthermore, only with the building of tramways, enabling large loads to be carried down the mountains to the sea, did any attempt at creating an industry commence. Although slate was, for example, carried down from Corris to Derwenlas in the sixteenth century, and subsequently exported by sea, these were isolated instances of a trade in the material.

When viewing the topography of the North Wales valleys, one obvious characteristic is the residue from the many small slate quarries that litter the area. For, although these days we talk as if slate came from one of a handful of land sites, the actual case in the late eighteenth and early nineteenth centuries was that dozens of small enterprises shot up, extracting the rock in hillside sites away from any population. Wales began outstripping the production of the other areas of Britain in about 1793, a year that the Welsh output was over half of the British output of 45,000 tons.

With the development of tramways in the early nineteenth century – the first brought slate down from the Penrhyn quarry to Bangor in 1801 – the Welsh trade flourished. In the 1820s Caernarfon and Port Dinorwic were connected to quarrying areas of Nantlle and Llanberis, the Ffestiniog Railway to Porthmadog opened in 1936, the Corris railway to the Dyfi in 1859, and the Talyllyn in 1865. At the same time the mainline railways were expanding fast, so that roofing slates could be quickly sent to the fast growing English towns and cities caught in the Industrial Revolution. The coastal trade declined at the expense of the rail network and England grew rich at the expense of its small neighbour.

While the local community saw some benefit from the spread of jobs, dangerous as they might be, much of the economic benefit left Wales. When one considers that the non-ratepaying multi-national supermarkets thrive in Wales today and the way their profit bleed out of Wales, I guess we shouldn't be surprised that this has long been the practise of business!

By 1882 Wales was producing 92 per cent of the 494,100 tons of slate that Britain either consumed or exported. But by this time over half of this tonnage came from the two super-quarries of Penryhn at Bethesda and Dinorwig at Llanberis. Not only was Welsh slate the best, but it also dominated the trade at its peak. However, it must be added that the Penrhyn quarry was financed with money from the family's Jamaican sugar plantations, which were themselves, built upon slavery. Considering that some 258 workers were killed at work between 1826 and 1875 at the Penrhyn quarry, it's likely that there were similar perils in working for this family in either business. In 1893 a Government report found that the death rate amongst slate mines was higher than in the coal mines, at 3.23 per 1,000 workers.

Because many mines were located high up mountainsides, many workers stayed in barracks close by during the week. In general the pay and conditions were not good, although some employers built model housing for their quarry workers. Out of these oppressive conditions came the *caban*, formal meetings of quarrymen with debates on current affairs or singing and poetry recital. Likewise, emerging from these came the North Wales Quarrymen's Union in 1874, and eventually radical politicians such as David Lloyd George. The *caban* was largely responsible for funding and the setting up the University College of North Wales at Bangor.

The Porthoer regatta with Aberdaron lobster boats competing.

Timber was sourced locally, with the larch coming from the slopes of Cefn Amlwch, further up the peninsular, the trees felled in person by the boatbuilder. Oak was bought in. Boatbuilding was in essence a local tradition, a localised design and, once the two main participants had died, it vanished suddenly. Unlike other parts of the Welsh coast, the fact that some twenty boats participate in the regatta and several more await restoration, proves the tradition itself isn't dead. Several years before, I'd witnessed the Sunday regatta during the preparation of an article on the vessels.

Davis, in *An Account of the Fishing Gear of England and Wales* (1937) noted 'within the memory of the present generation, an old man used to build small temporary stone weirs at Aberdaron'. The remains of another are said to exist off Porth Simdde at the west end of the beach. It was, of course, the beach that was the lifeline of the village with boats coming ashore to await low water to unload their cargoes of coal, limestone or salt and to take on cured herrings, butter, bacon, slate, cheese and kelp. Even the church, with its double nave, stands guard. Today it is the tourists in their search for sea and sand who patronise it, while the pubs, shop and cafés attend to their needs. It may have changed, as everywhere else, but Aberdaron, perhaps uniquely, has retained all of its positive charm.

DAY FIFTEEN

ABERDARON TO NEWBOROUGH

At Aberdaron dogs are allowed on the left side of the beach so, with the first rays of the sun warm on my back, the dog chased sticks I threw into the wavelets as they dashed themselves onto the beach. Afterwards we walked along the coastal path to Porth Meudwy to look at the Aberdaron lobster boats, neatly lined up on their trailers. Several larger more modern boats had already set out to check the trains of lobster pots that lie offshore. Further on, Borth Hen denotes an old port, signs of which are non-existent. Walking back over the headland, I was able to obtain fine views over the village.

Several writers including Pennant and Hyde Hall made extremely unenthusiastic observations upon the place. Pennant found it 'a poor village' while others found it 'a primitive fishing village' or 'a small and not very comely village'. Hyde Hall noted that only coals and groceries were imported, which was probably correct, but that nothing was exported. Presumably he came out of the herring season although to be fair he does say that some boats participate in the fishery in the season. If he'd arrived a decade or two later, he would have found that the nearby mines of Porth Ysgo were producing small quantities of manganese ore. By 1840 some fifty people were employed in the mining with the ore being shipped to Liverpool.

Again at Porth Smidde I looked for signs of the fish weir, but to no avail. Remains of a jetty can be seen, which, although its use is unclear, it might have been for the export of stone from the quarries on the slopes of Mynydd Mawr. I retraced back to Aberdaron, which was just waking up, and enjoyed a cup of coffee in the van gazing out over twin islands of *Ynys Gwylan-fawr* and *Ynys Gwylan-bach* in the distance. At the same time I attempted to imagine the village with a procession of pilgrims arriving and embarking on the small boat taking them to sacred Bardsey. Those here on their first visit must have wondered if they were about to embark on a trip to the ends of the world.

As I left Aberdaron along the narrow road west I was reminded of the entry in the 1907 *Black's Guide to North Wales* in which it declares of the village that there 'is no place in the three kingdoms the least like of it. It is a village transferred bodily from the operatic stage. The houses are toy like and unconnected'. This writer likened the place to Lilliput.

We drove to the car park at the top of Mynydd Mawr. I wanted at least to get some fine views of Bardsey, even if I had only been there in my youth. I've also sailed past it on a number of occasions. And there it was, almost at my feet, lying about two miles offshore, a bit in a haze, flat except for Mynydd Enlli at its nearest corner. The first religious order is said to have been founded by St Cadfan in the sixth century and the monastery became one of noted importance in the Middle Ages. Thus pilgrims flocked here, coming either from Caernarfon, in the north or Pwllheli, in the south. Legend has it that this is also King Arthur's Avalon, but having read various versions of the Arthur

Boats drawn up on the beach on Bardsey. (Courtesy National Library of Wales)

story, I wouldn't like to comment. As a final resting-place, though, he couldn't have picked a more tranquil and far away setting.

The island does have a notable lighthouse, which has the tallest square tower of any lighthouse in Britain. Built in 1820/1, it is set at the south-west corner of the island from where its red and white painted bands are visible many miles away. Until 1891 the tower was all white. At night I've seen it from over twenty miles.

Again I didn't want to linger and I don't want to burden readers with a catalogue of facts on the island as these are available in many other, if not better, books than this one. Try *Enlli ddoe a heddiw* edited by Peter Hope Jones in 1987 for it has some fine photographs of the past and present. One photo especially – number seven, showing what must be a boat of almost 30ft in length being repaired in 1934 – really sums up Bardsey's maritime prowess. Beach boats such as these are comparable to the open *Ness Sgoths* of Lewis, Outer Hebrides – regarded as Britain's largest beach boats – for their size and nowhere else in Wales can such large beach craft be found. Another photo (not in the book) shows several of these boats lined up along the beach. These exhibit a strong Norse influence in the same way that many of the Scottish craft do. As a form of classification, they have been termed 'western skiffs', and do bear many resembles to nineteenth-century craft working the Irish Sea and western seaboard of Scotland. From a Welsh perspective, once lobster potting surpassed the herring fishery, the boats were adapted to suit by being built with a transom stern so that none of these elegant double-enders have survived today. That is sincerely a great shame and perhaps one day soon somebody will build a replica vessel to prove their worth.

It was time to continue north, and over the next few hours we visited a number of bays which involved trying to find a place to park amongst the visitors' cars and walking a distance to find a beach not unbusy! So we saw Porth Oer (Whistling Sands), Porth

Iago, Porth Ferin, Porth Colman, Traeth Penllech, Porth Gwylan, Porth Ysgaden, Porth Llydan, Porth Ysgaig and Porth Towyn. Porth Ysgaden remains my favourite although Porth Llydan was glorious that day because of the fact that it was completely deserted, allowing me to swim in the flesh, so to speak, without any onlookers.

The north coast of the Lleyn was renowned for its quality of herring so that bays such as *Porth Ysgaden* (the herring port) had small beach-based fleets. Thomas Pennant noted in 1771 that herrings were in abundance, putting their value at £4,000 annually. Some was taken to Bardsey where they were cured and sent onwards to Dublin by Irish wherry. Some were cured on the shore locally. Again John Dory was taken but discarded for its ugliness. Lobsters and crabs were caught in baited traps. Hyde Hall observed that 'Porths Towyn, Colman, Gwylan and Isgadan' all had vessels which were involved in the herring fishery, some sailing as far as the Irish coast in their pursuit of the fish. He also found that the salt used in the cure was 'allowed duty free here as elsewhere', a fact that led to the repeal of the laws in 1825. Porth Colman was solely used as a place of shelter for the herring boats in times of gales. Limestone kilns were as universal as the stories of smuggling at all these bays. Coal was as likely to be shipped inwards for the kilns as was illegal salt for the herring until it was allowed duty free for curing.

Porth Ysgaden had been the site of a film setting two years previous when Scott Metcalfe had taken his converted Danish fishing boat, now rigged as a topsail schooner, and several small skiffs for the set. I'd gone along too as an observer, watching the antics of the actors and the professionalism of Scott and his crew. The film concerned the Quakers and we've already heard about a later sequence at Porthgain. We shall meet Scott soon. Today the little cove is home to a couple of crab boats. However, as a footnote perhaps, it is worth mentioning that one boat from here, with two locals aboard, unintentionally sailed over to Kilkeel in Ireland in 1933 after being forced to do so by an unfavourable wind shift. A feat of this magnitude was once almost a weekly occurrence if some of the historical evidence is to be believed.

At Porth Dinllaen, an extraordinary herring fishery emerged in the Middle Ages. In 1287 there were sixty-three nets in operation. In 1566 'Portynllayn' was a mere 'creke havyng a town nere unto hit called Nevyn'. A 1680 local inventory listed items associated with fishing along with oxen, sheep, cows and horses. By 1742 the lease of Cefn Amlwch confirms that both Porth Dinllaen and Nefyn were centres of free fishing. Six years later Lewis Morris found an unfinished pier, which he deemed would soon fall into ruin and the harbour ruined. He also observed an abundance of oysters and herring, of which 5,000 barrels were cured and shipped off in 1747, this figure not including that consumed in the locality. In the early nineteenth century, according to Hyde Hall, the pier was in use because he saw twenty-six fishing vessels behind it on his visit. Just around Penrhyn Nefyn, the bay of Nefyn was just as busy with curing houses lining the foreshore. There, he wrote, were forty fishing boats, each jointly owned by up to seven fishers. Initially it is thought the fishermen used similar boats to those at Aberdaron and double-ended fishing boats are depicted in photos but some of these suggest that they might have been bought in from outside. It is known that some were purchased from Matthew Owen of Menai Bridge in the early twentieth century. His boats were about 18ft long and cost £20.

Nefyn became the principal herring station of North Wales, overtaking Aberdaron, and its herring renowned throughout the area where the cry of 'Penwaig Nefyn' was well known. Also well versed was the fishwives' cry of 'Penwaig Nefyn, Penwaig Nefyn, Bolia fel tafarnwyr, Cefna' fel ffarmwrs' (*Nefyn herrings, Nefyn herrings, bellies like innkeepers, backs like farmers*). In 1679, according to the Estate Books, the nearby Glynllifon estate was supplied with herrings that cost between a shilling and 14*d* a Hundred. Cured herring were sent to Gwydir Castle, Llanrwst in 1623.

During the season that lasted from about September to January almost everyone was involved in the herring. Outside of that, it was the land that preoccupied these people and it was always vital to get the harvest in before the herring arrived. Even the quarrymen are said to have interrupted their work to help at harvest time, a sign that every able body helped at the important times of the rural calendar. Occasionally, if the moon was right, the fishing might begin in August although many believed it was wrong to fish prior to Thanksgiving Day. Most nets were 50 yards long with a one-inch mesh, these enmeshing the fish as they swam into the net and becoming trapped by the gills. These nets were either fixed at one or both ends, depending on the current so that at Y Gamlas they anchored both ends and at Y Swangins only one end was fixed at the other allowed to float free. Those unable to purchase their own nets were able to loan one from the net merchant who then took a quarter of the catch as a hire charge. These same fishermen obeyed unwritten laws that forbade a fisherman from one village encroaching on another's ground. This ensured there were no disagreements.

By 1910 there were still forty boats working at Nefyn but by Armistice Day in 1918 there were hardly any, a decline that the town never recovered from. Today the only sign that the fishery ever existed can be found at the Lleyn Historical and Maritime Museum in the old St Mary's church, easily recognised by the fully rigged sailing ship on the weather vane atop the tower. Here the story is told of the fishing, the shipbuilding and

The headland, Nefyn, from a postcard.

the coastal trade. It is well worth a visit and, for those unhappy to pay, is free, although donations are gratefully appreciated.

Shipbuilding flourished at Porth Dinllaen during the nineteenth century, during which period some fifty-eight vessels were built, although this figure is small compared to the other main Gwynedd ports. The last of these was the *Annie Lloyd* in 1878 and the largest *Robert Jones*, 495 tons, launched by James Owen in 1866. The same year the Harbour Company began the building of the breakwater and wharves for it was hoped to win the contract for the Irish ferry at the expense of Holyhead after an Act of Parliament had been obtained in 1806. Even though Hyde Hall had mentioned this possibility in 1811, it seems it took fifty years to develop any ideas, followed fairly quickly by the realisation that the plan was unacceptable and would never come to fruition.

We walked out to Porth Dinllaen via the golf course, avoiding the flying golf balls. At the tip is the Porth Dinllaen lifeboat station, which has been stationed on the same site since its inception in 1864. This was rebuilt before being extended for the first motor lifeboat in 1926. At the same time the slipway was lengthened to 351ft and remains one of the longest still in use. Further improvements were made prior to the stationing of the present Tyne-class all-weather lifeboat.

West of the lifeboat house the remains of a fish weir can be seen on the beach and west of this is the hamlet of Porth Dinllaen, which consists of hardly more than a dozen houses and one pub, the Ty Coch Inn. Luckily, the latter was open so I was able to purchase a pint and sit on the wall observing the activity in and around the bay. Holidaymakers dotted the whole sweep of the beach. Children ran in and out of the silky smooth water. Motor boats zigzagged around the harbour while sailing dinghies darted about the bay. A couple of windsurfers, obvious novices, were attempting to remain upright for more than a few seconds. Sunbathers I grouped in two categories: those baskers happy to lie and soak up the sun and those family members more concerned with casting a constant eye upon the antics of their offspring, thus becoming bad-tempered and ill at ease.

Not wishing to be biased to Porth Dinllaen, I afterwards spent a similar hour observing the beach goers of Nefyn. Here whitewashed cottages cling to the beach, competing with colourful beach huts for space. The pier, quite modern, had one fishing boat alongside and a few lobster pots were stacked nearby. Again sailing boats – possibly the same ones – sailed close to the shore, only just far enough off to avoid several swimmers in the sea. Sunbathers again clustered in groups, perhaps suffering the same concerns as their counterparts around the corner. I munched on a piece of bread and cheese, throwing lumps to the dog who seemed to be acceptable on the beach. Here, right in front of me, one source quotes that 191 ships were built during seventy years in the nineteenth century. John John Thomas, known as *Brennen Nefyn*, built thirty of these himself (with a bit of help from his 300 carpenters!) between 1813 and 1840. I later discovered that it was the eastern end of the beach that was 'dog free', according to the county council bylaw notice.

Afterwards, after visiting the aforementioned museum, I searched for a sign of three herrings I'd photographed a few years previously. It had hung over a doorway and was clearly obvious then. Today I could not find it. Was this a further sad reflection of the lack of awareness of just how great an industry once adorned these shores? However, after studying the herring fishery all along the British coast, it was a familiar situation. In my perhaps muddled mind, the herring fishery is just so much more interesting than the normal aspects of history that people immerse themselves in. But then, of course, I am completely biased on that score!

North-east of Nefyn the coast is cruel – sheer cliffs tumbling almost to the waves. Several quarries have dug holes into the mountainside of *Yr Eifl* and the stone carried away by boat, brought down the hillside on the many inclines that remain. Nant Gwrtheyrn was one such quarrying community where the workers were known to have turned to the herring during the season. Once the quarries were abandoned the village drifted into a deserted state before being converted into the present Welsh Language and Cultural Centre. A couple of ruined piers point to this exportation of stone by sea.

The harbour at Trefor stemmed from this same export, the first quay being built in about 1850 when the Yr Eifl quarry was opened by Samuel Holland. He also built the village for his workers and named it after his foreman Trefor. Initially the harbour was tidal until it was deepened in 1869, although the quays were still only 3ft of water above the high-water level. Stone was delivered by horse and cart until tracks were laid in 1873 enabling wagons to be pulled straight from the quarry to the harbour by the small engine – known as the *loco bach*. Between 1912 and 1914 a wooden pier was erected allowing loading on both sides. The quay was raised in height and hoppers built to store the stone. For some time steamers replaced the old sailboats in the trade and even diesel-driven ships. But the writing was on the wall for the sea trade. Although the railway never affected the trade, it was the advent of the lorry in the mid-twentieth century that did so, and the port became idle. The quarry itself closed in 1971. Today it is the habitat of a few local boats and some tourists who I found sunning themselves on the beach. The quays and *Doc bach* (little dock) were restored in the mid-1980s, at the same time that the lifeboat house was demolished. It remains a peaceful and pleasant place and, judging by the numbers of people walking their dogs along the track of the railway towards the older western pier, a favourite doggy spot!

The lifeboat *Cyprian* was stationed here in 1883. Known as the Llanaelhaiarn lifeboat, it was donated in memory of the captain of the steamer *Cyprian* that was wrecked here in October of 1881, causing a national outcry after the Porth Dinllaen lifeboat didn't set out to help the ship. Some of the quarrymen were said to have pulled survivors out after the ship foundered. The captain gave his lifejacket to a young stowaway who was thus saved whilst the captain, on the other hand, was not. The lifeboat was only launched to callouts twice and thus was closed in 1901.

In 1900 there were twenty fishing boats worked from here but, by 1950, this had fallen to eight. The only boat that could be classed as a fishing boat was a blue painted coble – a type native to Yorkshire and Northumberland. This pretty working vessel has been based here for several years although I've never seen it go out to sea. Presumably it does, though!

North of Trefor the coast sweeps up to the entrance of the Menai Strait. At Clynnog there's a huge church, noted as one of the largest and most elegant in Wales. On the shore there's also a fish weir – the Gored Beuno – thought by some to be the oldest in Wales. The village of Dinas Dinlle, named after the mound, which was once a fortification, is a one-horse type of place, which comes to life – a bit, anyway – in summer. It's a holiday kind of place as long as you don't necessarily need sun on your holiday. The long heatwave might still be continuing even if its intensity and length were indeed unusual. The 'Beachcomber' café was hectic, as were the other cafés and gift shops. Towels hung off balconies. In the hinterland I got my first view of Snowdon beyond little patchwork fields that led the eye up to the grey rock. The sandy beach here was lively but again the 'no dogs' sign meant he had to sit in the van while I had a short looksee. Later we drove past the airport towards Fort Belan, a fortification built by Thomas Wynn of Glynllifon at the western end of the Menai Strait in the late eighteenth century to ward off any seaborne attack upon the Strait. The dock and associated buildings were built by the second Lord Newborough (the family got the title for their contribution to the nation's defence) between 1824 and 1826 to house their private yachts. Opened as a tourist attraction in 1977, the fort was sold in 1986 and, a year later, an exhibition of the family's maritime artefacts, amongst them a few boats, opened. This sadly closed in the 1990s. In our attempt in reaching the fort we were thwarted by a gate at the end of a bumpy track with a notice 'Private Warren farm' and were forced to reverse. Fort Belan and Dock is, as are many of the estate grounds along the Menai Strait as I was soon to find out, inaccessible without a boat or an invitation – or probably both! I had neither.

Forydd Bay lies at the south-western end of the Menai Strait and is a sandy shallow inlet. From there the road clings to the Strait until arriving at Caernarfon. This is probably the least visited part of the Menai waterway that divides Anglesey from the mainland. Half way along is a slipway and a place for storage of boats. Further along is Coed Helen, from where a footbridge over the river Seiont connects to the town.

Almost any view of Caernarfon is dominated by Edward I's castle, which is situated close to the confluence on this river into the Menai. Completed in 1284, it is said that much of the stone for the castle came over from Anglesey, and that this trade led to the establishment of the Tal-y-Foel ferry, on the opposite side of the water. In 1566 it was described as 'a port or haven' with 120 households and ships, not owned there, that 'do lade and unlade by the Qwenes highnes authoritie'. Pennant suggested the town 'is justly the boast of North Wales for the beauty of the situation'. The town's maritime activity was centred on the slate trade from the Nantlle valley mines a few miles inland. Up to the last decade of the eighteenth century, vessels entered the river and loaded up as best they could, given that the facilities were next to none. However, in 1793 an Act for 'Enlarging, Deepening, Cleansing, Improving, and Regulating the Harbour of Carnarvon' was obtained, with another for further improvements in 1809. Thus when Samuel Lewis arrived in the 1833 he found 'extensive and commodious quays and wharfs' on the river below the castle as well as a new patent slip under construction. With the arrival of a tramway from the valley in 1828, slates were shipped out in quantity to various growing cities, especially Liverpool and Dublin. A new pier protruding out into the Strait, built to enhance the shipbuilding and ship repair facilities, later proved to exacerbate silting up problems and was subsequently demolished.

Copper ore from the Snowdonia mines accounted to some extent in the exports of the town. For this, sloops and smacks travelled almost continuously between the smelters in the Swansea area of South Wales and Caernarfon, bringing culm on the return trip. According to Lewis Lloyd in *The Port of Caernarfon 1793-1900*, these exports were of no comparison to the slate trade. Other exports he noted were pigs to Liverpool, some manganese ore and other sundries such as bacon, wool, oats, bricks, potatoes, calf skins, 'old iron' and furniture. Lewis Morris noted corn as an export. But the port never developed in a way through which the local hinterland was served. Imports generally consisted of coal, culm and North American timber for shipbuilding and the mines, a trade that developed after punitive import tariffs were introduced in 1812 on Baltic timber.

The Curing of Herring

Herring is a fish that deteriorates quickly once it is out of the water. The eyes go dull and grey instead of the bright red eyes that denote fresh fish. Once it is landed in the morning (usually), it has to be taken to market quickly. Obviously, in rural areas of the country where transport was limited, this was practically impossible. Local hawkers – most often fish wives – sold the fresh herring within the locality with their characteristic cries such as 'Sgadan Aberporth, sgadan Aberporth, dau fola ac corff (Aberporth herring, Aberporth herring, two bellies and one body). After the advent of the railway system into parts of Wales in the mid-nineteenth century, fresh herring could then be sent quickly to distant markets in the developing towns and cities on early morning trains. However, cured herring was a less troublesome and more profitable way of distributing the fish to a wider market.

The property of salt used as a preservative has been known to mankind for as long as history can remember. It was probably the only way early man could feed himself in winter, long before he discovered the benefits of smoking food to preserve it. Since man learned to travel about his globe, herring laid in a barrel between layers of salt has been one of the main ways of enabling food to be sent to distant markets he created. In the nineteenth century, the Scotch cure method of treating herring proved popular throughout Europe, Africa and the Americas.

Bands of Scots girls – the herring lassies as they were called – followed the fishing fleets around the coast and they spent their days gutting the fish and laying them into barrels. These were made by the resident coopers. The herring came direct from the boats and were tipped into troughs – farlanes – from where they were gutted and sorted, a lassie being capable of gutting sixty fish every minute. The fish were then place between layers of salt in the barrels and sealed once full. After several days they were reopened and packed tighter after the herring had shrunk. In Scotland, barrels were branded according to the age of the fish in the barrel, but this was not common practise in England and Wales.

Another avenue for the herring curers was to smoke the herring. All the herring ports in Britain had numerous smokehouses, which were constantly kept busy preparing a range of, smoked herring – kippers, bloaters, silver herrings, golden herrings and red herrings. Most fishermen also had their own 'backyard' smoker to prepare fish for their home.

To smoke kippers, herring were gutted and split along the back and placed into a pickle of brine. After a period of time the fish were removed from the liquid and left to drain in the air before being hung up in the smokehouse, over the oak chip fire, for a number of hours, depending on the degree of smoking.

If the gutted fish are not split but are pickled and smoked whole, they become bloaters, although there are regional variations in the preparation of this delicacy. In some parts of Wales the herring are left in salt for up to three weeks, usually on the floor of the salt-house. Sometimes they are smoked for a short time first. After another washing they are then smoked again for another short period, washed again and salted. In Nefyn they were dried before being laid out on a pile of ferns in the sunshine when, on rare occasions, the sun shines in autumn. In other parts of Britain the ungutted herring are salted and smoked.

Silver herrings are lightly smoked and were favoured by the Italians, while the Greeks preferred the golden herring, which were saltier with a longer time in the smokehouse. Red herrings were the most smoked variety, usually ungutted, after being left in the smokehouse between daily smokings of kippers, at which time they would sweat before it was relit.

Making Red-herrings.

Above: The author with a string of bloaters at the 2003 International Festival of the Sea, Edinburgh.

Left: Old print of 'making red herring'.

Sometimes they were left in for over three weeks and would keep up to a year after such treatment. The cliché 'red herring' comes from the fact that herrings so preserved were known to put a hound off its scent. They were also regarded as being beneficial in the treatment of gallstones and rheumatism. Similarly, a fisherman might hang herring high up in his chimney for weeks on end, producing a similar red herring for himself.

Some 225 vessels were built here between 1758 and 1898 which, although considerably less than at Barmouth, Porthmadog and Pwllheli, nevertheless was still of consequence, matched by the output of Nefyn and Porth Dinllaen together. The main boatbuilders responsible for these were Samuel and Richard Samuel, Roberts and Company, William Jones, Thomas Williams, Owen Barlow, Richard Edwards and Richard Price while a dozen individuals are known to be have built just one or two vessels in the 1800s.

Victoria Dock was planned many years before it actually opened for business in 1875. But it was three decades to late for the decline in the coastal trade had already onset helped on by the arrival of a branch line on the Chester & Holyhead Railway in 1852 and a further link to the Cambrian line south in 1867. Although the dock was said to be the finest achievement of the Harbour Trust, it took until 1907 to repay the debt of its construction and had already been the subject of dispute. When a couple of people fell into the dock while under the influence of drink, the *Caernarfon & Denbigh Herald* described it in 1881 as a 'man trap'. Sir Llewelyn Turner, one of the main driving forces behind its existence, replied, according to Lewis Lloyd, that these accidents 'were the results of over-indulgence in the low taverns and questing for prostitutes'. A sure sign, then, that some of the traditions of a seafaring town had still survived!

Samuel Lewis also noted 'the salubrity of the air, the convenience of its situation for sea-bathing, and the beautiful scenery in the neighbourhood' which, he wrote, had made the town the permanent home of 'numerous respectable families' as well as attracting visitors. A hotel had been built with its own seawater bath supplied by an engine. The outdoor pool alongside the Strait I remember quite well in my youth. The town also boasted lodging houses, piped water and gas lighting.

Fish were landed in great quantities for the townsfolk and the neighbourhood and kept many people employed. Lewis Morris had found supplies of salmon, cod, whitings, all kinds of flatfish, oysters, mussels and cockles. In 1808 several local landowners such as the Buckleys, Wynns and the Marquis of Anglesey 'took shares in the scheme initiated by Caernarfon lawyer John Evans for the joint stock of trawlers and trawl nets for fishing the adjacent sea', wrote Dodds. The fish were sold into the English markets and was said to have relieved some distress. These people were most likely spurred on by Mr O' Williams of Llanidan who introduced the 'Torbay system of trawling' into Caernarfon Bay some years earlier, which had caused an influx of trawl-boats from Dublin and Liverpool. In 1883 there were 300 fishing boats registered in the town and neighbouring area which probably including the Lleyn.

Today's Victoria Dock, after years of disuse, is a marina at one end while the other, shallow, end has yet to be utilised. A gate installed in the 1990s allows the boats to stay afloat at all times. The slipway is run by Arfon Oceaneering and enables boats to be taken out of the water for repair and/or winter storage. The excellent research centre at Gwynedd Archives is housed in a building almost next door to the boatyard while at the west end, under the castle walls, the Caernarfon (Seiont II) Maritime Museum can be found in the former mortuary. Here, displays tell something of the 'hardships and dramas of the maritime and industrial developments of the area'. Until recently, the 1937-built steam dredger, always a necessity in the harbour, was also on display. Outside of the museum several maritime artefacts, such as one of the anchors from HMS *Conwy*, are on display.

Caernarfon once had its small fleet of seine-net fishers who worked four stations between the mouth of the river and Abermenai Point. In the 1930s there were seven licensed teams of four men – two who rowed the 14ft open boats, one to pay the net out and a shoreman – who were full-time fishermen based at Victoria Dock. By the 1970s this number had decreased to four part-time teams and within a decade or two to none. The only netsmen working these days are of the illegal variety, and occasionally the local papers mention those up before the magistrates after being picked up by the Sea Fisheries Committee patrol boat or on-shore bailiffs.

Port Dinorwic – or *Y Felinheli* as it is sometimes known – mirrors Caernarfon in that it too developed through the slate trade. Originating as the creek of Aber Pwll, the embarkation point for the Moel-y-Don ferry to Anglesey, it later replaced Caernarfon as the loading place for slate from the Llanberis mines. This was at first brought by donkey to be loaded onto carts for the journey to the creek until boats were used to tranship it across Llyn Padarn to Cwm-y-Glo from where it was carried down to Port Dinorwic, often to be carried out to waiting ships by lighter. Improvements were made to Aber Pwll under the 1793 and 1809 Acts to improve the facilities at Caernarfon, and by 1802 Aber Pwll received the bulk of the Llanberis slate, the mines being owned in part by the Assheton-Smith family of the Vaynol estate, close to the creek. In 1809 docks and quays were built at the head of the creek and an artificial waterway built to connect these to the sea. Three years later a 'Slate road' connected mine to port and in 1824 the Dinorwic railway replaced this road and the formal name of 'Port Dinorwic' was adopted, probably spurred on by the Assheton-Smiths gaining full control of the mining activities. Four years later dock gates were fitted to enable vessels to remain afloat in the dock, and a dry dock for shipbuilding and ship repairs built in 1835. Over the next twenty years several factors helped the port to flourish. Firstly a new railway, with horse-drawn wagons, was built alongside Llyn Padarn and from there down to the port, replacing the former Dinorwic railway that had been unsuited since opening, largely due to some of its route towards the port being uphill. Then the shipbuilder Rees Jones moved his business from Barmouth to the port, where he subsequently built twenty-eight ships including the 825-ton barque *Ordovic* in 1877, the largest sailing ship built in North Wales. Lastly, the building of the new outer basin was completed in 1854, thus increasing enormously the capacity of Port Dinorwic. Whereas Caernarfon's fathers were thinking about it, here they did it, and benefited. This railway remained in use until its closure in 1961. Ultimately, though, it was the arrival of the Chester & Holyhead Railway that resulted in a slow decline in the port's fortunes when a separate extension was built down to the port, along ironically part of the original 1812 'Slate road'. However, unlike many other ports, it was a gradual decline for port extensions continued, suggesting a confidence on the part of investors. By 1863 the railway accounted for 15 per cent of export and in 1895, 339 loaded ships left the port in comparison to 764 in 1864. This figure, though, must take account of the fact that ships were becoming larger, thus more capacious, but still leads to the assumption that the trade was in decline, something which progressively increased until trade almost had all disappeared by the mid-1950s. With the closure of the rail link and the subsequent closure of the mine in 1969, slate exports from Port Dinorwic came to a complete standstill.

A word about the water-borne trade of Llyn Padarn and Llyn Peris. The recovery of a wreck of a flat-bottomed slate boat, complete with its cargo of slates, in 1977 in Llyn

Padarn confirmed aspects of the transport of slate across the lake. Research resulted in a building date of the late 1780s and a sinking date between then and 1824 when the Dinorwic railway was built, and the practise of carrying slate across the lake ceased.

When the remains of another boat were discovered in neighbouring Llyn Peris in 1979, it was first assumed that this, too, was a slate carrying vessel until its shape proved to be of a double-ended type of hull with a round bilge. Indeed, research also discovered that slate was never transported across Llyn Peris, although there is of course the supposition that such a boat might have come to grief in the lake for completely different reasons. The general consensus was, however, that this second vessel certainly predated the slate vessel. That the movement of copper ore across the lake occurred in Llyn Peris is known, but archaeological research found no stains of suggestive copper oxide although animal, possibly pony, droppings were found in the vessel, which led to the suggestion was that the vessel was used to transport animals upon the lake. When more timber was found three months after the first boat, this was discovered to have come from an entirely different vessel, a log boat with extended planking, which was deemed to predate the first Llyn Peris wreck. All three vessels have added much to our understanding of how mankind used such inland lakes to facilitate his movement of goods and animals (and perhaps people). Some have gone even further to make comparisons in boat construction between certain types of boats throughout Europe and America. In my opinion, this is perhaps drawing too many conclusions.

Today, just as almost every dock we've visited these last two weeks, both docks at Port Dinorwic are a mass of the masts of pleasure boats. Bill and Jean Dawson run a sail loft alongside the dry dock at the head of the original slate dock. There's the yacht broker, restaurant, marine engineer, chandlery – everything a yachtsman could possibly need in fact – which shows that this once quiet creek has joined the twenty-first century. The eminent North Wales maritime historian Aled Eames, it seems, had plenty to say about these 'waterfront' developments that have sprung up everywhere from Cardiff to Port Dinorwic. In *Shrouded Quays* (1981) he speaks disparagingly of the 'incongruous holiday type homes' at Porthmadog and of the success of a campaign by residents who 'opposed a grandiose scheme by developers to reclaim and in-fill part of Hirael Bay so as to create a marina surrounded by some three hundred 'yuppie' houses, offices, hotel and a large supermarket'. Even so, we allow these unsightly, unsuitable and unnecessary developments whilst at the same time wondering why the face of Wales has changed. Capitalism survives on being at the forefront of progression but it never fails to amaze me that we let corrupt officials escape with their back-handers and the developers run with the profits from such deplorable schemes.

Moving on from Port Dinorwic the Vaynol estate, with its own private dock, blankets the Strait from view until the second of the bridges that connect Anglesey to the mainland is reached. Built by Robert Stephenson and opened for rail traffic in 1850, the Britannia Bridge was set alight in the 1970s and subsequently altered to allow the passage of road traffic upon a second tier over the rail track.

Pwllfanog is a tiny creek that probably mirrored Aber Pwll until the latter was expanded into a port. Flourishing until about 1900, it was engaged in producing slate writing tablets. Slates were carried over from across the Strait, the wreck of one such vessel having been found in the adjacent waters. Subsequently, bacon, flour and margarine have been produced here.

Sitting in the van watching dog paddle around on the water's edge, I wondered how to proceed. Something was troubling me. Having already written a previous book about the coastline of Anglesey, it seemed that I was about to repeat this earlier work. Then, of course, it occurred to me that I was already repeating the work of many other writers, so concluded that it would be unreasonable not to include the island. A quick circumnavigation was therefore justified before we proceeded east towards the ultimate goal of the river Dee. For now, with the day's end imminent, a good night's rest in a bed at a friend's house seemed just the thing to raise the spirit. And, having lived in this part of Anglesey for over thirty years, I knew just where that bed lay.

DAY SIXTEEN

NEWBOROUGH TO TRAETH LLIGWY

Before Thomas Telford built the suspension bridge across the Menai Strait in the early nineteenth century, the only way across the hazardous waterway was by ferry except for the rare occasions that a horse was able to cross at its shallowest point over the Lafan Sands. I've already mentioned the Tal-y-Foel ferry that closed down in 1953 and another existed at Abermenai which was often used by the inhabitants of Newborough on their way to the Caernarfon market to sell their baskets, ropes and mats woven from the marram grass collected locally. Much of this was harvested on what is now Newborough Warren and Forest. Beyond the dark forest of conifers, and along the wide, sandy beach, lies the island of Llanddwyn, a jewel upon the coast.

It's rare that it is actually an island for it's only at very high tides that the causeway across is flooded by the high tide. It's a popular spot at all times of the year, and because parts of the beach are 'dog free', we drove to the residents' car park which is situated closer to the causeway. Locals from the village have a key for this, and I still had mine although I'd moved a few months earlier!

Llanddwyn has, quite rightly, been described as one of the most beautiful areas of Britain. The remnants of the church of St Dwynwen, the patron saint of Welsh lovers, dates from the fifteenth century. Beyond are the pilots' houses and the towers of two lighthouses – the smaller one dates from 1819 and the larger from 1846. Two lifeboat houses, both in a reasonable state of repair, stand close to the beach, the earlier one of the two set almost into the rocks by the remains of the pier.

The Caernarfon Harbour Trust established the first lifeboat here in 1825 at a time when that harbour was undergoing expansion. The pilots on duty were paid an extra £5 a year to man it when necessary. However, by 1831, after virtually no launches because of the lack of manpower, it had been taken to Caernarfon for repairs, where it seems to have remained. However, in 1840, the Anglesey Lifesaving Association financed another to be placed at Llanddwyn, with more standby crew supplied. From then until 1907 this service saved over a hundred lives, at which time trade in the port of Caernarfon diminished to make the service unnecessary. The Harbour Trust's lifeboat at Caernarfon remained in service until possibly 1891, although this is as yet unclear.

Malltraeth Bay is shallow and sandy but nevertheless Lewis Morris advocated the building of two piers for the exploitation of the coal deposits under the Malltraeth Marsh in his 'Plans' – almost a third of these plans were of the Anglesey coast. He also suggested the closing off of the whole bay to create a meadow with a superb harbour at its entrance. Furthermore, he reported 'most kinds of Fish' as well as a green stone with white and red spots at Llanddwyn.

The next bay is Aberffraw where he suggested the building of another pier. Sloops frequented the place to load up with corn, butter and cheese as well as there being a plentiful supply of fish, including oysters. Samuel Lewis, almost a century later, found a 'small harbour capable of receiving vessels of forty tons' burden' which exported oats and barley.

The coast road treks north again to Rhosneigr, which has been renowned for its lobsters for generations. As far back as 1600, George Roberts noted that these lobsters were 'very sweete and delicate meate and plentie taken'. Until the 1880s this was a tiny sleepy hamlet of scattered cottages whose inhabitants survived from the sea. The lobsters were sent to Liverpool by boat that sometimes brought in limestone and coal. Butter, cheese and corn were also exported and the village was largely self-sufficient for its own needs while during the summer large catches of mackerel were taken. Furthermore, there were good catches of whiting, plaice, bream, conger eel, seatrout and prawns. Herring, it seems, was rarely landed, owing its scarcity because of the strong tides on the West Coast of Anglesey.

The first of the visitors then came in the 1880s, encouraged by the fact that there was a small station on the main Holyhead railway nearby. Their arrival heralded an abrupt change from the traditional way of life. The visitors came and built houses to use in summer, enjoying the lovely beaches that the West Coast continues to be renowned for. Then came the hoteliers, constructing their hostelries, bringing in more visitors. These very same people later opposed the building of an armaments factory nearby that could have given work to 300 locals. This sort of outside influence upon the traditional way of life of rural Wales has, over the course of a century, brought about many changes in patterns that had, previously, extended back generations. And with it has come the downside of social change that has to be weighed up against the incoming wealth and human interaction.

Rhosneigr from Beach

JV 46188

Rhosneigr from the beach, from a 1904 postcard.

Old print of Holyhead harbour.

The Rhosneigr fishermen used boats of 15ft in length that had a small beautifully shaped 'wine-glass' transom. Twenty pots was the average number for each man, and these were hauled each day except Saturday and Sunday, each baited with the preferred salted gurnard. Crabs didn't like the salted fish and were usually taken with fresh fish heads. The pots used for the fishery were the traditional Cornish willow ink well pots, which were often made up by the fishermen themselves. In the early twentieth century the average annual catch was in the region of 400 lobsters, a greatly reduced figure of a century before.

The lifeboat was established in 1872 with the cost of £680 for both boat and boathouse being contributed by Mrs Thomas Lingham in memory of her husband who was drowned in Caernarfon Bay. The first boat, the *Thomas Lingham*, was perhaps famous for the most famous of rescues the station ever undertook. The *Norman Court* was a tea clipper on route from Java to the Clyde when she was driven onto rocks in Cymran Bay during a storm in 1883. On the third attempt at reaching the vessel, with the crew of the Holyhead lifeboat aboard because of exhaustion amongst the Rhosneigr crew fighting the storm on the first two unsuccessful launches, they managed to get twenty of the ship's crew off, a magnificent feat of seamanship. Two years later the *Thomas Lingham* was replaced by a slightly larger vessel bearing the same name. This, in turn, was replaced by another of the same name in 1904 until the station finally closed in 1924 after saving seventy-three lives on twenty-nine launches. The lifeboat house still sits atop the harbour beach.

The Crigyll Robbers – *Lladron Crigyll* – were a group of renowned eighteenth-century gangsters who survived by looting vessels that had become wrecked on the shore north of Rhosneigr. Their name comes from the little Afon Crigyll, that flows into the sea here. Stories abound of cattle having lanterns tied to the horns to mislead passing sailing ships – that's an old story probably with some element of truth – yet this band of mercenaries certainly seem to have only plundered vessels and hid the booty amongst the dunes. They did not, it seems, actually ever lure ships to their fate. According to Ian Skidmore who has a fascinating account of them, and other shipwrecks for that matter, in *Anglesey and Lleyn Shipwrecks*, these robbers were from all walks of life. Amongst their fold were '*wealthy landowners, farmers, tailors, a weaver, a fuller, servants, even children*' as well as a group of Calvinistic Methodists during one looting! For years they operated without much hindrance with the local magistrates unable to convict those found with stolen goods. Three men were eventually committed for trial in Beaumaris Gaol and were found guilty of raiding the sloop *The Charming Jenny* that was stranded in the river in 1773. One of these fellows, John Parry, was hanged in 1775 for his crime. However, it seems they came from all around the vicinity and operated for more than two centuries up to the end of the nineteenth century before finally being forced out of business.

Rhoscolyn lies across the bay to the north and here another lifeboat was stationed between 1830 and 1929 in the lifeboat house that still sits on the western end of the semi-circular beach. The first lifeboat on station, a 25ft Palmer-type, was built by Henry McVeagh of Holyhead. Tragically, five members of the lifeboat *Ramon Cabrera* – the sixth lifeboat at the station – were swept overboard during a launch to the SS *Timbo* in 1920, after the ship had been driven off course into Caernarfon Bay during a north-westerly gale.

According to Samuel Lewis, Rhoscolyn quarried a particular type of green variegated marble known as 'verd antique', which surpassed similar Italian marble for colour diversity and intensity. He also tells us that the same quarries gave up 'veins of beautiful asbestos, of soft and silky texture, and of a very superior quality'. In today's world after countless deaths from the stuff, it is hard to imagine anybody describing asbestos as 'beautiful'. How things change, eh!

From Rhoscolyn it's a short drive to Trearddur Bay which was once a small hamlet home to a few lobster boats. Now it's a holiday centre and an eyesore with unsympathetic housing and caravans. Many are strange buildings totally out of keeping amongst the traditional dwellings of the island. With their weird rooflines, obscenely large windows and unnecessarily grandiose structure, it really does amaze me how they were ever given planning permission in the first place. Nowhere else on Anglesey is the anglicisation of the community as apparent as it is here. Mind you, having been in the building trade for many years on the island, and knowing something of the attitude of the local council – some call it totally corrupt – it doesn't really surprise me. These same people encourage the installation of plastic windows and exterior coatings of the ghastly pebble dashing when traditional houses are given a makeover. Corrupt, inefficient and inept perhaps would be a better description! Thankfully some of us chose to paint our houses otherwise Anglesey would have become uniform throughout.

South Stack lighthouse sits on a tiny island at the bottom of a cliff, a few miles north and has acted as a magnet for visitors since it was first illuminated in 1809. One unusual feature of the light was another small clockwork lantern that was fitted to an incline leading down to the sea. When the cloud was low and the main light was thus obscured, this was lowered to within 50ft of the sea. Today signs of the incline remain but there's a fog signal instead, replacing the North Stack fog station that has been sold off.

To say it's dramatic is perhaps an understatement when you first arrive and catch a glimpse of it 300ft below. To reach it, over 400 steps lead down the cliff and a bridge spans the bubbling cauldron between mainland and island. When we were kids we went on windy days, down the steps, always counting (I forget the actual number now), and across the earlier suspension bridge that swayed as it was buffeted, while the sea frothed wildly below. That was the days when the keepers lived on site for now the light is automated and rarely open to the public. The steel door was firmly closed today.

And so, sitting in the van, coffee in hand, staring out over the lighthouse, I considered Anglesey. Successions of writers have visited the island over the centuries and their observations have not been particularly encouraging. Leland found 'a good commodite for fishing about Tir Mon but their lacketh courage and diligence' while Defoe found that 'there is nothing of note to be seen in the Isle of Anglesea, but the town, and castle of Beaumaris' although he did add that the land 'is fruitful and pleasant' for corn and cattle. George Lyttleton, in his *An Account of a Journey in Wales*, suggested the island didn't produce goods anywhere near its potential and that the population were content with this state of affairs, being simply happy to be self-sufficient. Another traveller went as far as describing it 'naked and unpleasant' while Joseph Hucks thought it 'a picture of desolation'!

But the island has for ages been known as '*Mon, mam Cymru*' – Anglesey, the mother of Wales – as a reflection of its ability to supply the whole of Wales in grain. In 1770 alone more than 90,000 bushels of grain – mostly barley and oats – were produced from over fifty windmills. No wonder it was regarded as the 'granary of Wales' until cheap imports in the second half of the nineteenth century forced farmers to turn to animal husbandry.

As to the sea, Aled Eames found that many of the seamen aboard the ocean-going Welsh sailing boats were from Anglesey – folk who were 'prompted by economic necessity rather than romance'. Their choice was to work the land or the sea.

As we progress around the island we will see that Lewis Morris was optimistic as to the amount of fish available. In 1775 Nicolas Owen, in *The History of the Island of Anglesey*, noted that the herring fishery had failed 'with which these coasts were abundantly supplied'. The potato had been planted, becoming a principal part of the local diet. He went as far as to suggest that the population had increased because of the potato supplanting the salted herring in their diet. He continues 'the islanders frequently live to eighty or ninety years, are generally healthy and long-lived. The air of Anglesey is keen, but seldom tainted with infectious vapours'.

Less than fifteen years later Warner found huge shoals of herring that 'sometimes visit the Anglesea coast, which are taken, dried and exported: being considered by the knowing ones in delicacies, as particularly excellent'. This suggests that the shoals lived up to their tradition of being notoriously fickle in their appearance.

We drove to Holyhead, a place of mixed opinions, for it was once voted as the worst town in Britain, which, considering some other English towns I've visited, does seem a tad unfair. It has a port, a huge breakwater, a lovely vista, great surroundings and a depressing centre that has become less depressing and airier in recent years. It also has history, which is so often overlooked.

When Suetonius brought the Roman army over to Anglesey in flat-bottomed boats at Moel-y-don (a ferry crossing point used by many of our quoted travellers) in AD 61 he began an occupation that lasted over 300 years. The Romans built a fort 'above a creek on a small island off the West Coast of Anglesey' which was the foundation for

Holyhead. After the Romans came the Irish Picts and about AD 550, as Britain was converting to Christianity, a monk called Kebius came to settle in a monastery, which later came to be known as Caergybi. At the time the inhabitants were said to be farmers and fishermen. When the Vikings came to attack and plunder in the tenth century, the town was growing in both population and stance.

But it was the 'post' that really enabled the port of Holyhead to develop. As a stepping stone to Ireland, the town was a perfect haven for sailing vessels and soon became an embarkation point. In the late sixteenth century it became a 'post town' to enable the state papers – or 'packet' – to pass over to Dublin. In 1625 a vessel was engaged to ply the route across to Dublin by post barque – later packet – for a sum of £10 per lunar month. This service was formalised in 1656 by Queen Elizabeth and Holyhead soon found itself the principal Irish passenger and mail port. Thus travellers wishing to reach Ireland from Britain found they had two options – either to take the erratic boat service from Chester or to journey through North Wales to Holyhead. In 1688 this coastal route was described as some of the 'most heathenish country man ever travelled' for rivers and the Menai Strait had to be crossed before achieving their goal. It wasn't until the Britannia Railway Bridge was completed in 1850 that the journey from London could be made without stoppages, other than to rest the horses. Letters between Ireland and Holyhead often took six days and cost 8*d*. During times when Holyhead was inaccessible because of the weather, vessels would land and embark around on the West Side of Holy Island at Porth Dafarch, a tiny cove we'd passed on route to South Stack.

Lewis Morris noted that 22,000 bushels of grain were shipped out, mostly to Ireland. Fish was, seemingly, plentiful while he also mentioned 'sampier', a particular pickle found on the cliffs of Holyhead Mountain (*Mynydd Twr*). A salt house manufactured salt from the seawater, with rock salt being added to improve the flavour. This fell into disrepair after the management failed to oversee its success, though not before a substantial amount of salt was smuggled in from the Isle of Man to avoid the salt tax. Smuggling – or 'free trade' – was, of course, practised on the coast of Anglesey as elsewhere.

The harbour was expanded in 1821 explicitly for the packet. In 1847 work commenced on the one-and-a-half-mile-long breakwater, designed by James Meadow Rendal, who was also responsible for the docks at Birkenhead. He died in 1856, midway through the construction and, although he is said to have died from natural causes, rumours suggested he took his own life because of alterations to his original design which increased the overall length of the breakwater from 5,360ft to 7,860ft, while his East and Mail Packet piers were never built. The final cost of the structure was £1,285,000, a considerable sum 150 years ago, but the port became the only refuge for ships between Milford Haven and the Clyde. In 1917 some 250 ships took shelter in the huge harbour over a period of eleven weeks, according to a crewmember of the schooner *John Gibson*, which was also forced to shelter whilst under passage between Runcorn and Ireland with coal.

Holyhead has always enjoyed some of the benefits of lying in the proximity to the rich fishing grounds of the Irish Sea. Well, that is they were rich grounds, until twentieth-century fishing depleted them! As I mentioned above, fishermen lived alongside farmers before the Vikings came, although it is perhaps more accurate to say that the inhabitants were both farmers and fishermen, working the land and sea as seasons dictated.

Lewis Morris and his Maps

The son of a carpenter and cooper from northeast Anglesey, Lewis Morris was born in 1701 to later become the eldest of four brothers. In 1724 he went to work as the estate surveyor for Owen Meyrick at Bordorgan, on the other side of the island. During the four years spent making surveys on the estate lands, he must have considered the plausibility of making maps of the coastline. In 1729 he went to work as a customs official, based in both Holyhead and Beaumaris and, as such, came into contact with ships' captains who probably filled his mind about the dangers lying off the coast and the inadequacy of the existing charts.

Having put proposals before the Admiralty to survey the whole of the coast of Wales, it came to Morris to fund the expense of hiring a vessel because of the lack of interest from the authorities. Thus, in 1737, taking on a boat at a cost of five shillings a day, he set out on his own. Later that year he sent eleven charts to the Admiralty but received little interest. He continued on his own the following year and, in 1739, was informed that his employers were unwilling to allow him further leave to complete his surveys. It was Owen Meyrick who came to the rescue, using his contacts in the Admiralty Office to persuade the Lords Commissioners of the validity of Morris' work and thus allowing him to proceed once again in 1742. Two years later he had reached Tenby when war with the French broke out, and work was halted, never to be resumed and completed. Hence his maps of today finish with Tenby and Caldey.

Even though he completed the maps from his surveys when back in Holyhead, the Admiralty was too concentrated in war to take concern. Morris considered publishing them himself until the Admiralty changed its mind in 1748 and insisted he publish not only his chart of the whole coast but the individual harbour plans that he had originally intended as an aid his memory in preparing the larger plan. In September 1748 the twenty-five small plans were published along with his general chart of the Welsh coast. There were 1,230 subscribers and stocks had run out by 1761. Over the next few years he prepared further plans of Liverpool Bay and Amlwch

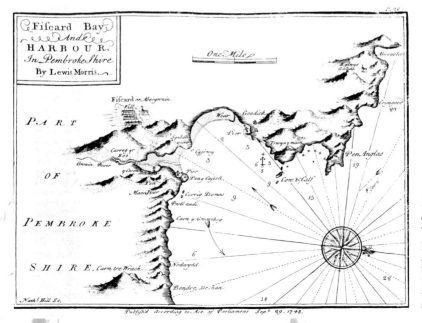

Left and opposite: Three of Lewis Morris's plans, Fishguard, Aberystwyth and Dulas Bay.

harbour which were not published until after his death. In the 1760s he went to live in Cardiganshire and produced a number of plans of the mines of that area. To illustrate the quality and detail of his work, several are reproduced here.

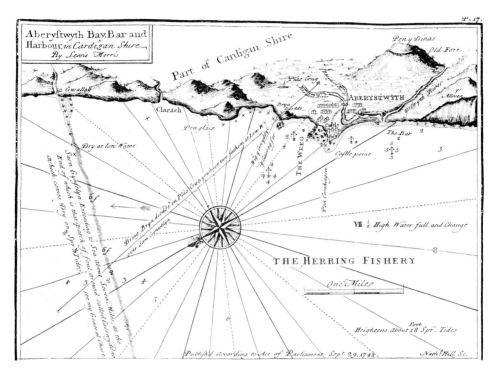

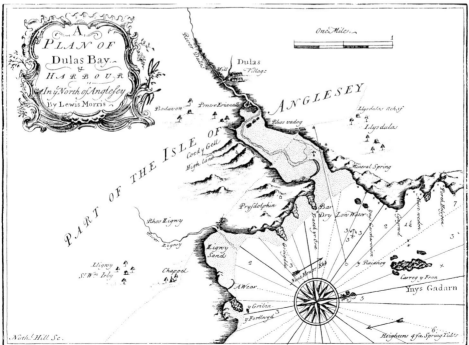

In more recent times the packet trade, the coastal trade and shipbuilding, dwarfed fishing. In the case of the latter, the seafront was a hive of shipbuilding activity in the eighteenth and nineteenth centuries, with various ships being built at any one time upon the slipways that adorned the area. Boats of 200 tons could be accommodated, and vessels also came here from all over the West Coast for repairs.

In the early twentieth century herring boats from the Isle of Man and Scotland landed their substantial catches here to be cured by the roving Scottish women – the herring lassies – who travelled all over Britain following the herring fleets. Holyhead herring was sent to the West Indies, Russia and Germany at one time. After the First World War the trade died to be briefly reinstated in the 1930s and again in the 1950s, when herring was cured on Salt Island. With the fish all but fished out or killed through pollution by the nuclear establishments around the Irish Sea, Holyhead's fish harbour was very quiet when we arrived. Two or three boats lay alongside the quay but there was no sign of activity.

I took the dog for a run along the seafront, passing the Maritime Museum which was closed, unfortunately. I counted about fifty yachts lying at moorings in the bay while more were stacked up at the new marina at the West End of the bay. Beyond the harbour wall I could see the Skerries lighthouse, another important navigational mark for ships making their way in or out of Liverpool. This lighthouse was built in 1716 by an Irishman, William Trench, the tenure of which, at his death in 1725, passed to his widow's son-in-law. Trench's own son had been drowned whilst delivering coal for the beacon. Five years later an Act of Parliament allowed for the collecting of light dues from each passing vessel which in effect became light dues. It was eventually taken over by Trinity House in 1841, the last lighthouse in the country to come under their jurisdiction.

Of course, Holyhead has a lifeboat and has had since 1828. In fact it's had several boats, not just lifeboats. The first boat was kept in a stone house close to the Pier Head in the summer and under cover on the pier in winter and craned into the water when needed. This boat alone saved 139 lives under the management of the Anglesey Lifesaving Association. When the running of the station was taken over by the RNLI in 1858 a new Peake-type lifeboat was brought on station, housed in a new lifeboat house on Newry Beach. Over two days in December 1863, during a particularly violent storm, this boat rescued forty-eight persons from four separate call-outs, while the crews of another two vessels in distress in the bay were unable to be saved, although the lifeboat attended. This lifeboat was replaced the next year, and a new lifeboat house built with a wooden slipway in 1870. In 1890, because it was apparent that one lifeboat alone could not undertake all the work it was being called upon to attempt, a second lifeboat was established, with the house being extended to accommodate it. Two years later Holyhead received one of the first steam lifeboats in Wales. This, the *Duke of Northumberland*, was the first steam lifeboat built by the Institution.

In 1891 another lifeboat was established at Porth Rhuffydd, a small cove on the West Side of Holy Island – close in fact to Porth Dafarch – so that the port had three lifeboats for a short time. However, this one was short-lived because of the shortage of crew and the fact that the newer steam lifeboat was able to give sufficient coverage on the west side of the island. It was closed in 1904. The second lifeboat was kept on station until 1930, two years after the arrival of the first motorised lifeboat, the *H.C.J.*, which was kept afloat. Although a new house was built on Salt Island in the late 1940s and used until 1980 and again from 1984–1997, today's lifeboat is kept afloat alongside the Old Admiralty Pier, while an inshore boat is stationed in the old Trinity House building at the western end of Newry Beach.

A ferry came into port while we were ambling along the seafront. I noticed the funnel above the breakwater first and within minutes the great big thing appeared around the end. Both B&I Ferries and Stena Line operate services over to Dublin and Dun Laoghaire respectively, both with traditional displacement vessels and the high-speed catamarans – or super ferries as they are called nowadays. When these super-things were first introduced in the 1980s (I think) they were not allowed out to sea when the waves were something like one and a half metres high which, when considering what the Irish Sea can be like in winter, didn't seem to make much sense to me. Presumably the operators knew something we didn't!

We left Holyhead and stopped briefly to have a look at the fish weir in Beddmanarch Bay, close to the outflow of the Afon Alaw, Anglesey's major river. Shipbuilding flourished at this quiet spot too in the eighteenth century, much in the same way as we've seen shipbuilding at other out of the way, desolate places along the Welsh coast. The remains of the fish weir are pretty obvious, a low wall of stone along the bed of the river when seen at low water. I guess many people will have mistaken it for a simply boundary wall although I wonder if those same people stop to wonder why anybody would build a wall in a river! Oak posts would once have raised the height of the weir to six or seven feet and the fish collected in the pool left behind once the tide had receded. Today it is simply just another one of those relics of a bygone era that few care to bother with. It's a surprise that a substantial part of the wall still remains for many another structure has been dismantled and the stone used elsewhere.

This part of Anglesey has a succession of sandy beaches and Church Bay – *Porth Swtan* – is one of these, a quiet tranquil cove with a stone slipway leading down to the beach. *Swtan* translates to 'whiting' which points to the fact that fishermen once worked from here. The nearby Lobster Pot restaurant also adds to the general impression that fish were landed here. The recently restored thatched traditional fisherman's cottage is another pointer.

From Church Bay we drove north along winding roads up to Cemlyn Bay, the home of the first lifeboat to be established on Anglesey. One tragedy that acted as a catalyst was the sinking on the West Mouse Rock of the *Alert* in March 1823 in calm conditions. Becalmed and drifting, the ship hit the rock and, out of 152 passengers and crew, only seven escaped on the ship's rowing boat. Even though locals looked on, they were helpless for there were no boats around to go to their assistance. Then, over a period of a few years, some twenty or more ships were wrecked on the north coast of Anglesey. Two people had who witnessed the sinking of the *Alert* were Canon James Williams, rector of Llanfair-yng-Nghornwy, and his wife Frances, both of whom were chiefly responsible for the foundation of the Anglesey Lifesaving Association in 1828. A new Palmer-type lifeboat was delivered in November that year, and within a year £160 had been raised for its cost and another £60 for its annual upkeep. The rector's son, Owen William, himself a Reverend, became the coxswain. After six lifeboats, several reserve lifeboats, over thirty lives saved and dozens of call-outs, the service was terminated in 1918.

The massive bulk of Wylfa Nuclear Power Station stands just east of Cemlyn, a dark threat to all inhabitants of Anglesey, but still in service thanks to public relations, government spin and the promise of benefits to the local economy. I still remember as clearly as yesterday the effect that radioactive fallout from Chernobyl had on North Wales and don't dare to imagine what terror Wylfa could instil on us if an accident happened. Some folk think the financial gain is worth the risk. It seems that the station is often shut down for various reasons and personally I'd prefer to see it shut for good. You never know, even the fish may stop their genetic malfunctioning.

The village of Cemaes sits under the shadow of the power station. Nestling at the head of a small bay, it has a maritime tradition stretching back centuries. Although it has been said that the fishermen of the village were salting herring, it seems that the harbour developed through the export of stone from nearby quarries. Lewis Morris notes another 'famous Quarry of the Stone Asbestos'. He also lists other exports as corn, cheese and butter. The harbour wall was reputedly destroyed in a gale sometime before 1828 and the present one was rebuilt in 1935. Limestone and coal were the chief imports. Shipbuilding had a brief flutter when Ismael Jones was employing, so it is said, sixty people in his yard, although records only account for three ships he launched between 1825 and 1840. Once the railways arrived at Holyhead and Amlwch, the port fell into disuse. Today it is home to a couple of fishing boats and small pleasure boats.

Cemaes lifeboat was established in 1872 and kept in a lifeboat house at Porth Ogof, a mile or so west of the village. The wooden building was built on a wooden ramp, the stumps of which still stick out of the beach. It closed in 1932 after attending sixty vessels and saving thirty-two lives.

The coastal footpath leads past the ancient port of Llanlleiana from where locally dug china clay was exported, to Porth Wen where remnants of a brickworks can be seen and onto Bull Bay (*Porth Llechog*). Another lifeboat was stationed here between 1868 and 1926, during which sixty-three lives were saved. It's a short hop on to Amlwch.

Amlwch was once described as 'one of the most important ports in Wales', even if it was merely a tiny natural creek frequented by the odd fishing boat in the mid-eighteenth century. Lewis Morris thought it so insignificant he didn't think it worthy to produce a plan in 1748. But it was the copper mines of nearby Parys Mountain that led to the later growth of the port. Copper had been mined here since Roman times but when a second, larger, mine was opened in 1775, the amount of ore being extracted dramatically jumped up. The same year the harbour was recorded as being forty perches long and five perches wide. When the tide was in 'it was nothing strange to see men fishing while they stand only at the brim of the cavation: in this agreeable pastime they avoid those commotions often concomitants of sea-fishing'. Until 1781, when they were moved to nearby Porth Eilian, the Liverpool pilot boats were based afloat in the harbour.

Then, in 1792, an Act of Parliament for 'enlargening, deepening, cleansing, improving, and regulating the Harbour of Amlwch in the Isle of Anglesey' to facilitate the loading and carriage of the ore to the smelters in Swansea Bay. Nor surprising, then, Hucks found 'a small sea port' with copper mines appearing as 'a vast yawning chasm'. Between 1786 and 1825 some twenty-nine ships were built on Anglesey, but only one of these was built at Amlwch. By the time the nineteenth century dawned, though, there were twenty smelters working in the town as the annual production from the mines increased to 44,000 tons. Trade exploded and, in 1825, James Treweek opened a

The harbour at Amlwch, *c.*1890.

shipbuilding yard and launched his first vessel, the 68-ton sloop *Unity*. More ships quickly followed including the 130-ton brigantine *James and Jane*, the largest wooden boat ever built at the port, in 1830. Treweek's sons later joined him in the enterprise and one, Nicholas, opened a yard at Hirael, Bangor, in 1842 but only appears to have built one vessel, the 74-ton schooner *Mary*.

The Treweeks built the 160-ton *Mary Catherine* in 1859, the first iron ship constructed in Wales. Later the same year they moved into new premises while the old yard was sold to William Cox Paynter who, although he concentrated on ship-repairing, continued the building tradition at the yard until his death in 1881. Captain Thomas Morgan took over, again focusing on the repair side of the business even if he did build three vessels between 1884 and 1898.

Old Treweek had died a few years after the 1859-move and his sons took control with Nicholas, so it seems, in charge. Captain William Thomas, who sailed many of the Treweek-owned ships, bought out what had become a prestigious business, with its carpenters' shop, smithy, counting house and sail loft, in 1872. It is thought that he already owned another yard in the village because, when he ran an advert in the local paper to highlight his purchase, he mentioned 'yards', as well as another yard in Duddon, Cumberland, he had obtained in the buy-out.

Thomas died in 1893 and the business passed to his sons Lewis and William. These two produced some of 'the finest vessels built of their time'. The port itself, with dry docks that enabled three ships to be built side by side, peaked in about 1890, and afterwards slipped into decline after imports of foreign ore had a major impact on all the Welsh copper industry. However, W. Thomas & Sons continued building up to 1908, when their last sailing vessel, the *Eilian*, was launched. A lull intervened until a hospital ship was built four years later, added to which a few ammunition barges were produced during the war. By the end of hostilities in 1918 work had finally ceased. Between 1825 and 1918 some seventy new vessels were launched from the port. Today the signs of prosperity and activity at the port are all but gone. A few boats lie alongside the walls and I managed to say hello to one person, also out with her dog. Otherwise the harbour was as dead as the brickworks at Porth Wen.

We proceeded on to Point Lynas, where the 1835-built lighthouse marks the northeast tip of the island. Prior to that, a beacon was lit on the headland to direct the pilot boats back into the bay. From there it's a run over Mynydd Eilian to the main circular road around the island, upon which we headed south. Traeth Dulas once had a thriving shipbuilding industry and herring fishery while the remains of a fish weir can be seen at Traeth Lligwy. The latter is popular with the holidaying set but, with the heat of the day now past its prime, most of the beach-goers had, it seemed, gone, leaving behind their physical evidence – sand castles, plastic bags of rubbish and the lingering smell of suntan lotion. The last stragglers exited as I let dog loose on the beach. I'd reached a stage of not caring any longer about 'no dog' signs, irresponsible as it might be, because my dog doesn't shit on beaches! If he did, then that might smother the smell of the suntan lotion!

Sitting on that beach, watching the last vestiges of those in holidaying mood on their way home, I decided I'd had enough. Enough of writing about lifeboats, of shipbuilding in wild places, or driving at pace along endless roads and fed up of watching these carefree people. Fed up, too, of the sense I'd had from the beginning of this journey that almost all the traditions of these maritime communities had disappeared and nobody seemed to care. Even the heat was becoming boring and I yearned to return to my past habit of discovering these maritime communities when they had at least some appearance of their former self. Winter is always best for this. A split decision was made. I'd stop right now, return home, write up, fall back into normality, go shopping or whatever is meant to be normal, get a life. And then I'd resume the trip when the weather wasn't so glorious. I'd view the rest of the North Wales coast in December with the wind in my hair. I whistled the dog; we climbed into the van, and drove off to the beckoning distant mountains, away from the sea.

DAY ONE/SEVENTEEN
MOELFRE TO PRESTATYN

When Richard Ayton and William Daniell set out on their voyage around Great Britain in 1814 they didn't journey continuously, rather taking two summers to reach Kirkcudbright in Scotland. There Ayton decided to proceed with the project no longer, so that it was Daniell who set out alone the following year, producing his fine aquatint illustrations and the accompanying text himself. Again in 1818, then in 1821, 1822 and finally in 1823 did he set out, completing the circumnavigation of Britain in September of that last year. Although my observations are nowhere near as succinct and elegant as theirs, I rest easy that I'm not alone in completing a coastal journey in more than one stage. This trip was meant to be organic, after all!

It was a matter of days before Christmas that I was able to rejoin my track around the coast. Standing at the memorial to those lost during that fateful night in 1859 when the *Royal Charter* ran onto rocks just yards away, it was easy to imagine the Moelfre villagers watching helplessly from this very spot as the ship struck, not far away from their homes. Gazing out to sea, Lligwy was to my left and Dulas beyond. Offshore, the 1824-erected beacon with a shelter for any sailor unfortunate to find himself stranded on Ynys Dulas stood out clearly. A large red ship lay at anchor, awaiting clearance to enter Liverpool presumably. A glint in the sky announced the true arrival of dawn. We walked, dog and I, along the grassy path back towards the village, past the lifeboat house, and the 'Moelfre Seawatch' centre. This was obviously closed at this early hour – it's only open between Easter and the end of September – although I peered through the window to see the lifeboat *Birds Eye* on view. The centre, run by Isle of Anglesey County Council, boasts of telling the 'life and history of the sea', a bold claim I thought. Beyond is the older lifeboat house. Walking back to the beach, I noted signs over two adjoining houses declaring 'Anchor' and 'The Old Crown', presumably the old pubs, havens to the fishermen.

Moelfre is a gem of a place, once just a small hamlet hugging around the cove, although now it has spread inland. It still retains a charm almost irreplaceable these days. The small stony beach (dogs not prohibited!), now miniaturised by a car park, was once home to Anglesey's major herring fishery. For decades, centuries even, small open boats with names such as *Seagull*, *Sovereign*, *Stag* or *Shamrock* sailed out to check the nets, returning in the early morning loaded with the silvery fish. Moelfre men were fine seamen too, many of who sailed the seven oceans aboard large trading vessels. Many returned specifically for the herring season when two or three months of fishing could earn them the equivalent of a year's salary on the deep sea.

Their nets were taken out each Monday, shot and fixed with large stones to the seabed because of the strong tides, unlike the drift-netters. They would be checked daily and brought ashore each Saturday. If a seasonal gale rose up – they fished from October to

The beach at Moelfre with herring boats drawn up, *c.*1920.

February – and they were unable to launch the small boats, the nets became twisted so that they had to be brought ashore as soon as the weather allowed, to be sorted and repaired, often by the women folk. These nets rarely lasted longer than five weeks of works for they were never barked in preservative to help them last longer.

Some years ago, while following the story of the herring around the Welsh coast, I met Dick Evans, Moelfre's renowned lifeboat coxswain who gained two gold medals, the first for saving the crew of the *Hindlea* almost a century to the day after the wreck of the *Royal Charter.* By the time I met him Dick was in his nineties, but his mind must have been as sharp as the day he went out in the temporary lifeboat *Edmund and Mary Robinson* in what has been described as 'one of the finest rescues ever accomplished by any North Wales lifeboat'. He remembered going out fishing with his grandfather. The 16ft boats were prepared for the season for the preceding month, all coal-tarred beneath the waterline and painted white above and inside. Sometimes the herring shoals were a mile offshore in three fathoms of water while at other times they had to sail over to Benllech to find them, the village having its own small fleet of boats and fishermen as well. Dick remembered earning £3 10s a week as a ship's officer later in his life, and came home for the herring season and remembers earning £50–60 a week. At that time a barrel fetched £3 10s. Much of this was sent by train to the Liverpool market and Dick remembered the salesman, Patrick Hogan, who paid Dick an extra £1 to load the barrels onto his lorry. This was later raised to £2 after Dick went on strike!

Dick has sadly passed on since then, although his memory lives on in the village and around the lifeboat. The road upon which he lived has recently been named after him. Today a younger set of men crew the lifeboat.

Moelfre received its first lifeboat in 1830, according to the RNLI, although other records state 1848. The site of the boathouse is unknown but a second lifeboat house was built in 1875 while the present boathouse stems from 1909, substantially altered to house the present Tyne-class boat and an inshore boat.

From Moelfre it's a short walk along the coast to Traeth Bychan where the remains of a little harbour once described as being perfectly 'positioned for sloops to load and unload away from the swell'. These craft came to collect millstones from the nearby quarry, which were of an excellent quality. In 1314 the Royal Mill in Dublin purchased one for the sum of 28*s* 9*d*. Around the corner is Benllech with its fine beach, which would have been crowded during the summer. This beach is also known for being the place where the ill-fated submarine *Thetis* was beached after she had sunk soon after leaving the Birkenhead shipyard where she was built in 1939 and had been subsequently raised soon after.

Traeth Coch (Red Wharf Bay) was, according to Lewis Morris, a hive of activity in the eighteenth century. He suggested the building of a small pier, using local stone. Furthermore he noted that herrings were 'in plenty, and other Kind of Fish, of which the Inhabitants here make great Profit', possibly with the help of the fish weir he found at the eastern end of the bay. In 1812 a scheme to build a tramway to bring coal from the Pentre Berw mines, and some quays at Porthllongdy was devised but never taken up. Another proposal was made in 1947 for a pier, but again never surfaced into reality.

The Vikings came here in about 1170, attacking the inhabitants so that the beach ran red with blood, giving the bay its name of Traeth Coch – literally 'red beach'. In 1407 it is said that the port received 16*s* 8*d* in dues. Many vessels came to load up with stone from the Castell Mawr quarry – stone that was used to build Caernarfon and Beaumaris castles, and later Liverpool Docks. Morris suggested that the local marble 'would make Columns for Public Buildings'. The sand he found perfect to use as manure. Shipbuilding briefly flourished here, as on the many other beaches as we've seen, with the 81-ton sloop *Eleanor* being built in 1786. She spent much of her working life carrying copper ore from Amlwch to Liverpool. Between 1766 and 1840, eight vessels are known to have begun life upon these sands.

There's another lifeboat station at Penmon. When we arrived, the unpleasant man who had accosted me a few years previously was not there. Nobody wanted my £1.50 this time! I was free to photograph the 1838-built, black and white painted, sea-washed lighthouse at Trwyn Du, the name of the actual tip of land at Penmon. Designed by James Walker with a stepped base to deflect waves, it is regarded as a prototype for his Smalls light.

The reasoning behind both lighthouse and lifeboat was a particular disaster that occurred during gale-force winds in 1831. The wooden paddle steamer *Rothesay Castle* was on route from Liverpool to Beaumaris when, due to her design, which was for estuary work, she became flooded and went aground on the Dutchman's Bank and eventually broke up with 140 passengers aboard. Although there were twenty-three survivors in all, such was the shock and outcry that the Anglesey Lifesaving Association opened a station the following year, stationing a 26ft Palmer lifeboat there. Within the first seven years of operation, the Penmon lifeboat is credited with saving eighty lives.

By 1859 this lifeboat was almost unserviceable so a new 30ft Peake was brought on station. This was replaced again in 1880, at which time a new boathouse was built until the service was transferred to Beaumaris in 1914. The lifeboat house has since been converted to a dwelling, as have the nearby coastguard cottages. Across from the lighthouse and coastguard cottages is the island known by the Vikings as Priestholm, the Welsh as Ynys Seiriol and the English as Puffin Island, the latter on account of the large number of these birds that nest there in April, 'displacing the rabbits from their burrows who flee to the other side of the island' according to Thomas Pennant. These puffins were caught and pickled in barrels about twelve inches long and fetched between three and four shillings apiece. Lewis Morris noted the large amount of millstones being shipped out of the nearby quarries. In 1775 it was also reported that 'Penmon has a good

The Girling brothers with some of a catch from the Gorad bach fish weir. (Courtesy Bridget Dempsey)

harbour and plenty of oysters, remarkably large: the poor find constant employ in the dredge, and in pickling the fish for foreign consumption'. Today the Dinmor quarries remain as gigantic amphitheatres gouged out of bare rock. A few buildings remain, as does the small quay for the output's export.

Between Penmon and Beaumaris the coast is flat and the foreshore stony and muddy. The remains of two fish weirs can still be found, the smaller of the two being worked up to the 1960s by two brothers John and Wilf Girling. Alongside it was once the Beaumaris lifeboat house and slip, built in 1914 to replace the Penmon station, and closed amid local fury in 1991. Before that, a lifeboat had been kept briefly off Beaumaris pier between 1891 and 1896. Today only an inshore lifeboat is stationed in the town.

Beaumaris was born out of Edward I's castle that he commenced building in 1296 and finished thirty years later. At the time boats could sail right to the castle walls but today the sea has regressed so that only a shallow moat surrounds the castle. Herring fishing was prosecuted in those days and a tax of one penny a mease was levied on all fish landed. Some £60 a year was raised from the fishermen, which went to help with the castle building. When it was completed, Edward repaid the local inhabitants by forcibly removing them to Rhosyr, into the 'new borough' that soon became Newborough (*Niwbwrch*). Edward later contemplated building a bridge across the Menai Strait, keen to imitate Alexander the Great. I wonder how he would react to the reality that no such bridge happened for another 500 years.

Pennant found 'a very good anchorage for ships in the bay... the town has no trade of any kind, yet its custom house for the casual reception of goods'. This suggests that, although the customs house was situated here, most, if not all, of the goods passing through were from outside the town. *The Welsh Port Books* show that salt was imported from Cheshire while salt herring was exported back that way, to Liverpool and Chester in the second half of the sixteenth century. Between 1722 and 1723 Richard Morris and Lewis Davies were employed as fish packers, presumably overseeing the quality of fish thus exported. Lewis Morris noted a thriving herring fishery and well as various kinds of shellfish. No doubt this supply was supplemented by fish from the fish weirs that had existed on the foreshore below the town since medieval times. When Hucks arrived in 1795, he described it as 'a dirty sea-faring town'.

Shrimps, too, were caught off the town in later years by nobbies, the traditional boats of the northwest. When the Victorian trippers started coming to the coast from the Lancashire cotton mills, many chose Beaumaris. Shrimp teas – boiled shrimps, bread and cup of tea – became a firm favourite. George Borrow noted in 1862 that the town was second to none as a watering place, with steamers bringing visitors from Liverpool and Llandudno. The pier to accommodate these steamers was first built in 1846 – as far as I can ascertain the earliest in Wales – and was developed in 1872 and again in 1895. Herring continued to be landed from nets in Fryar's Bay in the twentieth century. However, any fish bought in the local fish shop these days is as likely as not from far away.

West of Beaumaris is Gallows Point, the place where men were taken from the town gaol and hanged. It also has a tradition of shipbuilding that goes back centuries. Today there is still a boatyard, presently stuffed full of boats over-wintering, and sheds housing individuals willing to undertake repairs on boats. At the Gazelle Hotel, a couple of miles further west, the Garth ferry used to run over to Bangor pier, the ancient quay being visible at the lowest of tides. The remains of further fish can be seen at Menai Bridge

(*Porthaethwy*). The local fishermen used to keep their boats at Porth Lladron while today's' boatmen use the slip at Porth-y-wrach. Next to Porth Daniel is the timberyard of William Roberts & Co., which has been importing timber to the island since the nineteenth century. Commanding the waterside view above the town is the Menai Suspension Bridge, from which the town gets its name, and by which we left the island.

Bangor is, according to the brown sign on entering, the 'City of Learning' which seems a somewhat melodramatic description even if it is home to a university. Indeed, many British towns and cities have universities, but I think this is the first place I've seen such a road sign. Obviously the city fathers are extremely proud of the establishment that sits atop one of the two hills between which the city is located. Along the foreshore below is the remains of a fish weir, a tiny boatyard, a pier – opened in 1896 and still in good order since its refurbishment in the late 1980s and the larger boatyard of A.M. Dickie & Son. Yachts galore stood in the waterside yard while the firm undertakes repairs. The business originates from Tarbert, Loch Fyne, where they used to build fishing boats, yachts and launches until that yard's closure in the early part of this century. However, the main port for Bangor lies across Hirael Bay at Port Penryhn.

For an apt description of the port I shall rely upon Richard Ayton who, with William Daniell, arrived in 1815:

> About half a mile from [Bangor] is Aber Cegin, or Port Penrhyn, a grand emporium of slates procured from the quarries of Lady Penrhyn. A fine quay, projecting several hundred yards into the strait, was built here by the late Lord Penrhyn, on each side of which vessels of three hundred tons mat lie and receive their lading. The slates are exported in immense quantities to Liverpool, Bristol, Dublin, and indeed to all parts of the kingdom. They are of an extremely fine texture, and are made of various sizes, from thick slabs for tombstones and pavements, to the thinnest plates used for roofing. There is also a very extensive manufacture of cyphering-slates established here, which the Welsh have advanced to such a degree of perfection, that they have altogether eclipsed and reduced to bankruptcy the more bungling manufacturers of Switzerland, to whom we were formerly indebted for our principal supplies of these useful articles... The quarries are about four miles distant from the port at Dolawen, from whence the slates are brought down with great facility and rapidity in waggons, which run upon iron rail-roads, three horses being able to draw twenty tons.

Port Penrhyn has the distinction of having had the first tramway in Wales, constructed in 1801 from the quarries down to the port five miles away. Horses were used to pull the wagons. It also has what has been described as the most exquisite ten-seater round privy – today a listed building – where the port workers held their own debates, much in the same way as the slate miners held their *caban*.

I took dog for a walk along the foreshore to the fish weir close to the mouth of the river Ogwen, one of two that Hyde Hall found in the proximity. The other was presumably the Gored y Gilt that was working in 1588 – the year of the Spanish Armada – and last worked in 1852, after which it was used as oyster beds. The Ogwen weir, on the other hand, was still in operation in the 1960s and consisted of a stone wall with a wattle fence, some eight feet high. The cost of building such a weir Hyde Hall estimated as £800 with some ten percent of the catch going as rent. Much of the fish – salmon, herrings and flat fish – he added, went to Bridgenorth and Shrewsbury 'whence regular fish carts arrive in season', although some went to a nearby recent curing house which supplied the poor with salted herring at an affordable price.

Between Penrhyn and this weir lie the remains of a building. Ayton described this as 'Lady Penrhyn's Bath – an elegant little building, designed by Wyatt... stands at the extremity of a road, carried out about two hundred and twenty yards into the strait, raised nearly thirty feet above the level of the water...has much the character of an Italian building'. Staring at it, I was only able to amaze at the way those rich landowners spent their wealth so frivolously. Still, it gave the dog plenty of scope to sniff whatever he could smell!

Port Penryhn is also home today to Waterfront Marine, which is run by Scott Metcalfe, who's been here for over fifteen years. Luckily Scott was working aboard his converted Danish kotter *Vilma* when we arrived unannounced. Working from two railway sheds, Scott has built up a successful business in boatbuilding and repairs. *Vilma* was the culmination of a dream to build a Welsh topsail schooner. He found the fishing boat in Scotland in 1995 and over the next six years restored the hull, fitted her out below decks and fitted a schooner rig. Scott's reputation for quality boatbuilding is reflected by the fact that a boat had recently arrived from Greece. The owner, having read about the yard, brought the vessel by sea and road, and was awaiting a surveyor's report on whether to proceed with a rebuild. Alongside lay other boats in Scott's newly acquired hard standing that allowed him to offer winter storage to a number of yachts. 'I've now got a crane capable of lifting 18 tons and a 20-ton trailer – the biggest investment I've ever made, bigger than the house!' Scott told me.

Today Penrhyn Dock, lying in the shadow of Penrhyn Castle, is home to a collection of different boats. *Letty*, a Bristol Channel Pilot Cutter, has been here for years. Three

Scott Metcalfe (in boat) on the set of a film in which he supplied the small skiffs for S4C.

ex-Scottish fishing boats, other than *Vilma*, lay alongside. The much larger mussel dredgers lay along one side, two belonging to Myti Mussels, a company purifying and processing huge amounts of mussels and exporting much of the end product to the European continent. A whole host of small boats fill in the gaps between the bigger boats.

From Bangor we headed due east. We whizzed past Aber on the A55 Expressway and turned off into Llanfairfechan. In the days when the pubs in Anglesey were closed on a Sunday we used to drive here to get a drink. The town grew from the export of granite from the quarries on the Penmaenmawr Mountain, as did its neighbour Penmaenmawr. Tourism then followed, gleaned from the railway in the mid-nineteenth century, but today the bypass means that the majority of travellers simply miss the small attractive town. The beach is pleasant, with fine views across to Anglesey and Puffin Island. Dog ran out onto the sand while I observed the beauty of the tall four-storied terraced houses standing separated from the promenade by a grassy green. Some had lovely gable frontages and curved windows, which reflected their Victorian past. Dogs had to be on a lead on the prom during the months of May, June, July and September. To the south-west was the Traeth Lafan Local Nature Reserve with its intertidal mudflats, bird-life and expanse of mussel and cockle beds. On the other side, the Penmaenmawr Mountain seemed to almost cast a shadow over this, a once thriving resort town.

The road skirts the bulk of the Penmaenmawr Mountain, on whose slopes, and top, are the Graiglwyd Quarries. Granite stone comes down the mountainside in a conveyor system that is the modern equivalent to the tramway and wagons of old. The stone either is loaded into railway wagons or directly onto small ships that still come alongside the jetty that protrudes almost to the low water mark. This granite was once exported all over Britain, and was used in the building of the Mersey Tunnel. In 1870 between 60,000 and 70,000 tons were exported down the mountainside and away by boats.

The Penmaenmawr railway station was opened in 1849, and encouraged some tourism so that the town became a resort after about 1860. Today though, like Llanfairfechan, sandwiched between mountain and sea, it doesn't seem to have much of an air of a resort. It's funny to think that these two places were made fashionable simply because of Prime Minister Gladstone's preference for Penmaenmawr as his favourite holiday resort.

From Penmaenmawr we ascended the Sychnant Pass which, before the construction of the road around Penmaenbach (which was heavily congested once again due to seemingly constant roadworks), was the main route to Conwy. At low water, before construction, travellers could circumvent the bulk of the mountain upon the sands, heading parallel to the coast before heading off across the Lafan Sands to cross over to Beaumaris. Hucks thought this area once dangerous for the wary traveller – he doesn't really explain why – but added that it 'is now perfectly safe'. After a short stop to allow dog to run about the hillside, and a few minutes taking in the view even if a grey mist did obscure much of distant Anglesey, we arrived in Conwy, described by Defoe as 'the Poorest but Pleasantest Town in all this County… a noble Harbour for Ships'.

Entering the town through one of several gateways in the ancient town walls, we drove back out of the boundary protection of these walls to the harbour, on the periphery. 'Keith the fish' was in his tiny mobile fish shop at the far end. He filled me in on the local gossip that had occurred since I'd seen him last – I used to bring the 'Herring Exhibition' here every year until vandals attempted to tip my smokehouse up one night.

Keith has been rolling his trailer out each day from across the road onto his pitch on the quayside ever since anyone can remember, it seems. Christmas Day is his only exception, although, with sales well down, he wondered how long he could continue. As we spoke, a Canadian woman came up, not to buy as she said, but to ask questions of Keith about the harbour. Perhaps the local authority should pay him as an information centre to supplement his income and keep him here.

Conwy is obviously dominated by the castle, another of Edward I's, built in 1294 by the same architect Edward employed for Caernarfon. However, the town is noted for its fine castle walls and the three bridges that span the river Conwy. Before the first of these was built in 1826, the first fixed crossing point upstream was at Llanrwst. Ferries existed at Conwy and Tal-y-cafn, the former crossed by Ayton and Daniell only a decade before the bridge was built.

Alongside the quay were two fishing boats while a collection of boats in various states sat on the foreshore north of the quay. Pontoons in the river are crowded with vessels in the summer. Another, more grander (more expensive) marina was been created in the hole in the bank used to construct the massive sections of tunnel that have been sunk into the river to form the new Conwy crossing for the A55 Expressway.

In 1566 Conwy was only one of four havens recognised as such in Caernarfonshire. There were threescore households and only 'one barke belonging to the same port or towne comonly called the Katheryn of Conwey of the burden of fourty tonnes the owners thereof Robert Wynn, William Holland and William ap Richard and is comonly occupied in the trade of merchundise'. Lewis Morris found, 'In this Place Corn, Timber, and Oak-Bark, are in great Plenty'. Some 12,000 bushels of different kinds of grain were exported. The pearl fishing that was prevalent some time ago he found to be neglected.

The pearls were coming from locally fished mussels and the fishing must have recovered from its decline for Halliwell, travelling in North Wales in 1860 found the mussels were 'found in considerable abundance at low water all along the shore at the entrance to the river, and are dredged by boatmen along the course of the river, as well as collected on the mussel banks. I tried my fortune with a dozen of them, a number yielded nearly a dozen pearls, two of these the size of a pin's head; the others were exceedingly minute'. In the late nineteenth century, though, 160 ounces were said to have been collected in one week, fetching 2s 6d an ounce.

By the 1880s mussels were being collected for human consumption. Before the age of mechanism these had to be dredged by hand. Two methods were adopted – either using a hand rake from a small rowboat, or simply by harvesting them by hand. In the latter instance, the pickers, often women, made their way to the chosen spot by boat and gathered by hand, using a small knife called *twca* to cut clumps of mussels away from the rocks. These were then bagged and put aboard the boat for carriage back to the quay. On the other hand, those dredging from an anchored boat use a rake with eight or so prongs – nominally not bigger than 3ft across the mouth – with a bag-net along one edge and the whole implement is attached to a long pole up to 30ft in length. The mussels are forced into the prongs of the rake by pulling it along the seabed towards the boat. Once the handle is vertical, the rake is flipped over so that the molluscs fall into net. These are then hauled to the surface and dumped into the boat. Once the boat is full, the fishermen returned to quay to offload. This method has an added advantage in that it does less destruction to the mussel beds.

Wrecks Around Wales – The Royal Charter

The coast of Wales is simply littered with wrecks – too many to count. However, few have attracted as much attention as the wreck of the *Royal Charter*. Even such a distinguished writer as Charles Dickens was minded to rush up and write about it.

What has been described as 'the hurricane of the century' began on 23 October 1859. Two days later the first of 135 ships that this one storm caused to sink floundered in the English Channel. Later that night winds of over 100mph hit the Anglesey coast. Port Penrhyn, Bangor, was devastated, with boats smashing into each other and sinking. At Holyhead, the steamship *Great Eastern* was in danger of breaking away from its mooring and all but sank.

The *Royal Charter* was on her way back from Australia with miners bringing home the successes of the gold rush. The clipper ship, built at Sandycroft on the river Dee, was iron-built and fitted with an auxiliary steam engine. She had only been launched four years previously and had not been lucky. At first she refused to budge, and when she did enter the water she was towed down river, where she grounded, damaging the keel. On her maiden voyage she almost sank in the Channel, due to being over-ballasted, and had to return to Plymouth. When eventually she did sail to Australia, she completed the voyage in amazing speed – in just under sixty days.

She arrived off the Skerries on the evening of 25 October, just as the hurricane was about to hit with its full strength. The Liverpool pilot boat was unable to leave Amlwch harbour, such was the wind. However, around 10 p.m. that night, with the ship off Point Lynas, the wind changed direction, from the previous SE to ENE. Thus the ship was sailing into the wind and it soon became apparent that she was being driven towards the Anglesey coast.

The captain attempted to manoeuvre into deeper water but found that he couldn't make way, even with full power and added sail. Thus he decided to anchor, laying out both anchors. Two hours later the port cable snapped and, an hour later, the starboard. At 3 a.m. the ship's bottom scraped the rocks of Anglesey. Half an hour later she was stuck fast, beam on to the sea in some four fathoms and only twenty-five yards from the coast. Once the tide had gone down, the captain reassured the passengers, they would be able to walk ashore. However, 60ft-high waves were pounding the ship.

One seaman, Joseph Rodgers, managed to reach the shore with a line. Villagers from nearby Moelfre had been aroused and helped bring sixteen passengers off in a bosun's chair. But, at around 7.30 a.m., a huge wave tore a hole in the side of the ship and within several minutes she began to break up so that, in the space of a short time, some 450 people on board were drowned or smashed to death against rocks. Out of an estimated compliment of some 100 crew and 390 passengers, only around forty survived. Some half a million pounds worth of gold bullion was lost to the beach.

Although much of this has been salvaged over the years, stories still abound of gold coins appearing in the sand. One tale tells of Will and Jinnie Jones who lived closeby. Out winkle picking one day, Will chanced upon some gold sovereigns under seaweed. Unbeknown to them, wily village butcher-cum-coastwatcher Dan was watching as removing gold was illegal. Jinnie took the booty home while Will continued picking. Dan confronted Will who denied any knowledge so Dan hastened after Jinnie who arrived home with a bit of time to spare, with Will hard on his heels. Dan insisted on searching the house while Jinnie went about stewing the gastropods for dinner. Eventually Dan admitted he must have been wrong and the two invited him to share their meagre meal. Soon afterwards Dan left and Will, hardly able to contain his excitement, wondered where his wife had hidden them. 'Heb fod ymhell', she

Poster advertising the
Royal Charter, which
was wrecked in 1859.

answered – 'not very far away'. 'Oh, Will Bach,' she added after a few minutes, 'they've been lying at the bottom of the stew pan under the winkles all the time!' They both laughed so loud they were afraid Dan would return.

Whether this story is true or not, it does highlight the fact that there were many keen to plunder the gold while the authorities were keen to protect it. For many years the arguments ranged about the villagers who risked their lives that fateful night and the latecomers who were only set on benefiting from the wreck. That hurricane certainly was of unusual strength and is still known as the *Royal Charter* gale, even if it did culminate in over 800 deaths at sea. Almost exactly one hundred years to the day, another hurricane hit the Anglesey coast in which the Moelfre lifeboat was launched into horrendous seas. Coxswain Dick Evans managed to reach the stricken ship and come alongside over ten times to take the crew off the *Hindlea* before it was ultimately dashed to pieces on the rocks that had destroyed the *Royal Charter*. For this feat of seamanship Evans was awarded the first of his two RNLI gold medals. He was, in fact, descended from Richard Matthews, a Moelfre villager who led the rescue attempt that night in 1859 when the *Royal Charter* ran aground.

Both catches were then sorted and washed before being purified by immersion in sterilized sea water containing chloride of lime to flush out their stomachs. Regulations stated that this process should take place two days before they were bagged, carried to the railway station by horse and cart, and sent to the markets in the Midlands. The first purification plant opened in 1916 after national health scares.

Each family in Conway had their traditional point of embarkation and there were two fishermen in each boat in 1929, the year of the earliest available records. There were fifty-five mussel fishermen and ten years later this had increased to seventy-five, including eight full-time women. During the war years when the men went off to fight, the women ran the entire fishery.

Of course, the fishery has changed a bit these days. Even though the fishery is still going and well managed, more modern dredges are used, although some are still picked by hand. I'd been out twice dredging on mussel boats from Port Penrhyn. The first time was aboard the 1905-built Dutch general-purpose cargo boat converted dredger *Tannie Christina*, BS98, and the second time on Myti Mussels new dredger *Mytilus*. On both trips it became obvious that, although the fishing process is simple – dredge over the size, trawl, haul and empty into the hold – the job is both monotonous and tiring, much more than any other fishing.

A new purification plant has been opened upon the quay where fifty baskets of mussels are placed in four tanks at a time. These are left for forty-two hours, ultraviolet light being used to kill off the bacteria. From these tanks the mussels are fed into a conveyor system which cleans, riddles, scrubs, brushes and finally bags them. Overall, three tons can be processed every two days before being sent to market. 'Keith the fish', I noticed, had some bags of Conwy mussels on his display.

The river at Conwy and the shipyard in the background. (Courtesy National Library of Wales)

Conwy was heaving with the rush of Christmas shoppers but the quay was almost deserted. In summer it's busy with visitors, many of whom come to see 'the smallest house in Wales' at the other end of the quay. However, it is easy to imagine the harbour full of sailing vessels, some sailing up as far as Llanrwst to carry coal upstream and local goods back down. The river has also been famous for its sea trout, and there were six seine nets in operation in the 1970s, the fishermen using small 10ft boats. Further upstream coracle fishing had been a common practice since at least the sixteenth century. Later, in 1819, Michael Faraday had written of observing two-man coracles on the river but within a few decades coracle fishing seems to have disappeared.

Across the river from Conwy the old quay at Deganwy was in the process of being developed into a marina with the proverbial housing, so it seemed pointless to stop there. Richard Ayton observed some of the remains of Deganwy Castle. We pressed on to Llandudno, described as 'the queen of Welsh resorts'.

Up to the nineteenth century Llandudno was an isolated hamlet located on the rim of the eastern slopes of the Great Orme. Miners, farmers and fishermen living in tiny primitive *tai-un-nos* or one-night cottages inhabited it, as they have since been called since they had to be built in one night under ancient laws. Ayton described it as 'rude and romantic'. However, with control of much of the land passing to Edward Mostyn under the Enclosure Acts, the houses were cleared and the beginnings of the resort of Llandudno laid in the 1840s. Hotels were built, a water system, sewerage, gas lighting installed and roads improved. The population increased rapidly and by 1859 visitors were being encouraged to take '15 to 20 minutes in the sea' unless they suffered from 'apoplexy, epilepsy, hysteria, fainting fits, incipient pulmonary consumption, chronic bronchitis, dysentery, diarrhea, spitting of blood, organic diseases within chest and

Beach and Pier Pavilion at Llandudno.

abdomen, valvular disease in the heart, inflammation in the kidneys, enlargement of the liver, spleen etc or anyone who did not see a flow on the skin after sea bathing'. A brisk walk up the Great Orme should follow.

There had been plans to build a harbour of St George in the 1830s by almost enclosing the bay between the Great and Little Ormes with a breakwater put forward by the Chester & Crewe Railway. This was at the same town as plans to develop Porthdinllaen by the Irish Railway Commission. As we know, Holyhead was the favoured option.

And so Llandudno prospered as a purpose-built resort. The first pier was built in 1858 in another vague attempt to entice the Irish packet boat here, but was severely damaged the next year in the same storm that wrecked the *Royal Charter*. It was repaired and survived several more years until the present pier was built and opened in 1877.

Up on the Great Orme copper production between 1830 and 1850 was at its highest and was exported by sea. Current belief, though, suggests mining first began here in the Bronze Age. The semaphore station, part of the signaling link between Holyhead and Liverpool alerting the port of approaching ships, dated from 1827 and was converted to a hotel in 1909. Other places of interest attracted the visitors. St Tudno's church was built to replace the church built by the saint of that name who came here in the sixth century and from whom the town took its name. Happy Valley was a limestone quarry, closed in 1887 and subsequently developed into a sort of fun park where, in 1890, 'a large concourse of pleasure seekers meet daily in the season'. A Camera Obscura was built in 1860 and destroyed by vandals in 1966, another being built recently. Cust's Path around the edge of the Orme was built in 1858 but twenty years later was widened and turned into the circular Marine Drive. Guiding ships away from its coast, the castellated, fortress-like Great Orme's Head lighthouse was built in 1862 but the light was finally extinguished in 1985 and is now run as a private hotel. The mountain railway leading up from the town dates from the very beginning of the twentieth century.

In 1864 the *Liverpool Mercury* bestowed upon Llandudno the accolade of being the 'Queen of Western Watering Places' while Arnold Bennett, in his 1911 novel *The Card*, wrote that the town 'is more stylish than either Rhyl or Blackpool, and not dearer'.

The lifeboat station was opened in 1861 in a boathouse close to the railway station. Some of the cost of the Peake-type lifeboat was borne by the Misses Brown, frequent visitors to the town. A new boathouse was built in 1903, enabling the boat to be launched from either the West or East Shore, but by the 1950s, it was only possible to launch on the East Side. Today's lifeboat is a Mersey-class all-weather boat, and an inshore lifeboat has been on station since 1965.

Llandudno was the forerunner for seaside resort development right along the North Wales coast. From there we drove to Rhos-on Sea (*Llandrillo-yn-Rhos*) St Trillo's tiny chapel stands close to the road and is normally open to view. St Trillo, son of Ithel Hael of Llydaw, was possibly of Breton descent and probably educated on Bardsey. He established his 'cell' here in the sixth century on a small island at the mouth of the river Ganol. At the time the coastline was very different, with the river Conwy emerging seaward on the east side of the Orme and not the west, following the route of what is now the river Ganol. Close to where I was standing now was the island with the nearby fish weir on the eastern side of it. However, this is conjecture, as differences in sea level seem to contradict this. For William Ashton argues that the coastline was several miles out to sea and that the Menai Strait simply did not exist, while the river Ogwen as the river Ell, flowing out from its present confluence along the Anglesey coast and out between Puffin and Trwyn Du. Everything else was fertile land. In 1812 Pugh reported during his tour that he 'found a causeway pointing from Priestholme island to Penmaenmawr easily visible' while Ayton noted that, according to tradition, a great plain of land filled up the space between here and Priestholm (Puffin Island).

The fish weir at Rhos Fynach – the 'monks' promontory' – probably dates back to the time of the Cisterian Monks who had settled here in the twelfth century. Two weirs once existed, either side of Rhos Pier that once ran out from the point. The one to the east was destroyed while the west weir was working up to the First World War. This was one weir that was specifically exempted from the provisions of the 1861 Act abolishing these 'fixed engines' after submissions to the Royal Commission proved its existence for many years. On one occasion 35,000 herrings were taken in the weir in 1850 while 10 tons of mackerel was caught in 1907. In the 1860s, the celebrated dog fisher Jack was presented with a solid silver collar by public subscription. The dog, it seems, was excellent at catching salmon and thus spent his days at the weir. He ultimately died after receiving wounds after killing a small shark in the weir. Norman Tucker, who recounted the story in his *Colwyn Bay, it origin and growth*, noted that he had seen Jack reposing in a glass case at his owner's daughter's house, as well as the silver collar.

The pier is unusual in that it was bought second-hand from the Isle of Man by William Horton in 1896. It was demolished in 1954 after being partly destroyed by fire a few years earlier. Today only the entrance ticket office has survived, turned into a museum (closed), a shop and restaurant. In 1908, seventy-five passengers waiting to embark on the approaching 196-ton paddle steamship *Rhos Neigr*, calling here on route from Llandudno to Blackpool, watched in horror as the ship flooded and was beached. All eighty passengers and nineteen crew aboard were saved.

Steamers called in at all the North Wales resorts. From 1821 to 1963 these pleasure steamers cruised from Lancashire to the Menai Strait, sometimes providing day trippers with spectacular views of the coast and at other times bringing in holiday-makers in the busy resorts. I remember well being taken on a day cruise around Anglesey on the *St Trillo*, the last of these ships to exist before being scrapped.

Colwyn Bay (*Bae Colwyn*) has its own pier, at 900ft long, which opened in 1900 and was named Victoria Pier. It had a pavilion capable of seating 2,400 people but this was destroyed by fire in 1922. Another, smaller one was built to replace it the following year, but this too was destroyed by fire in 1933. The third was opened in 1934 and remains, although the pier was closed in 1993 and was in danger of being demolished until being sold into private hands.

Colwyn, as it was then called, was part of the parish of Llandrillo in 1801, the population of which was 769. There was no shortage of fish and the people survived on oats, milk, butter, family reared pigs and potatoes. Turnips were introduced in 1765, which enabled the animals to be fed all winter. No development occurred when the railway was carried through in 1848 but ten years later this happened, leading to the spread of the town now visible today. In the 1880s the first of the limestone quarries opened at Penmaenhead, followed by those at Llanddulas and Merllyn. The rock was blasted, broken up, graded and loaded onto wagons capable of carrying 4 tons before

PRICE SIXPENCE.

Official Guide

OF THE

COLWYN BAY & LIVERPOOL STEAMSHIP CO., LIMITED.

THE "RHOS COLWYN"

Sails from **LIVERPOOL**
Along the **NORTH WALES COAST**
To **COLWYN BAY** (RHOS PIER).
LLANDUDNO,
MENAI STRAITS, AND
HOLYHEAD.

The official guidebook for the Colwyn Bay & Liverpool Steamship.

being pushed along tramlines to the top of the jetty. Flats, sometimes called 'hoppers', came from the Mersey. These were beached alongside the rickety jetty until mechanisation increased efficiency, deeper jetties were built and coasters came to pick up the stone. Although some is transported by rail, some still leaves by boat.

The North Wales coast, from Bangor to the river Dee, is almost one continuous stretch of sand, one of the deciding factors that led to the growth of the resorts. Llanddulas perhaps never developed into a resort, perhaps being better known for its limestone quarries. The first jetty was built in 1822 to ship the stone out. In 1869 a lifeboat was stationed here in a new lifeboat house, but, after only saving twenty-one lives, this was closed in 1932. It had been stationed for the previous year at nearby

The Colwyn Bay & Liverpool Steamship Company. Ltd

Registered Office: RHOS-ON-SEA. Colwyn Bay.

The New, Fast, Cross-Channel Saloon Paddle Steamer

DAILY SERVICE

S.S. RHOS COLWYN

· BETWEEN ·

LIVERPOOL..
COLWYN BAY.
LLANDUDNO
· AND ·
MENAI STRAITS

Advert for the Colwyn Bay & Liverpool Steamship Co.

Abergele before Llanddulas, the latter being more centrally placed between Llandudno and Rhyl. Abergele, although half a mile from the sea, was another small watering hole where, according to Hucks, they had a strange custom. This, he wrote, 'has an air of great indelicacy to a stranger; which is, that the inferior orders of people commonly bathe, without the usual precautions of machines or dresses; nor is it singular to see ten or a dozen of both sexes promiscuously enjoying themselves in the lucid element, regardless, or rather unconscious, of any indecency. Not being myself accustomed to this mode, I chose to retire farther up; but it is very unpleasant bathing, being a flat level beach, and necessary to wade a quarter of a mile into the sea before one can arrive at any comfortable depth'. Echoes of Aberystwyth or what?

We drove east, not stopping at Abergele beach, and passed through Pensarn and Towyn. Both sides of the road were carpeted in caravans. Caravans galore! The river Clwyd is crossed at Foryd, an ancient fishing hamlet that was also the ancient port of Rhuddlan. In 1566, 'Vorryd adoineth the towne of Rudlan which is a little village so named Rudlan conteynyng in it aboute 40 housholdes which are pore people yet not lacking habitcones'. In 1800 the fishermen lived in 'tiny miserable thatched cottages with turf or cobble-stone walls' which were in constant threat from the high tides and the sand dunes. Pennant found a flourishing fishery with 'flounders, plaice, small sole, ray, dab, cod, weaver, and even anchovy', as well as mackerel and herrings. Of the latter he wrote that these 'in this sea are extremely desultory. At times they appear in vast shoals, even as high as Chester. They arrive in the month of November, continue until February, and are followed by multitudes of small vessels, which enliven the channel. Great quantities are taken and salted but are generally shotten and meagre. It is now about 10 years since they have paid us a visit'. Record amounts, it seems, were landed in 1766 and 1767.

Rhyl's lifeboat has been kept at Foryd since 1856, although the first lifeboat had been established six years earlier by The Shipwrecked Fishermen and Mariners' Royal Benevolent Society. Between 1856–1939 the tubular-type Richardson lifeboat on station proved extremely popular with the crew who preferred the type to the

Rhyl beach with donkeys lined up for rides and a fishwife in background.

self-righting boats after six lifeboatmen drowned after one such boat, the *Gwylan-y-Mor*, capsized in 1853. The station's third and final tubular lifeboat, the *Caroline Richardson*, remained on station for forty-two years, and had the distinction of being the longest serving lifeboat in the annals of the RNLI. However, the boat had only been launched seventeen times. She was replaced by the station's first motor lifeboat, today which is a Mersey-class boat and which is housed close to the beach with an inshore boat.

Rhyl was one of the last ports of North Wales to be called in at by sailing ships, bringing in Scandinavian timber to the sawmills of Charles Jones & Sons. This company was established in 1870 and specialised in 'Archangel Reds, Floorings, Bathurst Spruce, Mobil Pitchpine & English Cement'. Shipbuilding at the old Foryd yard commenced in the mid-nineteenth century but didn't survive until the end of the century.

It was getting quite dark as we drove through Rhyl, even if the bright lights of a few of the amusement arcades lit up the promenade. Some quasi-Popeye structure, part of it named after Noah, sprawled along the seafront close to the centre. Large four-storied houses lined the road, renowned as being rented as bed and breakfast hostels for homeless people, many coming from Manchester and Liverpool. Illuminated signs enticed me to play superbowl or enter into Pleasureland. Robin Hood was advertising free sites for 2004. We passed the Sun Centre where I remember taking my son for a birthday treat many years ago. We didn't stop, making Prestatyn in time to park up and run the dog on the seafront as the waves thrashed and splashed. The lights of Liverpool brightened the eastern sky while offshore a gas flare pinpointed one of the gas wells. Behind, the headlights of a car stabbed the darkness of the hillside behind the town. Somewhere up there, between Prestatyn and Gronant, is the old Voel Nant telegraph station, the last in the chain of Welsh semaphore stations giving Liverpool advance warning of ships approaching Holyhead on route to the port. But it was too dark to make it out. I went to eat in the nearby Indian restaurant housed in a converted school. Fireworks announced the approaching Christmas festivities. I climbed into a damp bed just as the rain began its all night onslaught on the tin roof of the van. Sleep, though, came easily.

DAY TWO/EIGHTEEN
PRESTATYN TO THE RIVER DEE

The rain rattled the roof almost all night. Emerging into a dank grey December day, I found a flood of water almost a foot deep beneath the van. Much more and we'd have floated away! The dog stuck his nose out, sniffed and jumped back onto the bed. It was going to be a very wet final day, a far cry to lazy sunny days fishing on the river Severn. I enticed him out for a walk along the beach.

From the Ffrith beach, the North Hoyle Offshore Wind Farm was just visible through the gloom even if these wind turbines were hardly more than a couple of miles away. Thirty turbines, each generating 2 megawatts of electricity for the National Grid were about to be brought on line, having been installed over the last year or so. According to the information board, these Vesta turbines would prevent some 160,000 tonnes of carbon dioxide being put into the atmosphere each year.

Through the blinding rain and blustery wind I gazed out. Somewhere beneath these waves lay the wreck of the *Resurgam*, the world's first mechanically powered submarine that was invented by George William Garrett. Launched at Birkenhead in December 1879, the vessel stayed underwater for thirty hours on her maiden voyage to Rhyl, where she arrived for minor repairs. Keen to get the submarine to Portsmouth to show her off to the Admiralty and earn a hopeful £60,000, Garrett decided to tow *Resurgam* south using the steam yacht *Elfin*. However, on his second attempt, he set out in the following February with a gale warning imminent. When this sprang up, Garrett and his crew moved off the submarine onto *Elfin* and continued the tow until the towrope parted, the submarine drifted away and later sank. The *Elfin* was later wrecked in the river Dee after having trouble with her boilers. The *Resurgam* was located off Rhyl late in 1995 by a trawlerman called Dennis Hunt. She was snagged in his nets and a local diver, while freeing the nets, realised what the wreck was. A replica is to be found on Woodside ferry terminal, Birkenhead.

The Point of Ayr lighthouse, some four miles east, was our next stopping point. Driving to Talacre, and the Point of Ayr Holiday Park, dog and I had a good walk over the sand dunes. Here Liverpool evacuees lived during the Second World War in temporary houses behind the dunes. I found a brick chimney sticking out of one dune and wondered whether this was part of such a dwelling. The lighthouse itself stands alone on the sandy beach, and marks the entrance to the river Dee. The first lighthouse was built in 1777, and Edward Price was paid 16 guineas a year to be the keeper. His job was to keep the two tar buckets on top alight. Ayton described it as having 'two windows in the light-room, one shewing a light to the eastward into the river Dee, and the other pointing to the W.N.W. as a guide over Chester Bar'. Each tar bucket illuminated each window, but it seems it was never very effective. The ships were more likely to see the light during the day, not because of the actual fire, but the smoke from it! In 1819, when Trinity House took over its running, it was altered. It was then used intermittently after the 1840s when another piled structure, since demolished, was built. In 1903 a lightship was moored offshore so that it had fallen into total disuse by the 1920s. Judging by photographs from that era the sand dunes have moved back from the sea for, although the lighthouse is situated well out onto the beach, it used to be alongside the dunes.

It is possible that a lifeboat was stationed here by the Mersey Docks & Harbour Board in the very early nineteenth century but details are unknown. That one was established across the estuary at Hoylake in 1803 is known. Records, though, do confirm that a lifeboat was on station at Point of Ayr between 1839 and 1923 and presumably earlier for this lifeboat was known to have rescued the three crew of the flat *Thomas* in April 1835. For a while, it seems, two boats were kept side by side in a boathouse, with horse teams available to draw them to the most convenient launching spot on the sands.

Just around the point are the docks at the Point of Ayr colliery from where coal was exported to Ireland, North Wales, Cardigan Bay and Lancashire. In 1566 Picton Pool was mentioned as having two deputies and was regarded as being a small creek capable of receiving 'barges and botes'. The hamlet of Picton lies half a mile inland from the colliery. Output from the colliery reached its peak in 1915 and it wasn't until 1996 that it closed. The workings are said to reach over two and a half miles out under the sea.

Mostyn Docks have been expanded over the last few years to provide new port facilities for the P&O Irish Sea ferry between here and the heart of Dublin as well as the import of timber, scrap metal and wood pulp, and export of rolled steel. However, it is much older, being the site where Colonel Mostyn landed with 2,000 Irish volunteers in 1643 in support of the Royalists during the Civil War. According to Mike Griffiths, later that same century, Mostyn was used to bring in Irish girls to work as prostitutes in many small Welsh ports. Between 1835 and 1850 another lifeboat was stationed here. Its only known service was to the flat *James*, returning from Port Dinorwic loaded with slates, which was wrecked in 1839, with the ship's master being the sole survivor.

Between Mostyn and Flint there are three small inlets. A small private dock at Llanerch-y-Mor now houses the ex-British Rail Isle of Man ferryboat *Duke of Lancaster*, which towers above the surrounding topography. Privately owned, it has served as a casino, a theatre, a shopping centre and a fun centre. But small creeks such as these were probable landing places for smuggled goods, for this entire coast was once active in free trading. It has been said that the whole coast between Anglesey and Hilbre Island was a myriad of small coves ideal for smuggling due to the sparse population, and the nearby expanding towns keen to receive these cheap goods.

Greenfield was more active than Llanerch-y-Mor in that several boats lay in the river, even if the tide was out, including two smart fishing boats. The little lute-sterned boat *Little Wonder* intrigued me simply because the stern arrangement appeared similar to the Hastings beach boats – a digression from the Welsh coast! On a gate alongside the pool was a sign 'lifeboat launching keep clear'. Where was the lifeboat? In the village there's a pub called the Packet House, a reminder that several ferries across the Dee Sands carried passengers to Parkgate from where they could proceed to Liverpool. Parkgate was, of course, the birthplace of Emma Lyon who became Lady Hamilton after being the mistress of Charles Greville, Hamilton's nephew (remember Greville at Milford Haven and Nelson out with Emma in Tenby?).

LIVERPOOL
AND
Mostyn Packet.

THE
STEAM PACKET
HERCULES,

Has commenced running as a Regular Packet between *Liverpool and Mostyn Quay*, and will continue throughout the Winter sailing (for the present) every WEDNESDAY from Liverpool, and returning the same day from Mostyn at the hour stated below; but if sufficient Encouragement offer she will sail Twice in the Week. For Freight or Passage apply to

JOHN RICHARDSON, Liverpool, or THOMAS DAVIES, Mostyn Quay.

Packet Office, Liverpool, 5th November, 1829.

DAYS OF SAILING FROM LIVERPOOL,
For the Months of November and December.

Wednesday, 11th Nov. 7 o'Clock, Morning.	Wednesday, 9th Dec.	7 o'Clock, Morning
Wednesday, 18th ,, 11 o'Clock, Morning.	Wednesday, 16th ,,	11 o'Clock, Morning
Wednesday, 25th ,, 7 o'Clock, Morning.	Wednesday, 23rd ,,	7 o'Clock, Morning.
Wednesday, 2d Dec. 11 o'Clock, Morning.	Wednesday, 30th ,,	11 o'Clock, Morning

DAYS OF SAILING FROM MOSTYN QUAY,
For the Months of November and December.

Wednesday, 11th Nov. 11 o'Clock, Morning.	Wednesday, 9th Dec.	11 o'Clock, Morning.
Wednesday, 19th ,, 3 o'Clock, Afternoon.	Wednesday, 16th ,,	2 o'Clock, Afternoon.
Wednesday, 25th ,, 11 o'Clock, Morning.	Wednesday, 23rd ,,	10 o'Clock, Morning.
Wednesday, 2d Dec. 2 o'Clock, Afternoon.	Wednesday, 30th ,,	1 o'Clock, Afternoon.

The HERCULES also continues plying between Liverpool and Rhyl.

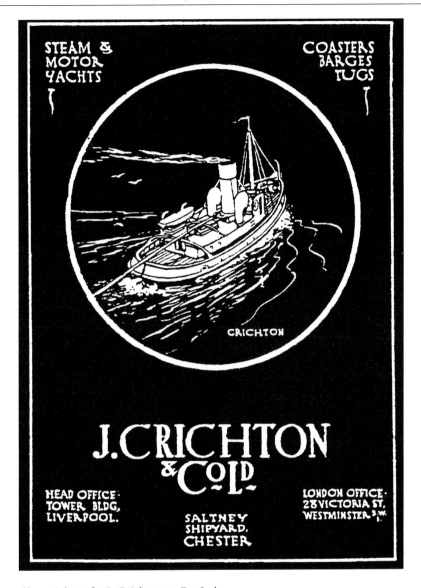

Above: Advert for J. Crichton & Co. Ltd.

Opposite: Advert for the Liverpool and Mostyn Steam Packet.

Crossing without local knowledge was perilous and many unwary travellers must have come trapped by the quicksands for which the estuary is renowned. Greenfield's development stemmed from industry being attracted to the short valley that leads down from Holywell. Lead had been mined in the Holywell and Halkyn area since Roman times and a lead smelter was said to be in operation here in 1590. Water-powered cotton mills sprung up in the later eighteenth century, harnessing the water supply from the river. Copper from Anglesey was sent to be smelted here and a brass foundry was established. Pennant found 1,250 people working in the cotton mills alone. A tramline ran from Holywell down to the port. However, by the end of the eighteenth century, cotton production had moved to Lancashire and the lead run out. Beyond Greenfield is Bagillt, another similar inlet upon a small river with two docks used primarily to export coal from nearby seams. Both had flushing-pools inland to keep the silt out of the docking area. Since the railway came in the 1840s these ports declined, although the main dock at Bagillt remains because of the flow of water through the surviving sluice gates. Like Greenfield, it is home today to fishing and pleasure boats.

Flint had been a port since Roman times as well, principally for the export of the lead from the mines and, later, coals. Today, like the others, it is home to a few fishing boats. Flint briefly became a seaside resort after the building of the railway for the waters were claimed to have miraculous healing powers. Today the tourists have gone, to be replaced by industry. Indeed, almost the whole of the coast between Greenfield and Queensferry is a strip of thriving industry, adding to the general wealth and high employment of north-east Wales, when considered in comparison with other parts, especially the north and west.

Flint has its own lifeboat and this was first purchased with money raised locally. After a man was lost upon the sands on a foggy, freezing cold Boxing Day night in 1957 – those searching could hear his cries until they suddenly ceased but could never ascertain his whereabouts – several of those involved in the fruitless search realised the urgent need for a boat. £365 was raised locally to buy a small boat with a 1½hp outboard engine, which was kept in a fisherman's store. Over the years several rescues saved lives that would otherwise have been lost on the treacherous sands. In 1966 the RNLI took over the station and £18,000 was raised for a new station. However, for some reason a builder could not be engaged, so the crew built the station themselves. Today it houses an inshore boat, complete with tractor for towing the boat about the sands.

Fishermen have been setting stake-nets on these sands for generations. These had been introduced to Rhyl in the 1820s by Scottish fishermen from the Solway Firth and were effective at catching salmon. However, largely because they were considered so deadly in their catching ability, many of the fishermen objected to these nets, and many were destroyed by these locals in the 1850s. By 1870 most were replaced by seine-nets, although some were retained for a fisherman who was recorded as almost drowning after becoming lost on the sands; he was later rescued by the lifeboat crew. The reality of these stake-nets was noted by Charles Kingsley in his poem *The Sands of Dee*. Mary went off to call the cattle home but got lost on the sands. When they found her: 'Oh! It is weed, or fish, or floating hair-/A tress of golden hair,/A drowned maidens hair/Above the nets at sea?/Was never a salmon yet that shone so fair/Among the stakes on Dee'.

Cockles are abundant in the Dee estuary as well, and rumours abound of unemployed persons who both claim dole and fish wearing facemasks and hoods. It is said that one officer from the benefit office was beaten up with a baseball bat on one occasion. Although many parts of the Welsh coast seem to suffer from sudden visits by groups using quad-bikes to gather cockles, it does seem that the problem of working on the dole and fishing is highly exaggerated. I guess, like anything else, there's a thread of truth in the gossip.

Upriver from Flint, the river Dee was canalized in the late 1730s all the way to Chester, which led to a flurry of dock building along the river's edge. Connah's Quay dock was built in 1760 and described by Pennant as 'a handsome pier... built by the River Dee Company, jutting into the channel for the protections of ships bound to and from Chester under which they take shelter in bad weather or adverse winds'. This was the New Quay. Previously, it was only the Wepra Pool that had been anything relating to a creek – in 1566 it had two deputies. By the early 1780s the place had become Connah's Quay and was being advertised as a seaside resort where lodgings could be had at the Connah's Quay House.

Today this is the Old Quay House pub, which is situated by the one remaining dock, the other two having been infilled. I entered the pub, leaving the dog in the van. Immediately I knew this was the haunt of the local fishermen so that it didn't take long to strike up a conversation with them. Individuals were arriving and swapping Christmas cards. The seaboots and wisened, weather-beaten faces gave them away! In the middle of the room was a skittle table. The walls were adorned with wonderful photographs portraying the river a century ago, with as many as six sailing ships alongside the quay. Next door to the pub was the old shipyard of J. Crichton.

Malcolm Williams and his brother Ken, known as 'Conger', told me about their fishing life on the river. Well, just that little bit of it that they didn't mind me knowing. The occasional question was met with a blank stare, but I don't mind that, expect it even. Most people wouldn't entertain a prying stranger but these guys seemed really happy to talk about the river.

We discussed the salmon fishery. Two methods were used – the seine-net and trammel net. The seine-net was worked on the river Dee in the same way as we've already discussed. In the 1980s there were thirty licences issued whereas today it is limited to

Dee salmon boats at Chester, *c.*1930.

sixteen – eight above Queensferry and eight below. Trammel nets, on the other hand, are fished in a similar manner to drift-nets. The trammel net consists of three walls of netting. The central wall – the lint – being too small to let a fish become trapped by the gills while the outer two walls – the armouring – are of a much larger mesh and is hung more loosely to allow the fish to swim through but not out. The 'Connah's Quay Trammel' was said to be different to many other trammel nets in use about Britain. The outer armouring is usually of a square mesh as against the commoner diamond mesh. The nets are drifted downstream on the ebb as far as Greenfield before drifting back to Flint on the flood.

The boats these fishermen use are unique to the river and are called Dee Salmon boats or 'draft boats'. At approximately 17ft 6in in length and 6ft 3in in beam, they are open boats with three thwarts and a shute over the rear of the boat to hold the net. It is said that the design evolved from Mersey sprit-rigged boats, although sprit-rigged boats, some with three masts known as 'grabs' which were used mostly for shrimping and prawning. Most of these draft boats emanated from the Chester boatyard of J.H. Taylor & Sons that opened at the Old Dee Basin in 1916. The only difference between the boats of the upper and the lower reaches was that those fishing the more exposed waters of the river had a smaller transom to cope with the choppier waters.

In an earlier article of mine that appeared in *Watercraft* magazine some years ago I mentioned that Old Boaty built the draft boat *Coronation* in 1911 as well as a few others. The *Coronation* was about to be destroyed at the time and I since learned from the two brothers that she had indeed been burnt by her owner George Latham a few years ago. The only surviving working wooden draft boat was the *Pride of the Dee*, one of the last to be built by the Taylors in the 1950s. Today the majority of the working boats are fibreglass. These wooden boats have the distinction of only having one knee per side to strengthen each thwart whereas most boats had two. It seems the owners couldn't afford two when the boat was being built!

It appears that Old Boaty was in fact a fellow named Roberts who had a boatyard in Connah's Quay and was renowned for the fact that not only did he built these boats but also the oars and mast, setting up the nets and sewed the sails. One story that Malcolm Williams told me concerned another of his boats. When asked what he was going to name a particular boat as he was making up the name-board for the transom, he answered, 'I don't know!' The same person returned the next day to see what he had decided upon and there, on the back of the boat, was the name-board with the name brightly painted in new paint. He had called it *I Don't Know*!

Salmon fishing on the Dee can only be practised between midnight on Sunday night and midnight Thursday night. In other words there was no fishing Friday, Saturday or Sunday. To compensate the fishermen for a shorter week than in other areas, the season lasts from 1 June to 31 August. A licence was currently costing £480. If you listen to the fishermen, they never catch enough fish to warrant that outlay, yet they return year after year. That's the canny nature of fishermen!

The two brothers suggested I contact Vic Williams who had written a few local books, and I did visit him soon afterwards. He has been writing the history of the differing aspects of life in Connah's Quay for a number of years and spends hours pouring over old newspapers to glean his interesting facts. He had recently discovered that Connah's Quay got its name from James Connah, a fisherman with eight children, who lived in the Quay House. Three of his children were called William, Edward and Mary and the date stone on the Quay House bears the initials W.E.M. The youngest George is believed to have taken over the running of the pub.

I managed to purchase a copy of one of Vic's books in the Connah's Quay library. Entitled *The Old Quay House and Riverbank Tales 1751-1914*, this book gives much of the background to the quay, fishing and shipbuilding during that period.

Shipbuilding flourished right along the Welsh side of the Dee. It dates from the medieval period but was stimulated by the building of the canal. Between the end of the eighteenth century and the First World War it has been estimated that there were some twenty shipbuilding yards building vessels of all sizes from Talacre to Chester. During the early nineteenth century the yards were mostly small, building schooners, flats and sloops and many ceased working after about 1860. Perhaps the best known of these was J.Crichton who opened a yard at Saltney in 1913 and subsequently took over the Connah's Quay yard of Ferguson and Baird (the yard next to the pub). They built trawlers, tugs, paddle steamers and floating grain elevators. Many went to the tropics to work in shallow waters. They ceased work in 1935. The last builder to operate was the Brimscombe, Gloucestershire, firm of Abdela & Mitchell that began work at Queensferry in 1908, building trawlers, coasters, barges and oil tankers. They closed for the final time in 1938.

However, it was the sailing ships that the Dee was better known. The most renowned of course is the *Royal Charter*, launched from the Sandycroft yard of George Cramm in 1855 before being wrecked off the coast of Anglesey four years later. Ferguson and Baird opened up in Flint in 1852 before moving to Connah's Quay six years later. There was originally another partner named McMellon, but he died soon after. Their first vessel was a two-masted schooner *The Charles Edward*, launched the same year. James Reney and David Jones had already established themselves by that time.

In April 1900 Ferguson and Baird launched the three-masted schooner *Lizzie May*, 98.4 feet in length and 136 tons gross. On her first commercial voyage she carried 226 tons of firebricks to Kent, thence to Plymouth with cement, Cardiff with pitch, Falmouth with coal and Weston Point with clay before returning home to Connah's Quay. In her first year she sailed over 3,000 miles. By 1908 this had increased to over 40,000 miles, at which time she was sold to Ireland and name-changed to the *Kathleen & May*, the name that she sails under right up today. Based in the West Country, she has recently undergone a total refit, and remains the only Connah's Quay ship in existence.

I leave the last few words of Connah's Quay to the fishermen. When I asked Malcolm Williams what he did throughout the rest of the year, he smiled. 'Flukes [flounders] we net, and eels in conical nets that we send to the market in London. Sometimes shrimps.' But what about in winter? Nothing, it seemed, for they hang up their seaboots to over winter in their sheds. 'Now's not the time to be out on the river, perhaps stranded on the sands, in the freezing cold, with the wind blowing froth and the mist in'. I was reminded on those last lines of Kingsley's poem: 'But still the boatmen hear her call the cattle home/Across the sands of Dee'.

From Connah's Quay we drove to Queensferry (previously known as Kingsferry until the new bridge was built) to photograph the draft boats in the mud alongside it. Crossing over the river, we drove towards Chester along the A548 before turning off to the Higher Ferry.

Dog and I would walk along the river for a while. This ferry, being established in about 1740 after the canalization of the river, survived until 1968. The amazing thing is that throughout this period it was always operated by members of one family. When the river authorities wanted someone to run the ferry they gave the job to a salmon fisherman named Manifold from Saughall – where ironically fishermen were compensated because of the loss to their fishery by the canalization. Bob Manifold was the last ferryman when it closed in 1968. It seems that the local council was oblivious to the fact that the ferry was still in existence until someone from the council called round. Their first act of goodness was to supply Bob with an outboard to replace the oars in his rowboat. Then they decided on a footbridge, which was duly built, thus throwing Bob out of a job. They said he could use the boat for fishing but it seems they later came and took it away. They said it was progression. I agree with Bob who reckoned it was a waste of time. Everybody liked the ferry. Now the bridge just brings trouble. The only reminder of the old ways was a salmon boat lying beneath the bridge.

We drove into Chester to the boatyard of David Jones, which was closed. Phoning David on his mobile, he said he'd gone to Dorset for Christmas, visiting family. I'd met him a few years before whilst preparing the article on the salmon boats. I asked him how he was getting along. No more salmon boats since the last ones he'd built in the 1980s. Boat repairing was the mainstay of the business although he'd recently acquired a river launch, the *Lady Edwina Grosvenor* so that he had run river cruises for visitors in summer. Just outside his yard was the salmon boat *Jubilee of Connah's Quay* that appeared to be in dire need of restoration.

Greenaway Street, Handbridge, was the traditional home to the Chester salmon fishermen. A few years before, on my last visit, I'd found several boats both afloat and lying on the riverbank. Dog and I walked along the wet, grassy bank and found none, except for a couple of fibreglass wrecks. I threw sticks for him in every direction except for into the murky but fast flowing water. Across the stream a motley collection of boats were moored in the river and a few others sat on the opposite bank. I wasn't sure whether this was a sign of a decline in the fishery or that they kept their boats elsewhere.

We were, of course, now in England, although the border was only a mile or so away. Upstream, over the weir that has caused so much aggravation over the years, the river flowed from Welsh mountains, to only kiss the English ground for a matter of a few miles. In places the river was the border. Coracle fishing was once practised in these higher reaches, although today the fishing is in the realms of the anglers. Two types of coracle once existed – the Lower Dee coracle in use between Bangor-is-y-coed and Overton and the Upper Dee coracle used between Bala and Llangollen. The latter was broader for holding two men and the construction was, likewise, stronger and consisted of stout lathes. The Lower Dee coracles were constructed of lathes that were narrower and thinner than in any other coracle. Their use had long disappeared from river activity.

We were now at the end of the journey. I thought about the salmon and eels that Malcolm Williams caught. For here was the connection between the beginning and end of the story. Autumn was the time for the departure of those migrating eels for whom the time had come to swim back to the Sargasso Sea to mate, and ultimately die. Some might have spent twenty years foraging out of sight around the river bed of the Dee – unless they were the unlucky ones to be caught and subsequently jellied or smoked – before they get the summons to return. Thinking about the slimy beady-eyed creatures and remembering lifting those eel pots six months before on the river Severn, I somehow felt both relieved and overjoyed. Several hundred miles of driving were over yet I'd discovered so much of a country I loved. I'd seen parts of it I'd never seen before, learned new stuff about it, and, all the while, unearthing bits of myself I never knew existed!

I walked back to the van, noticing that the red brick buildings of Greenaway Street that I'd seen in a photograph had been demolished, replaced with modern bright red brick houses. I called the dog who was trying to climb a tree, adamant as he was that there was a squirrel up it. There was no squirrel, indeed no life around at all; no one else walking their dog, no one cleaning their windows. Perhaps they had all gone Christmas shopping (the squirrels too, maybe!). There was certainly no movement up the tree. We retraced back to the van. I turned around for a last glimpse of the river now that the journey was over. In front of me was a sign with big black words: 'No Dog Fouling Area'. Some things never change, I thought. Perhaps, though, it was as the council said of the footbridge over the Dee: progression. Fair enough, dogs shouldn't shit where we can tread in it. But we can see and think for ourselves, and avoid it, just like we can think for ourselves in every avenue of our lives. The trouble is that politicians today often leave all their shit lying about and we can't always avoid that. Without them the world would be a much better place. Through progression we've forgotten how to live.

List of some Museums, Heritage and Information Centres in Wales

These museums and centres have a degree of relevance to this book. Some of the establishments offer free admission while others charge for entry. Details were correct at time of writing although a phone call is suggested to check these details. Remember that some establishments have a last admission time before closing.

Chepstow Museum, Gwy House, Bridge Street, Chepstow, Monmouthshire, NP6 5EZ. Tel: 01291-625981. Open: Mon.–Sat. 11–1, 2–5. Sun. 2–5 Extended hours July, August and September 10.30–5.50 Mon.–Sat.

Caldicot Castle & Country Park, Church Road, Caldicot, Monmouthshire, NP26 4HU. Tel: 01291 420241. Open: 1 March to 31 October every day from 11–5.

Newport Museum & Art Gallery, John Frost Square, Newport, NP20 1PA. Tel: 01633 840064. Open: Mon.–Thurs. 9.30–5, Fri. 9.30–4.30 and Sat. 9.30–4 Sun. opening over Christmas period.

Glamorgan Coastal Heritage Centre, Dunraven Bay, Southerndown, Bridgend, Glamorgan. Tel. 01656 880157. Open: Mon., Thurs. and Fri. 9–3 during the season and when rangers are available at other times. Ring before visiting for confirmation.

Porthcawl, The Old Police Station, John Street, Porthcawl. Tel: 01656 782211 Open: Easter – Christmas daily 2–4 and winter Thurs., Fri. and Sat. 2–4.

Swansea. The museum is currently closed and the National Waterfront Museum is due to open in 2006.

Gower Heritage Centre, Parkmill, Gower, Swansea, SA3 2EH. Tel: 01792 371206. Open all year 10–4 November–March, 10–5.30 April–October, closed Christmas, Boxing and New Year's Day.

Kidwelly Industrial Museum, Broadford, Kidwelly, Carmarthenshire. Tel: 01554 891078. Open: Easter, May Bank Holiday and June–September inclusive, 10–5 Mon.-Fri. and 12–5 weekends.

Carmarthen County Museum, Abergwili, Carmarthenshire. Tel: 01267 228696. Open: Mon.–Sat. 10–4.30, closed between Christmas and New Year.

Dylan Thomas Boathouse, Laugharne, Carmarthenshire. Tel: 01994 427420. Open: Easter & May–October 10–5.30, November–April 10.30–3.30 (last admission half an hour before closing).

Tenby Museum & Art Gallery, Castle Hill, Tenby, SA70 7BP. Tel: 01834 842809. Open: 5 April–7 December 2003, every day 10–5, 8 December–Easter 2004, Mon.–Fri. 10–5, except Christmas.

Caldey Island Museum, The Post Office, Caldey Island. Open: Mon.–Sat. in summer season during Post Office hours but only two hours a day in winter.

The Gun Tower, Front Street, Pembroke Dock. Tel 01646 622246. Open: April–September inclusive 10–4 daily.

Milford Haven Museum, The Old Customs House, The Docks, Milford Haven. Tel: 01646 694496. Open: Easter–end October, Mon.–Sat. 11–5, Sun. 12–5 on Bank Holidays and school holidays.

National Coracle Centre, Cenarth Falls, Carmarthenshire, SA38 9JL. Tel: 01239 710980. Open: Easter to end of October, Sun.–Fri. 10.30–5.30 and other times by appointment.

Cardigan Heritage Centre, Teifi Wharf, Cardigan. Tel: 01239 614404. Open: daily in the season 10–5.

Newquay Heritage Centre, Newquay. Open: Sat. and Sun. 12–4 in season.

Ceredigion Museum & Art Gallery, Coliseum, Terrace Road, Aberystwyth, SY23 2AQ. Tel: 01970 633088. Open: Mon.–Sat. 10–5.

Fairbourne & Barmouth Steam Railway Museum, Beach Road, Fairbourne, Gwynedd, LL38 2PZ. Tel: 01341 250362. Open when trains are running and at other times when someone is available. Generally Easter, 1 May–end September and October, half-term daily 10.30–4-30.

Barmouth Museum, Ty Gwyn, Barmouth. First-floor room with exhibits opened by someone locally, hours unknown. Ask locally.

Shell Island, Llanbedr, Gwynedd, LL45 2PJ. Tel: 01341 241453. Open: daily from 1 March to 30 November.

Porthmadog Maritime Museum, Oakley Wharf, Porthmadog. Tel: 01766 513736. Open: Easter Week and May Bank Holiday to end of September daily, 11–5, or by appointment.

Lloyd George Museum, Llanystumdwy, Criccieth, Gwynedd LL52 0SH. Tel: 01766 522071. Open: Easter, Mon.–Fri. in May & daily July–September 10.30–5 and Mon.–Fri. in October 11–4.

Lleyn Historical & Maritime Museum, Old St Mary's church, Church Street, Nefyn,

Tel: 01758 720270. Open: beginning July to end September Mon.–Sat. 10.30–4.30. Sundays 2–4.

Caernarfon (Seiont II) Maritime Museum, Victoria Dock, Caernarfon. Tel:01286 675269. Open: daily Spring Bank Holiday to mid-September.

Holyhead Maritime Museum, Newry Beach, Holyhead. Tel: 01407 769745 (out of hours 01407 764374). Open: Easter to end of October, Tues.–Sun. 1–5.

Amlwch Industrial Heritage Centre, The Port, Amlwch. Tel: 01407 832255. Easter–end September 10.30–5 but phone to check.

Moelfre Seawatch Centre, Moelfre, Anglesey (contact Isle of Anglesey County Council, Leisure & Heritage Department 01248 750057). Open: Easter–end of September, Tues.–Sat. 11–5 and Sun. 1–5.

Conwy Mussel Centre, The Quay, Conwy, LL32 8BB. Tel: 01492 592689. Open: during working hours in the mussel season, which lasts from about September to April.

Llandudno Museum. Open: Easter to end October Tues.–Sat. and Bank Holidays 10.30–1 and 2–5, Sun. 2.15–5.

BIBLIOGRAPHY

Ashton, William, *The Battle of Land and Sea*, Southport, 1909.

The Evolution of a Coast-line Barrow to Aberystwyth, 1920.

Bainbridge, Cyril, *Pavilions of the Sea*, London, 1986.

Benham, Hervey, *Essex Gold*, Chelmsford, 1993.

Bennett, C.J., *A Pedestrian Tour through North Wales*, London, 1838.

Bennett, P. & & Jenkins, D, *Welsh Ports of the Great Western Railway*, National Museums of Wales, 1994.

Bennett, Tom, *Shipwrecks around St. David's*, Newport, 1994.

Bingley, W.A., *A Tour around North Wales performed During the Summer of 1798*, London, 1800.

Breese, Gwyndaff, *The Bridges of Wales*, Llanrwst, 2001.

Campbell-Jones, S., *Welsh Sail*, Llandysul, 1976.

Chappell, Edgar L., *History of the Port of Cardiff*, Cardiff, 1939.

Clarke, E.D., *A Tour through the South of England, Wales and part of Ireland made during the summer of 1791*, London, 1793.

Craig, R.S. et al, T*he Industrial and Maritime History of Llanelli and Burry Port 1750-2000*, Carmarthen, 2002.

Cradock, Joseph, *An account of some of the most romantic parts of North Wales*, London, 1777.

Daniell, William, *Voyage Round Great Britain 1814-1825*, (8 vols),London, 1978.

Davies, H.R., *The Conwy and Menai Ferries*, Cardiff, 1996.

Dawson, J.W., *Commerce & Trade, A History of the Ports of Newport and Caerleon*, Newport, 1932.

Defoe, Daniel, *A Tour thro' the whole Island of Great Britain*, 2 vols, London, 1927.

Dixon, J & Pickard, G, *Crichton & Co, Shipbuilders of Saltney & Connah's Quay*, Chester & Ellesmere Port, 2002.

Dodd, A.H., *A History of Caernarvonshire*, Wrexham, 1990 edition.

The Industrial Revolution in North Wales, Wrexham, 1990 edition.

Eames, Aled, *Ships and Seamen of Gwynedd*, Caernarfon, 1976.

Ships and Seamen of Anglesey 1558-1918, London, 1981 (2nd edition).

Twilight of Welsh Sail, Cardiff, 1984.

Ventures in Sail, Caernarfon, 1987.

Shrouded Quays, Llanrwst, 1991.

Edmunds, George, *The Gower Coast*, Abergavenny, 1986.

Edwards, Sybil, *The Story of the Milford Haven Waterway*, Almeley, 2001.

Evans, Revd John, *Letters written during a Tour through South Wales*, London, 1804.

Description of North Wales, London, 1810.

Farr, Graham E., *Chepstow Ships*, Chepstow, 1954.

Wreck and Rescue in the Bristol Channel – the story of the Welsh Lifeboats, Truro, 1967.

Fenton, Richard, *A Historical Tour through Pembrokeshire*, London, 1811.

Fisher, J. (ed), *Tours in Wales 1804-1813 by Richard Fenton*, London, 1917.

Fletcher, H.L.V., *The Coasts of Wales*, London, 1969.

Gilpin, William, *Observations of the River Wye and several parts of South Wales in the Summer of 1770*, London, 1782 (facsimile reprint 1973).

Griffiths, Mike, *The History of the River Dee*, Llanrwst, 2000.

Gruffydd, Elfed, *Llyn*, Llanrwst, 2003.

Hadfield, Charles, *The Canals of South Wales and the Border*, Cardiff, 1960.

Hague, Douglas B., *Lighthouses of Wales*, Aberystwyth, 1994.

Hall, S.C., *The Book of South Wales, the Wye and the Coast*, London, 1861.

Hampson, D.G., *The Story of St. David's Lifeboats*, St. David's, 1989.

Harris, D.W., *Maritime History of Rhyl and Rhuddlan*, Prestatyn, 1991.

Howells, Brian (ed), *Pembrokeshire County History Vol IV*, Haverfordwest, 1993.

Howells, Roscoe, *Old Saundersfoot*, Llandysul, 1977.

Howson, J.S., *The River Dee*, Clwyd County Council, 1992.

Hucks, J., *A Pedestrian Tour through North Wales in a Series of Letters*, 1795.

Hughes, Eric   *Kidwelly, a history*, Kidwelly, 1999.

Hughes,E & Eames,A., *Porthmadog Ships*, Caernarfon, 1975.

Hughes, Wendy, *The Story of Gower*, Llandysul, 1992.

Hyde-Hall, E.E., *Description of Caernarvonshire (1810-11)*, Caernarfon, 1952.

Jenkins, J.G. et al, *Welsh Rural Communities*, Cardiff, 1960.

Jenkins, J.G., *Nets and Coracles*, Newton Abbot, 1974.

Life and Traditions in Rural Wales, London, 1976.

Maritime Heritage, The Ships and Seamen of Southern Ceredigion, Llandysul, 1982.

Cockles & Mussels – aspects of Shellfish gathering, Cardiff, 1984.

The Coracle, Carmarthen, 1988.

The Inshore Fishermen of Wales, Cardiff, 1991.

Llangrannog, Llangrannog, 1998.

John, Arthur H.(ed), *Industrial Glamorgan 1700-1970*, Glamorgan County History vol. V, Cardiff, 1980.

John, Brian, *The Ports and Harbours of Pembrokeshire*, Fishguard, 1974.

Jones, Ivor Wynne, *Colwyn Bay, a brief history*, Clwyd Library Services, 1995.

Llandudno – Queen of Welsh Resorts, Ashbourne, 2002.

Jones, Peter Hope (ed)*Enlli ddoe a heddiwi* (Bardsey past & present), Caernarfon, 1987.

Jones, Thomas, *Brut y Tywysogyon (The Chronicles of the Princes)*, Peniarth MS20 version, Cardiff, 1952.

Jones, W.H., *History of the Port of Swansea*, Carmarthen, 1922.

Leach, Nicholas, *For those in Peril*, Kettering, 1999.

Leland, John, *The Itinerary of John Leland the Antiquary*, (9 vols) Oxford, 1769.

Lewis, E.A. (ed), *The Welsh Port Books*, London, 1927.

Lewis, Hugh M., *Pages of Time – A Pictorial History of Aberdyfi*, Aberdyfi, 1989.

Aberdyfi: The Past Recalled, Talybont, 2001.

Lewis, Ivor, *The Afan Fisheries*, Aberafan, 1999.

Lewis, Samuel, *A Topograhical Dictionary of Wales*, (2 vols), London, 1838.

Lewis, W.J., *Born on a Perilous Rock, Aberystwyth Past and Present*, Aberystwyth, 1980.

The Gateway to Wales, Cardigan, 1990.

Lloyd-Hughes, D.G., *Pwllheli*, Llandysul, 1991.

Lloyd, Lewis, *The Port of Caernarfon 1793-1900*, Harlech, 1989.

Wherever Freights May Offer – the Maritime Community of Abermaw/Barmouth 1565-1920, Harlech, 1993.

A Real Little Seaport – The Port of Aberdyfi and its People 1565-1920, (2 vols), Harlech, 1996.

Lodwick, M. & E., *The Story of Carmarthen*, Carmarthen, 1954.

McKay, Ken, *A Vision of Greatness – A History of Milford 1790-1990*, Haverfordwest, 1989.

Miles, Dillwyn, *The Ancient Borough of Newport in Pembrokeshire*, Haverfordwest, 1995.

Morgan, Prys (ed), *History of Wales*, Stroud, 2001.

Morris, Lewis, *Plans in St. George's Channel – 1748*, facsimile reprint edited by G. Budenberg, Beaumaris, 1987.

Morton, H.V., *In Search of Wales*, London, 1938.

Nat. Mus. of Wales, *The Maritime Heritage of Dyfed*, Cardiff, 1982.

Nicholson, C, *Rock Lighthouses of Britain*, Latheronwheel, 1995.

Owen, George, *A Description of Pembrokeshire*, Llandysul, 1994.

Owen, G. Dyfnallt, *Elizabethan Wales*, Cardiff, 1962.

Parry, Henry, *Wreck and Rescue on the Coast of Wales*, (2 vols), Truro, 1969.

Radice, Betty (ed), *Gerald of Wales – the Journey through Wales/The Description of Wales*, London, 1978.

Raggett, Paul, *Solva*, Solva, 1996.

Rees, J.F., *The Story of Milford*, Cardiff, 1957.

Rees, P.H., *Gower Shipwrecks*, Swansea, 1978.

Roberts, Ann, *Estuary People – Penclawdd 1900-1970*, Newport, 1975.

Roberts, E. Roland, *Elizabethan Wales*, Newtown, 1924.

Roberts, Tony, *Porthgain*, Cardigan, 1996.

Roderick, Alan, *The Newport Kaleidoscope*, Newport, 1994.

Simpson, A.C., *The Lobster Fishery of Wales*, London, 1956.

Skidmore, Ian, *Anglesey & Lleyn Shipwrecks*, Swansea, 1979.

Gwynedd, London, 1986.

Smith, Carol, *Mumbles Lifeboat*, Swansea, 1989.

Smylie, Mike, *The Herring Fishers of Wales*, Llanrwst, 1998.

The Traditional Fishing Boats of Britain & Ireland, Shrewsbury, 1999.

Anglesey and its Coastal Tradition, Llanrwst, 2000.

The Slopemasts (unpubl. MPhil thesis, St Andrew's Univ.), 2002.

Herring, A History of the Silver Darlings, Stroud, 2004.

Spurrell, William, *Carmarthen and its Neighbourhood*, Carmarthen, 1879.

Stuckey, P.J., *Sailing Pilots of the Bristol Channel*. Bristol, 1999.

Takel, R.E., *The Story of the Ports and Shipping of South Glamorgan*, 1982.

Thomas, Dilys, *Memories of Old Colwyn*, Wrexham, 2000.

Thomas, Norman L., *Mumbles – Past and Present*, Llandysul, 1978.

Thompson, M.W. (ed), *The Journeys of Sir Richard Colt Hoare through Wales and England*, Gloucester, 1983.

Thorne, Roy, *Penarth – A History*, Newport, 1975.

The Ports and Creeks of South Glamorgan, County of S. Glamorgan, 1981.

Troughton, William, *Aberystwyth Harbour – An Illustrated History*, Aberystwyth, 1997.

Waters, Brian, *Severn Tide*, Letchworth, 1947.

Waters, Ivor, *About Chepstow*, Chepstow, 1952.

A Chepstow Notebook, Chepstow, 1980.

The Port of Chepstow, Chepstow, 1989.

Williams, C.J., *Industry in Clwyd*, Hawarden, 1986.

Williams, Stewart (ed)*Saints and Sailing Ships*, Cowbridge, 1962.

Williams, Vic, *The Old Quay House & Riverbank Tales 1731-1914*, Connah's Quay, 2000.

Periodicals

Folk Life, published annually as the Journal of the Society for Folk Studies, St Fagans

International Journal of Nautical Archaeology, published annually by the Nautical Archaeology Society

Mariner's Mirror, published quarterly by the Society for Nautical Research, London

Maritime Life and Traditions, published quarterly by Le Chasse Maree, Douarnenez

Maritime Wales – *Cymru' A'r Mor* – published annually by Gwynedd Archives, Caernarfon

The Carmarthenshire Antiquarian, published annually by the Carmarthenshire Antiquarian Society

Transactions of the Anglesey Antiquarian Society and Field Club, published annually

INDEX

If you are interested in purchasing other books published by Tempus,
or in case you have difficulty finding any Tempus books in your local bookshop,
you can also place orders directly through our website

www.tempus-publishing.com